Developmental Dynamics and Transitions in High School

Transitions in Childhood and Youth

Series Editors: Marilyn Fleer, Mariane Hedegaard and Megan Adams

The series brings together books that present and explore empirical research and theoretical discussion on the themes of childhood and youth transitions. Special attention is directed to conceptualizing transitions holistically so that societal, institutional and personal perspectives are featured within and across books. Key to the series is presenting the processes of transitions between practices and activities and their relationship to the person in contexts such as intergenerational family practices, the processes of care, a person's development, the learning of individuals, groups and systems, personal health, labour and birthing and ageing. All books take a broad cultural-historical approach of transitions across a range of contexts and countries and when brought together in one place make an important contribution to better understanding transitions globally. Books in the Transitions in Childhood and Youth series offer an excellent resource for postgraduate students, researchers, policy writers and academics.

Advisory Board:
Anne Edwards (University of Oxford, UK)
Fernando Gonzalez-Rey (University Center of Brasília, Brazil)
Jennifer Vadeboncoeur (University of British Columbia, Canada)
Anna Stetsenko (City University of New York, USA)

Also available in the series:
Children's Transitions in Everyday Life and Institutions, edited by Mariane Hedegaard and Marilyn Fleer
Qualitative Studies of Exploration in Childhood Education: Cultures of Play and Learning in Transition, edited by Marilyn Fleer, Mariane Hedegaard, Elin Eriksen Ødegaard and Hanne Værum Sørensen
Supporting Difficult Transitions: Children, Young People and Their Carers, edited by Mariane Hedegaard and Anne Edwards

Forthcoming in the series:
Exploring Young Children's Agency in Everyday Transitions, Pernille Juhl
Pedagogical Transitions in Post-Apartheid South Africa: A Cultural-Historical Approach Towards Inclusive Primary Education, Joanne Hardman

Developmental Dynamics and Transitions in High School

Sofie Pedersen

BLOOMSBURY ACADEMIC
LONDON • NEW YORK • OXFORD • NEW DELHI • SYDNEY

BLOOMSBURY ACADEMIC
Bloomsbury Publishing Plc
50 Bedford Square, London, WC1B 3DP, UK
1385 Broadway, New York, NY 10018, USA
29 Earlsfort Terrace, Dublin 2, Ireland

BLOOMSBURY, BLOOMSBURY ACADEMIC and the Diana logo are trademarks of Bloomsbury Publishing Plc

First published in Great Britain 2022
This paperback edition published in 2023

Copyright © Sofie Pedersen, 2022

Sofie Pedersen has asserted her right under the Copyright, Designs and Patents Act, 1988, to be identified as Author of this work.

For legal purposes the Acknowledgements on p. xv constitute an extension of this copyright page.

Series Design: Joshua Fanning
Cover image © Ababsolutum/Getty Images

All rights reserved. No part of this publication may be reproduced or transmitted in any form or by any means, electronic or mechanical, including photocopying, recording, or any information storage or retrieval system, without prior permission in writing from the publishers.

Bloomsbury Publishing Plc does not have any control over, or responsibility for, any third-party websites referred to or in this book. All internet addresses given in this book were correct at the time of going to press. The author and publisher regret any inconvenience caused if addresses have changed or sites have ceased to exist, but can accept no responsibility for any such changes.

A catalogue record for this book is available from the British Library.

Library of Congress Cataloging-in-Publication Data
Names: Pedersen, Sofie, author.
Title: Developmental dynamics and transitions in high school / Sofie Pedersen.
Description: 1 Edition. | New York, NY: Bloomsbury Academic, 2022. | Series: Transitions in childhood and youth | Includes bibliographical references and index.
Identifiers: LCCN 2021026031 (print) | LCCN 2021026032 (ebook) | ISBN 9781350141728 (hardback) | ISBN 9781350141735 (ebook) | ISBN 9781350141742 (epub)
Subjects: LCSH: Youth development. | High schools–Social aspects.
Classification: LCC HQ796.P384 2022 (print) | LCC HQ796 (ebook) | DDC 305.235/5–dc23
LC record available at https://lccn.loc.gov/2021026031
LC ebook record available at https://lccn.loc.gov/2021026032

ISBN: HB: 978-1-3501-4172-8
PB: 978-1-3502-1689-1
ePDF: 978-1-3501-4173-5
eBook: 978-1-3501-4174-2

Series: Transitions in Childhood and Youth

Typeset by Integra Software Services Pvt. Ltd.

To find out more about our authors and books visit www.bloomsbury.com and sign up for our newsletters.

To Anna, Peter, Lisa, Emily, Matilda and Mia, for inviting me in.

And to my younger self, who at times struggled to make sense of the contradictory standards woven into the fabrics of everyday life – and to my current and future self, who may, at times, continue to do so.

Contents

List of Illustrations	x
Preface	xi
Series Editors' Foreword	xiv
Acknowledgements	xv
Note on the Text/Copyright	xvi
Introduction: Developmental Dynamics and Transitions in High School	1
1 Setting the Scene – Invitations and Expectations	29
2 Becoming High School Students: Entering New Activity Settings *Case Study 1: Anna, Mia and Lisa*	47
3 Becoming High School Students – Entering New Activity Settings *Case Study 2: Emily and Matilda*	87
4 Eco-niche Variability: The Meaning of Where Youth Life Is Lived	105
5 Standardizing the Body? – Negotiating the Meaning of Health	121
6 Exploring Subjective Processes of Transformation	135
7 Negotiating Self within a Multitude of Invitations and Possibilities	165
8 Interweaving Analytical Threads	195
Concluding Thoughts and Perspectives	209
References	224
Index	234

Illustrations

Figures

6.1 The dialectical-ecological model of subjectified subjectivity (Pedersen & Bang 2016a). 144
7.1 The dialectical-ecological model of subjectified subjectivity (Pedersen & Bang 2016a). 166
7.2 The dialectical-ecological model of subjectified subjectivity (Pedersen & Bang 2016a). Analytical emphasis on the 'personal side' of the person-environment dialectic. 167
7.3 The dialectical-ecological model of subjectified subjectivity (Pedersen & Bang 2016a). Analytical emphasis on the negotiation of meaning. 183
8.1 Anna's directedness. 197
8.2 Peter's directedness. 199

Table

4.1 Eco-niche variations 107

Preface

During a research stay at CUNY in the fall of 2013, I was following a seminar by Anna Stetsenko, on the notion of development. One of the first things she had us read concerned Darwin and his study of earthworms, which I found puzzling: how could this possibly be of relevance for a bunch of postgraduates and Ph.D. fellows who were studying child and youth development? Little did I know that this text would inscribe itself in my thinking, as a simultaneously fundamental and curious depiction of a constituting factor in development: *reciprocity*. Hence, to introduce a basic principle of this book, we must return to Darwin.

In 1881, Darwin wrote his final book, titled: *The formation of vegetable mould, through the action of worms with observations on their habits* (Darwin 1881). According to Costall (2001), it never received the same attention as some of Darwin's other writings, but for present purposes it is perhaps his most interesting contribution to psychology. Darwin conducted his studies of earthworms over many years and was very dedicated to this study; he was sure that worms were one of the most important species in terms of their important impact in the development of the landscape. An important insight brought about by the study of the worms 'in their world' was that the earthworms and the surrounding mould had co-evolved: '*vegetable mould did not exist before earthworms. Their relation is mutual*' (Costall 2001:478). This concrete and practical study of developmental processes enunciates the interdependency – the reciprocity – of organism and environment, which is a central tenet in cultural-historical psychology, and perhaps the very heart of ecological psychology. Yet also within ecological psychology it '*is easy to slip into a kind of environmental determinism, and treat the environment as an "independent variable", ultimately separate from the animal in question*', as Costall (2001:478) infers. Through their collective activity, earthworms '*have both transformed and sustained their circumstances*' (ibid.).

Inspired by Darwin, Dewey states in his 1884 article, titled 'The New Psychology', that '*the idea of environment is a necessity to the idea of organism, and with the conception of environment comes the impossibility of considering psychic life as an individual, isolated thing developing in a vacuum*' (p. 56, also cited in Cahan 1992:206). Dewey further states that the '*individual is born into an "organized social life ... from which he draws his mental and spiritual substance"*' (Dewey 1884:57). These thoughts resonate in Vygotsky's (1994) conceptualization of the environment, or rather, of the person-environment relation, as one can hardly separate the two in terms of their meaning. I shall return to Vygotsky in the Introduction. The point here is that this book concerns *person-environment reciprocities* in the pursuit of comprehending developmental dynamics, as they unfold among young people in their everyday life at high school. It is thereby my attempt – and hope – at contributing to a wholeness approach to the study of youth development, and to insist on comprehending developmental phenomena in their institutional, material, societal and ecological embeddedness.

However, this book is not just about theoretical ventures relating to the study and comprehension of person-environment reciprocity (or earthworm-vegetable mould reciprocity, for that matter). It is also, and perhaps first and foremost, a book about being young, starting high school, and trying to figure out 'who you are' or 'who you ought to be' in a myriad of invitations and possibilities to become anew, while – strangely – feeling like 'yourself' most of the time.

And despite more than twenty years having passed since I graduated high school myself, being a high school student is not an 'outside' perspective to me. I began high school when I was fifteen. This was back in the year 1997, and I was the youngest one in my class. I was used to being the youngest, as I had started school early; however all of the sudden, the oldest one in my class was three years older than me. He was already eighteen and had a driver's licence – and a car.

I never gave my choice of high school much consideration; I simply chose the one that was closest, and where most people I knew attended. Growing up in a small-town village in the countryside, the nearest high school was located in the nearby town 10 km away. Alternatively, I would have to commute to a larger city, even further away, but I had no need to expand my world to that level just yet. The bus connection ran once an hour, so to be at school on time, I had to leave the house at 07.05, only to arrive at the school around 7.25. I got used to my alarm going off at 5.50 every morning, just as I got used to finishing some of my homework in the early morning hours before classes that began at 08.15. Again, I did not think much of it – it was just the way things were.

I do not recall being particularly aware of my own development during my three years at high school – I was constantly *in* my own existential life situation, trying to make sense of all the things that were happening around me – of bigger and smaller nature – and to meet the demands that high school undeniably threw my way. These demands were both of academic and of social nature. In elementary school, there were fourteen pupils in my class with another twenty in the parallel class, which meant that I was roughly relating to thirty+ others in my daily life, plus/minus some from the year below and the year above. And even though my high school was amongst the smaller schools, each year still boasted around 120 students, which meant that my social world had expanded exponentially overnight. Not to mention the students from the two years above me at high school, some of whom I would send long glances across the hallway to admire their cool clothing style – or I would swoon over a particular guy from the third year – others I would get to know through my engagement in the school choir and the school musical, and they soon became friends, which added even more people to my new (and still analogous) social network.

I do not recall thinking I changed. But I recall the feeling of entering something unknown – a feeling of more explicitly striving towards something, though this 'something' was somewhat elusive. An increased independency perhaps. I remember drama – my own and that of others. I remember the self-awareness, the sense of competition and positioning, of finding good people to collaborate with, of the need of not standing out and being unique at the same time, of trying to acquire a better sense of what direction to pursue in life. And I remember encountering contradictory categories or standards that implied deciding 'where' one wanted to belong, or letting others decide for you.

Looking back at my time in high school twenty+ years later, I have forgotten the details, but I still remember those three years as important. This was where the contours of my future adult life became visible – although they later deviated much from the original vision – and social life suddenly felt of utmost importance. I do not intend to enforce a nostalgic glance upon my own youth, but merely to say that I am not an outsider to the field of study – I was also a high school student and I carry with me implicit ideas of what high school life is like. Therefore, writing this book also brings about a new level of reflection in relation to my younger self and the developmental dynamics I took part in back then.

Undeniably, a lot has changed from my high school years (1997–2000) and up until today. Or at least up until the school year 2012/13, where I carried out the ethnographic study that provides the empirical basis for this book. And at the same time, a lot remains the same in terms of the dynamics that are at play among young people in high school. High school still constitutes a space that is full of standards and ideas of 'who' and 'how' to be, and I think that most people attending high school will find various aspects challenging at some point in time, because high school opens a new developmental space where one cannot take part unaltered, nor is one supposed to.

This book is about trying to learn from practice: it is about understanding how developmental dynamics unfold in times of (longer) transitional periods in youth, as well as in the micro-genetics of everyday life – and it is about insisting on the complexities that are involved in such processes and dynamics.

I went into this study with a genuine curiosity concerning the developmental dynamics that unfold in the lives of young people, and a desire to explore these dynamics from a wholeness approach – in a time where increasingly individualized understandings (of youth) seem to be enforced, also in relation to responding to the problems that young people at times experience. My exploration of the respective everyday life settings of the young people in the study implied being directed by that which *came to matter to them*, primarily. As I chose to embark on the fieldwork, and explore the life-worlds of the participants, as openly as possible, the participants self-enrolled in the project which created a gender imbalance among the participants. In part this approach meant that intersectional parameters such as gender, ethnicity and socio-economic status were not explicit focus points. That is not to say that such aspects do not matter or that they are not potentially important parts of the developmental dynamics that unfold in young people's lives. As I have not pursued analyses of such aspects myself, I fully acknowledge that such readings of the material (e.g. with an emphasis on gender) may offer and enable other – or supplementary – analyses and understandings or give rise to further nuancing. I therefore encourage others to contribute to such analyses.

Series Editors' Foreword

In this book series we have chosen to focus on transitions through the lens of cultural-historical theory. Specifically, transition is conceptualized to encompass the changes in daily activity settings, the changes in everyday moves between different institutional practices and the changes on entering new practice through life course trajectories, such as going to school, leaving school, entering the work force or entering into parenthood. Through transition into new practices, children and young people meet new challenges and demands that may give them possibility for development.

Important for a cultural-historical conception of transition is the person's agency or intentions, which can be used as analytical tools for gaining the person's perspective during microgenetic transitions between activity settings within an institution, such as indoor play, lunch and outdoor activities in kindergarten, in daily moves between home and kindergarten, school or work, and during macro-transitions that involve new practices. As the person or people take forward their intention within the daily transitions or the new institutions that they attend, a dynamic interplay between the person and the institution can be observed. Cultural-historical studies of transitions across a range of contexts and countries are brought together in this book series, where they can make an important contribution to better understanding transitions globally.

Acknowledgements

This book would never have come about if it was not for the openness and willingness of Lisa, Emily, Anna, Matilda, Mia and Peter (including their families and their respective schools) to let me take part in their everyday lives throughout their first year of high school. For that, I am forever grateful.

I also want to thank Mariane Hedegaard, Marilyn Fleer and Megan Adams for inviting me to publish this book in their series on Transitions in Childhood and Youth. And Mariane Hedegaard in particular, for seeing the potential in my work and encouraging me along the way. I also want to thank Evangeline Stanford at Bloomsbury for impeccable editorial assistance.

A special and deepfelt gratitude extends to Jytte Bang, who was not only my supervisor during my PhD project (that provides the foundation for this book), but with whom I have also co-developed some of the theoretical work that appears in this book, and who continues to be a close collaborator.

The research project on which this book is based was financed by The Danish Council for Independent Research, as part of the SUBSTANce Research Centre, and to me, it is a reminder of the importance of independent research, which seems to become increasingly rare.

Furthermore, this book was written in *my* concrete environment, and so somehow it is co-constructed by the many miles of pavement and communal paths that laid ground to my running shoes, and by the ducks who (a bit hesitantly) agreed to momentarily share their eco-niche (read: the local lake near my parents' place) and its icy waters with me for my morning winter-bathing routine in January 2021. Not to mention the significant amounts of freshly ground coffee beans (and, let's face it, jars of instant coffee as well), and Japanese matcha, or the tranquillity at Solveig's summer cottage or at my parents' house when I needed a break from the constant background noise in Copenhagen. In that sense, this book is the result of multiple interacting aspects of my lifeworld and an abundance of mutually co-constructive processes and relations, to which I – very concretely – owe this publication.

Thank you to my wonderful, supportive and ever-inspiring colleagues, and to my cherished friends, and especially to M. Dressler and S. Roepstorff for sharing the (writing)ride.

To my family and loved ones …

Note on the Text/Copyright

Chapter 3: Parts of the chapter (concerning the theoretical propositions) have previously been published: Pedersen, S. (2019): Not Just a School: Explorations and Theoretical Considerations in Relation to the Human Eco-niche. In: Murakami, K., Cresswell, J., Kono, T. & Zittoun, T. (eds.): *The Ethos of Theorizing*. Canada: Captus Press, pp. 212–221.

Reprinted with permission from Ethos of Theorizing, The – ISTP 2017, by Kyoko Murakami, Jim Cresswell, Tetsuya Kono and Tania Zittoun (Concord, Ontario, Canada: Captus University Publications, 2019). Permission to use has been granted by Captus Press Inc. <http://www.captus.com>

Chapter 6 is a reprint and an elaboration of previously published work: Pedersen, S. & Bang, J. (2016a): Youth Development as Subjectified Subjectivity – a Dialectical-Ecological Model of Analysis. *Integrative Psychological and Behavioral Science,* 50(3), 470–491.

It appears with the permission of Springer Nature. The original work is co-authored by Jytte Bang and reflects our collaborative work. In this chapter, I have expanded the analysis to include additional empirical material to further elaborate the analytical points.

Introduction: Developmental Dynamics and Transitions in High School

UNDER CONSTRUCTION – BEWARE OF DANGER!

This statement is written on the back of Lisa's vest, one that she carries daily in the colder months of the year. I ask her about it; is it a quote from somewhere, or perhaps a reference to something specific? No, she says, *'that's just how we are ... under construction'*, and in many ways this statement provides an excellent opening line for this book.

This book is about Lisa, Matilda, Mia, Peter, Anna and Emily,[1] and their first year in high school. It is about how they relate to and try to make sense of their new respective high school environments – with its myriad of possibilities, its invitations to 'be young' in certain ways, as well as its institutional demands and expectations. Through their efforts, and their respective processes of becoming high school students, we are able to explore and theorize about the developmental dynamics that unfold in the lives of young people in their transition from one educational setting to another, and, in a larger existential perspective, their transition from childhood to adulthood.

Let us return to the statement on Lisa's vest for a second. 'Beware of danger' connotes a double meaning: in the first sense it signals 'watch out', this process of becoming could go anywhere, conveying a message to the world of perhaps expecting the unexpected. And, as Lisa herself puts it, that intense emotional outbursts are possible. And in a second sense, it can be read as an appeal to the world of approaching the subject with cautiousness, as in being mindful and caring. That the person is not yet fully developed and thus in need of understanding and compassion. Undeniably, this might be an overinterpretation on my part; however the image of this statement on the vest stuck with me, long after my time spent with Lisa and the other high school students. Perhaps because it somehow depicted so well what I was trying to explore – being 'under construction'– and perhaps because it made it clear that this question transcended an abstract research agenda and presented as a highly relevant question or awareness among young people as well, including Lisa.

Regardless of what we may read into Lisa's statement, it is fair to say that this book is about young people's processes of *construction* or *development*. It concerns young

---

[1] The names of the participants and high schools in this book have been altered for the sake of privacy.

people being in process or in transition; from childhood and adulthood, from one educational setting to another, between different activity settings, and, perhaps, in a process of being or becoming 'me' in new ways. The aim of the book is to illustrate young people's development of self-understanding, subjectivity and new motive-orientations, by exploring how such developmental processes unfold and take shape, as intimately embedded in and intertwined with the concrete conditions of everyday life as it unfolds in the institutional settings in which they participate.

Over the course of a little more than a year, I took part in the everyday lives of Matilda, Lisa, Mia, Peter, Anna and Emily, from they finished elementary school in the spring of 2012, and throughout their first year in high school, from the summer of 2012 to the summer of 2013. These six young people were dispersed at four different high schools at different locations in Denmark, and so the book not only provides insight into youth life in high school in a singular sense, but also explores the variations and diversity of high school youth life by exploring the differences it makes to attend high school, e.g., in the countryside versus in the inner-city or the suburb. The empirical foundation of the book is based on an ethnographic study where I took part in the lives of the aforementioned six young people throughout their first school year. I took part in classes, hung out at recess and after school; this involved skipping classes, hanging out at the mall, stepping outside school premises for a cigarette, discussing appropriate outfits for the upcoming party, trying to avoid sitting on chairs 'reserved' for senior students in the canteen, playing online games during class (when the teacher did not notice!) and at times being called out for a student myself (although I was in my early thirties at the time of the study). This ethnographic approach allowed for me to be part of the actual everyday life of these six young people, and to acquire an insight into how they experienced and made sense of their new high school environments, what they found challenging, what they saw as norms and standards of how they ought to be, and how their relations to others, as well as themselves, changed over time. Through their way of encountering the particular demands of their respective high school settings, we are invited into the developmental dynamics of youth life as it unfolds in relation to the institutional practice of high school. We encounter the invitational character of the various high school practices alongside the young people, and we see their struggles to fit in while remaining unique, and how these somewhat ambiguous attempts are nested in institutional and social standards of youth life.

By exploring and theorizing the developmental dynamics that occurred over the course of the first school year, this book thus places itself in between grand theories of development and anthropological description, and as such aims at offering an in-depth contextual and situated comprehension of the developmental dynamics of youth life in a high school setting. The book explores the dynamics of youth development by delving into transitions in a double sense: firstly, by explicitly exploring youth development in the transition from one institutional setting to another (from elementary school to high school), and secondly, by exploring young people's everyday life in a time of general transition, moving towards young adulthood. The understanding of transition that is employed in this book builds on Vygotsky's theory of development (1932/1998), and the further development proposed by Hedegaard (2012, 2014) as well as Hedegaard and Fleer (2019). Here the notion of transition refers to the new demands that, in this case, young people are faced with, both directly and indirectly, when entering new institutional settings, and how this correlates with – and necessitates – new motive orientations. It further encompasses how young people, through their participation in new settings, are not only faced with new demands, but also place new demands on others and change their environment – and by doing so, also contribute to the shaping of their own developmental conditions (see Hedegaard 2014; Hedegaard & Fleer 2019). Hence, individual development cannot be understood apart from the concrete environment in relation to which it occurs (cf. Vygotsky 1994, 1998; Leontjev 2005; Bozhovich 2009) or as reduced to the result of meeting new demands alone, but rather it becomes a question of concurrently comprehending the activity settings (in which the young people participate) as dynamic and ever-changing as young people actively relate to them and negotiate their meaning, *as part of* meeting new demands, pursuing various motives and trying to make sense of the world – together and on their own. In this sense, transitions are not regarded as problematic in their own right, but rather as spaces of possibilities; for potential development of new relations to self, others and the world (see also Hedegaard & Fleer 2019; Winther-Lindqvist 2019).

By diving into everyday life as it unfolds for our six young high school students, we are invited to take part in the multiple transitions that occur on a daily basis, between different activity settings. As we shall see, high school in itself offers a variety of options to participate in settings that have their own internal logic or values. For example, there is a difference between being seen as academically skilled in French class and mastering a Kendama or knowing how to relevantly talk about upcoming parties in recess. In that sense, transitions between various activity settings at the high school premises feed into the co-construction of developmental space of opportunities, just as, of course, the transitions between a new high school setting and a familiar home setting do (see Winther-Lindqvist 2019 for elaboration).

This implies that being 'under construction', as put forth by Lisa, is not understood in a passive sense, but in *dialectical* terms. In relation to the notion of transition, the book is not intended to dwell on the concept in itself; rather it is intended to explore and illustrate how developmental processes occur and unfold in *a time of transition*, relating to multiple transitory processes, to better understand what such a time in young people's lives entails, how they continuously co-develop their relation to the world and themselves, and eventually, why this may be experienced as challenging or even difficult at times. The young people in the study are in a process of becoming familiar with, and making sense of, not only institutional but also social demands when transitioning into being high school students. This has implications for their ways of orienting themselves, participating in high school life, and ultimately for their self-understanding. Hence, development is studied as a dialectical relation between (always developing) personal motives and ways of participating *and* institutional activity settings and standards for youth life. Hence, the book offers a theoretically and empirically grounded qualification of transition as a developmental process in the lives of young people.

The analyses presented in the book focus on approximating a first-person perspective on developmental processes as they are experienced by young people, and to relate these perspectives to the particular environmental conditions and standards that the young people are facing in their everyday life at high school. This allows for concurrent micro-genetic studies of development of 'self', and studies of variations in youth life across different places. By integrating subjective and institutional levels of analysis and by insisting on seeing the developmental dynamics that unfold in the lives of young people in relation to the particular environments in which they participate, this book proposes a dialectical-ecological understanding of youth development. The theoretical dimension of the analysis conceptualizes youth development as a two-sided, reciprocal and transactional movement between persons and environment, and the argumentation points out in detail how development is a process in which the individual subjects are actively involved in the continuous creation and recreation of their everyday living with institutional demands and standards. As such, the book offers a renewal of our ways of understanding youth development, in order to avoid or overcome the potential reductionism of only (or mainly) studying youth development as an intrapersonal, decontextualized or universal phenomenon. More than being a book about six persons and their individual development in an isolated manner, it is a book about the invitations, expectations and demands that young people encounter when they start high school, and how they relate to and make sense of them. This implies that the developmental dynamics that occur in young people's lives must be understood as entangled with – and inseparable from – concrete places and materiality, as well as social dynamics, individual motive orientations and preferences. By exploring the everyday lives of Peter, Emily, Lisa, Matilda, Anna and Mia respectively, the book contributes to a theoretical further development, specifically considering the meaning of the person-environment reciprocity in relation to youth development. This theoretical endeavour will gradually be unfolded throughout the book, closely intertwined with the exploration of the concrete life-worlds of these six young people as they become high school students.

Before I return to Lisa and one of the other young people, Anna, I will briefly outline a contextual backdrop for this book, regarding the study of youth and high school as an institutional setting.

Youth: A Time of Developmental Tasks, Challenges and Transitions

In general, youth is thought of as a longer transition-period from childhood to adulthood. Undoubtedly, it can be debated from here to eternity at what age youth begins and when it ends, and this would surely require a culturally sensitive and dynamic definition. Also, the definition or demarcation of youth is largely susceptible to historical developments and furthermore depends on *what* and *who* are defining the concept and for what purpose (see, e.g., Jensen 2010). In this book, focus will be on young people who are transiting from elementary school[2] to high school, which

---

[2] The last years of elementary school in Denmark correspond with Junior High (in an American school system). When I write elementary school, I mean to refer to the ten years of consecutive schooling that are mandatory in Denmark.

means that they are between fifteen and sixteen years old.³ In that sense, they will not be defined by age, but by their age period in the sense that they share mutual circumstances of transitioning from one institutional setting to another and therefore find themselves in similar developmental situations, in relation to facing similar institutional demands (Vygotsky 1998; Hedegaard 2012).

Previous youth research has appointed a central development task of young people to consist of promoting '(..) *the development of qualified self-determination and social relations to be able to, individually, handle an adult life*' (Mørch 1994:40, my translation). Such a developmental task, whether we refer to it as 'qualified self-determination' or not, must be handled in a society highly focused on the development of individuality, and on the expansion, optimizing and pursuit of possibilities for oneself (Aaberg 2005, see also Rose 1996). Youth is no longer perceived as the 'difficult state of emergency' largely defined by chaotic and unruly hormones as it was in previous generations – today it is rather a desired label for the categorization of self, upheld and nourished by, e.g., the media, commercial. Whereas youth was earlier mostly regarded as a sort of waiting room before entering adulthood and becoming a proper member of society, it is now, according to Nielsen and Rudberg (2006), for many considered to be the best years of life. Such expectations – of youth being the best years of life – may indeed influence young people who find themselves in the middle of the transition from child to adult which includes multiple transitory processes; from dependency to greater independence and responsibility for others; from preparatory steps towards economical and societal participation to actual participation, for example, the transition from the educational system to the labour market (see Arnett 2004; Resnick & Perret-Clermont 2004; Furlong, Cartmel & Biggart 2006; Smith, Christoffersen, Davidson & Herzog 2011). Today – as opposed to a few generations ago – young people are expected to take responsibility for many aspects of their lives on their own: their learning process and outcome, their social life, their health and general well-being. This suggests that identity is turned into a project, as something young people can – and ought to – construct and optimize ('to succeed') in a certain and rather conscious way, which, according to sociologists such as Rose (1996), often refers them to the guidance, counselling and help of various more or less formal experts in the field (this can be anything from teenage magazines, Youtubers or other social media personages, to psychologists, coaches or psychiatrists). All of which provide different kinds of information concerning what constitutes 'normal' youth life.⁴ When addressing youth life or youth development in a current context, it is difficult – if not impossible – to

---

³ As an 11th school year is optional in Denmark, some students are older when they start high school. However, all six participants in this project proceeded straight from 9th grade (the 10th school year) to high school.
⁴ One could, with a reference to Rose (1996), stipulate that young people are controlled by their own choices, made under guidance from various experts and authorities, in a regulated, but free, space. This 'regulated free space' in itself represents a longer line of research and knowledge production concerning the influence and government of political levels, in terms of afflicting and controlling the subjective possibilities for development and action. In this sense, the book inevitably also connects to both relevant psychological and sociological research traditions on this matter; see, for example, Foucault 1995, Rose 1999, Bauman 2005 and Dean 2010.

circumvent the fact that an increasing number of young people are experiencing various kinds of challenges that result in an increase in high school dropouts and mental health problems such as depression, anxiety or stress. Stress has in itself become an increased and rather common phenomenon among high school students, and it is not unusual to hear of high school students taking various kinds of performance-enhancing or anxiety-reducing drugs during times of examinations (see, e.g., Mainz 2014a, 2014b). Recent research in the area found that around 25 per cent of nineteen-year-old girls in Denmark report having suffered a mental illness and that many girls show depressive symptoms. Depending on age, 26–35 per cent of girls have received psychological counselling, whereas the numbers for boys range from 15 to 19 per cent. For boys the tendency points towards excessive smoking and drinking, combined with unhealthy eating habits, and research demonstrates that these numbers tend to rapidly climb (Ottosen et al. 2010, 2014). Other reports and analyses document that a decreasing number of young people manage to complete a youth education (Ugebrevet a4 2009), and that drop-outs from youth educations are posing an increasing problem in a socio-economic perspective (AE 2011a). These numbers suggest that youth as a life period may be experienced as challenging, and that the expectations or ideals of who and how to be might be difficult to meet. The grand narrative of youth as endless possibilities and the best years of life does not necessarily translate into the subjective experience of everyday life, nor does it automatically mean that the navigation of a discursive space of endless possibilities is easy and unequivocal.

The question of 'who' and 'how' to be – and not to be – is not just a question of interest to the adult outsider: the teacher, the parent, the school psychologist or the researcher. It is also often a pending question for young people, as it presents itself with its often-conflictual dynamics and ambivalences. As one high school student expressed it in a newspaper reader's letter:

> *Look at me, hear me; I am important, I need to be the centre of attention. (..)I may have problems, but to the outside I need to appear as someone in control of things. (..) I will spend a lot of energy on meeting the ideals that I assume my surroundings are measuring me against. These are my thoughts about myself; a 19-year-old woman, attending high school. There are many ideals among young people. They are made by our surroundings, but we also take part in their construction ourselves. The ideals are mainly about 'being turned on and tuned in', having energy (for everything) and looking good. There is no room for a day where everything collapses; we dare not show our weaknesses.*
>
> (Schou 2012, my translation)

As Schou calls our attention to, there is a multitude of ideals and expectations at play in the lives of young people, telling them how to do and who to (desire to) be(come). And evidently, this nineteen-year-old high school student feels under pressure, or even trapped, between the ideals that she is surrounded by, and her subjective experience of being. She is aware that the ideals that dictate her appearance to the world are not only imposed on her by the surroundings but co-constructed by herself, in her continuous reproduction of them in her everyday life. The ideals that she refers to indicate notions of how '*one is supposed to be*' when being a high school student, in order to fit into locally developed ideas of normality. The author of the reader's letter quite precisely points out the inherent paradox of co-creating and reproducing such ideals, or standards as I would call them, that are at the same time problematic to her, without being able to change the situation. I propose that a rise in the experience of mental health problems among youth cannot be understood apart from such paradoxical conditions in which young people have to meet, embrace and handle the developmental tasks of youth.

If we return to the universal ideas of youth, one could claim that the transition from elementary school to high school contains, among other things, increased demands for autonomy and self-government, and it is expected that young people are, to a larger extent, capable of making independent choices. In addition, the transition from one societal institution to another – such as that from elementary school to high school (representing two independent school systems) – contains a considerable social challenge given that social bonds may be discontinued in the new social setting where new friendships and a sense of social belonging may have to be reconfigured. All in all, the transition to high school in most cases marks a shift in everyday life conditions which forces upon the person a re-orientation in, and negotiation of, standards – standards for clothes, political opinions, health preoccupations (and priorities), sexual activity, alcohol consumption and time spent on homework, just to give a few examples. In other words, standards for manners in which to behave, participate and relate, for perspectives on everyday life and for what constitutes normality; *for how to be 'me'*.

High School as a Framework for Developmental Processes

As this book targets the institutional setting of high school in particular, high school as a framework for developmental processes deserves some contextualizing considerations as well. In the Danish school system, the first ten years of (elementary) schooling are mandatory. An eleventh year (which is called 10th grade) is optional, and mostly attended by those students who need an extra year to develop either their academic skills or a general maturity. After elementary school comes a level of youth education, which consists mainly of three-year educations: high school, business school or vocational school. A completion of this educational level is needed to proceed to further education, such as university. In general terms, high school is a highly recognizable educational setting for young people between the ages of approximately fifteen and twenty. It is also the most commonly sought kind of youth education in Denmark with, according to The Ministry of Children & Education (2017), approximately 73 per cent[5] of a year group applying every year. High school thus represents the most general form of youth education in Denmark. Furthermore, this book's emphasis on youth life in high school settings to a large degree implies an exclusion of other central settings in the lives of young people, such as 'the home' or the 'afterschool workplace'. Arguably, this emphasis is to some extent arbitrary in the sense that with the aim of

---

[5] In this statistic, the percentage includes all high school-level youth education, including business school. It distinguishes solely between high school educations and vocational schools.

studying developmental processes from a wholeness approach, high school as a setting will only provide partial insight into the environment in a person's life. However, at the same time the choice of focus is not arbitrary at all, but rather deliberate for a number of reasons: (1) high school constitutes a new activity setting for the young people in the study (whereas, e.g., 'home' does not), and therefore a new (and perhaps unfamiliar) practice to orient and engage oneself in (also referring to the institutional demands that co-constitute this age period, cf. Vygotsky 1998; Hedegaard 2012), (2) it is an institutional setting shared by all six participants in the research project which therefore offers comparability, and finally (3) high school is the setting where young people are spending the largest number of waking hours during the weekdays (Collins & Coleman 2008). In addition, it represents a societal institution to which value is ascribed. This makes it a significant setting in terms of new orientations and possible new self-understandings and, in many ways, makes high school (as a setting) the *least* arbitrary choice of focus in the study of youth life. In effect, high school is an institutional setting where youth life concurrently is practised, lived out and negotiated, as social processes among young people, and institutionally arranged, influenced and governed in relation to political objectives. It is the intersection or coherence between these two aspects that this book will seek to unfold.

In the time of being a high school student, most of the waking hours of the day are spent at school and it is theoretically well-established that young people are to a large extent influenced by and oriented towards their peers. In the study of developmental dynamics, this book does not single out the influence of peers, but explores it as entangled with societal pressure and demands that are built into and represented by the specific institutional setting of high school, as well as the meaning of the concrete possibilities offered by the (local) environment. This implies an emphasis on how young people actively meet and engage with new institutional demands, social others, and shared ideals or standards of how to enact youth life, and how their motive orientations develop in relation to the concrete activity settings of high school.

Young people are not 'blank pieces of paper' or 'empty vessels', as previous conceptualizations of youth seem to suggest (see Lesko 2001, see also Chapter 8) when they enter high school. Rather, they start high school full of hopes and dreams, and ideas about who they are and where they are going. They are already shaped (in terms of, e.g., their motive orientations and self-understanding) by the different practices in which they have previously participated; this of course includes both the specific family practice and different institutional settings such as kindergarten and elementary school. The book does not aim to provide a complete overview of everything that can affect young people's development, but rather to offer an empirically and theoretically grounded understanding of the developmental dynamics that unfold in young people's everyday life in a high school setting particularly, and what the transition from one major institutional setting to another entails in terms of development. This refers specifically to the common idea that young people are 'the same' regardless of where and when they are studied, and that we can know what the motives, concerns, etc., are like for people on the basis of their age alone (e.g. being a teenager, as is stipulated by earlier theoretical accounts of youth development). This implies that dominant understandings of youth are indeed often decontextualized and generalized (both in theories and in the media) in the sense that all high-school students are presented as being similar, with similar conditions and similar problems. Often the details that could serve to contextualize a phenomenon/situation/problem are omitted from the analysis and we are merely dealing with immediate representations. By attempting to comprehend developmental dynamics in high school in a coherent manner – by concurrently emphasizing the concrete environment and young people's agency and participation – this book seeks to overcome both the problem of decontextualization and the streak of determinism that might otherwise be insinuated with an ecological emphasis (by e.g. highlighting the significance of the environment at the expense of the active engagements, motive orientations, and meaning construction of the young people).

Historically, high school in Denmark comprised a structure of two equally qualifying academic lines; a natural science line and a humanistic-linguistic line, which gave equal access to further education. However, recent structural reforms[6] have transferred the pressure of making educational choices from a decision to make *after* high school, to a decision integrated in the choice of academic line *in* high school. Albeit the choice of academic line in high school is not final in the sense of being unalterable later on, studies show that these structural rearrangements of the high school organization have contributed to inclusion- and exclusion processes among young people (Zeuner 2009). Furthermore, it is well-established that high school, as an educational institution, sets the frame for negotiating and reproducing different kinds of standards of living; in relation to, for example,, socio-economic status and social class (Willis 1977), social categories and group affiliations (Eckert 1989), as well as habits (Ingholt 2008). This implies that the high school setting becomes an arena for social in- and exclusion processes among young people. In addition, it is well documented that divergences in relation to general standards, or discrepancies between, for instance, standards at school and the life of a particular young person (given their concrete conditions or way of living) may lead to problems, such as bullying, social isolation, mental health problems and the establishment of marginalized subgroups (Hundeide 2004; Kofoed & Søndergaard 2009). This may greatly influence the psychological well-being of a person and how she or he conducts her/his everyday life; not only at present, but for years to come. However, more knowledge is needed about the manner in which standards influence the lives of young people, and this requires a new perspective on developmental normativity.

Inspired by the research of Elder (e.g. 1974), this book thus connects to classical discussions of normal and pathological developmental paths in a life-span perspective, but it defines itself within recent theoretical attempts to get beyond ideas of uni-linearity and single causality. It can therefore be seen as a prolongation of a recent shift towards understanding development from a dynamic and complex wholeness

[6] The high school reform I refer to here was politically decided in 2003 and implemented in 2005. It was a major reform in the sense that it changed the dual structure system in high school to a system of multiple academic lines. This restructuring was instituted in order to facilitate the transition from high school to university and to encourage students to proceed directly from one educational institution to another, thereby reducing the number of gap years and speeding up educational progression.

approach already elaborated in recent Danish traditions (e.g. Hedegaard 2003, 2009, 2012; Hedegaard et al. 2008; Hviid 2008; Bang 2009b; Højholt & Kousholt 2014). The Danish traditions particularly highlight the child's perspective (motives, activities, agency) in relation to institutional demands and conditions.

Youth Life Variations

To illuminate and theorize about developmental dynamics, the book explores the everyday lives and transitions of six young people as they become high school students, at four different high schools. The high schools in this book are referred to in generic names: Northside-, Southside-, Westside- and Countryside High. In that sense they are thought of as exemplary, and their variety serves to outline differences that exist in practice. Evidently, there are variations of high school life that will not be accounted for in this book, yet an exploration of particular youth lives at these four schools tells us something about 'high school life' and about the developmental dynamics that unfold *for* and *with* young people who enter a high school setting.

To illustrate, we encounter Anna, who attends a provincial high school in a smaller town. Anna is, at the beginning of the school year, very directed towards becoming a pedagogue and spends most of her time engaged in activities that she considers relevant to this endeavour. As such, she presents what appears to be uncomplicated and very linear steering towards adult life, clearly motivated by her overarching goal for her future career. Anna is not particularly interested in boys (or girls, for that matter), nor is she interested in attending parties or engaging in drinking alcohol, as many of her peers. As a consequence, she does not participate in the extra-curricular social activities at school; they involve alcohol, and various degrees of acting out. Anna sees no point in this. In the first months of high school, a social gap appears between two groups of girls in Anna's class; on the one hand those who do not like to attend parties, etc. (including Anna), and on the other hand, those who seem to mostly be preoccupied with parties and the social life outside school. This social gap is also perceptible to Anna and it bothers her. It underlines a dominant standard in high schools about being social 'in a particular way' – a standard that is in some ways predefined, but also constantly negotiated and reinterpreted among young people. A standard that, despite its movability, also co-defines and restricts action spaces and hence 'who' may participate 'where' and 'how'; it contributes to the forming of social groups, and, in effect, processes of social in- and exclusion. This will be especially clear when following Anna's developmental trajectory over the course of the first school year. In that sense, the social interactions that unfold among Anna and her peers, as well as Anna's way of understanding herself, and the practice of high school, are to some extent co-defined by said standard.

In another part of the country, in the capital, we encounter Lisa who attends a private inner-city high school. To Lisa, it is all about standing out and breaking norms; she is doing what she can to own this agenda, for example, as the statement written on her vest, and other statements on her backpack also demonstrate. To her, very few aspects of her current everyday life situation are considered a given: she unceasingly reflects upon her choices, and happily makes a point of opposing something, just for the sake of opposing it. Her ideals of critical reflection and transcending norms correspond with fundamental values at her high school, which in turn support and encourage Lisa's attitude and approach to youth life, and at the same time present a challenge. Because how do you break norms when breaking norms becomes a norm in its own right? Lisa seems to struggle with this predicament along with her friends at school; this involves openly sharing personal stories of mental health issues and excessive daytime drinking on a public bench, all the while ensuring high grades at school and singing in the church choir on Sundays. She is, at the same time, seeking out 'the edge' and meeting standards of academic achievement and engagement. In many ways, she is struggling with remaining unique (to herself and the world) all the while being invited by and drawn to standards of youth life pertaining to social life and academic performance.

When spending time with the young people in this book, it becomes evident that youth life in high school is *not* the same regardless of where it is lived which emphasizes the meaning of place. No one would rightfully claim that Anna and Lisa, or any of the other four young people in this book, for that matter, are 'the same', and yet, there is a vast tendency to explain youth life, youth development and youth problems in general decontextualized manners. What Anna's and Lisa's stories demonstrate are two different ways of being young and meeting the different invitations, possibilities and demands that high school life offers, and we cannot sufficiently explain these differences, nor the developmental dynamics that unfold on a personal level, as simple mechanisms of socialization. This would not only oversimplify things, but also potentially blackbox important aspects of being young with the developmental challenges that this entails. Not only are these developmental challenges interesting in their own right, but they are also an important aspect to grasp if we wish to better understand the difficulties that some young people experience in their everyday life. This calls for a comprehension of developmental dynamics in youth life that emphasizes a global yet differentiated field of mutual reciprocities (dialectics) between a person and that person's (ecological) environment (see Pedersen & Bang 2016a; Bang 2009b). Such an aspiration furthermore connects the book to a long-standing tradition within developmental research that aims at establishing wholeness approaches to the study and conceptualization of developmental phenomena (e.g. Lewin 1935, 1946/1954; Vygotsky 1994, 1998; Hedegaard et al. 2008; Bozhovich 2009; Hedegaard 2009, 2012; Fleer & Hedegaard 2010; Hedegaard et al. 2018).

Towards a Dialectical-Ecological Comprehension of Youth Development

To comprehend developmental processes in youth from a wholeness perspective, we must be able to accommodate the fact that young people do not exist in environmental, societal or temporal vacuums (see, e.g., Ingold 2004); they are at all times surrounded by standards (as part of practices) that have been established and negotiated by others, and thus convey the accumulated intentionalities of other people (Busch 2011). By this I refer to the manner in which certain aspects of practice have been reproduced (more than others) and therefore over time become a standard of 'how we do high school here'. High school is therefore not just 'high school' in a universal sense, it is also a local institution for learning that is placed in a particular area and inhabited by particular persons (also historically); therefore, the high school practice reflects a conjunction of political rules and regulations (as standards), as well as locally developed standards for practice (Pedersen 2019). Part of the endeavour in this book is therefore to examine how differences between general standards for youth life in high school and particular possibilities and conditions may co-create a variation of subjectification processes among young people. Furthermore, it is necessary to examine the manner in which subjectivity (as the becoming of the human subject) is transformed through the concrete encounter with high school standards, and how subjectivity also has an influence on the form, meaning and transformation of standards. To explore these dynamics and transitory processes as they unfold concretely in the everyday lives of Anna, Mia, Peter, Emily, Matilda and Lisa, this book employs a developmental psychological approach, building on cultural-historical activity theory (Leontjev 1977, 2002; Vygotsky 1998; Hedegaard 2003, 2008, 2009, 2012, 2014; Bang 2008, 2009b; Stetsenko 2012, 2013; Pedersen & Bang 2016a, 2016b; Pedersen 2019) and ecological psychology (Barker 1968; Barker & Wright 1966, 1971; Gibson 1986; Heft 2001). In the following, I shall briefly present some foundational concepts that will drive my analysis as well as serve as the basis for theoretical further developments.

The outset of the book draws reference to Lewin's field theory (1935, 1946/1954), and his proposition to regard the *totality of the situation*. According to Lewin (1935:111), there is a 'circular causal relation' between the person and the environment, outlining the impossibility of singling out certain parts and attributing them to the environment *or* the individual. This means that we must study developmental dynamics as they unfold in the individual's *lifeworld,* inherently connected to the concrete environmental settings in which everyday life is lived (see also Heft 2001). Lewin thus outlines a wholeness approach that has later been further developed in different ways; as such he becomes a shared reference point in that both the cultural-historical traditions and the ecological psychological approaches that I draw reference to in this book build on insights proposed by Lewin.

According to Vygotsky, '*we can only explain the role of the environment in child development when we know the relation between the child and his environment*' (1994:338). And the child's environment is not static. For instance, it changes as the child changes educational setting, but it also undergoes continuous changes in the sense that the child relates to it differently. Accordingly, one cannot consider the environment a determining factor in the child's development but rather an integral part of a child-environment dialectic. To analytically grasp this dialectic, or the 'social situation of development' (cf. Bozhovich 2009), Vygotsky proposes the 'child's emotional experience' [perezhivanie] as an analytic unit for the child-environment relation, rather than a study of the environment as abstracted or detached from the child. Consequently, it is not possible to comprehend the influence of the environment irrespective of the child's relating to it. Later, Vygotsky's proposition of the emotional experience as the primary unit of analysis has been challenged and expanded by, e.g., Leontjev (2005) and Bozhovich (2009), who argue that *activity* should be the uniting factor, rather than experience. According to Leontjev (2005:20): '*Of everything that Vygotsky developed theoretically, the conception of the environment is the weakest*'. Development starts with material activity (2005:23) and by not acknowledging this, Vygotsky does not solve the problem of the relation between individual and environment in a theoretically consistent manner. 'Perezhivanie' is a compelling conceptualization, however, as Leontjev (2005:26) writes:

> *So, the influence of the external situation, just as the influence of the environment in general, is not determined each time by the environment itself, and not by the subject, taken in their abstract, external relation to one another, but also not in the experiencing of the subject, but rather specifically in the content of his activity. Consequently, it is in activity and not in social experience that the true unity of the subject and his reality, personality, and environment is realized.*

To comprehend developmental dynamics as they unfold for young people in a high school setting, we must therefore explore the *developing relations* between young people and their environments, through (with reference to Leontjev) their orientations and directedness, and their engagement in activities as part of concrete and ever-changing environments. This enables an analysis and comprehension of the meaning of the environment as intrinsically intertwined with the individual developmental processes that unfold.

What Vygotsky does draw our attention to is the importance of regarding development as qualitative leaps or changes rather than quantitative ones (see also Bozhovich 2009), and furthermore that development can be qualified as the developing relation between person and environment. His proposition of 'emotional experience' as analytical unit is but one attempt at a wholeness approach to the study of development. Another is proposed by Hedegaard (2009, 2012, 2014), who, building on Vygotsky among others, proposes to explore the relation between children's motives and the institutional demands they encounter and how these co-shape on another in concrete everyday life activity settings. Building on this groundwork, I wish to contribute to such wholeness approaches by further exploring developmental dynamics among young people in their *concrete high school environments* and hence propose new units of analysis that may add productively to already existing conceptualizations. In this book, I will draw extensively on theoretical insights from ecological psychology as a supplement to cultural-historical psychology with the intent of emphasizing 'the environment' in the person-environment dialectic.

Development, in this book, is thus explored as new motive orientations and qualitative transformations of activities in which the person is engaged (with reference to Hedegaard 2003, 2012), and by which the lifeworld[7] (with reference to Lewin 1935) of the person – including a person's self-understanding – is expanded and transformed. This implies that a person expands her or his *possibilities for life*, referring to the concrete possibilities for participation that a person has, is offered or that she/he creates her-/himself, along with the capabilities and directedness of the person towards an increased range of possibilities. In other words, development is explored as the *developing relation* between person and environment (Costall 2004), regarding both person and environment as dynamic. By emphasizing the importance of connecting societal values, embedded in institutional practices, with the concrete motives of the person, Hedegaard (2003, 2009, 2012) argues for a multi-dimensional, or multi-layered, comprehension of development (in line with criticisms directed towards uni-dimensional theories of development, as voiced by, among others, Riegel (1975) and Bronfenbrenner (1979). Consequently, the study of development entails a simultaneous comprehension of the person in the concrete socially and historically developed practices, the activities in which the person engages, subjectivity (personal agency and directedness), the meaning making- and negotiation processes that occur between people, in concrete environmental settings, with particular conditions and possibilities for action. As the philosopher Marx Wartofsky (1983:197) poetically argues:

> The <u>extended</u> or <u>social</u> self is not simply a creature of consciousness, but of practical activity. Thus, in this sense, my self exists for me in the artifacts and practices of my culture, my society, and my historical period. I am, so to speak, externally embodied in the products and practices that are shaped by my activity and that also shape it, serving as its means, or its objects. I <u>am,</u> in a manner of speaking, the automobile, the university building, the Houston traffic jam, the bad coffee in plastic cups, and this symposium itself, insofar as I both constitute, and am constituted by, my world.

By integrating cultural-historical activity theory and ecological psychology, it is possible to consider both the societal realities in which youth life in high school unfolds, the invitational character of the environment (as something that enables and conditions youth life in concrete and dynamic ways), and the subjectivity of individuals as they actively relate to and participate in a multitude of activity settings in their everyday life, thereby also shaping their environments and hence their conditions for development.

The Invitational Character of the Environment

The transition from one institutional setting to another, I presume, actualizes questions of 'who to be' or 'become' in a new environment, and as such this institutional transition in itself constitutes a natural experiment (acc. Bronfenbrenner 1977). The encounter with new activity settings will inevitably present new demands and lead to

---

[7] I am aware that Lewin uses the notion of life-space; however, I will employ a notion of lifeworld, drawing on Lewin's understanding, but emphasizing a phenomenological aspect.

new motives (or rearranged motive hierarchies) and, to explore 'the environmental aspect' of the transformations that occur on an individual level, I will theoretically work with concepts that elucidate the invitational character of the environment. Here, a central concept is Gibson's notion of *affordances* (1986). The core idea of Gibson's – that perceiving means the pick-up of information by an exploring organism – entails that the concrete environment facilitates and enables certain actions for the organism, whereas others are inhibited. And not only does the environment present itself as functional possibilities; it also invites certain actions qua its particular layout (or properties).[8] These must be understood concretely, as the invitational character of the environment relies on a person-environment fit (in terms of, e.g., the size one's body in relation to the height of a table), and so the environment does not invite the same actions for everybody.

A fair question would then be: *what does this have to do with young people's development in high school?* For one, it draws our attention to the fact that the environment is not just abstract surroundings, but rather concrete and specific conditions that make up certain spaces of possibilities (for action and for 'becoming') that exist as an integral part of a person's lifeworld. And secondly, it suggests a way for us to analytically explore these environmental features. However, as Gibson's notion of affordances is primarily directed towards the study of organisms, it proves insufficient for the study of human development (see also Heft 1989, 2007; Costall 1995, 2004; Pedersen & Bang 2016b); it cannot account for the societal, historical aspects of the human lifeworld, nor can it transcend a level of immediacy. To overcome these challenges while preserving the conceptual grasp of the invitational character of the environment, I will employ the notion of '*affording of societal standards*', as proposed elsewhere by Jytte Bang and myself (see Pedersen & Bang 2016b). When young people enter high school, they encounter a multiplicity of societal standards of how to be a high school student. These standards are not necessarily aligned, but often imbued with ambiguousness and ambivalence, if not downright contradiction in their invitations. Despite being encountered on a level of immediacy, these standards also reflect the mediated societal and historical character of the practice in which they are embedded. Therefore, the invitational character of the high school not only entails the immediate possibilities for action (as direct affordances), but also conveys different levels of expectations and demands to the students, which may be better encompassed by the 'affording of societal standards'. In addition, the change from the noun 'affordance' to the gerund 'affording' reflects how societal standards must be thought of as dynamic, negotiated and processual, rather than fixed and prefixing (if we were to slavishly follow Gibson). The environment is further conceptualized drawing on the work of Barker (1968), and Barker and Wright (1966, 1971), which I will further unfold in Chapter 1.

---

[8] Gibson was inspired by Gestalt psychology, mainly the work of Koffka and Lewin, and the idea that things have meaning in themselves. His notion of affordances thus builds on concepts such as 'demand character', and 'Aufforderungscharaktere' (which was later translated as 'valence'), which Lewin defined as follows: 'By valences, positive or negative, we refer to the meanings of objects by virtue of which we move towards some of them and away from others' (Lewin, as cited in Jones 2003:108). These early ecological terms imply the person and the person's perspective as an integral part of the environment (see also Pedersen & Bang 2016b for an elaboration).

Historical Time and Place

Furthermore, the environment is not something that is 'just there'; it must be understood historically. Here, the historical epistemology proposed by Wartofsky (1983) will serve as a backdrop for my exploration of youth life, along with the work of Elder (1974, 1998, 2001). This implies that the environment is not preconceived as an immediate availability of things or surroundings in a functional sense, but rather as concrete conditions for youth life to unfold in, saturated with historical meaning. In his seminal work, mapping the lifespan development of people from different cohorts over a prolonged period of time, Elder (1974, 1998) articulates four[9] principles in life course theory, to account for developmental trajectories:

(1) Historical time and place: [..] the life course of individuals is embedded in and shaped by the historical times and places they experience over their life-time.
(2) Timing in lives: the developmental impact of a succession of life transitions or events is contingent on when they occur in a person's life.
(3) Linked lives: lives are lived interdependently, and social and historical influences are expressed through this network of shared relationships.
(4) Human agency: [..] individuals construct their own life course through the choices and actions they take within the opportunities and constraints of history and social circumstances

(1998:3–4)

Based on my study of young people in high school, I will propose an expansion of Elder's principle of historical time and place, giving increased awareness to the notion of place.[10] To explore the meaning of place and the variations in youth life that seem to, in part, be connected to different high school practices, I will employ and further develop a notion of eco-niches (from Gibson 1986). Hereby, it becomes possible to grasp how young people take part in (local) shared life worlds where collective meaning is historically developed (and developing). This offers a way to comprehend the taken-for-granted-ness of the immediate environment and what matters in it, as a historical and social dynamic (between persons and their environment). Variations in youth life cannot be explained merely as a high school's way of practising high school, nor as reflecting the actions of individuals (the young people) alone, but rather they (the differences) must be comprehended in their dialectical and historical connection, where both high schools and young people have co-created (and concurrently co-create) themselves and each other – thereby reflecting locally anchored and mutual processes of becoming. This implies that 'place' becomes more than a geographical location, and as this book integrates the ecological perspective with a cultural-historical tradition, I

---

[9] According to Zittoun (2012: 514), a fifth principle is added by Elder, Kirkpatrick Johnson and Crosnoe (2004), namely that of *life-span development*, outlining that human development and ageing are lifelong processes.

[10] The study of young people's development in concrete high school settings – with the emphasis on place – also resonates with the field of human geography (see, e.g., Gallagher 1993; Collins & Coleman 2008; Karaliotas & Bettini 2013).

shall operationalize the human eco-niche by looking into the concrete *activity settings* (Hedegaard 2003, 2009, 2012, 2014), in which young people participate, thereby emphasizing subjectivity and motive orientation.

To fully account for the subject-in-the-world is to some extent a hopeless project, as, arguably, it may be virtually impossible to delimit the unit of analysis. Therefore, there are cuts to be made and analytical foci to be foregrounded, leaving other none-the-less-important aspects of the human lifeworld or the totality of the situation in obscurity. This book faces the same challenge, and it will be the reader's privilege to assess to what extent I succeed with my endeavour. Aspiring to contribute to a wholeness approach means employing approaches that seek to unite person and environment in their theoretical apparatuses. Such theoretical aspirations to unite person and environment inspire each other, overlap and promote various aspects of the person-environment relation by means of various conceptual propositions. My aspiration – and hope – with this book is to contribute to the development of such wholeness-oriented conceptual development that in turn builds on already exiting bodies of writing and theoretical developments and seeks to further develop them in relation to the specific task of comprehending developmental dynamics in high school youth life. However, despite employing, and attempting to contribute to, a wholeness approach to the study of youth development, I will not posit a comprehensive theory on *all* that may influence the developmental dynamics of youth. This is simply too great a project to take on. Rather, this book will explore and seek to theoretically qualify the dialectical intersection of the societal realities in which youth life in high school unfold, the invitational character of the environment (as something that enables and conditions youth life in concrete ways), as well as the subjectivity of individuals as they actively relate to and participate in a multitude of activity settings in their everyday life.

Methodology: A *Who* and a *How*

Engaging young people in a research project, especially one that runs over a prolonged period, can easily pose a challenge. Asking someone who is about to graduate elementary school if you – a stranger – can take part in their everyday life throughout the first year of high school is a delicate matter and a lot to ask. Hence, it was of utmost importance to me that the young people who would participate in this project would find it meaningful, in the sense that they also had an interest in some of the questions that guided the project. My initial research interest into developmental dynamics in youth life was guided by questions concerning how young people found out *who they were* and felt like they *were supposed to be*; who they were *becoming* and how they felt they *ought to become*. And how these questions and ideas (and their potential internal discrepancies) were being negotiated, shaped, asked and answered in the concrete everyday life settings in new high school environments. With reference to a co-researcher methodology, as proposed by Psychology from the Standpoint of the Subject (e.g. Holzkamp 1983, 1998, 2013; Dreier 1996; Højholt & Kousholt 2014; Chimirri 2015; Chimirri & Pedersen 2019), my approach to the field of study was, from the onset, open and exploratory, albeit at the same time guided by theoretical preconceptions and research questions, however open-ended they were. Participants were recruited via information meetings held in the early spring of 2012 in the 9th grades at various elementary schools, in different parts of the country and reflecting a certain variability in socio-economic background. Here I openly shared my research interest with the pupils, and we co-reflected about how to design such a project. Interestingly, quite a few of the participants suggested that to know about developmental processes in youth life, you would have to be present where young people live their everyday lives. Subsequently, a number of young people got in touch with me and expressed an interest to take part in the project. On the basis of various practical considerations, I included six of them, dispersed at four different schools. The open manner in which participants were recruited resulted in an unequal dispersion of sex; only one boy, Peter, signed up. Similarly, high schools were not preselected for their variety, but as a consequence of the young people's choices to take part in the project. My main criteria were a certain degree of geographical and socio-economic dispersion, and in addition, that those who would join the project were willing to let me take part of their everyday life throughout their first year of high school. Consequently, the six participants in the project are not equally represented. This reflects an ethical consideration in relation to doing empirical fieldwork of not burdening the participants unnecessarily and being aware that your presence in their everyday lives may also affect their spaces of possibilities or the dynamics that unfold in unforeseeable ways. The six young people who agreed to participate signed up while they were still in elementary school and high school was therefore a somewhat abstract feature in their lives. Engaging in practice research collaborations requires mutual and ongoing negotiation and, as a prerequisite, a genuine respect from the researcher (see also Højholt 2005). The participants therefore had a lot of say in relation to how much and where I was allowed to take part, and subsequently, differentiations arose in relation to my participation in the various high school settings.

An additional consideration extends to the position I was granted by participants, in relation to their peers. For some, it was somehow 'cool' to bring your personal 'psychologist' to school with you. For others, I was 'the researcher', whereas for one, I was positioned more as an older sister, even though to all (peers, teachers), it was completely transparent who I was and for what reasons I was there. I accepted and tried my best to meet the different positionings I was offered, all the while not attempting to be something I was not. Here I draw reference to the notion of relational expertise, as presented by Edwards (2010), along with Hasse's (2015) reflections about how the anthropologist participates in practice to learn with others and ask new questions. Furthermore, it goes without saying that the six young people in the study are very different; they have different concrete conditions in their everyday lives, they are preoccupied with different things and they may find the social dynamics at school more or less easy to engage in. All of these aspects of life play into how our joint participation evolved over the course of a year and therefore some of the young people are more dominant in this book than others. This is especially clear when it comes to Anna and Mia, who attended the same class: Anna (and her family) had no restrictions in relation to my participation and Anna was very open and relaxed about my presence, both at and outside school. Mia, on the other hand, was more reluctant, and her mother did not want me to visit their home. She was sceptical of the whole research agenda and what would come of it. This meant that I was allowed to follow Mia at school, but not at home. Finally, this book does not present an exhaustive account of the empirical work, but rather analytical cuts and selections that allow for various points to be made on how developmental processes occur in youth life in high school, which in itself contributes to an uneven representation of the participants.

Emergent Meaning and Multiple Perspectives

The comprehension of how developmental processes unfold in practice at the same time presupposes an open exploratory research approach, and theoretical conceptualizations that enable some sort of focussed presence. And so, I entered the field with theoretical notions of the reciprocal, dialectical nature of the human lifeworld, and an interest in approximating that which would acquire meaning to the participants over time, in the sense of having an impact on their developmental trajectories. Here I was particularly interested in what would co-construct ideas of *how one ought to be a high school student*. I refer to these ideas as standards, and I will introduce the notion of standards further in Chapter 1. However, my starting point was not a study of particular or preselected 'standards' – I was not looking for something specific and how this specificity would have an impact. That would have been quite a different study. Rather, it was the invitational character of the environment and how the environment is imbued with meaning, possibilities and demands, relating to who and how to be, that was the focus point. As an example, a standard of beer drinking and partying as part of 'doing high school youth' will appear several times in this book, and thus stand out as a 'dominant' or important high school standard. However, I have not been interested in pointing out or comparing the participants ways of relating to this standard; rather I have studied how particular and different aspects of practice became meaningful to each of the participants and in what ways. This implies that the standard of beer-drinking and partying will appear imbued with very different meaning and demonstrate different dynamic processes with some of the participants.

Adopting a curious and exploratory approach, rather than studying preselected standards or particular activities, enabled a comprehension of the lifeworld of the six participants, as it unfolded during their first year at high school. Over time, themes that became significant in relation to development arose, such as relating to beer and beer-drinking practices, health as a shared agenda, the rejection of ongoing invitations to take part in social life outside school, and a number of ambivalences in the ways in which high school institutionally arrange and set the frame for youth life. It also enabled the micro-genetic study of how young people actively relate to and negotiate the meaning of their environment, as well as concurrently try to look out for their own interests. To sum up, I did not enter the field empty-handed, nor equipped with pre-chosen standards to examine. Instead, I have entered the field with theoretical pre-concepts of inter alia 'standards' and 'subjectivity', and a comprehension of development as a processual and developing relation between person and environment (see also Hedegaard 2008).

Inspired by Hedegaard's interaction-based method (Hedegaard 2001), as well as recent strong developments in relation to the study of the child's perspective (e.g. Bang

2008, 2009b; Hviid 2008, 2012; Winther-Lindqvist 2014, 2012; Højholt & Kousholt 2014, 2018; Chimirri 2015, 2019; Højholt 2018; Hedegaard et al. 2018; Juhl 2019), this project employs a multiplicity of perspectives. With the intent of contributing to the comprehension of developmental processes, this approach enables the study of the interplay between young people's motives and their institutional or environmental conditions, as well as the intersubjective interactions between young people in the course of their everyday lives together at high school, as distinctive social situations and motive orientations. As Hedegaard (2012:135) writes:

> A cultural-historical wholeness approach to understanding children's development has to research the child's social situation in the activity settings that the child participates in. A child's social situation in an activity setting is characterized by the child being an agent, putting demands on another person as well as initiating activities.

The researcher participates in everyday life settings with the respective young person and focuses on understanding the person's perspective and orientations (Hedegaard 2001, 2009, 2012, see also Højholt & Schraube 2016). This entails a conjoint first-, second-, and third-person perspective, or a multitude of first-person perspectives, which briefly deserves a comment. To start with the first-person perspective, there is simultaneity of those of the participants, and mine. A first-person perspective refers to a first-person givenness, as found in the phenomenological tradition, indicating that people experience their lifeworld from a first-person perspective (Zahavi 2008; Schraube 2013). Through my participation with the young people in their daily life, I have the opportunity to observe and co-experience their actions, engagements in activities, their directedness in concrete social situations and environmental conditions, as well as their thoughts, feelings and reflections about themselves and their experiences (through our conversations and their conversations with others). My presence in these everyday life settings and situations enables a study of minor transformations in subjectivity over time, as subjectivity is not, acc. Schraube (2013:14) *'isolated and worldless'*, but rather *'contextualized and situated'*. My participation in everyday life thus implies a second-person perspective, or intersubjectivity, reflecting the fact that during my prolonged presence in practice there were numerous and inevitable direct exchanges with the participants, in the sense of co-participation in activities along with multiple conversations (a direct subject-subject perspective). Here, Edwards (2010), with her notion of relational expertise, argues how we each participate with the special knowledge that we have. This implies a presence as both a researcher and as a person; one cannot abide to the illusion of objectivity or neutrality, when it comes to researcher subjectivity. Finally, a third-person perspective is present, in the sense that I, from my researcher position, am also directed towards the wholeness, to the totality of the situation. Hence, I am at the same time directed towards the first-person perspectives of the participants, and towards the environmental and societal conditions for their daily life, and the variations that become visible in the intersection of everyday life conditions and the subjectivities of the participants. Such a third-person perspective permits a comprehension of the institutional settings, their materiality and their historically, socially developed meaning (Schraube 2010:101), which could otherwise be difficult to grasp. Schraube (2010) further points out that it is the simultaneity of the first-person perspectives of the participants and a third-person perspective on the participants' everyday life settings that enables a comprehension of the manner in which subjectivities are mediated in a societal world.

Being, and Not Being, a High School Student Anew – Conducting Research in High School

As previously noted, the study was carried out as participant observations and conversational interviews. Both demand a few comments. As Szulevicz (2015:83) writes, participant observations constitute an oxymoron in the sense that participation and observation connote two different things; participation connotes active involvement, whereas observation connotes a distant uninvolved position in relation to the researched phenomenon. Conducting participant observation thus presents the challenge of being both a participant and an observer at the same time, which arguably is a question of balance, and situational variations. Participation in practice may be more or less active, in relation to the situation, the relation to the participants and to the research interest (Pedersen et al. 2012; (Dewalt) & Dewalt 2010). In the study, I have been both (active and passive) and to varying degrees, depending on the situations and contexts. Some situations called for a more withdrawn participation, merely observing what was happening in the situation (e.g. in class when the teacher was talking, or students were presenting). Other situations meant engaging in conversations, in laughter, in working with French assignments in class, in drawing exercises in arts class and in engaging in longer conversations about the meaning of things. Over time, I increasingly became part of practice – and again here there were variations from school to school. The scepticism that I sometimes encountered from both fellow students and from teachers in the beginning of the school year gradually vanished, and my way of participating changed, in the sense that it became more natural, also to me.[11] My days were often rather unpredictable: sometimes my participation prevented notetaking in the situation, and notes were jotted down as quick keywords and conversations in a bathroom stall; other times teachers would call upon me in class, and the pressure of getting the answer right in physics class was just as nerve-wracking as when I was a high school student myself in the very last years of the previous millennium. At other occasions, a younger teacher would behave flirtatiously, I would find myself challenged by the use of slang and sense of humour pertaining to a group of sixteen-year-old boys, I would feel out of place or I would forget about time and engage in deep conversations about life. All of this to say that conducting field work is messy, demanding and exciting all at the same time (see also Law 2007 for an elaboration of this point). Inspired by the interaction-based method and the practice research tradition, I was preoccupied with trying to see the

---

[11] Grønborg (2012, 2013) provides an excellent account of this process of becoming part of practice in ethnographic research.

world 'through the eyes of the young people', which emphasized the perspective of the young people, at the expense of the perspectives of, for example, teachers and parents. Central awareness to guide my notetaking related to what was relevant or became meaningful for the young people – and in which way.

Part of my participation also involved longer conversations with the participants, which I refer to as *conversational interviews*. These were qualitative, informal and unstructured interviews based on situational or everyday life focus points. They were carried out *if* and *when* it made sense in the field work. This implies that the interviews usually took place after school, at a participant's home or at a café. The reason why I refer to them as conversational interviews relates to the fact that they were indeed *conversations*; conversations between me and a participant, co-reflecting upon the everyday life of the participant or some of our shared experiences in the high school setting. The conversations were open-ended, and depending on my relationship with the participant, they also contained a high level of mutual self-disclosure. These interviews contributed with elaborations of – and connections between – situations and provided valuable insight into the first-person perspectives of the participants. Also, they served as a way for me to question, validate or elaborate my understandings of the participants and the practices in which they participated, with a focus on motives, meaning, standards, scope of possibilities and self-understanding. When I present these conversations as interviews and not just part of a participant observation, it has to do with the liberty they contributed to (for me), in terms of not having to write thorough field notes, as the conversations were recorded. The reason for considering the conversational interviews a supplement to the participant observations is that the participant observations predominated. This relates to three issues: firstly, that I was first and foremost interested in the everyday life as it was conducted by the participants. This places an emphasis on what activities the participants were engaging in, how, with whom and in relation to what. Furthermore, it emphasizes 'doing' rather than 'reflecting about', just as a potentially decontextualized co-reflection on something (without a previous co-participation in the high school setting) would risk creating a separation between the participant's thoughts and feelings on the one hand, and the environment on the other. This would imply that the lifeworld of the person would potentially be reduced to the 'stories' or insights narrated by the person, and I would be prevented from obtaining valuable knowledge through observing the person participate in concrete social settings with other people and concrete material conditions (see also Pedersen 2012). Secondly, that it was not possible to make recordings in a high school setting, and thirdly, that it was sometimes difficult to produce the recorder as it automatically positioned me more formally as *a researcher* vis-à-vis a *participant*, whereas when the recorder was not present, the relation was usually more relaxed and informal.

Despite conducting an extensive fieldwork, there are delimitations to outline. And just as one can extend a criticism towards some research approaches, for example, decontextualizing, individualizing, objectivizing and so forth, employing and attempting to add productively to a wholeness approach is not automatically a methodological ticket to heaven. In my work, I have tried to insist on the interconnectedness and reciprocity of persons and their concrete environments. This comes with the risk of turning the unit of analysis into a never-ending quest of contextuality and complexity, which – admittedly – may also obscure the lens, so to speak. Therefore, analytical cuts are needed. Analytical cuts that illuminate some aspects all the while they tend to push others into obscurity. Law (2007) refers to this as the process of othering and argues that we ought to pay an interest in that which we do not put in writing. Not as an argument against claiming responsibility for the analytical scalpel, but to ensure that we indeed acknowledge and claim ownership of this responsibility. We, as researchers, make decisions on what is included and relevant, and what is not. In this case, this responsibility falls upon me. Following this line of thought, there are a few aspects worth mentioning here. As already noted, there was a certain randomness in the selection of participants, which is reflected in the uneven dispersion of gender among participants as well as the absence of ethnic differences. Also, this book is primarily about the life that goes on at the high school premises, among young people and the high school as an institutional setting. Therefore, family dynamics are not extensively explored and are not in focus. This in no way excludes their significance – neither in the book nor in the developmental dynamics in general – however, they have not been made a deliberate focus of exploration. Another aspect that is deliberately not explored concerns the teachers; teachers surely play a part in the dynamics that unfold in a high school setting, just as they will be part of this book. However, teachers' perspectives are not directly included in the study which, surely, may contribute to a perceptual sidedness – and this sidedness was a deliberate choice. A choice of solidarity with the young people, and from a young person's perspective, as an alternative to the much dominant standardized and normative 'adult' perspective on youth (according to Bang & Møhl 2010). There were numerous invitations to engage with teachers and to acquire teachers' perspectives on the young people, and in a few instances, these will be included. However, it was also my clear experience in practice that shifting between attentiveness to teachers and the young people when conducting field work was not an option; it was an either or, especially for the young people. Demonstrating solidarity was important, otherwise I was perhaps just another adult whose intentions were not clear.

What Do We Get to Know about Youth Development?

This book does not claim to present universal ideas pertaining to 'this is how *all* young people are'. That would violate the situated character of the study as well as the foundational understanding of the relation between the person and her/his environment (in accordance with Vygotsky 1994). However, it *explores, illustrates* and *theorizes* developmental dynamics that occur in the life of six young people as they find themselves in the midst of a transition from one educational setting to another, as well as in the more existential transition from childhood to adulthood. In this book, I propose that in order to comprehend youth development, we must insist on a wholeness approach, which in my take emphasizes the concrete environmental settings in – and in relation to – which development occurs. Therefore, I accentuate the invitational character of the environment, both in a direct and more material sense, but also, and nonetheless importantly, with an analytical gaze to the invitational character of that which does not directly materialize, but that all the same come to shape the developmental spaces in which young people participate. I will analytically unfold this as standards, and as collective ideality. The reason for doing so is to take seriously how young people are *always* in dialogue with the surroundings, and in that sense, subjectivity, including development, is not merely an individual matter (see, e.g., Stetsenko 2013). Through our taking part in the everyday lives of Mia, Anna, Lisa, Emily, Peter and Matilda, we learn about their individual transitory processes and the (potential) challenges that arise along the way. However, I will argue, we also learn about youth life in a more general sense, and about developmental dynamics that may prove relevant in other settings than the ones explored in this book. The exploration of high school life as it presents itself for the participants in this book thus enables me to propose theoretical concepts and analytical awarenesses that in an abductive manner emerged from the study. Theoretically, there is always an interchange between the specific or concrete and the abstract or general. In the framework of cultural-historical activity theory, we build on the knowledge we gain from specific cases and use this as a starting point for extrapolating aspects of the human lifeworld that are not limited to the specific situation (as situated generalization, see Axel & Højholt 2019; Dreier 2019). At the same time, we draw on well-established theoretical concepts that show their value through their relevance in relation to unfolding and comprehending complex social situations and phenomena. In the case of this study, we learn about various and specific conditions in relation to which the everyday lives of six young Danish people are unfolded, along with how the motive orientations and ways of relating to themselves, others and the world of these young people change over time. The theoretical concepts that are employed and developed in the book show their strength and general value through their relevance in relation to understanding the complex subject matter of youth development in a time of transition. This implies that the insights proposed here have the potential to transcend the specific situations of the six participants. As Valsiner (2011) points out, as a general idiographic science, developmental psychology generalizes from particular, individual cases that have unique histories. And as Molenaar and Valsiner (2008:25) write, *'behind that uniqueness are basic universal processes that have to be discovered'*. The study of the lives of particular young people (embedded in their everyday life settings) provides not only knowledge of those particular persons and the particular and situated manners in which their lives unfold but may also contribute with general knowledge about the processes of development that occur in the lives of young people in general. This means that generalization derives from the particular, a point also made by Lewin (according to Beckstead et al. 2009), as well as Flyvbjerg (2001). The book thus offers insight into, empirically speaking, the specific youth lives of young people in different locations in Denmark, and, theoretically speaking, into the developmental dynamics that occur – which are not limited to a specific geographical or cultural context.

Structure of the book

The book is structured so that we move from an emphasis on the invitational character of the environment to the developmental dynamics on a subjective level. Throughout the book, these aspects are considered inseparable; however in order to analytically tease out and discuss developmental dynamics, a certain structure has been imposed to – hopefully – gradually unfold the complexities of the person-environment reciprocity.

To begin our exploration, I will set the scene in **Chapter 1**, by inviting the reader to take part in three different introductory events at three different high schools. Here it is illustrated how concrete expectations and invitations are presented to prospective students, setting the scene for understanding the values and demands in the different high school settings. This illuminates similarities and differences between high schools on an institutional level. It also outlines the dominant standards or norms that frame youth life (in a high school context).

In **Chapter 2**, we return to Anna and Lisa, as well as Mia, who attends the same class as Anna and explore their everyday life at respective high schools. The emphasis here is to explore the values and orientations of the girls in direct relation to the way their respective high schools enact and enable 'high school'.

In order to unfold the dynamic interplay between the young people and their respective schools, the chapter presents and discusses the relevance of a concept of the *human eco-niche* and proposes for it to be studied as persons' participation in and engagement with various *activity settings*. The chapter will more explicitly examine the high school setting as part of the eco-niche and look into the manner in which variations in youth life are created in, and in relation to, a specific high school setting. The variations that emerge, and the difference they make, have implications for the ways in which young people are invited to participate and perceive themselves in these settings. This points to the situatedness of where one grows up and suggests that high school is not just a decontextualized institutional setting, but rather a setting that reflects collective idealities of actions, values and possibilities for action, on a local and situated level (which also relates to an overall societal and political level). The two case studies, or eco-niche portraits, show us something about the different ways in which young people are subjectified as high school students, and as many other positions, roles or qualities, depending on the availabilities of their respective eco-niches (e.g. as responsible gymnastics trainer, as baby sitter, as junior politician, as someone on top of fashion, as someone unique or different, as someone who can do what she wants, as a beer-drinker, a choir-singer). This implies that the eco-niche, as a concept, offers an important analytical tool in the pursuit of comprehending developmental processes.

Whereas Chapter 2 explores differences between two different high schools, **Chapter 3** delves into one school, Westside High, that Emily and Matilda attend and explores the connections between the high school as a practice and how the girls relate to the values, demands and challenges they encounter via-a-vis the ambitious and performance-oriented profile of the school. Here, specifically, it will become evident how individualized problem-conceptualizations are closely connected to the high school practice, and how young people are trying to cope with the challenges that this implies on a personal level. This demonstrates how variability is not only found on an institutional level, but also on an individual level, in the two girls' ways of relating to the same institutionalized pressure (e.g. to perform in certain ways). It demonstrates how the young people are constantly trying to navigate the myriad of invitations to perceive themselves and to participate in certain ways, and it presents an argument for why an understanding of developmental dynamics must be studied and understood in the intersection of young people's subjectivities and motives and the particular demands and values embedded in the institutional setting.

Chapter 4 discusses the implications of the eco-niche variability presented in the previous two chapters. The key point in the chapter is to discuss the meaning of *where* youth life is lived and the difference this makes. This aspect of youth life is often diminished or even black-boxed in dominant discourses of youth life; youth life is generally thought to be the same regardless of where it is lived. The meaning of place indicates that young people are offered different conditions and different possibilities for action depending on the location of their school. This refers to both the concrete availabilities in the environment (at, and in proximity to, the school), of the concrete architectural layout of the school and to an overall historically developed local set of objective meaning sets. Also, it indicates that the high school is part of a particular eco-niche in the sense that there are differences in the general conditions that the eco-niche offers and thus also what the available environment offers (as well as invites for and accentuates) in terms of conditions for orientation, participation and self-understanding.

In **Chapter 5**, I will further explore an ambiguity connected to the introduction of standardized health profiles in Anna and Mia's class at Countryside High. The reason for this is that it provides an interesting example of how the (social) meaning of introduced (politically motivated) standards is negotiated. The standard in question is represented by a health profile that students are required to complete (by various tests) twice a year. The implied expectation is that awareness of personal health will affect young people's behaviour in certain ways (in terms of health optimization). However, what we see over the course of the school year is how the content of the health profile is negotiated and acquires its own life, so to speak. This implies that the well-intended political agenda of drawing young people's attention to health issues by introducing mandatory health measurements cannot be regarded as a predictable outcome or effect. Rather, it demonstrates how meaning is continuously negotiated socially, and therefore we need to acknowledge the way in which young people actively make sense of the standards they encounter, including how they alter, or even pervert them. It exemplifies how politically motivated demands, as embedded in institutional practices, cannot be understood as directly influencing young people in a narrow and uniform sense (as determinism), but rather how these demands are met differently depending on personal motives, and the social setting in which they are introduced; it thus becomes a contextualization of standards of health and bodily normativity.

Chapters 6 and 7 invite us to co-experience high school at a subjective level, by exploring the life-worlds of Anna and Peter, respectively. In **Chapter 6**, we dive further into the subjective aspects of relating to the standards of youth life that are encountered in the high school setting, and how relating to these standards co-creates development on a subjective level, in relation to not only participation but also self-understanding. Here we return to Anna, and we follow her closely to see how her understanding of herself changes over the school year, and more specifically in relation to drinking beer, as representing a standard of social participation. What is interesting is that we can readily interpret Anna's development in relation to beer drinking and meeting standards of social participation as a case of simple socialization, where norms are gradually appropriated and internalized. However, what becomes evident over the course of the school year is that the change is not limited to Anna, but also the ways in which the others in her class participate and the very meaning of the standard of social participation itself. This allows for an understanding of youth development as a dynamic relation – a dialectical process of meeting societal standards and negotiating their meaning while acting on personal motives. This points to a theoretical development of a dialectical-ecological model of youth development to better grasp the subjective processes of transformation in relation to 'self'.

Building on the previous chapter, **Chapter 7** explores the lifeworld of Peter, and how he relates to, and negotiates the standards he encounters in the high school setting. The chapter will demonstrate how Peter does not merely integrate the dominant standards of youth life into his self-understanding, but rather how he challenges them by actively negotiating meaning and ways of participating. The chapter thus illuminates the subtle and ongoing negotiations of meaning that young people engage in, and how this relates to their self-understandings and intentionality. This reveals the efforts of young people to create a meaningful space for oneself, holding on to one's self-understanding while actively relating to the standards of the environment, as elusive as these may be.

In **Chapter 8**, I will gather the analytical threads and reflect upon their implications and possible contributions to a dialectical-ecological understanding of developmental processes. Here, I discuss the need to insist on a dialectical-ecological approach to the study and understanding of youth development, and what such an approach may tell us of the developmental dynamics of youth life. This entails the comprehension of youth development as syntheses of subjectivity and subjectification processes and implies that solely focussing on either comes with the risk of reductionism. It thus presents a counterargument to the aforementioned notion of regarding young people's development as simple processes of socialization. Here the notion of subjectified subjectivity (that is first introduced in Chapter 6) will be further qualified in relation to other prominent conceptualizations of youth development. The concept is proposed to sum up the concurrent developmental dynamic between a phenomenological experience of 'being me' (subjectivity) and the way in which we are acting in relation to the standards and invitations we encounter (in the environment) and to some extent integrate them into our self-understanding (subjectification).

Finally, in the last chapter (**Concluding Thoughts and Perspectives**), I draw concluding remarks and reflections in relation to the findings and theoretical propositions of this book and where this leaves us in terms of comprehending developmental dynamics and transitions in high school.

1

Setting the Scene – Invitations and Expectations

To understand the transition heralded by starting high school, we need to start our analysis *before* one is enrolled at high school. Starting high school is not restricted to the actual first day at school. The first day is preceded by a familiarization process that has often begun a long time before one becomes a high school student. For some, the choice of which school to attend is not difficult, and perhaps not even a conscious or explicit question. This may be the case when growing up in an area with limited choices of schools, or in case one has older siblings or another kind of precedence in the family or local community of attending a particular school. Here the choice is more likely a choice between different kinds of educational profiles: trade school, vocational school or high school. For others, choosing the right high school requires careful consideration and preparation. This implies an awareness and acknowledgement of the variations that exist between different high schools and that these variations make a difference, albeit one is perhaps not able to voice exactly why or how.

In this chapter, we look at the different invitations that young people encounter at the formal introduction events that high schools host annually to prospective students and their parents. These introduction events or information meetings are held at all high schools in Denmark in late winter (usually in January or February) prior to enrolment and school start in August. Prospective high school students attend these meetings with their parents and/or friends to get an idea of what the school is like – which academic profiles are offered, how is the atmosphere and what are the expectations? Some attend only one meeting at the school they have already set their mind to, whereas others shuffle around and attend several different ones to get an impression of the different atmospheres and possibilities.

Examining these introduction events gives us an idea of how high school as an institutional setting produces and conveys standards for youth life and installs expectations of *how to be* in high school. This happens through the way in which the school invites you to become part of the school. These introduction events demonstrate how high school is not a neutral space, but a space infused with historical and local meaningfulness – of *how we do high school here*.

In this chapter, I will start by examining the invitations given at the introduction events at three different schools. What will become evident is the multitude of *different* invitations that young people encounter, or the *variations* over the same kind of invitations. We will see how there are many similarities across the different schools, but also how the different ways of emphasizing aspects of high school life create variations in atmosphere; the schools are in many respects similar and yet very different.

Paying attention to the initial invitations presented by the high school as a setting provides insight into the school as a developmental space and gives a first glance at what is valued and what will be demanded from the school more formally, and not the least from its current students. It also outlines the dominant standards or norms that frame youth life (in a high school context); I shall return to this later in the chapter. I will start by introducing Northside High, followed by Westside High and Countryside High.

Northside High: *Youth Life Is an Important Part of Being Young*

Northside High is located in the suburbs north of Copenhagen in a mixed middleclass and upper middleclass area. It is a rather large high school with a little over a thousand students. Because of its location in the larger Copenhagen area, not only local students attend, but also students who live further away, e.g., in Copenhagen or in other suburban areas.

The introduction event at Northside High is officially initiated in the school's sports hall. To get there, one has to enter the main entrance hall, where the school choir is singing, and pass through parts of the school, which provides an opportunity to glance into classrooms and briefly study posters and decorations on the walls. In the sports hall, rows of chairs have been lined up and a stage has been set up in one end of the room. Around 800–900 people are gathered here: all young people with their parents. Some obviously know each other and talk in small groups. Current students and teachers are engaging in small talk here and there and handing out information pamphlets about the school. The event is about to start, and people sit down. In the back of the room, a large group of the school's current students gather. They are here to help out, entertain and explain, after the event in the sports hall.

The program is launched by two current students at the school, Martha and Daniel, who take the stage to tell the listeners about '*the school that they hold so dearly*'. They introduce themselves and Martha welcomes everyone with a slightly nervous undertone in her voice. They mention the particular school spirit, without going into details about what this means, and identity work, again en passant, as if everybody knows what this means and that we all agree that young people are in the midst of some sort of identity building process. Martha continues:

> *Youth life is an important part of being young ... and therefore ...* (she clears her throat and takes on a more formal tone in her voice as to underline the importance of what she has to say) ... *Dear parents. For the first couple of months that your children attend to high school, you will be 'childless', because your children will be out at parties. Either here at the school or at private parties, and it is very important that you allow them to attend these, because here they'll be forming important social relations.*

Daniel comments with a smirky smile:

> *Yeah, no one left our class, 'cause we are all very close ... eh, I mean ... eh ...* (he starts blushing and his fellow students in the back of the room start cheering) *... we get along really well. And there's been some kissing here and there as well.*

The current students in the back of the room start clapping and cheering, and Daniel and Martha blush and smile, and suddenly appear a little shy. They then go on to talk a little about school rules concerning smoking and Martha notes that '*it is good to have rules that are kept once in a while*'. They then leave the stage and are followed by Martin, the student council president. After introducing himself, he says:

> *We teach all subjects here at the school* (as to indicate that the school does not have a narrow academic profile). *We take care of you. You might get insecure or your home-base might get insecure, but regardless of what kind of problems you might have, we can take care of it here at school. Either from the school's side or from the people that surround you here in your daily life. Because here at Northside High, you make friends for life! There is room for everyone here, regardless of their background.*

He continues to introduce how the first months at school are planned to give the best start. And he presents the school slogan: *A good place to learn, a good place to be.* He then runs through more formal aspects of the school organization; there are fourteen different academic programmes to choose from, a homework café is organized twice a week throughout the school year, democratic influence for students is ensured via the student council, and there are numerous parties and cafes arranged throughout the year at the school premises. There are concerts: the annual musical, the spring concert and a church concert. There are mandatory school trips abroad, and on the last day of school, there is folk dancing. All this is presented as a high-speed information flow that appears overwhelming and appealing at the same time. Martin adds:

> *We also run a talent development programme. For this, we cooperate with The School for Talent Development and Team Denmark* (a sports related talent development) *... and we value health, so we organize a run in the spring, where we run in the nearby park. And the mayor of the city joins this run as well ... And finally, we have the alumni association that you can join, so that it is possible to attend our cafes, parties etc after graduation, because you miss the school so much.*

On a brief note, what is particularly noteworthy here is how the first part of the introduction event is led by students. *They* are in charge of welcoming and setting the scene, not only for the evening, but also for attending this particular high school. They present and represent a 'we'; how 'we' do high school and thus outline what one can expect and at the same time, what is expected of you, when you become part of this 'we'. As such, they become an authority, directly addressing the parents with clear expectations, and speaking on behalf of the school. And to the future students, it becomes an invitation to become 'like us'.

The second part of the introduction event is led by the vice principal, who briefly outlines the choices one has to make regarding academic profile, and when these choices have to be made. He then outlines the structure of the three years in high school and concludes with: *'and on June 24th 2016, the principal will be handing you your diplomas at graduation'*. This serves as an introduction to the principal, who, as the last speaker of the evening, comes on stage. She picks up on some of the points already made by Martin regarding talent programmes and how the school may be helpful in relation to all sorts of problems:

> *We want to help you stand on your toes, push you gently, challenge you and make demands. [...] Everyone will be screened, so that extra measures can be taken* (in relation to e.g. reading skills) *if need be. [...] The study counsellors can help you manage high school life as well as your private life ... perhaps!*
>
> *We have a high percentage of students who graduate; this is a very large school, but we take care of each and every one of our students.*

This affirms the impression already given by the students. As Martha, the principal also places a responsibility on the parents:

> *We know that attending high school can be challenging at times, and we need you parents to be supportive and respectful about this.*

She then addresses the prospective students with the same directness:

> *We expect you to show up prepared for classes and to hand in your things on time. That you engage yourselves actively in the classes. That you contribute to creating a good atmosphere here at the school, and that you show respect and openness towards everybody at school. [...] You will be forming networks and friendships for life here and it is an important choice you are facing* (regarding choice of school). *We want to help you figure out what you are good at.*
>
> *We will have 12 new first grade classes new year* (first grade refers to the first year at school). *We hope to be able to enrol everyone who applies but I cannot provide any guarantees at this point.*

The principal's speech completes the official part of the programme, and after a few songs performed by the school band, people are encouraged to tour the school and hear about all the different subjects that will be represented by teachers and students in various classrooms. Everywhere is packed with teachers and students who enthusiastically share their thoughts about the different subject matters to the prospective students and their parents.

Even though the above example presents only an excerpt of the introduction programme, it clearly illustrates how prospective high school students are bombarded with expectations, normative standards, possibilities and demands with their own more or less overt agendas built in. These are in no way homogeneous: students are expected to socialize in a specific way, which involves (a lot of) partying, some kissing and making friends for life. All the while they engage enthusiastically in finding their 'right path' academically, master classes and pursue talent programmes, indicating that there are differences to be celebrated and nurtured rather than ignored. The anticipated detachment process from the parents that one can find in traditional theories of youth development resonates here by a clear invitation to handle the problems that may occur at the school, rather than within the family. This instates a pressure on prospective students to free themselves from their parents in order to become full members of the community; high school will become the new 'home', and your new friends are expected to replace the meaning of the family, in terms of a secure base. Of course, this is not a requirement, or a demand set in stone, but an invitation to start thinking (oneself) along these lines. At the same time, a clear expectation is conveyed to the parents to 'set their children free' and accept that they will not see them as much. This message is given both as an information of how to expect the young people to be out partying or with friends, when they are not at school, and as a reassurance of how the school will provide a sufficient safety net from now on: 'you can let go, we've got this'.

The multitude of invitations offered here at Northside High first and foremost says something about Northside High and the specificity of how high school is enacted here. At the same time, it tells us something about high school life in general. And before I look more closely at the invitations more specifically, and what it tells us about high school life, we shall have a look at the introduction events at two other schools: Westside High and Countryside High.

Westside High: *You Create Westside, Westside Creates You. Together, We Create the Future!*

Westside High is an inner-city school, located in the bustling Copenhagen city centre. The introduction event takes place in the nearby sports facility, as the school itself does not have rooms that are large enough for such assemblies. The school has a little less than a thousand students and rejects a fair number of applicants every year, as it is a popular high school.

When arriving at the introduction event, one is first not sure whether one is entering a bigger sports event or another kind of cultural happening, as the location in no way signals high school. However, students are handing out printed programmes at the doors, and as one enters, live music is playing, and the choir is singing a groovy tune. Even though it is a very large sports hall, the place is packed, and people sit on chairs, on the floor or lean against the back wall. As was the case at Northside High, the event is launched by two students, who introduce themselves as the hosts of the evening, present the programme and guide the following sing-along. After the sing-along, the principal comes on stage, as the first speaker of the evening. She welcomes everyone again and emphasizes the strong globalization profile of Westside High, which means that internationalization and global citizenship are keywords for all the academic programmes at the school.

> *We want to awaken your appetite to study abroad – you should consider the whole world your playground. […] We will stimulate your international mindset. […] As a student here, you need to be ready to develop your global mindset. This requires engagement and a desire to give it your most. Choose carefully where you want to fit in!*

The principal makes it clear that at Westside High the academic level is high as are the expectations to the students; *you have to want it*. Knowledge, learning, democracy and community are the key values that are meant to shine through all school activities. Perhaps this is what is referred to as the school spirit, which is mentioned a lot. There is, however, no doubt that attending this school is tightly linked to being ambitious. The principal emphasizes the numerous collaborative projects that are carried out with both universities and the business world. The general academic profile is presented as creative, innovative and ambitious.

> *West Side High has become a campus.*

By underlining the campus-like structure of the high school, the principal refers both to the architectural layout of the school premises and – which is important here – to the university approximation that the school aims at. It is a positioning of the school as well as a clear invitation for students to consider themselves further on in the educational system than they actually are at present. And so, it underlines the connection between the high school and what comes after.

After the principal's speech, two students come on stage to give their account of student-life at Westside High:

> *(one) The school nominated me for the national debating team, where I was accepted. I now practice ten hours per week, and the school is making it happen both financially and practically.*
> *(the other) The talent programs offered by the school are among the things that I have appreciated the most here. The opportunities they provide are a true gift.*

Clearly, what is highlighted at Westside High are primarily its academic merits and ambitious expectations to the students. This overshadows any mention of the value of the social or a sense of community. These are somehow implicit or at least unnecessary to explicitly draw forth. And yet, there is a clear coherence between the school's expectation of students' engagement and the engagement actually demonstrated by the students on stage; it is convincing and very alluring. A very clear image is painted here of who you would want to be. A certain kind of successful.

After the formal part of the introduction event at the sports facility, people disperse into the different school buildings to hear about different subjects and academic programmes. I make my way to the music room, as the two girls who participate in my study at this school are attending the school's music line. A lot of people cram together in the smaller music room, and there is not nearly room enough for everyone. Two teachers talk about the programme more specifically and some of the current students perform a few pieces. The atmosphere is relaxed and warm, and people take the time to stay and hear all the details. In a way, this presents as a contrast – or a welcome supplement – to the cooler and more professional atmosphere displayed in the sport facility, where the invitational character was at the same time almost supercilious and yet convincing. Here, in the more intimate classroom setting, you feel a different kind of atmosphere that is social and more relaxed.

Already, there is a noticeable difference between the schools, but we also see how they connect with some of the same tendencies regarding high school life, albeit weighted differently. Let us see what impression we are left with at Countryside High.

Countryside High: *My Dad Used to Go Here*

Countryside High is a provincial high school in the island of Funen, a bigger island (population of little less than half a million) in the middle of Denmark. Countryside High is located in a smaller provincial city and drawing students from a large surrounding area of other smaller cities, villages and countryside areas. The school accommodates a little less than 600 students. The introduction event takes place in the large communal area in the middle of the school building, where rows of chairs have been lined up for the occasion. The area is the first thing one sees, when entering the main entrance, and one is therefore immediately drawn to the activity in the big open space. There is a turn up of perhaps 200 people, which is far from the numbers at Northside- and Westside High, but seems to meet the expectation of Countryside High, judging from the number of available chairs.

I sit down next to a prospective student, who attends the introduction event with his father. I take the opportunity to ask him why he is considering attending this particular school.

It is the obvious choice for me. My dad used to go here, so I can't see why I should choose somewhere else.

Countryside High is the only high school within a rather large radius, which makes it the obvious choice for many. Here the choice is less about the profile of the school and more about whether or not to attend high school, in the first place, and whether to choose the local school or go to the nearest bigger city to attend high school there. Countryside High is located app. 25 km from a big city. For many it thus becomes a practical question of transportation options and convenience.

At Countryside High, the introduction event follows the same pattern as at the other schools; the event is launched by two current students, Catherine and Jonah, who welcome everyone and initiate the sing-along of classical Danish hymn. Afterwards the principal takes the microphone: here there is no stage, but the speaker is positioned next to the grand piano in front of the rows of chairs.

> *Welcome! I will now present the school and this type of school. We are really proud of this type of school. [...] You will see that we have something really good to offer the young people. [...] Your biggest challenge this spring is to choose which youth education you want.*

Here the principal addresses first the parents and secondly the prospective students, making it unclear who is actually supposed to make the choice of school. He gives a longer speech addressing the need for young people to choose high school (as opposed to trade school or vocational school), in relation to the current and future labour market. This paints an image of the group or social segment he is addressing; here the question is not one of choosing between different high schools, as attending high school is not a given, and – perhaps – a higher number of prospective students here have parents who themselves did not attend high school. The difference brought on by the geographical location, compared to the status of Northside- and Westside High who are but two among many schools in the same larger area, implies that there is no real competition here. Rather it becomes a question of choosing high school at all. The principal continues:

> *We have the highest grade-point average and the lowest drop-out rate, and the highest rate of students continuing to further higher education. [...] We offer extra teaching sessions to students with special needs and we have counsellors who can help in case of special needs or problems, as well as a mentor system. [...] We also do talent work, in collaboration with The Academy of Talented Youth, who employ university teachers. The purpose of this is to motivate and prepare the young people for university. I can also mention the Budding Scientist Project, where we produced two winners two years ago. Other than that, we have Olympiads in math, physics, chemistry, philosophy and biology, where we have had several winners from here – and we are very proud of that.*

The range that is depicted here, in terms of 'the implied student', is rather broad. On the one hand, the principal positions the school among the elite by emphasizing 'the highest grade-point average' and 'the lowest drop-out rates' and highlights the possibility of talent programmes. He stresses the fact that the school produces talented students (who can compete and win). At the same time, clear measures are taken to ensure that those students who require extra assistance and additional teaching, or need help with various problems, are looked after and their needs met. This implies that the school is addressing students who consider themselves both academically strong and academically weak. At Countryside High, it is clearly emphasized that one is supposed to feel good at school. As the principal points out:

> *In the national well-being survey that is conducted every third year, Countryside High came in 6th on the question of student satisfaction in 2013 (the most recent poll).*

And amidst the tendency to position the school on all sorts of surveys or scales, he further emphasizes that the best choice for students is the choice that resonates with one's interests, when it comes to academic focus:

> *My number one advice to you is to choose according to your interest – choose with your heart! That is, when choosing your academic line of study here, your choice is temporary and can be altered after the first six months.*

Here, the principal acknowledges that making choices – that have consequences for one's further education – can be difficult. It is hard to know what one will want further down the line, and where one will thrive, both academically and socially. Therefore, he encourages the prospective students to go with the interests they have now and then adjust them further down the road, if need be. In contrast to especially Westside High, Countryside High does not present a clear image of who, how or what it expects its students to be and become. Rather, one is left with the impression that everyone is a potential fit, and that everyone is welcome.

What stands out at Countryside High, in comparison to the two other schools, is the way specific details about the everyday life at the school are made explicit at the introduction event. These details are interesting, because they contain highly relevant information on a practical level, and, at the same time, to many may seem redundant, as the information given is assumed obvious knowledge.

> The principal: *We stress the importance of being a modern school; with high academic and pedagogical standards. All classrooms have smartboards, and all papers are handed in electronically. […] The school has recently been thoroughly modernized.*

Again, this might be addressed to the parents primarily, where some have attended this school themselves many years ago. The principal goes on to show an overview of the bus connections and timetables on the mobile fold-out screen positioned behind him:

> *The bus connections will be adjusted this summer to fit the new school reform, but this is just for the better* (for us).

This information clearly relates to the geographical location of the school and indicates the large area that the school is recruiting from – and the limited transportation options in the countryside. Many students live quite far away and are very dependent on the local bus routes that usually only run once an hour, potentially giving students a lot of waiting time. These latter points are important, as they tell us something about the school-identity. I will return to this in Chapter 2, where I will explore the school further, as an eco-niche.

By the end of the formal part of the event, a former student comes to 'the stage' to share her story. She is now studying law in Copenhagen and is about to finish her bachelor's degree. She emphasizes the strong sense of community that she experienced at Countryside High, and the profound sense of respect and security that it provided. She also shares that her friends at other high schools would refer to Countryside High as a 'hippie high school'.

Finally, Catherine and Jonah, who host the event, return to 'the stage'. They introduce the students in the music class, who perform an Eric Clapton song. The atmosphere is warm and relaxed, and the students take advantage of every opportunity to make joking comments, e.g., on the principal's speech being boring.

> Jonah: *Here dreams become reality. Is that really true, you ask. Yes, it is ... So why choose Countryside High? There are two main reasons: an academic and a social. There is room for everyone here and everybody will make good friends during their time at the school. It is a small school, and you'll make friends across the different years. I see it as an advantage that your friends live close by and are part of the same local community. Academically, there is also room for everyone. It is possible to keep up with the teaching and also to be(come) among the best. Here you have a ton of possibilities and there is room for everyone. That's what makes the school so good!*
>
> *[...]*
>
> *And this sounds almost too good to be true* (people, including Jonah, laugh) ... *but I can assure you that we also have highlights such as study trips abroad – that often have an academic content* (he smiles) *– language study trips, academic trips, parties, cafes ... Personally, I am always looking forward to the parties. What is cool is that we then have a bar over here* (he points to the side of the room), *where our amazing teachers will perform as bartenders and sell us beer.*[1] *Sometimes it will be parents as well, but not many of us* (students) *willingly want our parents present, so ...* (people laugh).

After the formal part of the event is finished, people disperse into classrooms and corridors, looking at teaching materials, talking to students and teachers. The atmosphere is relaxed and almost homely, as quite a few make a stop by the picture wall next to the principal's office to find the graduation photos of their siblings, or parents. Here you have a clear feeling that many already know the school, and everyone knows someone who already attended. It is not *a* high school, but more so *the* high school in this area.

---

[1] In Denmark, the legal age limit for buying alcohol with a lower alcohol percentage (such as beer and wine) is sixteen years, whereas the age limit is eighteen years for alcohol with higher percentages (such as hard liquor). However, in practice, Denmark has always had a very liberal alcohol policy when it came to young people's alcohol consumption. People under the age of eighteen are not allowed in bars or discotheques, so it is a common practice that youth educations and, e.g., local sports associations host parties where teachers, parents and/or other members serve as bartenders and thus create a somewhat safe environment for the young people. In addition, all high schools host monthly café-events after school hours, where students sell beers to other students. Such events are supervised by teachers or the management but run by student organizations.

High School Settings: Similar, Yet Different Frames for Youth Life

When one walks into a high school in Denmark, there are many features and practice elements that are recognizable and similar; they all fit with an overall idea of what high school is. And so, the high schools in this book share a considerable number of similarities in terms of structure and practice: they all have lessons of fifty minutes, smoking inside is not allowed, they use the same grading system, they follow the same curriculum guidelines, the same regulations, etc., just to mention a few similarities. At the same time, there are significant differences between the schools; the manner in which they create possibilities for actions for the students, and in the way that high school as a practice unfolds for you, when you enter as a newcomer to the school. From looking at the manner in which the schools, as institutional settings, invite prospective students into the school, we see how there are also many similarities in the ways in which *how to be a high school student* is depicted or which standards are being presented. And again, there are local differences.

By looking at the introduction events, we acquire a sense of the *multiple invitational character* of the environment. Entering high school does not equal entering a 'free space' of development. There are social standards of what to do, how to feel and think, what not to feel and think, what not to do, what to do while perhaps not feeling like it (or feeling like doing something else), how to think about oneself and others, etc. The total set of such standards is what actually constitute the everyday life of the high school youth; it may be dealt with in different manners and negotiated in different ways, but the culturally and societally (historically) embedded character of high school life is inescapable (see also Pedersen & Bang 2016a). What is being conveyed at the introduction events at the different high schools can readily be regarded as *standards* of youth life. But what do I mean by standards?

Standards and Standardization

The concept of standard comes from the area of productivity and grew out of the need to replicate the same item over and over again; to make standard sizes that would fit with other standard measurements, in order to facilitate, e.g., construction work (Busch 2011), and to regulate activity in the sphere of production (Bowker & Star 2000). It follows that standardization is the process of 'fitting-something-to-a-standard', which implies a *stabilization, generalization* and *unifying* of forms of manifestation. If we transfer this image to the high school as a societal institution, what is being standardized is not the production of metal screws or the soles of shoes, but different aspects of youth life, in terms of the orientations, activities, behaviour, knowledge level, priorities, appearance and so forth of the high school students. In a production metaphor, high school as an institution becomes the constructing agent, taking young people in and sending them out three years later, somewhat shaped and modulated to meet a certain standard. In that image, high schools *produce* a *particular standard* of youth. Or, in other words, the subjectification processes that occur in high school are mediated by standards – this means that, for instance, specific aspects of agency are *facilitated*, whereas others are *restricted* and *constrained*.

Standards are thus understood as generalized models for practice that have been culturally and historically developed. This implies that standards present and represent socials norms and meanings (as these are built into artefacts and social institutions) (see, e.g., Timmermans & Epstein 2010), and therefore something that structures our expectations to the world. Examples of standards could be, e.g., school performance tests (such as the PISA[2] tests), health standards integrated in the BMI calculations (Body-Mass-Index) or the national grading system (the 7-point grading scale). But standards are also more intimately interwoven into practice as norms: of how many beers to drink at a party, what clothes to wear, how much time to spend on your homework, how active to be class, what political orientation to have, when to lose your virginity and so forth.

In different ways, standards may come to work as ideals that we strive for and try to build our lives around or towards. They become ideas and ideals of *how* and *who* to be in a certain setting. According to Busch (2011:28), this makes standards powerful because they have the ability to '*set the rules that others must follow, or to set the range of categories from which they may choose*'. However, the power they exert is often indirect and anonymous because standards take on a life of their own. This means that they are ever-present and somehow ungraspable at the same time. They are dynamic yet seem to persist across time and place. This is clear when looking at the three different high schools and the way in which they draw forth similar standards of youth life, e.g., regarding expectations of being social in a particular way. Adopting this line of understanding contains a potential determinism of standards preceding the actions of people. Therefore, this represents only one aspect of the totality of the situation (with reference to Lewin 1935). The other aspect of the dynamic relation, which constitutes the basic assumption of this book, is that standards are constantly produced and reproduced by individuals, in the course of their daily life. This implies that high school does not alone standardize subjectivities, or young people's self-understanding and social orientation, but rather that high school provides a particular institutional setting in which different standards for youth life are *negotiated*, *appropriated* and *transformed*, in the concrete encounters between young people and the societal expectations and values embedded in the high school structure. Standards are not one-dimensional determinant conditions; they are created and re-created by people participating in practice and they come to work as standardization processes, by which they stabilize, generalize and sanction subjectivity across contexts and practices. This entails that 'the other side' of standardization processes are the subjectification processes – the becoming of the human subject (that in turn shapes its environment and (re)produces standards) (Pedersen & Bang 2016a). It is this 'totality' or dialectical relation that this book tries to unfold and examine.

---

[2] The PISA test is an abbreviation for Programme for International Student Assessment. It is a student assessment test developed by the OECD in 1997 and widely used in OECD countries as means of comparison of educational standards across the world.

The Question of *How to Be*: Contradictory Invitations and Expectations

As we saw from the introduction events at the different high schools, young people, when starting high school, encounter clear standards of 'youth life' (to party, drink (a lot!), make best friends for life, embrace the open possibilities before them), and at the same time they meet clear expectations of superior academic performance (to follow talent-programmes, know what they want later in life (and pursue it!), be prepared for class, hand in papers on time, aspire to be better, or to excel as individuals). Some may resonate with standards they are already familiar with from elementary school, while others may be new. Here there is a lot of variation on an individual level. However, these standards are not aligned or unidirectional, as we could see from the introduction events. On the contrary, they are often contradictory or conflicting. It may, for instance, be challenging to meet standards of social life with excessive partying and drinking, all the while pursuing extracurricular activities, such as talent-programmes or joining the national debating team. This presents a developmental challenge for a young person, on an individual level, of how to meet these different invitations to be part of a standardized youth life and at the same time, this is also where a new developmental space opens up, as one is faced with new demands and possibilities (see, e.g., Hedegaard 2012).

Thus, starting high school is – as I will argue – not about blindly adapting to dominant standards, but rather about navigating through – and negotiating – a myriad of invitations and possible self-understanding and self-realization options in concrete practices. Examining the invitations more closely, we see how they position young people in very different ways. There is an interchange of addressing the parents and the prospective high school students, which means that the young people are being positioned both as *nearly-adults*, and someone who can make well-considered choices regarding their future, and who know what they want, and, at the same time, as *still-children*, whose well-being and interests are (still) best taken care of by parents. This is illuminated in the way in which both students and principals address parents directly, and sometimes before addressing the young people, and in the small 'Freudian slips' that occur here and there, as, e.g., when the principal at Northside High addresses the students as '1st graders', instead of, e.g., freshmen, juniors or simply 1st year students. In Danish, the term '1st graders' refers specifically to year one in elementary school, and as such it offers an interesting slip of the tongue or infantilization of the prospective high school students. The explication of clear expectations for students to 'show up prepared for class, hand in things on time, and engage actively in classes' follows the same line in turning something that should be self-evident at this educational level into a formal institutional expectation. Contrary to this, we see, at all the schools, how talent programmes are being promoted with a naturalized emphasis. This entails that students are expected to know what they want – even before starting high school – and that they are expected to actively pursue it, also at the expense of potential other interests, as high school alone is not enough. Talent programmes are thus not reserved for the elite; it is promoted almost as a mandatory part of what the school offers, and one gets the impression that the schools themselves also experience a certain pressure to integrate the talent programmes into the 'high school package' they are promoting. Of course, this is a recent development, also in a Danish context, and it falls in line with neoliberal tendencies of regarding oneself as a project to perfect, to better one's chances in a competitive capitalist society (see also Rose 1996, 1999; Harvey 2005). Whereas this pressure to position oneself in society was earlier reserved for post-high school considerations of what further education and career to pursue, it has in recent years been naturalized as something to be reflected on and considerate about even before high school starts. This development was instated with the high school reform of 2005, where students were expected to choose between a large number of (more specialized) academic programmes that were to align them more directly with the university educations that they were aiming for. Whereas before this reform, high school only comprised two academic programmes – a humanistic/linguistic and a natural science line, respectively – that were equally qualifying for further education.

The mentioning of talent programmes resonates across all three schools, and thus paints a picture of a general trend. However, there are variations in the way the schools relate to these extra-curricular options. At Northside High it is mentioned a bit en passant, woven into information about other aspects of high school life. Also, it is mentioned by Martin, the study council president, whereas the principal is more preoccupied with ensuring that relevant measures will be taken in relation to students with special needs, so they can be offered the appropriate help. She does not talk of talent programmes, but takes it upon her, as a spokesperson for the school, to communicate that the school's task is to push, and support, the students further towards what they are good at. This delimits a range: the possibility of excelling, and wanting more than the high school offers, exists, just as the school is mindful of taking care of everyone, both academically and personally. However, the endpoints of this range are more outlined than made explicit, which means that the clear majority of students falls somewhere in between.

At Westside High, the atmosphere is different. Here there is a clear expectation of 'engagement' and 'giving it your most'. The school is ambitious as are its students, and various talent development aspects are presented as the norm rather than the exception; one is expected *to want* to do more than what high school offers in itself. A grand image is painted at the introduction event of preparing oneself to 'consider the whole world your playground' and the students on stage, who you are expected to mirror yourself in as a prospective student, tell you of their successes at the National Debating Team, and how awesome the talent programmes are. A lot of time is allotted for speaking of talent programmes and individual success. Needless to say that this instates a somewhat elitist atmosphere, which will appeal to many. At the same time, the school presents itself as a very encouraging school who will go out of its way to support the students' endeavours. As one of the students says, the school has made it possible for her to take part in the National Debating Team both financially and practically. This implies that the school may act as a buffer to ensure that its students have equal opportunity to excel, despite potential differences in background and family resources. There is, however, no mention of 'special needs', 'study counsellors' or the fact that youth may be a challenging period in one's life. Instead, the principal emphasizes that one should consider carefully where one wants to fit in; indicating the importance of *the choice* and that if choosing to attend (or apply for) Westside High, one understands what is expected. The standard is set high, and expectations and demands made explicit.

In comparison, the contrast to Countryside High could not be more outspoken; here the atmosphere is down to earth and there is a clear emphasis on local and pragmatic matters, such as how often and to where the bus connections run. It is the local community school, even though 'local' here covers a rather big geographical area. Everybody here knows someone who attended the school before or attends it now, and it is not uncommon that other family members have attended a generation earlier. The main question here is: 'do you want to attend high school?' and as we saw from the introduction event, the principal was concerned with arguing for choosing high school (over other kinds of schools). Here the parents are addressed much more directly than at the other introduction events, and one is left with the impression of a school that values a sense of security or a homely atmosphere. I will return to this point in a later chapter. As at Northside High, we are here presented with a broad range of invitations and values: from 'pursuing talent programmes' and 'winning national competitions' to 'extra teaching sessions and counsellors' and the placement in the national survey of student well-being. In that sense, the school appeals to everyone or no one in particular, which fits with its status as a regional high school that is the unquestioned choice of school for many young people, with reference to geographical placement alone. Again, as at Northside High, the social life is emphasized as important and many different aspects as drawn forth, such as 'friends for life', 'parties' and 'study trips'. However, whereas at Northside High it was pointed out that 'parents would be without children' due to the fact that their children would attend parties (where parents were clearly not invited), at Countryside High, it is emphasized how the school parties involve teachers *and* potentially parents as in integral part of the setup. In reality, the school parties at Northside High will also involve teachers; however, this is left unsaid. The small difference in emphasis here indicates different ways of positioning prospective students; as more or less independent from their parents. We could say that at Northside High, prospective students are invited to think themselves as nearly adults to a much greater extent than the prospective students at Countryside High. It is these minor variations in the way in which students are invited to think themselves (and others) that I am interested in; what difference do such variations make in terms of developmental dynamics, and why do we need to care about this if we want to understand the totality of the developmental situation?

Differentiations in How One *Ought to Be*

Despite (mostly) presenting a broad range of opportunities at the introduction events, the high schools do not present the same possibilities, nor do they present the same possibilities in similar ways. This informs us about the differences in what is valued at a specific high school, and about the 'implied student' that the school wants to appeal to. In that sense, the schools are not neutral spaces; their way of presenting high school and youth life in a high school setting to prospective students reveals a historically developed way of practising high school. The way in which various aspects of high school life are presented invites for prospective students to think themselves in certain ways, and I would argue that a certain image is being painted of how one *ought to be*. And here, evidently, the lines of this image can be more or less clearly drawn. For example, there is a big difference in presenting high school as a place for those who already have the skills and want to excel, or as a place for those who do not necessarily possess all the (academic) skills yet but need a little extra support to get through.

The invitational character of the high school, which in the above has been referred to also as at the school atmosphere, co-constructs the idea of how one ought to be. When choosing high school, young people are concurrently invited to think themselves along certain lines and thus to some extent conforming to the school's depiction of the norm, all the while they choose a school that seems to fit with their current ideas of self – and perhaps, with their wishes for who and how to become in the future. This illustrates a difference between, e.g., youth life conditions in the bigger cities and in the countryside: the city contains the possibility of cultivating the particular, special or unique in a way that may be more difficult outside city limits. In the bigger cities, young people get to choose from a range of schools and have the possibility of seeking out the school that seems just right for them, as we shall also see being the case for some of the young people in this book. This implies that choosing a school may, and may not at the same time, be a way to enhance particular aspects of one's self-understanding. A possibility that seems less available in the countryside where this kind of choice may be perceived as a luxury, or, if one chooses to travel far to attend school in a bigger city, it may be a way of distancing oneself from the local community.

When attending introduction events across the three (public) schools presented in this chapter, the similarities outweigh the differences, in the sense that the similarities are more prominent and easily noticeable. It is the same dominant standards of youth life that we encounter with expectations of being social (in a specific way), pursuing individual talent and displaying academic ambition, while detaching from parents. The difference is mostly made up by the truisms and taken-for-grantedness that exist in practice and that colour the atmosphere, so to speak. And although I have tried to make some of these differences visible to the reader in this chapter, one must also recognize that for the most part such aspects are difficult to fully grasp and put into words. In that sense, I was drawn (in)to the respective atmospheres of the schools in the moment, thinking 'oh, I sure would not mind if this was my school' and 'how cool'. It was not until later, when I read my fieldnotes and had the chance to distance myself a little, that the differences started to protrude, allowing for a space to critically reflect upon the ways on which these differences manifested, and how they co-constructed variability in the invitational character of the environment.

Returning to the concept of standard, it is evident that the different high schools tap into and reproduce the same general ideas and images of how one ought to be as a high school student. Or how one ought to be as a young person, attending high school. At the same time, we have to acknowledge that there are differences and variations in the atmosphere of the schools, and in the way in which various standards and norms are emphasized and presented. And all the while such variations are visible to the researcher who attends introduction events with the purpose of noticing such differences, in the everyday life, these variations are subtle and unvoiced. How high school is enacted, from an institutional side, is most likely perceived as a taken-for-granted-ness. Something that is not questioned. When students present their schools, they try to present the high school as a kind of positive and open-minded non-judging community. However, the talent programme indicates that there actually are differences that are not being ignored but rather celebrated (talents versus non-talents); furthermore, a pressure is put on the coming students to free themselves from their parents in order to become 'full members' of the community. In other words, the 'invitations' offered to the coming students are ambivalent and contradictory. They afford certain actions from the students. As simplified and rigid as the production metaphor of high school is, it nevertheless points to a relevant question: how does high school afford developmental processes from young people, and what role do the subtle variations in the conditions that are offered for these developmental processes to unfold in play? How one ought to 'be' or 'do' high school student is not arbitrary, but the result of multiple interacting aspects that are historically situated and temporally extended. There is no simple version of high school as a developmental space, and to further comprehend 'high school' as part of the person-environment reciprocity, we must explore it concretely in relation to young people's ways of taking part and making sense of it – as developing person-environment relations.

2

Becoming High School Students: Entering New Activity Settings

Case Study 1: Anna, Mia and Lisa

As we saw in Chapter 1, high school as an institutional setting is in many ways recognizable across different schools, and yet there are variations in the concrete ways in which high school is enacted, and in the different ways in which students are invited to participate and to see themselves. Already at the introduction events, subtle variations emerge which brings about the question of how such variations play their part in the developmental dynamics that unfold in high school. Returning to Elder's (1998) first principle, of the meaning of historical time and place, it is evident that the historical time and the places we inhabit in our lifetime shape our life course. However, we tend to apply this knowledge as a more broad and general awareness of historical time and the difference this makes, often as generational comparisons. We often hear parents saying something along the lines of 'you have so many opportunities compared to me, when I was your age', or 'it is so much easier for you than it was back in the days'. Although the analysis also may sway the other way: 'life was much simpler when I was young – there was less pressure back then'. Such analytical comparisons are thus often retrospective ventures on more general terms.

In this chapter, I will delve into the institutional setting of high school as a concrete place – as concrete surroundings – and explore the manner in which the young people become high school students in specific schools that offer their own historically developed situatedness and meaning. Often development is thought of as an individualized process which neglects the fact that development is always unfolding in relation to historical, societal, relational and material aspects. Or as developing relations between person and environment if we think along the lines of Vygotsky (1994). A consequence of this dominant individualized gaze is that the variations we see among high school students are predominantly attributed to individual psychological aspects or perhaps to a relational interplay with family members or close peers,

> Parts of this chapter, concerning the theoretical developments of the concept of the human eco-niche, have previously been published (Pedersen 2019) and are reprinted with permission from Ethos of Theorizing, The – ISTP 2017, by Kyoko Murakami, Jim Cresswell, Tetsuya Kono and Tania Zittoun (Concord, Ontario, Canada: Captus University Publications, 2019). Permission to use has been granted by Captus Press Inc. <http://www.captus.com>

meaning that the concrete surroundings or material conditions are often left out of our understanding. This calls for a way to analytically enlarge our comprehension of these variations and the difference these variations constitute in terms of developmental conditions and possibilities for young people. In other words, what a particular high school affords, and thus *who* the high school is inviting its students *to become* (reflecting what activities are possible), varies from school to school: we could say that the schools are the same, yet different. This implies that there are variations in the schools' ways of co-creating developmental spaces and in their ways of subjectifying students. To be able to comprehend these environmental variations as dialectical and dynamic relations of persons, places, materiality and history, a concept is needed that can provide an analytical basis: here James Gibson's (1986) notion of *eco-niche* has potential and will serve as the main analytical concept.

This chapter will thus 'widen the lens', and focus on that which *surrounds* the individual, namely the environment. A focus on the environment does not imply an analysis of what exists in the environment as isolated entities, disconnected from the individual. Rather it refers to macro-levels in which the individual is embedded in a dialectical sense; the environment being understood as what the individual interacts with and develops through – and through which concrete possibilities for action, and, in a larger perspective, possibilities for new motives, and for life in general, evolve (see also Vygotsky 1994; Leontjev 2005; Bozhovich 2009). Considered this way, the environment contains several analytical 'levels', ranging from concrete material conditions, to standardized behaviour patterns and eco-niches, all of which are levels that imply each other just as they imply the individual. In other words, we could say that in this chapter I will attempt to unfold the person-environment dialectics with an emphasis on the environment. However, the dialectical relation remains intact, reflecting how the lifeworld and the eco-niche can in fact be seen as different ways of analytically approaching the same dialectical phenomenon: the lifeworld reflects how concrete social, material, cultural and historical conditions for life appear for the individual person (a subjective first-person perspective), whereas the eco-niche reflects how the same conditions appear from the outside (a third-person perspective).

Conceptualizing the Environment: New Activity Settings and Possibilities for Life

To be able to examine the dynamic constitution of 'possibilities for life' – as they appear as part of the environment – theoretical concepts that allow for such analyses are necessary. Ecological psychology offers two main concepts that I find relevant in this pursuit: (1) *eco-niche*, as presented by Gibson (1986), and (2) *behaviour setting*, from the work of Barker and Wright (1966, 1971). These two concepts refer to different environmental levels, so to speak, and therefore offer different analytical perspectives in relation to the environment. Examining the possibilities for life, as they emerge in the lives of young people, necessitates the employment of a notion of *niche* that is both dynamic and dialectical; the niche constitutes the conditional frame of meaning-connections from (and in and through) which the possibilities for life are created. The concept of *eco-niche*, derived from Gibson, contributes with an analytical level that enables the study of 'environment' on a supra-individual level, offering the possibility to examine variability among different high schools as representing different eco-niches. This is relevant in order to shed light on the extent to which standards in, and for, youth life, along with conditions for development on an institutional level, are not necessarily identical everywhere in Denmark, even though we are often offered this impression from discourses on youth and high school life, delivered by, e.g., media and politicians.

If we are to stay with ecological theory for a minute, the *behaviour setting* is, in my understanding, subsumed in the eco-niche, and I will therefore spend a little time introducing insights from Barker and Wright, as a way of nuancing what 'environment' means. Referring to a supra-individual level of analysis, the concept of behaviour setting from Barker and Wright allows for a study of standardized behaviour patterns, or, in other words, 'what people do'. In Barker and Wright's work, behaviour patterns, which are recognizable independently of individuals, are studied. This approach enables the study of social standards of behaviour in connection with societal institutions, in this case high school. However, as I wrote in the introductory chapter, I will mainly employ the notion of *activity setting*, as proposed by Hedegaard (2012), to avoid a separation of young peoples' actions and their subjectivity. The notion of activity setting enables an exploration of young people's actions, not only as *behaviour-as-actions*, but as *behaviour-as-part-of-activities* that are motivated and directed towards something; this allows for intentionality and subjectivity to shine through in the analysis.

After laying the theoretical ground (as indicated above), this chapter re-introduces Anna and Lisa who we briefly encountered in the introduction of the book, along with Mia who attends the same class as Anna. The chapter explores the values and orientations of the girls in direct relation to the way the respective high schools enact 'high school', by looking into their everyday life at their respective high schools. Here the emphasis will be on exploring the reciprocity of high school setting and the young person as part of, and constituting, an eco-niche, along with the variations between the two different high schools, in order to see in which way, the high school acts as a constraining (and enabling) institutional setting for the young people in relation to developmental possibilities. This actualizes questions on how high school is practised in different (geographical) high school settings, and how the way of 'doing' high school is connected to the activities and values of young people (as new high school students). The variations that emerge, and the difference they make, have implications for the ways in which young people are invited to participate and perceive themselves in these settings.

Human Eco-niches

Let me start by introducing the notion of an eco-niche and see what it offers in terms of analytical value.

Gibson's Eco-niche

James Gibson was primarily concerned with affordances and the direct exchange between individual and environment (through perception), but he also contributed to an ecological understanding of a broader structural level surrounding the individual. To account for this, he proposed the concept of *niche* or *eco-niche* – a general term from ecology referring to *how* an animal lives, more than to *where* it lives (Gibson 1986:128). The eco-niche refers not only to a geographical location, as the term may indicate, but more so to a set of affordances (ibid.) reflecting the concrete possibilities for action (the *how*). Niches are constructed through the dynamic interplay between individuals living their life *in* and *with* the environment and each other. In Gibson's writings, the concept of eco-niche is primarily employed as a concept regarding animal environments; however, I suggest for it to have potential in relation to human environments as well. Humans alter the environment to fit their needs, and hence create eco-niches reflecting the persons who inhabit them. Niche construction thus reflects the ongoing construction and reconstruction of the specific, particular and local conditions that uphold and support the everyday life conducted by people. As Kono (2009:365) writes: '*Many animals can modify the surroundings to construct their niches; but human construction is considerably large-scale, thoroughgoing, collective, successive, and historical*.' In that way the eco-niche reflects a societal and historical developmental dynamic, as also described in cultural-historical psychology.

Humanizing the Eco-niche

As briefly outlined, the 'human eco-niche' becomes a relevant analytical concept in relation to the exploration of how possibilities for life are created, shaped and offered to young people in a high school setting. This calls for an elaboration. As Kono (2009) writes, human niche construction is collective and historical. It is important to emphasize that the eco-niche does not merely refer to a mechanical human-environment fit; that humans live a certain way because the environment (that they have co-constructed themselves) permits it. Rather I would propose the *human* eco-niche to reflect collective ideality, a dynamic dialectical relation between persons and their environment.

The notion of ideality is borrowed from Evald Ilyenkov (1977, 2014), who writes: '*Ideality is a kind of stamp impressed on the substance of nature by social-human life-activity, a form of the functioning of the physical thing in the process of social-human life-activity*' (Ilyenkov 1977:86 and 2014:58). Ideality is thus inherently connected to the ongoing (re)production of material life (what Marx terms 'labor'), in a social, cultural and historical world, where persons are part of collectives with each other, creating a shared world of collective meanings. Ideality is embedded in human activity and as it reflects objective reality, social and historical processes of meaning production are automatically embedded in the ideal form. By collective ideality I mean to imply the collective – and thus historical – processes by which persons ascribe meaning to their shared lifeworlds. It refers to the manner in which humans are engaged in ongoing processes of producing and reproducing their own conditions, and thus their environments. Through this production/reproduction process objective meaning is created where objects, artefacts, places, etc., acquire their own quasi-independent meaning, as ideality.

The human eco-niche has the quality of representing the collective *'social-human life-activity'* (Ilyenkov 2014:68) that is embedded in the 'ideal' in Ilyenkov terms. It is collective meanings that are present in the environment without necessarily being something we can point out. It arises from people's concrete activities and thus can be accounted for perhaps as a taken-for-granted-ness of the meaning we ascribe to things, artefacts, situations. It is in this taken-for-granted-ness – the (mediated) immediateness with which the environment presents itself to us – that variations exist in the different high school settings. I propose for this to be theorized as variations in human eco-niches, as variations in collective idealities.

The Generation of Collective Objective Meaning

With reference to Ilyenkov, the human eco-niche thus reflects a shared world of collective meaning. To better understand the process by which such collective meanings are generated, I will briefly turn to Leontjev. Leontjev (1977, 2002) distinguishes between objective meaning and personal sense, where objective meaning refers to the general over-individual meaning that is both connected to and embedded in concrete societal practices. Vis-à-vis this, personal sense is meaning as it appears to the subject (subjective meaning), and there may be more or less overlaps or differences between objective meaning and personal sense. Personal sense is developed through the life-course in concrete practices and relations and thus automatically reflects participation in a variety of social settings (Leontjev 2002). Leontjev further describes how consciousness (subjective awareness/experience) cannot be *'reduced to the functioning of externally assimilated meanings'* (Leontjev 1977:194), which is what would be implied if we understood the eco-niche as a one-way determinant of human behaviour (and meaning making). The individual contribution to the wholeness is important to include in this calculation.

The human eco-niche is therefore not to be comprehended as a specific 'space' of collective meaning sets that are superimposed on the person. Rather it refers to collective processes of production and reproduction of meaning to which a person actively contributes. A comprehension of the human eco-niche (and its variations) thus implicates a study of the generation of objective meaning as a continuous process in practice (e.g. at a high school setting). Meaningfulness, on the level of the eco-niche, relates not only to the individual person, but to a larger collective of people's meaning-making generation over time. This way meaning becomes idealized – and thus something that influences others, without being a specific point-out-able 'thing' in the environment; an object of *'quasi-independent existence'* in Leontjev's terms (1977:194), referring to something that is at the same time external to the individual person, and reflects the collected subjectivity of persons (a dialectical relation). Here, we perhaps approximate a grasp of the elusive atmospheres that were somehow present, but not necessarily directly point-out-able, at the introduction events.

This understanding of the human eco-niche as over-individual collective meaning refers to an analytical 'layer' in between societal institutions and society at large. A human eco-niche contains several social institutional settings, such as school, kindergarten, family; in that way one could argue that the concept of eco-niche transcends institutional boundaries. It refers to the manner in which meaning is ascribed to different aspects of everyday life – to material objects as well as to the way in which ways of relating to each other are valued. Drawing on Leontjev's distinction between objective meaning and personal sense, I would propose that the human eco-niche translates to the objective societal meanings, without turning these into abstract societal relations. Studying the human eco-niche enables a comprehension of how variations on the level of objective societal meanings occur, albeit these of course also contain general and more abstract societal meanings (on a national level).

When I enter a high school, or the home of one of the participants in the project, I am aware that I am entering a specific setting, such as a concrete 'high school' or 'home'. What happens over time is that patterns of meaning-generations start to become visible; you can observe how people more specifically arrange their daily lives, how different aspects of this daily life are valued, how particular possibilities for action are created (or prevented), and one is thus left with an image of how people practise their lives in this particular constellation of persons, place and time. There are differences and variations in these ways of conducting life that cannot be ascribed merely to individual persons alone, nor to geographical or institutional differences alone, and they appear within the same societal frame. Perhaps this 'image' could be explained as human eco-niches: as a super-individual globality of meaning connections offering a specific arrangement of possibilities for life, that are, at the same time, both offered and in the making.

Operationalizing the Human Eco-niche

The concept of eco-niche is, admittedly, a relatively general concept, which implies that, for analytical purposes, it can be qualified further. Also, as I have noted before, an eco-niche is not something that is directly perceivable in the immediate environment; it does not come with fixed boundaries or clear signs. So, in order to study it, an operationalization or concretization is needed that translates central aspects of the eco-niche into observable phenomena; that allows me to study how the eco-niche is realized in practice. To do so, we shall first briefly swing by Barker and Wright, and their notion of behaviour setting, to fully comprehend the power of the invitational character of the environment.

Barker and Wright proposed the concept of behaviour setting[1], which they (1971:45) defined as follows: '*a standing pattern of behavior and a part of the milieu which are synomorphic and in which the milieu is circumjacent to the behavior*'. And further: '*They are also community areas which individuals can enter and in which they behave*

---

[1] Although I shall primarily use the notion of activity setting in this book, I will keep with the concept of behaviour setting as I present the work of Barker and Wright. This allows for an opening into the meaning of the environment from a different angle than provided by cultural-historical psychology and therefore contributes to the qualification of the person-environment dialectic.

in accordance with forces that produce the characteristic behavior pattern' (1971:458). The behaviour setting is 'coercive', according to Wright et al. (1951), however only indirectly. They fully acknowledge what they refer to as 'the psychological habitat' of the person thereby recognizing that in any behaviour setting anything *can* happen: '*the coercive effect of a setting upon behavior, then, is indirect. It stems only from the fact that every setting tends to bring about certain psychological habitats rather than others*' (Wright et al. 1951:189-90). Barker and Wright thus attempt at theorizing the reciprocal person-environment relation, as did Gibson. In their study of behaviour, Barker and Wright understand 'behaviour setting' as 'supra-individual behaviour phenomena' (1971:46) consisting of, and discriminable in relation to, various characteristics. First and foremost, it denotes a behaviour phenomenon that is directly perceivable; this means that it exists without the researcher's manipulation of persons or environment. Furthermore, as the 'supra-individual' indicates, it refers to behaviour patterns of persons en masse, and is therefore not dependent on the individual (Barker & Wright 1971) – and so it abides to the over-individual level of analysis enabled by the eco-niche. In Barker and Wright's understanding of the milieu, it can comprise both 'natural' and 'cultural' components. They exemplify 'natural' with '*hills, storms, and July 4*th' (1971:46), and then add '*parts that are the products of behavior such as buildings, streets, and baseball diamonds*' (ibid.). There appears to be no real distinction between what is natural and cultural but from their examples follows that humans are considered as also producing their own environment, hence providing a bridgeway to cultural-historical psychology[2]. A behaviour setting does not refer to fixed structures in the environment exclusively, but also momentary behaviour settings, that appear briefly when, e.g., one approaches the street vendor who walks the beach selling ice cream, or reappearing traditions such as Halloween. Some behaviour settings also appear as intersections of particular persons, places and time. If we, as an example, follow Anna to her gymnastics practice, this particular behaviour setting occurs in a particular room (the sports hall at the local school), at a particular time (every Tuesday at 18.00), and it involves an arrangement of particular behaviour objects (e.g. music, mats and balls) to provide for a recognizable behaviour setting for the fifteen girls who are part of the local gymnastics team. Outside this particular time frame the room and facilities are used for other purposes and provide for different behaviour settings, such as theatre group meetings, school plays, yoga class for the community seniors, etc.

Surveying the behaviour settings[3] of Midwest provided Barker and Wright with thorough data on the availabilities and resources of the community. For instance, that

---

[2] There are clear overlaps, albeit also notable differences, between ecological psychology and cultural-historical psychology. I have addressed this issue specifically with J. Bang elsewhere (see Pedersen & Bang 2016b), providing an argument for why an integration of the two perspectives may be fruitful if not necessary.

[3] The concept of behaviour setting is analytically operationalized as distinguishable in different 'layers'. A behaviour setting (or unit setting) can consist of different sub-settings. A sub-setting is a setting within another setting, containing sub-settings of its own. And finally, cyto-settings, that are settings within another setting, with no further sub-settings. In their study of the town of Midwest, Barker and Wright find that the school (as a behaviour setting) has almost 200 sub-settings (Barker & Wright 1971:50). Barker and Wright suggest seeing the sub-settings as 'inclusiveness hierarchies' (1971:49), depending on the diversity and possibilities offered in a certain sub-setting.

there were numerous basketball and baseball games, but no lacrosse (Heft 2001). This entails that a certain space of possibilities for action was created, which did not in itself exclude or prevent an interest in lacrosse, but that did not invite for it or present it as a possibility. This brings about valuable information of not only the possibilities for action and participation in this given eco-niche (that is Midwest), but also insight into what is valued in this specific eco-niche. In the same way high school, as a behaviour setting within the eco-niche, presents itself as a particular space of possibilities, where certain actions and ways of behaviour are facilitated, promoted and invited for. As I will argue in this book, one of the ways in which this occurs is through the dynamics of standards that dominate, both on a more general level (such as general discourses on youth) and on local standards at a particular school. This does not mean that other types of behaviour (than what fits the standards) are impossible, but rather it implies that the way in which high school as a behaviour setting is structured and organized provides a specific frame for behaviour that the persons who occupy it relate to in different ways. It tells us something about the invitational character of the environment.

A central finding of Barker and Wright, which in part helped shape the research interest behind this book, is that changes in behaviour *'can be ascribed to conditions in the behavior setting'* (Barker & Wright 1971:53). The concrete and situated invitational character of the environment, and its concrete conditions, plays a huge part in determining the possibilities for action and thus for directing actions and activities in certain ways. At the same time, Barker and Wright do not succumb to environmental determinism, but fully acknowledge that two persons may depict very different behaviours in the same setting, which can only be ascribed to individual differences in preconditions and agendas. I will pick up on this shortly.

High School as Behaviour Setting

If we take a look at a typical high school – and for a minute consider it a behaviour setting, focusing solely on the supra-individual space of possibilities that it entails – it consists of numerous sub-settings: music class, the canteen, the teachers' room, Friday bar, communal meetings, smoking area, gym class, choir practice, recess and so forth[4]. Each of these sub-settings has their own rules or standards for behaviour and participation, reflecting specific conditions and possibilities for action. However, they all adhere to the same overall behaviour setting, that of being and (re)producing 'high school'. This means that general rules and standards apply in terms of behaviour, participation and possibilities for action across the different sub-settings, yet with minor differences in what is customary behaviour. If we take the classroom as an

---

[4] In their studies of elementary schools, Barker and Wright found in the area of 200 different sub-settings within the school premise. One could assume that a similar number could be found in a high school setting.

example; during math class, students sit at their desks all facing the teacher, who is located in one end of the room, and who is using the whiteboard to go through mathematical proofs. The students take notes on their computers (and some are on Facebook). However, there is a general implicit rule about not playing music, not playing with toys or gadgets, just as eating is prohibited. These rules are not written down anywhere, but everybody knows them anyway[5]. This does not exclude occasional diversions from the common practice in math class, but when observing many math classes, there is an explicit and easily recognizable behavioural pattern. Then when the bell rings, and marks the end of class and the beginning of recess, the same room is immediately used in new ways; new rules and standards apply. This means that people are now sitting on the tables, playing loud music from their computers, shouting, eating, laughing and playing. Finally, when there is a Friday bar at the school, the classroom often serves as a private room to sneak into, for a private conversation or a secret kiss. Then the otherwise public room suddenly is perceived as a private place that allows for intimacy.

In terms of understanding young people in their high school environment, Barker and Wright's work provides a relevant background for comprehending how concrete surroundings invite for, enable and somewhat restrict behaviour in certain – and often unarticulated – ways. As such, their work helps unfold the *environment*-aspect of the person-environment relation. Trying to grasp the totality of the situation (acc. Lewin 1935, 1946/1954), an analytical emphasis on the concrete environment and the way in which standards and possibilities for action are reflected in the patterns of behaviour is important. And this is an aspect that would be difficult to examine, not to mention comprehend, if I were to remain solely on a first-person perspective (in a more phenomenological sense), in terms of analysis. Conducting an analysis of young people in their respective high school environments on the basis of Barker and Wright's approach permits for a concurrent third-person perspective on the conditions and standards offered at a particular high school. This substantiates an analysis of the influence and significance of the concrete environment, in terms of what activities the high school setting affords, and which possibilities are created for the students (for participation, for action, for development). However, if we translate the human eco-niche to behaviour settings alone, we might end up with an understanding of eco-niches as produced and upheld through persons' assimilation to existing behaviour patterns, which might leave little room for agency and subjectivity. Therefore, I shall proceed with the notion of *activity setting*.

---

[5] Here there are of course variations, which I became aware of when I visited an American high school around the time when I was doing my empirical work. Here rules for appropriate behaviour in class were explicitly written on a poster on the wall: 'Don't be tardy; Don't talk when teachers talk; Keep your hands to yourself; No foul language; No hats', etc. Even though these rules were explicated and present in the classroom there are still rules regarding behaviour that are unwritten and that are not questioned in the everyday practice.

The Notion of Activity Setting

Barker and Wright's work has been continued and elaborated, both within an ecological framework, by, e.g., Bronfenbrenner (1977, 1979)[6], and within cultural-historical activity theory (e.g. Hedegaard 2008, 2012; Bang 2009b). As previously noted, their approach does not integrate a phenomenological or subjective aspect, although they recognize the importance of it. This implies that subjectivity can only be assessed as an outside perspective of how the person is subjectified through the concrete possibilities for action offered in a concrete behaviour setting. For example, when young people start high school, they are met from the school's side (primarily through the teachers) with certain expectations and demands, subjectifying them as 'high school students' in a specific way that corresponds with the high school practice and with overall political agendas of how young people are supposed to develop to meet larger societal interests (e.g. by already knowing what academic further education they wish to pursue, and that they will pursue it directly and not take a gap year). And although the work of Barker and Wright sheds (important) light on the invitational and potentially coercive character of the environment, their notion of behaviour setting will not suffice for my current endeavour, as we need to further embrace subjectivity in our analysis. Therefore, I shall proceed with the notion of *activity setting*[7], as proposed by Hedegaard (2012), approximating the subjectivity of the participant in a given setting. This enables a focus on the person's social situation in a given activity setting, with an emphasis on the (mis)congruence between institutional demands, concrete activities and the person's motives. It further enables an analytical comprehension of *why* people behave the way they do, as well as *for what purpose* (both a retrospective and prospective directedness[8]). As Hedegaard (2012:132) writes: '*By introducing the concept of activity instead of behavior, the concept of historically anchored recurrent cultural traditions is related to a person's appropriation of these traditions.*' In so doing, Hedegaard highlights the entanglement of institutional practices and the activity of concrete persons: '*Activity settings are not the single person's settings, but an activity setting is conceptualized as societal traditions realized within an institutional practice as concrete historical events*' (ibid.).

With the notion of activity setting, Hedegaard focuses on the child's activity in a given institutional (and thereby societal) setting, making the environmental conditions

---

[6] Both Bronfenbrenner (1977) and Hedegaard (2012) propose the term 'activity setting' to replace behaviour setting. For Bronfenbrenner this proposal originates in two accounts: (1) a criticism of the concept of environment as employed by Barker and Wright, and (2) that *behaviour* does not sufficiently encompass the content and the purpose of what people do (in his opinion). More specifically Bronfenbrenner's criticism towards Barker and Wright's conception of environment extends to their analogy to ecological descriptions of animal environments found within biology. Applied to a human context it provides for analysis limited to *immediate settings*, and the behaviour of people studied relatively isolated from each other and from societal (macro) levels (Bronfenbrenner 1977; see also Hedegaard 2012).

[7] Others also work with the notion of activity setting: e.g. Bang (2009b) and Farver (1999). Farver (1999) proposes the concept to draw on the work of Vygotsky, along with a behaviour setting concept derived from Whiting, and ecological cultural models. See Farver 1999 for an elaboration.

[8] Alfred Schutz has proposed motives to be either retrospective; that something is done 'because of something', or 'in order to' obtain something. See Schutz 2005 for an elaboration.

more subordinate, or at least emphasizing the environment as societal institutions, reflecting societal values (and thus a more cultural-historical take on the environment (in line with Wartofsky 1983), than, e.g., that of Gibson, who focuses mainly on physical and material aspects). This is where *activity setting* adds productively to the original behaviour setting conceptualization: 'activity setting' emphasizes the level of *societal practice*. The notion of practice, and the theoretical perspective it reflects, may open the analysis to the dynamic interplay between persons and high school (as a societal institution) with mutual processes of co-creation. In line with Hedegaard, there is a constant reciprocal and dialectical relation between person and activity setting; the activity setting accounts for the extra-individual situation that contain one or more people that each have their own unique social situation, in said activity setting. Understanding development dynamically therefore involves a concurrent comprehension of an activity settings, and the concrete possibilities and demands that it conveys, and the motives, agency and self-understanding of the person (the social situation). One could argue that 'behaviour setting' and 'activity setting' denote two different emphases on the person-environment dialectics: with its explicit focus on super-individual behaviour patterns the behaviour setting points to an analysis of the *actions* that appear in relation to *concrete environmental possibilities*. This reflects an analytical awareness of how the person adapts or assimilates to the affordances of the environment (albeit without succumbing to environmental determinism!), and thus highlights the meaning of concrete conditions in relation to understanding developmental processes. Activity setting, on the other hand, points to the *subjective* and *agentive* side of the person-environment reciprocity, which enables an analytical grasp on values as well as the way in which people are intentionally directed towards – and actively construct – their environment, and, through their participation in practice, negotiate the meaning of the environment (including the meaning of standards). In this way, the two concepts feed into the same overall person-environment dynamic where eco-niches are co-constructed by dynamic (temporally extended) interconnections between actions, values and possibilities. In the remains of the book, I shall primarily employ the term activity setting, so as to highlight the dynamic interplay of subjectivity and environment.

Eco-niche variations: Inner city ambitions and provincial proximity

The environment often becomes a fuzzy mélange of materiality and social institutions, which can make it hard to point out exactly what the environment means in terms of conditioning developmental processes for young people. It easily becomes abstract matter, rather than concrete aspects of the wholeness. For that reason, I will now explore the lifeworlds of some of the young people, intertwined with the respective eco-niches that they inhabit. The eco-niches will be qualified through an analysis of the activity settings that the young people participate in and co-create; and the dynamic that arise between the young people and their respective high schools. As such the eco-niche becomes a synthesis that enables an analysis of the space of possibilities created in the high school setting, or as part of youth life in high school, as concrete interactions between young people and high school conditions and practices. The remains of this chapter, as well as the following chapter, will therefore explore how high school is enacted as a dynamic reciprocal relation between the school as an institutional setting and the young people who attend it. In this chapter, I will focus on two different high school settings, namely Countryside High and Southside High. Not only do the two schools embody different geographical locations, but they also represent provincial- versus inner-city life, and give us an idea of the variations co-constituted by this condition. As we shall see, this entails rather different collective meaning sets and values. By exploring how different eco-niches are realized, we get a glimpse of the subtle variations that exist among young people, and we may acquire new insight into how such variations make a difference in relation to development. In Chapter 3, I shall explore two different young people in the same high school class, to further nuance variations within the same eco-niche. I will refer to these explorations as eco-niche portraits[9].

The portraits thus attempt to present the high school practice as closely connected and interweaved with narratives of the young people who attend them – who are they, what do they care about, who are they becoming – as this is understood as inherently entangled with the possibilities afforded by the specific setting. By doing so, my hope is to take seriously the ecological reciprocity, as instated by Gibson and Barker and Wright – as well as the cultural-historical dialectics, sensu Vygotsky and Hedegaard among others – and try to examine the way in which the concrete high school setting serves as co-constructor of developmental processes as they unfold in the lives of young people[10].

Each portrait begins with a presentation of the particular high school on a geographical and material level; because even on a material level high schools are not similar, and I wish to analytically demonstrate the way in which there may be coherence between the high school (on a material level) and the way in which one can become a high school student at that particular school. As Banks (2005) points out, school hallways are not just means of physically connecting classrooms, but rather they are where important social interactions take place (Banks 2005, and Collins & Coleman 2008). This implies that the material conditions of the school matter beyond the level of materiality. From here, I will proceed to explore how the material and geographical characteristics are related to – and enacted by – the young people who

---

[9] Methodologically, the portraits are inspired by the 'practice portrait' (Markard et al. 2004), which is an approach to explore the manner in which conditions present themselves to persons as constraints and possibilities, and how these fit (or do not fit) with the intentions and capabilities of said persons.

[10] The portraits have come about as impressions accumulated by me through the time I have spent with my participants in practice. This implies that the portraits consist of several entangled perspectives: (1) the self-presentations made by the schools, (2) thoughts and reflections from the participants in the project and (3) my participant observations. Together these perspectives are intended to highlight and describe the high school practice in terms of conditions, possibilities and invitational character; all in all, leaving an impression of the collective idealities (or objective meanings) as a conjoint production by the school and the young people. This implies that the schools are presented largely through the daily life activities of the young people, as I primarily wish to acquire insight into *how* possibilities for life are co-created in the high school setting.

attend this particular school. This means that I will be moving from a super-individual description to a level of subjective value, meaning making and activity, in relation to the high school practice, emphasizing the manner in which a particular high school practice presents itself and unfolds for a young person who is becoming a high school student. The aspiration is to try to grasp that which is elusive: the eco-niche does not have visible borders, road signs or clear indications of membership. No way to tell where it begins or where it ends. It is a subtlety, and yet a concrete doing – a practice – continuously produced and reproduced, negotiated and slightly altered by people, living their everyday lives with one another, pursuing goals and gradually transforming the world. Hence, the eco-niche becomes illuminated in the study of subtle movements and interactions between agency, values and possibilities, as they relate to each other in dynamic ways in the course of daily life. To study this, we must then study how the young people act and participate in concrete activity settings over time. So, let us begin by exploring the eco-niche of Countryside High.

Eco-niche Portrait of Countryside High: Close-knit Communities and Down-to-earth-ness

Countryside High is located in a small provincial town, surrounded by fields and agricultural farms. Even though the school is placed in the centre of town, it is at the same time placed on the outskirts of town (which indicates the small town-size) and is thus neighboured by fields on two adjacent sides. On the other sides, you find an elementary school and a kindergarten, and finally the local school dentist. The school is located up a blind road, meaning that the people who pass here usually have a purpose in connection with either one of the institutional settings located here.

The school building is a large one-floor building, although with a basement floor under a part of the building, housing classrooms for creative subjects, such as art and music. The building is predominantly constructed of concrete, wood and with large floor-to-ceiling windows, and it has various sculptures placed out front and in some of the smaller atriums that can be found in between the building's 'arms' and hallways. The heart of the building is a big communal room in the middle of the school, which serves as connecting point for the four adjacent 'arms' of the building that are symmetrically placed in each corner of the communal room. The main entrance leads right into the communal room, and it is therefore a natural meeting point for the students. In one end of the room, opposite the main entrance, there is a large greenhouse and the sides of the room consist of large windows to atriums with ponds, sculptures and benches. Alongside all the windows are hallways, separated from the centre (of the room) by big moveable bulletin boards. The greenhouse in the one end functions as a natural separation from the canteen area that is on the other side of the green house. The green house is large enough for people to hang out in, and a few chairs are placed in there. The separations made by the green house and the moveable bulletin boards create a 'room within the room'; on the 'inner' side of the bulletin boards are large groups of couches and small tables, where the students hang out before, between and after classes, and in the middle of the room there is an open floor space. Here you find the grand piano that is used for communal singing at school assemblies, and often one or two ping pong tables are set up as well (they are easily folded up and removed). School assemblies are held here a few times a month: an approximately fifteen-minute event consisting of the delivery of communal messages, information of upcoming events and perhaps an interlude of entertainment. Often, the different classes take turn in being in charge of some sort of entertaining input, such as a song or a small play. At these events, the students hang out in the couches and on the floor, and all the teachers stand in the background. One noticeable thing here is the clear division of *where* people hang out. The couches are divided according to school year; first-year students occupy the couches closest to the entrance and – if one wishes to apply a critical glance – the coldest part of the room, as there is often a draft from the constantly moving doors. One notices in the wintertime. In the middle of the room – alongside the corridor – are the couches for the second-year students, and in the far end – adjacent to the lush and warm greenhouse – are the couches for the third-year students, the seniors. Of course, this is not marked anywhere but an informal information that is passed on from one generation of students to the next as the naturalized order of things. In this way a hierarchy is supported by the structural layout of furniture and architectural lines, in a way that can only be comprehended as a historical becoming. Of course, this hierarchical division of space is visible at school assemblies, where classes usually sit more or less together, but it becomes even more outspoken when the room is almost devoid of people: in the middle of the school day, when some students are sent out to do group work or people pass time in between classes. Here one seldomly sees a first-year student hang out in the couches by the greenhouse, the senior's couches.

All classrooms are located in the adjacent buildings ('the arms'), connected to the centre by wide hallways, also containing classrooms. Each adjacent building is constructed the same way with classrooms of varying sizes surrounding a larger communal room, equipped with couches, and sets of tables and chairs. These communal spaces are often used for group work during class, and also serve as hang-out place during breaks. Most classrooms have large window sections towards the centre-room, creating a sense of transparency and openness. In the beginning of the school year, the first-year students are located in a block to themselves, with a 'home classroom' assigned to each class. On the door to each room, their tutors have made a welcoming sign, hand-written and decorated with coloured pens: 'Welcome 1.A' and then all the names of the people in the class. This creates an immediate *sense of belonging* as well as a welcoming feeling. However, at the same time it may signal childishness, or informality, as this resembles welcoming signs from kindergarten or first-year primary. Having a 'home classroom' means that all the classes, except the ones that require specific artefacts and conditions (physics, chemistry, music, arts and sports), take place here. After the first six months when the students have settled in their final classes (according to their final choice of academic line), this arrangement ceases and the students have to orient themselves for each class as to which room they will be in.

There is a general spacious feeling to the school; classrooms are rather large and most often fit all students in horseshoe-formation of the tables, which allows for students to all see one another. What stands out when spending time at the school, in terms of materiality and location – and the immediate feeling that the high school affords – can be summarized as a sense of transparency and openness (large open spaces, lots of light, glass walls), which contributes to a strong feeling of *community* and *proximity*.

I shall now proceed with introducing Anna and (to a lesser extent) Mia, who attend Countryside High, and through them I will examine the manner in which these key features of the school are integrated and reflected (and actively produced), on a subjective level, in the daily life of the girls. This will allow for Countryside High to unfold as a high school *practice*.

Proximity across Generations: Anna's Close Family Ties

Anna[11] lives with her mother and younger brother in an average-size terrace house in a fairly new housing area, mostly inhabited by elderly people. Anna's parents got divorced when she was six years old and ever since she has been living with her mother and younger brother. The divorce brought about a close relationship between Anna and her grandmother, since the grandmother would come over and help out at least once a week, when they were younger. That practice only ended a few years ago when Anna and her brother started feeling that they *had* to spend the evening at the house *because* of their grandmother. Family, which is mostly oriented towards Anna's mother and her side of the family, is very important to Anna and she often goes to the nearby bigger city, where her grandparents live to meet up with her grandmother. They usually meet at the mall, because her grandfather can be a bit grumpy and he prefers some peace and quiet in the house. Anna's grandmother used to work at the mall and refers to herself as a 'mallrat'. Anna and her grandmother have a joint practice of roaming the mall and looking for the best offers in DVD's and fast-food, preferably pizza-slices. Anna spends time with her grandmother several times a month, sometimes up to twice a week – she thinks it is important to have a close relationship to one's grandparents and she does not understand why this is not a common practice for others her age:

> *Some people my age, they do not want to hang out with their grandparents – at all. But me, I love it. I also spent days there in my summer holiday and then we went to the zoo.*

Spontaneously going to visit her grandparents is something that occurs rather often, especially if Anna has an early day at school – it is one of her ways of adding meaningful activities to her day. This emphasizes the value Anna ascribes to her family relations.

Proximity and Distance: A Practical Concern

Anna lives in a small town about 10 kilometres from the high school. This means that she takes the bus to school every day; it leaves near her home around 7.40 in the

---

[11] Anna, in comparison to Mia, will be more thoroughly represented in the following, due to her larger degree of involvement in the research project.

morning, and she usually arrives at school ten minutes before class starts, at 8.20. At this hour (early morning), it is mostly high school students who are on the bus, along with a few teachers, who live near the bus route as well. That a large percentage of the students (and some teachers) arrive by bus means that there is flexibility in case of the bus being delayed; then students are not marked for late attendance.

As Countryside High is the only high school within an approximately 25-kilometre radius, and the only high school in between two large provincial cities at the island of Funen, it has a rather large geographical coverage area. The students come from a range of small towns in the area, or from the countryside. Despite the large catchment area covered by the school, the *local* and *proximate* stand out as values in many ways. For instance, many of the students see the advantage of living close to their friends from school; though there may easily be 20 kilometres or more to where the other person lives. This gives some insight into the perception and meaning of physical distances when one lives in the countryside; most of the students are used to having to travel rather far for school or leisure time activities, but still within what they refer to as 'local'. In the sense, 'local' becomes opposed to living in the bigger cities that are not considered local, even though one is only 15 kilometres away. As we saw from the introduction event, the local aspect presents itself as part of the school's self-presentation: here the principal showed an overview of the bus connections to the school and emphasized the *accessibility* of the school with public transportation. The timetables of the buses are coordinated with school hours and vice versa. This is a practical concern of great importance to many in the local area, as they depend on the buses for transportation. Proximity and concrete connections (by bus) also influence the choice of high school for some, as, e.g., Mia:

> Mia: I may have been influenced by what my older brothers have done ... The oldest went to Alphaville High (in the bigger city), but I think that would be too far away for me. Especially now, that we moved. And my other older brother attends Countryside High now (as a senior). However, he started out at another high school in a bigger city as well, but **he didn't like it,** so he quickly changed. So, yeah, I believe that has influenced me. ... And then I went to Countryside High to visit it, and I **immediately just felt at home** there. Like I belong there. It seems like a **good place**.
>
> (emphasis added)

The practical arrangements around the high school, such as bus schedules, contribute to a feeling of connectedness with the surrounding communities (e.g. the small villages), and the high school is experienced as a place that *immediately* feels like somewhere where *one belongs* (unlike the schools in the bigger cities).

Community, Social Familiarity and Friendships

At Countryside High it is very common to have older siblings or even parents who have attended the school before you. Everybody knows someone who has gone there before them. This helps to underline the feeling of *familiarity* and *belongingness*. To Anna, Countryside High is perceived as a more social school (in the sense that people know each other) than the inner-city schools. This is mainly why she has chosen to attend it. In her mind, people who attend the inner-city schools spend too much of their time caring about what brand their handbag is or who owns what – she does not want to be influenced by this kind of thinking (so to Anna, specific schools are related to specific values and ways of thinking). Also, she feels that she already knows a lot of people who will be attending the school (before she starts), and then she will most likely have friends in common with the rest of them, she says; this makes the proximity factor very relevant and meaningful in the meeting between Anna, Mia and the school. Anna and Mia attended the same elementary school, and they know each other well when they start high school.

The school has a little less than 600 students. Growing generations and a larger demand for a high school education among Danish youths have resulted in an expansion and renovation of the school over the past few years. Yet the school has kept its reputation as a *smaller school* in the countryside. This identity is mainly due to a comparison with the inner-city schools that are considerably bigger. In this area high school is not necessarily the most obvious choice (of youth education), as a majority of the parents are working class without higher academic degrees. This means that high school competes with trade schools and vocational schools for student uptake. Therefore, the introduction events are partly advertising for high school in general, and secondly advertising for the particular high school.

It is well integrated in the atmosphere of the school that things are 'down to earth'; already in the presentation of the school (at the introduction event), students draw forth how this is a place of sociality and friendship: that it is a small high school and that *everybody has friends* across class-structures. The monthly parties at the school are very popular and the teachers (and occasionally parents) will perform as bartenders throughout the night and serve alcohol for the students. This emphasizes a safe environment, where you are *taken care of* by the people around you and where there is a large degree of familiarity with one another. This does not mean that everyone cares about the same things or hangs out with each other. Especially in the beginning of the school year, there are significant differences in the motives and interests displayed by the girls in Anna's and Mia's class, which becomes the cause of tension and a rather explicit informal group formation. I will return to this and unfold it in Chapter 6.

The dominant sense of community is not an automatism. The school has deliberately incorporated a structure to enhance and support the social integration at school. It implies that a person is assigned to a class on the basis of preliminary choice of academic line and attends this particular class for the first semester (from August until Christmas). Then at the end of the first semester, the students can reevaluate their choice and freely switch to another academic line[12]. This means that the first semester is a bit more basic and students are mostly concerned with finding out what high school is about. Anna and Mia both start out with attending the humanistic, creative line; in this class most of the students have music as their creative subject, whereas Anna and

---

[12] This structure is built into the current high school reform, and therefore not an opportunity limited to this particular high school. However, high schools in general emphasize this structural opportunity to various degrees.

Mia have art. They do not particularly like art class; they are only in this academic line because they also wanted English and social sciences. As Anna aspires to become a kindergarten teacher, she also found art to be a relevant subject. That Anna and Mia do not attend music as the most of their classmates means that they feel somewhat outside of the dynamics created in connection with music. And after Christmas they both change to another academic line, with a base of English, social science and psychology. Anna finds that this combination is ideal in relation to her future goal of becoming a kindergarten teacher, and Mia has chosen it as she found it the most relevant line in relation to pursuing a career as either a journalist or working in a clothing shop. The school's intention of this structure is revealed in the social practice of Anna and Mia: their switch to another academic line after Christmas means that they get to know more people and that the dynamics in the class change, in a way that makes them both feel a lot more integrated socially. They both still keep their relations with many of their former classmates, so they feel that this structural arrangement has increased their social integration at school – just as the school intended. As an overall setting, Countryside High affords highly social behaviour and activities that are directed towards the community of the school. This fits well with both Anna and Mia and what they value in their everyday lives.

Keeping the World Small and Proximate: Hello Kitty Socks and the Royal Family

At the school it is common practice to use the big open cloakroom near the main entrance. Here everybody hangs their coats, leave gym bags and so forth. In the winter Anna usually leaves her winter-boots here and puts on slippers that she wears throughout the school day. It is not uncommon to see students in socks or slippers at school. This year the student council decided that for two consecutive weeks during the fall, all students *had* to wear slippers indoors at school, as they found that students in general had become too careless in terms of putting their feet up on the furniture. This was considered disrespectful towards the cleaning staff at school and the other students in general.

The collective thus becomes a very concrete matter that is actively perceived (in the large open spaces), just as it is structurally enacted in various ways. This is also something the girls have to get used to:

A conversation between Anna and Mia:

Mia: *Did you hear that they are raising the prices for the school parties?*
Anna: *I did ... to 75Dkr[13], right?*
Mia: *Yes*
Anna explains to me that the price increase is due to the fact that some of the classes that were chosen to assist with the cleaning (after the party) failed to show up, and therefore the party committee has decided to raise the prices so they can afford to hire professional cleaning in the future.

---

[13] 75Dkr is equivalent to €10.

Anna: *They're punishing us collectively and that really sucks!*
Mia nods and declares that 75Dkr is way too expensive for this kind of party.

The community feeling thus set new conditions that the girls do not necessarily find reasonable, albeit they do understand the rationales at play. However, it is not only in relation to cleaning matters and wearing slippers inside that the sense of belonging and a being part of a community is denoted. The proximity principle also shines through in ways of relating to bigger issues in the world. The following conversation between Anna and her friends is rather exemplary:

'Have you heard that Korea has exploded a nuclear bomb on the size of Hiroshima?' Charlotte asks and the other girls confirm. *'Yeah, Obama wasn't too happy about it either,'* Charlotte continues. *'And the pope resigned!'* Charlotte says. *'That's crazy,'* Anna says. Maria comments: *'Yeah, it's insane – it's the first time in like 600 years!'* *'Well, how do they usually resign?'* Clara asks. *'Well, they usually stay on until they die,'* Charlotte replies and continues, *'but this guy he kind of abdicated like if queen Margrethe resigned ... '* *'No! She wouldn't do that!'* Anna says in a firm voice indicating a hint of panic; *'or at least that wouldn't be fair to (crown prince) Frederik and (crown princess) Mary!'* *'And why is that?'* Charlotte wants to know. *'Well, because they live such a happy family life,'* Anna says. *'Alright, little miss Tabloid[14]'* Charlotte says in a teasing tone.

Here, international, and perhaps slightly abstract, matters are directly connected to homely conditions in order to ensure comprehension. And in this specific case, it is coupled to one of Anna's main interests, the Royal Family. Anna is a big fan, and she is always up to date on what they are doing. Usually, the others tease her about it, as this is not a common interest among her peers, but they also admire her detailed knowledge that she mainly acquires from Billedbladet (a Danish tabloid magazine). Anna is not ashamed to admit that she reads this magazine although it is not at all considered 'cool' among her peers. Coolness or appearance is not a high priority for Anna – she does not care much for fashion or how you are supposed to look. She prefers to wear what she feels like and then sometimes thinks that maybe she should put on another top, but then is too lazy to do so. It happens that other people tell her that her outfit does not match or that her top is see-through, but she really does not care. Mia, on the other hand, is a lot more fashion-conscious and Anna does not always get it; she cannot see why the importance. For instance, Anna prefers clothing items that are comfortable, as, e.g., her pink Hello Kitty socks. She and one of the other girls in the class have a thing for Hello Kitty socks, mostly because they find them 'super soft' and 'extra thick'. To Anna they have a special meaning; she works as a gymnastics trainer for younger children every week and the children love when she is wearing her Hello Kitty socks. This ascribes meaningfulness to the socks that she brings with her to school, even though the school practice and the gymnastics practice are completely

---

[14] The term 'miss Tabloid' here indicates that Anna is always keeping up with celebrity gossip, especially concerning the Royal Family.

separate activity settings, and she is the only person who connects them. However, it demonstrates how meaningfulness and self-understanding are not fragmented aspects of her everyday life, but rather something she carries across different activity settings as part of the narrative of who she is and of what matters.

Valuing Local Community and Working Actively to Realize Motives

Anna is a determined girl; she has a clear idea of what she wants with her life. Her goal of becoming a kindergarten teacher is reflected in many of her choices regarding high school and how she structures her time. After high school she plans on working as an au-pair in the United States. To her, this is the ideal way of combining the desire to go to the United States with her love for children.

> *So, I have always thought about it like this, that if I do not want to be a kindergarten teacher anymore, then I would want to be a private child-minder or something like that; but it's **always** something that has to do with other people. I want a job that **involves people;** I would not be able to have a desk job, like my mom.*
>
> (emphasis added)

Just as Anna's dream is reflected in her choice of academic line in high school, it is also evident in her activities outside school: she is baby-sitting regularly and helping out at the local kindergarten. She is also very much engaged with the local gymnastics' association, where she is part of a team herself, and also coaches younger children. Her way of engaging in these various activities implies that she is active in the local community and has many contacts. In some respect her local engagement is slightly untypical for her age group, where many seem to prioritize time with their peers at the expense of time with other family members. For Anna, this seems to be the other way around. At least at the beginning of the school year. Besides seeing her grandmother frequently, she practises zumba[15] with her mother in the local sports facility every Monday night, although she prefers not to stand next to her mother during class. It is evident that Anna values her local community highly and especially the activities that involve children. The activity settings she engages in are thus very much about being close to other people and meeting motives of developing her skills as a child-minder, as means of realizing her overall goal of becoming a pedagogue and working as a kindergarten teacher.

Contradictory Practices and Institutional Double Standards

In the last part of this eco-niche portrait, I will draw forth some ambiguities that became apparent at Countryside high. Here I refer to aspects where the invitational character of the environment became ambiguous or contradictory; not necessarily in

---

[15] Zumba is a fitness form similar to aerobics, while drawing heavy references to Latin dance moves.

its own right, but in the meeting between the school (as an institutional setting) and the young people's understanding of the school and themselves as students. The first relates to the atmosphere of openness and inclusion, and the second point to what I will refer to as an institutional double standard. It relates to a tension in the manner in which the high school invites the students to participate and the way high school ascribes meaning to the academic choices made by the students. It therefore points to a tension in the way high school unfolds as an activity setting.

Perhaps It Is Too Airtight ...

As a special feature, Countryside high offers a class specifically tailored for students with Asperger syndrome. This is a relatively new initiative at the time of my presence at the school, and something the school is rather proud of, according to one of the teachers who is assigned to this class. Not many schools offer such classes, and it is seen as an important integrative venture that allows for students who may normally have difficulties in attending regular high school classes to attend the same school as everyone else, albeit with careful consideration and special measures taken to ensure that they feel comfortable in the environment. This falls in line with an overall political agenda in Denmark regarding inclusion in the schooling system, where the aim is to ensure that the public schooling system is for everyone, also those who are dealing with various difficulties and mental issues. This year, approximately 170 new students entered Countryside high. They were divided into eight first-year classes, and one of these were a class for young people with Asperger syndrome.

One day in English class, I am sitting in the couches in the communal area in one of the 'arms' with Anna, Mia and another girl from their class, Maya. They are doing group work and talking about an upcoming English assignment.

> A teacher comes out from one of the adjacent classrooms and asks them to quiet down. When she has left, Anna sighs and says: *'It is because of them Aspergers. They are sitting in there!'* She nods in the direction of the room from which the teacher came. The two others nod. *'I really don't get why they haven't installed soundproof doors or why we are even allowed to sit here, when the Aspergers are in there,'* Anna says, again nodding in the direction of the classroom door. *'Do you think it is more annoying for the students with Asperger than it would be for you?,'* I ask. *'Definitely, yes,'* she says. *'We are used to it, but their heads cannot handle the sound, I think ...,'* she says and looks thoughtful. Anna and Mia continue the conversation: *'I mean, why don't they just make soundproof room down here* (in this section of the school)? *I mean, I'm not saying that they shouldn't be here ....* (she contemplates a little) *... but perhaps it is too airtight for them in that room that is actually soundproofed?'* She points to the room next door that has new doors and according to rumor is more soundproof. Maya comments: *'But the problem is that they cannot handle changes, so they cannot just move to another room'*. *'No, but ....,'* Anna says, and appears annoyed at the situation.

In a way, we could infer that there was nothing to remark about this small exchange. And at the same time, it points to a doubleness relating to the school's valuing of openness and inclusion. The atmosphere at the school is characterized by a down-to-earth-ness, as we, e.g., see from the way in which students walk around in socks at times, and a general homely feeling, where you get the feeling that everybody knows everybody, more or less. The school values inclusion and actively wants to accommodate a wide range of students; both the academically skilled ones, as well as the ones who need extra teaching, and then a smaller group of students who are dealing with Asperger syndrome. However, despite the school's effort and desire to include the students with Asperger, it seems from the empirical extract above that the students in the other classes are struggling to make sense of their presence. And this in a double sense: on the one hand, it seems to annoy the girls that they must take special considerations when doing group work outside the room where the Asperger class is located, and the students with Asperger are primarily understood based on their diagnosis, and thus someone positioned in a marginalized position in relation to the other students. Hence, a qualitative difference is pointed out as a natural thing. At the same time, we see a certain expression of care and consideration in the way the girls are trying to think what the school should have done to take better care of the special needs of the students with Asperger, or how the school could make better conditions for them. Here we see how it is more the school's solutions or concrete material conditions that are problematized, rather than the students with Asperger. From the girls' way of talking about their fellow students with Asperger, one can speculate if the school has actually managed to integrate the students with Asperger, or merely succeeded in creating a marginalized parallel existence for them within the school premises. I never had a chance to talk to any of these students, and all in all, what was most apparent about their presence at school was their 'non-presence', which could either indicate an integration to an extend that they were undistinguishable in practice or, the contrary, that they did not really take part in high school life as it presented itself to other students, such as Anna. I can only wonder.

The More Peculiar Types Attend the B-class

There are a lot of choices to be made in high school regarding which classes to take and which academic profile this provides you with. It is of special relevance if you wish to pursue further academic education, and it is a choice that needs to be made when starting high school. At some schools, including Countryside High, the choice can be altered after the first term (five months into the first school year). Aspiring to become a kindergarten teacher, it is of no real importance to Anna which academic line she chooses, as long as she graduates high school. However, she finds that psychology is clearly more relevant than mathematics in relation to her long-term educational project. In addition, she does not find mathematics interesting which makes math class a waste of time. Therefore, she is happy that there is no math in the psychology line, but instead English and social science. She has discussed her decision of not having math (except for the mandatory first year) with her mother, and they both rely on what the headmaster said at the introduction event: '*Always choose with your heart!*' He had pointed out to them that enthusiasm for the subject was more important than rationality and reason, and it would always to be possible to take supplementary courses after high school, if needed. This means that on the basis of the initial encouragement from the headmaster (to choose with your heart), Anna chooses to pursue her overall motive (related to her goal of becoming a kindergarten teacher). She thus complies with the school's valuing of 'enthusiasm', and she tries to combine her own interests with the interest of the high school – or we could say that she tries to align her motives with the demands of the school.

At some point in the middle of the school year, when I am doing field work at Countryside High, I take a break (as I recall, from a never-ending math class) and go to the teacher's room to grab a cup of coffee. Otherwise, I tend to avoid this area (at all the schools) as my main interest is getting close to the students' perspectives rather than the teachers' perspectives, and because spending time with teachers tends to create insecurity about the purpose of my research to the students. But as we are in the middle of class, the chance of encountering teachers is minimal. Perhaps this is the reason why the following conversation arose, as I and the Social Science teacher, Annie, who I had not met before, were the only two people hanging out by the coffee machine.

> Annie: *Are you the new substitute?*
> Me: *No, I am ....*
> Annie interrupts: *Oh, are you here for the teacher's training program then?*
> Me: *No, I am here as part of a research project, where two of the students take part ...*
> Annie: *Ah. What's it about then?*

I then briefly tell her about the project.

> Annie: *Well, I'm asking because I teach Social Sciences and it might be of interest to us, you know ... But tell me, which class are you in then?*
> Me: *1.B*
> Annie: *I see! That makes sense. Well, the B-class is a bit heavier, you know, academically ...*
> Me: *What does that mean?*
> Annie: *Well, everyone knows that students attending the B-class are somewhat behind academically in comparison with the other students at school. These students need an extra push or need to be 'pulled' more. You know, they are not as bright as the others. You won't find the best grades in here. I mean, this is the class you chose to attend if you want to avoid math and such. And that's how it is in the B-classes on all levels – they are just somewhat 'heavier' and this is where you attend if you need a little more help (academically), or ...*
> Me: *Okay, this is new to me ...*
> Annie: *Actually, in a Social Science class of mine, we once did a survey on social inheritance. Here in this school that is. And it showed that the B-class was a 'heavy' class, in the sense that relatively few of the students' parents (in this class) had a high school diploma. And it was the same pattern several years in a row!*
> Me: *okay*

Annie makes a few additional comments on what I ought to look at (rules, eating habits in class etc.), and then leaves. I head back to class.

The information provided by Annie is surprising to me, as I have heard no mention of this correlation or lack of academic proficiency in the classroom. I therefore choose to examine this further by discussing it firstly with Anna and Mia, and secondly with the school principal:

> Later that day I ask Anna and Mia whether they recognize any differences in academic performance between students in their own class and students in other classes – are there any known tendencies? Not to their knowledge, they say. Many in their class get really good grades and they have the impression that grades are dispersed relatively equally between classes. No class sticks out as either really good or really bad. I then ask why they chose the B-class, and I get the answers that I already know: this was the academic profile that they found most interesting and relevant in relation to their long-term motives of studying pedagogy and journalism, respectively.

This marks an incongruence between what the teacher told me about the B-class and what Anna and Mia told me. I find it interesting, so in my next small break I pass by the school principal's office and knock the open door.

> (at the principal's office):
> I start out by asking the principal how students are assigned to the various academic lines that the school offers. He explains that this is done solely by the students' own choices that they mark in their initial application.
>
> Me: *OK, so there is no specific assessment involved in this process, in relation to the academic levels and needs of the students?*
> Principal: *No, absolutely not!*
>
> I then tell him that I am puzzled by this general impression that I was made aware of by a teacher, stating that the B-classes are academically behind in relation to the other classes, and that I am unsure of how to make sense of it.
> This upsets the principal, and he denies that there is any truth to it, although he is aware of the rumor. Apparently, he was recently contacted by a concerned parent asking into the very same thing. He is very keen on shutting the rumor down and he says that he might write something about it in the next newsletter: '*it is important that rumors like these do not flourish*'. I thank him for his time, and as I am halfway out the door, he says:
>
> *That being said, there is a tendency to find some more peculiar types of students in the B-class ... you know, the ones who choose an academic line of English, Social Science and Psychology, and actively avoid math, I mean, it's just ... I mean, that is a fact, but it is not something the school is creating.*

The conversation with the teacher, and later the principal, brings about an interesting contradiction in the school practice, in relation to standards and values. The official story is that young people are free to choose the academic line they find most interesting, and they are even encouraged to do so. We recall the very same principal telling prospective students to 'choose with their heart' at the introduction event and encouraging their enthusiasm. Unofficially, however, and at the same time there appears to be an assumption that the bright students automatically choose math and physics (natural science); or that natural science is the standard choice at high school, especially for ambitious students. Humanistic subjects are somehow lower level, reflect a personal flaw or problem or a peculiar personality. I refer to this as a double-standard: it is clearly something working as a standard (among teachers in their evaluation and subjectification of students), but at the same time it is non-existing and in contrast to that which exists (the clear invitation to 'choose with your heart'). The double-standard creates an interesting tension, when contrasted with the atmosphere at the school: on one hand the school, as an institutional setting, invites for community, proximity and familiarity (which is also reflected and integrated in the activity settings that students engage in), and on the other hand the high school practice reveals hidden, but working, standards of natural science students being 'the norm', indicating that other students are somewhat problematic or deviant from the average or idealized student. This creates a potential tension in the way that students are subjectified, a tension that may readily be difficult for students to make sense due to its elusive character.

Recapitulating Countryside High

Having spent time with Anna and Mia at Countryside High throughout their first year at the school, I am left with a persistent impression of both the school and its students as being very oriented towards local community and a principle of proximity in the everyday life. In my exploration of Countryside High and the everyday life of Anna (and to some extend Mia) as part of an eco-niche, the proximity in particular emerges as imbued with meaning – both in the manner in which high school is practised, and also in the daily life of the girls in general. A high level of engagement with local community life is reflected on many levels, both within the school practice and the self-understandings of the students at the school. The proximity and the sense of community that are invited for by the school (also in terms of architecture and materiality) are reflected in the school practice: when school hours are coordinated with the local bus routes, with areas to hang out in that affords and supports community, and when students have to wear slippers at the school for two weeks (decided by other students). The high school practice (as an overall behavioural setting, in Barker & Wright's terminology) co-creates and offers specific conditions and possibilities for participation (in the different activity settings available at school), as well as for the way in which to be and become a high school student.

Similarly, the proximity principle resonates in Anna's way of conducting her everyday life outside the school setting: when she teaches children's gymnastics at the local gymnastics' association, when she attends zumba-classes with her mother, when she spends several afternoons a month with her grandmother at the mall, and the way in which she makes sense of international politics through associations with the Danish Royal Family. Just as it stands forth in the open ways in which the girls discuss and negotiate meaning with each other, about things that matter to them (I shall return a bit more to this in Chapter 4). This implies that proximity and close relations become significant keywords that resonate in most of the activity settings that the girls participate in – it is something they are directed towards in their actions, and it is meaningful to them.

By and large Countryside High, almost as an organism, 'breathes' transparency and community: this is what resonates in practice and, I would propose, reflects parts of the collective idealities that characterize Countryside High as an eco-niche. However, there are a few challenges to this that comes across as tensions. I understand these tensions as a result of the school's way of balancing its own historically developed self-understanding and meeting political and societal demands and trends. This is what comes across in the ambiguous manner in which the school invites students to choose freely (with the heart), signifying that all choices of academic career (in high school) are equally good, and then at the same time ascribes generalized assumptions to the students based on their choices (students are 'slow' and 'behind'). Additional ambiguities or tensions, concerning the integration of health profiles as individualistic self-monitoring tools, present themselves, but I shall explore these more explicitly in Chapter 5.

Eco-niche Portrait: Southside High

Southside High is a private high school located in Copenhagen in the midst of an area historically known as the cradle of the autonomous and radical groups. Now the area consists mainly of trendy bars, cafes and shops, along with Middle Eastern food shops, and an abundance of small kiosks. The school is housed in an old building in between ordinary residential buildings, and most of the school area is not visible from the street, as it is accessed through the courtyard. Being a private high school – which is not so common in Denmark, as most schools are public and therefore free to attend – the school also houses the last two years of a private elementary school.

Most of the school walls, inside and to some extent outside, are covered by graffiti; this includes classrooms, communal rooms, toilets, staircases and hallways. Each class has its own homeroom that the students are allowed to decorate and personalize as they please. This requires first painting over the decorations made by the previous class who resided there, and then deciding for themselves on how to decorate. Usually, decorations consist of graffiti paintings and various tags. Tables and chairs also get decorated throughout the school year. In the classroom, there is a little shelf system on the wall, where students can keep a book or papers or the like. The shelves are open and accessible to everybody, and no one worries about theft or things disappearing, which reflects a high degree of mutual trust.

As an older town house, the school appears almost majestic and with a historic character. Both the main building that is visible from the street and the building in the courtyard consist of several floors. On the ground level, via the courtyard, you enter directly into the heart of the school: the big communal room where all school assemblies are held. School assembly is a particularly important organizational organ at the school, as it is mainly here the ideals of the basic democracy, that the school values and is based on, are practised. Here decisions regarding both major and minor issues are discussed and put to a vote, and binding decisions are made by majority vote.

This includes the hiring of new staff or basic rules of the school. Democracy is a key value, and it is practised extensively. The communal room itself is large and open, and only divided by tall pillars here and there that support construction. Tables and chairs are spread around in what appears to be a random mess, and obviously the formation of tables and chairs is reconfigured often, according to purpose. At one end of the room, there is a small canteen that sells a daily hot meal, cake, coffee, tea and drinks at student-friendly prices. When first visiting, the room more resembles a student house or a sort of cultural venue than 'high school', based on material appearances; however when one starts noticing people's behaviour, the similarities to other high school reemerge. To an outsider or newcomer like me, the room appears messy or perhaps even disorganized; however, when observed in use it becomes evident that the room is highly flexible in terms of furniture arrangements. This provides for an organic feeling, where the room is organized depending on the purpose of use. On the upper floors of the main building are classrooms and there are couches, tables and benches in various arrangements on the hallways that provide places to hold meetings, or to do group work. Stairwells seem endless and are climbed several times during the day. Floors are organized so that all the first-year classes are on the same floor, which increases a sense of belonging and facilitates getting to know one another across class configurations, albeit it concurrently contributes to a division between the different years. Ground-floor rooms hold facilities for drama and music classes, and extra music facilities are placed in industrial containers in the courtyard, due to limited space in the building. The container rooms are used as rehearsing rooms and are sound insulated. However, in the wintertime they are relatively cold as the electric radiators hardly suffice for heating them. The containers in the courtyard give the school a certain Klondike-like feeling, as the industrial containers seem out of place amidst the old majestic town house that make up the school. The widespread graffiti contributes to the Klondike-feeling and, for a Copenhagener like me, it draws clear reference to Freetown Christiania in Copenhagen that was founded in 1971, or to the various popup street food courts around town, for that matter. The atmosphere of the school area reflects a similar sense of autonomy and potential revolt against the establishment as one finds in Christiania. The discrepancy between the invitational character of the historic majestic building and that of the containers and the graffiti is outspoken, and it fosters an interesting atmosphere of new possibilities, autonomy and ownership.

The school is organized by a principle of basic democracy which implies that everything is decided in a democratic way and everyone, both teachers and students, has an *equal vote*. Academic requirements are decided by the school, but students are involved in a series of decisions on how to work with different subject matters, whether they want grades for their assignments or not, what the school spends money on and who gets hired as, for instance, a new principal. And, as a recognized high school, the school also adheres to certain standards of academic levels and teaching content. The school is referred to as an elite school by people from the outside. It is hard to say to what extent this is true as the student population is fairly mixed in terms of socio-economic backgrounds and orientations – that being said, it is clear that the fact that the school is private in itself implies that parents can afford to send their children here, as opposed to having them attend a public (and free of charge) high school (that is financed by the tax system). The elite predicate does however not seem to resonate with the students; neither in their way of dressing, nor as something they seem to find particularly accurate as a denominator. They do not seem to embrace this outside attribution of value. Some attend the school because of its political orientation that is outspokenly leftist and its very profound valuing of democracy and social engagement. Others attend because it is a very artistic school. And finally, some because they hope to feel like they fit in here, as opposed to feeling like outsiders at other (more mainstream) high schools. The majority of the students come from resource-rich families; a mix of creative working- and middle class and upper middle class with academic and political orientations. Some students come from far away to attend the school. One example is Maria, who lives about 60 kilometres away. This means that she stays at a relative's place in town during the weekdays, in order to be closer to school. Maria's mother is unemployed, and her father has an ordinary working-class job at a hospital, which means that Maria's attending this school requires a lot both financially and logistically from the family.

At Southside High what stands out in terms of materiality and location, and the immediate feeling that the high school affords, can be summarized as *alternative normativity* (conveyed by, e.g., the abundance of graffiti everywhere), which is deeply intertwined with the basic democratic structure of the school practice and the flexible and open rooms for sociality.

I will now proceed with introducing Lisa, who attends Southside High, and with her I will explore the manner in which these key features of the school are integrated and reflected (and actively produced), on a subjective level, in her daily life.

Lisa: My Middle Name Is 'Different'

Lisa attends Southside High, but as she has already attended the last two years of elementary school here, the high school setting is not particularly different from what she is used to. Mostly she has to relate to new teachers, new classmates and new subjects, but the schoolground in itself is familiar territory.

Lisa is an only child. She lives with her parents in an apartment in the centre of Copenhagen, within walking distance of the school. Her mother is a pedagogue, and her father is an artist, who is often unemployed. Lisa considers herself to be different from others, which she traces back to the fact that she was conceived by IVF (in vitro fertilization). Being different is both something she has been attributed (according to herself) – as being conceived by IVF – but it is also of importance to her in relation to her self-understanding: it is something she is very aware of and takes great pride in, in her everyday life, and it comes out in various ways. The most obvious way is perhaps the way she dresses: she has long bright-coloured dreadlocks that often change colour, and she has several piercings in her face. She always wears strong eye make-up, and sometimes paints dots in her face. This often gives her a rather dramatic look. She cannot wait to become old enough to get tattoos (the legal age for tattoos in Denmark is eighteen), and she is saving up for this whenever possible. She is usually wearing two pairs of stockings (as the outer is either deliberately torn or a fishnet stocking), a short black skirt, a hooded shirt and military boots. Mostly, the outfit is black mixed with a strong colour such as pink, purple or turquoise – also colours that you often see in her dreadlocks. This look clearly makes her stand out from the crowd when she walks on the street; however, at the school this is a fairly normal dress code. Not everyone at school dresses this way though, and there are variations within the degrees of extremes. Skulls and peace-signs are seen side by side with hearts and Hello Kitty, on jackets, bags and clothes. Also, piercings are the rule rather than the exception. The following example demonstrates how knowledge about piercing practice is carefully distributed among the students:

> In the classroom Alexander has noticed that Sara has used an ordinary stick that she picked up from the ground as a piercing in her ear. *'You have to watch your ear, he says, it is the only left ear you have'*. On her permission he removes the small stick, takes one of the expansion earrings that he has in his own ear out, and inserts it into her earlobe. He tightens it quite hard and it is obviously hurting Sara, whose face is distorted in pain. *'Not too hard ... then the skin will break!'* says Lisa, who has been watching the operation. Sara wipes a tear off her cheek. *'In a week or so, you will be able to turn it all the way in!'* one of the other girls says encouragingly. Sara cautiously feels her ear with her fingers. *'But never again use a wooden stick that you found on the ground!'* Alexander says in a lecturing tone.

The interesting thing here is the way in which the young people are helping each other in careful ways, albeit taking an expansion ring from one person's ear and directly inserting it into another person's ear is not a very hygienic thing to do. This, however, does not seem to occur as a reflection for either Alexander, Sara or Lisa. The excerpt shows how there is a shared value ascribed to adorning oneself with piercings and that rough or dramatic expressions are considered cool. At the same time, it shows how the young people care for one another: 'it is your only left ear', as Alexander points out, emphasizing that Sara would not want to get it infected. Just as Lisa points out that Alexander should not insert the expansion earring 'too hard', as the skin might break.

In general, Lisa comes out very conscientious, responsible and dedicated; she always does her schoolwork, and she is a high achiever in terms of grades. She refers to herself as rather 'nerdy', and she often hands in extra-long reports in biology because she gets so caught up with the topics. Despite there being a practice of not getting grades for papers at Southside high, she prefers to get grades because she likes to reflect her performance level in the number.

> Lisa: It's usually those who anyways get good grades who want to know. Meaning me. I mean, I don't have a problem admitting that, even though it might seem as if I'm showing off. But I've just always done good and that's why I want my grades. I am after all a little stressed out, you know. So, I actually do want to know, especially now when moving from elementary school to high school, if I'm doing just as good, or if my grades have dropped. That is interesting to me. Also, in relation to the rest of my time at high school, like what should I work harder at, how much should I prepare and stuff?

Me: *Do you have a set goal for your grades that you want to achieve, or ... ?*
Lisa: *As long as it is above 7 (C)*
Me: *As long as it is above 7 ... you know that you will get above 7, right?*
Lisa: *Yeah, or like in relation to grades, I feel that as long as it is above 7, then it's good. If it is above 4 (D), or 4, then it's acceptable. If it's below, then I cry.* She strikes a brief laughter.
Me: *Do you ever get (a grade) below?*
Lisa: *No, I have never gotten below 4.*

Lisa feels at ease with her academic ambitions. It is neither particularly encouraged, nor looked down upon at school. The school atmosphere seems to instate an openness to personal meaning in relation to academic achievement, concrete efforts and outcome:

Lisa: *People never went around asking (about grades). Instead, they would ask Hey, did you choose a topic?, what kind of feedback did you get? or What did you get? I think it's always been like that here. People are more relaxed, they don't gloat. Nor do they brag. It's more like they ... rejoice. They rejoice on behalf of each other and themselves. And then, if someone has done less well at something, they're like ah, too bad, and then moving on.*

The feeling of mutual care for one another that we saw in relation to the piercing practice seems to resonate in how the young people at Southside High collectively ascribe meaning to grades and assessment practices. Lisa feels free to pursue her ambitions, and excel at school, without feeling categorized on the basis of it, nor that it is something to try to hide or diminish, and yet, it appears that there is no pressure to perform. At least it is not experienced as an outside pressure for Lisa, but as a very personal meaningfulness in academic achievement that is directly linked to the love of knowledge. She loves physics and chemistry, but as she attends the creative/humanistic line at school, she has neither of those subjects. To compensate, she plans to take them later on or perhaps as simultaneous classes outside school hours, as part of a talent programme. The school itself does not run talent programmes, but they cooperate with the School of Talent Development that comes to the school to advertise their programmes and possibilities once in a while. Lisa finds this option of extracurricular classes appealing; however, she does not think that she has the time for extra classes while she attends high school. Evidently Lisa puts an effort in standing out in relation to mainstream societal norms, and at the same time she fits in well with the alternative normativity at school, in terms of appearance, just as she indeed meets societal ideals for school performance all the while she manages to remain rather reflected about her own ambitions and the value of not adding pressure to others.

'If Only I Were Older'

Lisa spends much of her time outside school with her boyfriend. He lives with his parents in a suburban neighbourhood and is educating himself to be a carpenter. He is a bit older than her, and they have been together for two years. They like to spend time doing large jigsaw puzzles together. Lisa handles his finances for him, and she is very keen on saving money herself. As mentioned, one thing she is saving for is tattoos; another is for a deposit for an apartment. Lisa dreams of moving from home. Her room in the apartment is small and placed next to the kitchen, and her parents often complain of her and her boyfriend having too loud sex. Lisa knows that it will be very difficult to move from home until she is eighteen (she is sixteen at present), so saving up money already is her way of working towards that goal and feeling like she is actually doing something to realize her motive. To earn money, she sings in a church choir, which brings her a little money, but far from enough. For this reason, she plans on taking on an extra job of some sort; however, she knows that a job can be difficult to find with her current number of facial piercings. She has also managed to save the money she gets for her birthday every year from her grandmother, as well as money she earns from collecting empty bottles around town. Sometimes she even manages to put money aside from the pocket money she gets from her parents every month. She tries to keep her budget to a minimum, and only spends money on cigarettes and beer. Her parents make her lunch to bring to school, so she does not have any unnecessary food expenses.

Lisa's way of conducting her everyday life is thus highly oriented towards her future dreams, of financing tattoos and moving from home. She engages in different activities (e.g. church choir, collecting bottles, economizing her expenses and saving up) to move closer to achieving her goal and realizing her profound motive of increased independency. Now and then, her priorities outweigh social participation, although her motive is not necessarily shared with others, as we shall see in the following excerpt:

> '*I'm feeling completely knackered,*' Lisa says. Maria adds: '*Yeah, I also found it nearly impossible to get out of bed this morning.*' '*Me too,*' Lisa says, and continues: '*and I snapped at my mom which was totally unjustified.*' There is silence and the girls seem thoughtful. Lisa rolls a cigarette, and we go outside the school premises to smoke (smoking is no longer allowed on the school premises, e.g., in the courtyard, as it was before, due to new national regulations of smoke free schools). Class has just ended. A guy from another class joins us: '*Hey Lisa, you're totally going on the annual skiing trip!,*' he says, more as a stating of the obvious than as an actual question. '*Nah, I cannot afford it,*' Lisa says in a dismissive tone. '*Hm ... well, then we'll just have to smuggle you along somehow,*' the guy says, hopeful. '*Well, if you can smuggle me along, that would be just fine ... or if you pay for me,*' Lisa says in a somewhat cheeky tone. '*Don't wanna do that!,*' he answers. '*Are you coming to Prague, then?,*' Maria wants to know ('Prague' refers to an annual trip around Easter where many Danish high school students, especially from the Copenhagen area, meet in Prague, in the Czech Republic, and party for a week. The reason for this destination is that the price levels are relatively low compared to Danish standards). '*Nah, I can't afford it,*' Lisa says and adds: '*I think I will pass this year and wait until next year.*' She changes the subject.

Here Lisa's tendency to insist on being opposed to what everyone else wants shines through – both Maria and the guy seem enthusiastic about the respective trips, and perhaps therefore, Lisa is not – as well as her priorities with her money. Her savings are meant for other purposes than travelling, which shows her dedication and motive hierarchy that directs her actions and priorities in her everyday life. However, in this situation at least, her reasons for saving are not made public, and the invitation to take part in the skiing trip or the trip to Prague is dismissed with reference to not being able to afford it, which in fact, she very well could, if her priorities were different. We thus get a glimpse of the persistent character of her dedication to her future plans.

Resisting Standards and Being in Opposition

Lisa's self-understanding as *being different* largely resonates with the school practice in general, and with her way of relating to people around her. For instance, she categorically rejects what others like and places herself in opposition to their views or preferences. This dynamic is especially outspoken towards her friend and classmate Maria. When Maria talks enthusiastically about her favourite food, Lisa says she does not like that food in particular; when Maria talks about places she wants to visit, Lisa wants to go somewhere else or makes sure that they have different angles on it; and when others talk about the upcoming skiing trip, Lisa prefers to stay at home. A similar dynamic appears in relation to the social dynamics in her class. An example is illustrative of this:

> One day in class the students are trying to organize a social gathering after school. One of the boys proposes a meeting place, which raises a discussion of relevance etc. in relation to current weather conditions. After a while Lisa says: '*Well, I just wondered if we could agree on saying out loud in the classroom whatever we end up deciding on? Because I am not often active on Facebook, so I don't keep myself updated there.*' She pauses and looks around. People are nodding here and there, and some just look surprised at her, with disbelief even. She continues: '*Or perhaps someone would please remember to send me a text message, in that case?*' she asks and looks around. '*You see, I would like to participate, but I just don't check my Facebook account and it sounds like things will be coordinated through Facebook?!*' she adds. In the end one of the boys promises to send her a text message.

Lisa does have an active Facebook account, but she only checks it if there is something specific, she wants to see, and apparently, the social gathering is not specific enough for her to stay updated via Facebook. To her, Facebook easily feels like a stress factor, as she feels it forces her to keep up with what everyone is doing all the time, for no reason. It is clear that Facebook serves as the standard medium through which social life is organized; it is implicit among the people in the class (and in this sense young people in this high school does not stand out from the young people at the other schools). To Lisa, being different is an important, if not central, part of her self-understanding and thus affects the way in which she relates to different artefacts and standards: in this case Facebook and its use in relation to sharing and organizing social life. It seems that Lisa is very much preoccupied with an awareness of herself as someone who tries to fight or oppose a standard. However, she shows some interesting contradictions in the sense that (1) she actually has an active Facebook profile, and (2) she says that she *does* check Facebook, but only if she knows that she has to keep track of something important. In that sense she is not only opposing the use of Facebook as a standard for social organizing, but also negotiating the importance of the social organizing in itself. And since the social gathering does not qualify as important enough for her to check Facebook, she is also negotiating the importance of the social gathering, thus displaying her own standards for what qualifies as important (her values). In this way, Lisa is enforcing reflections (upon her classmates) of the immediateness by which Facebook comes to serve as a platform for social organization in the class, and although this (Facebook as a platform) does not change, she co-creates a potential space of reflection for the concurrent immediacy and mediacy of this practice.

Lisa's actions can also be understood as a way of insisting on a position as 'I-am-not-like-you' or someone who is, by her own choice, on the margins of the social group – a way of saying 'I am certainly not mainstream'. This is a way of performing 'self', as Lisa's experience of 'self' is continuously being defined in relation to what everyone else is not, and at the same time she meets and reproduces societal demands on young people to do well at school and plan for the future. What is worth noting is how Lisa's need to be different poses a challenge to her in an institutional setting, where 'being different' is the norm; it is integrated in the alternative normativity at the school. Lisa therefore spends energy on positioning herself as different on a daily basis, because this is of particular value to her. However, this may be a time-consuming job, as she has to stand out – and in opposition – to both mainstream society *and* to the norms at school, all the while her actions and activities weave in and out of generalized norms and standards: e.g., her relationship with her boyfriend in some ways bears resemblance to a more conservative lifestyle or values (prioritizing twosomeness, doing jigsaws, planning and saving for the future), and at the same time challenges norms (by having loud sex despite her parents complaints; in that sense defying the shame often felt by teenagers in relation to sex). In some respects, in her way of deliberately trying to steer clear of normativity, Lisa in many ways embodies a conservative normativism; however, she does so not out of the need to fit in or meet demands, but because it makes sense to her – all the while, her way of conducting her everyday life is full of activities that in many ways transcend norms. In that sense, the narrative of being in opposition is perhaps more important than the actual actions constituting opposition, or at least it does not seem clear in relation to what opposition is defined. Rather this appears fluid and full of contradictions.

'Not Giving a Shit'; Defying or Bending Rules as a Value

> I am standing outside the school with a couple of the girls, who are smoking. '*Hasn't class already started?*' One of them asks. '*Probably, but I am going to finish my cigarette first*' the other one answers, '*This is my morning cigarette, and I need to take my time for that one*'.

Rules or no rules, there seems to be a tendency for the students at Southside High to be very much aware of their own needs and rights, just as they seem willing to debate and challenge the rules. This becomes apparent in a number of ways: both in relation to school practice and to bigger societal issues, and in ways of relating to rules, ranging from following them, to bending, debating and defying them. As an example, Lisa spends a lot of time programming on the computer and playing online games (e.g. World of Warcraft). Online gaming is a regular hobby of hers outside school; however, at school she also frequently plays online games during classes. This is her way of concentrating the best and she often manages to participate in ongoing discussions and answering questions, while playing online. Lisa knows that teachers do not accept students playing online games in class, and it happens that a teacher confiscates a computer or two during class because they catch someone playing. Lisa usually hides her computer behind her bag (on the table) so that her gaming activities are less obvious. And even though democracy is a key value at the school, there are still rules to be followed, and the teachers at Southside High have very different ways of assuming positions of authority. Casper, their teacher in Danish, prefers to be familiar with the students, calls most of them nicknames, surprises them by suddenly throwing a candy stick out in the room, or brings cookies for everyone. At the same time, he is not afraid to confiscate computers, and the students respect him. His style of teaching and relating to them fits well with the overall values of the school, of everyone having an equal say. However, to Casper this particular class, that Lisa attends, is difficult to teach: he finds that most of the students do not know what it means to attend high school – what it requires from them. Apart from that he loves teaching at Southside High in particular because of the easygoing and relaxed atmosphere. Another teacher, Christian, approaches the teaching situation from a different angle, and gets easily frustrated with the students, when they do not abide by his more classic question/answer teaching style. He sometimes yells at the students, which results in even less active participation from them. Almost like dominos, the students lean back, fold their arms in opposition, or simply disengage and start small conversations in the corners. Much to Christian's frustration. In Lisa's opinion the strength of the school is the open and inquisitive approach to the world that it fosters; that everything is up for discussion and that rules are not necessarily pinned down in advance or predetermined by authorities. However, she finds it frustrating that some teachers do not really embrace this school atmosphere, and instead seem too fixated on following their own plan, regardless of the inputs they receive from the students. This implies that even though key values at the school are openness and democracy, the high school practice reveals ambivalent teaching strategies and ambiguous rules.

Creating Alternative Normativity

The alternative normativity that is emphasized at Southside High is fully integrated in Lisa's daily life, and she finds her own ways of practising it. For example, when spring starts Lisa acquires a new habit of hanging out on benches in the city and drinking beers in the sun: sometimes on her own, sometimes with others. She drinks between two and eight beers on an everyday basis, she says, and she describes it as an old habit that she has picked up again. Her parents are aware of this practice, since she brings home all the bottles and she does not want to lie to them; they think it is a bit too much but does not restrict her drinking-practice. Her motto is that *'rules are meant to be broken'* and she prefers drinking beer over soda anytime. Contrary to what could be expected, her alcohol intake does not affect her school performance, so she finds it hard to see a problem in this behaviour. She argues that in old days, everybody drank beer all the time, so she *'doesn't give a shit'* about the official guidelines on alcohol consumption. And in that sense, normativity becomes a topic in its own right – the question of who and how to be is ever present and almost an agenda of its own, at least to Lisa.

> Lisa: *It's not that I have to be unique and special. I just hate being told that I resemble someone else, 'cause that's like …. I don't look like anyone, I am me. I mean, I do not want to look like anyone else, like other existing persons. […] To me, I think it's about trying to represent myself through my appearance and I don't feel like representing others … besides myself. So, basically, that is what all my body-decorations and my clothing style are about – it's about me showing that I am me. Basically.*
>
> Lisa: *This also explains why I change my look all the time. Because I evolve too, you know, and that is on ongoing process. […] Also, you know, people they tend to categorize me all the time, or at least they try to, and I am not particularly fond of that.*
>
> Me: *As what for instance?*
>
> Lisa: *Well, sometimes someone yells 'punk (rocker)' at me, other times 'emo'*[16]. *I've also been called 'rocker' (as to insinuate being member of a bike gang), which is rather inappropriate, I think.* She strikes a laughter.

This points to an interesting tension, as Lisa at the same wants to avoid resembling anyone else all the while, she does not have to be unique or special, and she hates when people try to categorize her. In that sense, it becomes evident that Lisa is actively and constantly (re)producing her 'self', often in slightly different ways that may not be noticeable to others but that serve as important and meaningful denominators of her self-understanding, as someone undefinable, yet always recognizable to herself. To some extent it seems that the production of her self-expression, rather than the expression in itself, is the meaningful aspect to her, as this is her way of keeping in control of who she is. She often refers to 'who she is' and at the same time acknowledges that her 'self' is constantly in the making, and something that requires 'figuring out', without the expectation of ever succeeding in this endeavour. However, her outspoken motive 'of being different' implies that sometimes this 'different' is determined by what others are not, as we saw in relation to her conversations with, e.g., Maria. And in

---

[16] Here 'emo' refers to a subculture grounded in communities related to certain emo-bands that had their break-through around the year 2000, as a prolongation of the 90s grunge wave. Emo is usually associated with black clothes, hair and make-up, and is predominantly a teenage culture.

spite of her efforts, Lisa's motive of being different cannot be understood apart from dominant standards of youth life, and the effects of standardizing practices:

> Lisa: *There is so much to live up to. Also, for instance some of the things that we have an active stance on here at Southside High, like grades etc. I mean, this is a pressure that one has to live up to at many other places, and we also have that going here (at Southside High). And even though we don't get many grades, we get still get some and we also receive written feedback, and either you get a good or a bad feedback, right.*
> Me: *So, what you're saying is that there is still a lot of comparisons … ? And perhaps there is something about being governed without being aware of it.*
> Lisa: *Very much so! The worst part is actually when being aware of being governed but still doing it (conducting one's everyday life accordingly).*
> Me: *Yeah, can you elaborate on that?*
> Lisa: *Sure! I mean, we're fucking controlled by beauty ideals, food ideals and all sorts of measurements, like BMI etc., telling you how to be or how to look.*

Despite the quest for establishing an alternative normativity, some aspects seem inescapable, such as general beauty standards or ideals. The atmosphere at Southside, resembling that of a free-space in many ways, and practising democracy in the daily conduct of school-life serve both as a temporary or 'as-good-as-it-gets' free space from societal pressure, while at the same time perhaps co-creating or facilitating the narrative, or the alternative or opposed norm. The awareness of societal pressure, of power structures, possibilities and lack thereof does not in itself dissolve the influence of standards or societal pressure; however it may support students' own and active stance in relation to such matters – or at least it seems to invite them to do so. And for Lisa, this resonates profoundly with her self-understanding and ways of conducting her everyday life.

The outspoken political awareness and engagement among students (and teachers) at Southside High mean that classes are often cancelled when there are big demonstrations, and the students spend their time in school preparing banners and flags for the demonstrations. The cancellations are not official from the school's side, but due to the fact that the students democratically decide to block the school facilities for political purposes. Such activities are largely supported by the teachers, and, by matter of principle, by the basic democracy that is valued at the school. Lisa is very preoccupied with social injustice and politics in general. She often participates in demonstrations and has been arrested once (for demonstrating against police violence). As the arrest was unjustified, she received a compensation from the police of 4000 DKK.[17] This money was put straight to her tattoo-savings. In her own words, she is rather paranoid towards police and any kind of control authorities, such as in

---

[17] 4000 Danish kroner is approximately €537, and a considerable amount for a sixteen-year-old. Here I am not commenting on whether or not it is a fair compensation for an unjustified arrest, but only that this amount of money would take a sixteen-year-old quite an effort to acquire through an after-school job for instance.

the airport. This means that she plans vacations that do not involve flying (for the sake of avoiding airport authorities) and last year she stayed away from a guided tour at the parliament (with her school), because the very sight of guards and police officers makes her want to scream, she says. This sort of behaviour – and the choices that come with it, such as deliberately avoiding places like airports – is rather common among Lisa's friends. It is also rather common to be open about your problems, such as mental illness, and Lisa and her friends at school openly discuss the medication they are, or have been, taking for example, depression or anxiety. It is as if things that are taboos in other places become 'the new normal' or an alternative normativity in the social setting that Southside High constitutes. In a way, this also implies that if one cannot boast a personal history of depression, anxiety or some sort of paranoia, just to exemplify, one might be deemed rather boring, or 'not normal'. An alternative normativity, or perhaps rather an active seeking out of the borders of what constitutes normality and pursuing a collective meaningfulness thereof, is thus emphasized in the school's political engagement, in Lisa's opposition to established law enforcement, and in the open manner in which Lisa and her friends discuss and compare psychopharmacological drugs. It shows us that there are considerable correlations in the way the high school, as an institutional setting, co-creates possibilities for the students (and invites for them to participate), and the way in which Lisa subjectively engages in the high school practice; the continuous co-construction of the school as an eco-niche with a certain invitational character is evident. In spite of Lisa's attempts to stand out and avoid categorization, she still very much fits in at Southside High. We could think of this as a balancing act of constantly negotiating and reflecting upon the meaning of things. She is in no way an outsider, neither socially, nor academically, and yet she is very much 'herself'.

Recapitulating Southside High

After having spent time with Lisa at Southside High, it is evident that the school places itself as an alternative to regular high schools. The alternative element mainly consists in the different way of organizing the school, embracing a basic democratic structure and creating more open spaces for actively negotiating and defining learning-forms and outcomes. As an example, the students are decorating their own classroom and in so doing are co-constructing their material conditions (as a joint project), which affects the atmosphere and the way of relating to each other in that particular social setting. They literally co-create (parts of) the materiality of their learning space together. Hence, they are creating a sort of participant-identity of 'who are we' in this particular activity setting of the classroom. It is a way of co-creating and co-developing participation, belongingness and meaningfulness in the teaching situation and in the school practice in general. This feeds into a strong sense of autonomy, ownership and empowerment that is equally facilitated by the basic democracy practised at the school. To exemplify, during my time at the school, a new headmaster was hired: a process that involved all students and took a long time, as space for negotiations and questions was deemed important. This sort of organization and student-involvement is practically inconceivable at other (public) schools. But the sense of ownership has other and more concrete material components as well. The decorating-the-classroom-activity supports a feeling of the school being a reflection of its current participants; that it is in fact an ongoing co-construction of priorities and learning spaces. For this to succeed, students need to be aware of their own responsibility to contribute to the outcome of their time spent at the school. Something that, according to the teachers, might take some time to realize, and identify with. This is also a learning process.

It is implicit in the school's way of practising high school that it tries to expand or transcend mainstream normativity, and in so doing it creates a space for critical perspectives on societal norms. This co-creates an overall behavioural setting (in Barker & Wright's terminology) that affords participation on many levels of 'doing high school', and it creates a free space for self-realization projects that do not comply with mainstream standards. This is reflected in – and to some extent co-constructed by – Lisa's self-understanding as being 'different'. In her own way, she constantly recreates this image of herself, in her way of behaving and relating to others. However, in doing so, she also challenges stereotypes by combining excessive beer drinking (on weekdays) with academic performance and engagement, singing in a church choir *and* being responsible with money. She is aware of the need to continuously perform in a certain way to be able to maintain her position as different, since most students at the school consider themselves different to some extent: this makes 'being different' the norm rather than the exception. In trying to transcend societal standards of normativity, an environment is created where new standards arise (from the dust of the old and rejected ones) and with them a local sense of normativity, which implies that trying to transcend or challenge societal standards becomes a standard in its own right. As a consequence of the continuous quest to stand out, dominant standards, e.g., academic performance, are integrated with an awareness of the inherent societal governing that is implied. To Lisa it almost becomes a predicament: she is at the same time aware of how she is meeting such standards (and thereby subjecting herself to a standardization process), all the while she tries to oppose their influence on her priorities and self-understanding.

All in all, there appears to be very close connections between the manner in which Southside High creates possibilities for participation and conditions for producing (and reproducing) an alternative normativity (as a standard), and the manner in which the students value and practise 'being different' in their activities. This resonates with and is continuously negotiated across various activity settings at the school. Southside High as an eco-niche may therefore be summarized by the importance of being different and the way in which contractions are openly embraced: by the outspoken collectivity, basic democracy and political awareness, the need to be free of categories and control, and the radical way in which norms are challenged and negotiated (and re-created in local ways).

Different Eco-niches, Similar Dedication

Looking at Southside High and Countryside High as two distinct econiches, we can easily point to their internal differences. Countryside High is surrounded by fields and other educational institutions, whereas Southside High is characterized by inner-city roughness (graffiti and containers) and historical buildings. The atmosphere in both places conveys an openness, albeit in rather different ways; the openness and invitation to contest and negotiate norms found at Southside high are rather inconceivable at Countryside High. Here there appears to be little awareness of a need to contest norms, and the openness in terms of atmosphere is more of an outspoken down-to-earth-ness and a sense of proximity and close community in the everyday life. The need to stand out and display independency that appears evident among Lisa and her classmates is contrasted by a directedness towards the community among Anna and Mia at Countryside High – which is interesting, as the strong sense of community is part of the DNA of Southside High with its basic democracy. Countryside High tries to create room for everyone and invite for a broad academic spread among students, albeit as we saw from the excerpt with the social science teacher, there may be ambiguities in the way in which the school actually values different academic profiles of the students. At Southside High, the emphasis seems not to be on the academic achievements, in spite of the school's reputation for being an elitist school. Here, the invitational character of the eco-niche and the collective idealities embedded in the school atmosphere relate primarily to pursuing and supporting a basic democracy as a fundamental value and practice, along with a profound societal engagement in social injustice and political matters. And yet, to Lisa, academic performance is a central part of her self-understanding. In that sense, despite the schools being different, there are a lot of shared aspects, although they are realized with variations and embedded in different collective meaning sets.

In spite of the distinct eco-niche profiles of the two school environments, we see how Anna and Lisa respectively display very similar dedications. They both have strong motives relating to future goals – that lie well beyond the scope of high school years – and they are very engaged in conducting their everyday lives in manners that facilitate their respective pursuits and realization of these motives. For Anna, it is the goal of becoming a kindergarten teacher that impacts on her choices for academic profile in school, as well as her priorities of how to spend her spare-time outside school hours. For Lisa, it is the longing for independency in her living situation, along with her (more short term) desire for financing tattoos, once she is old enough to have them done. These motives clearly impact her priorities, both in terms of social participation (e.g. saying no to trips (skiing, Prague)), her priorities for securing a steady income (by singing in the church choir), and her dedication to saving up money (by regularly collecting bottles, and saving up money from her grandmother, etc.). In like ways, Anna and Lisa are showing us how they are actively engaging in their everyday life conditions in ways that at the same time relate to the concrete demands they meet, all the while they are trying to furnish their surroundings in ways that fit their pre-existing motives, and therefore also preserve their self-understanding, that is constantly undergoing smaller alterations. They are bringing their subjective meaningfulness and orientation with them in their meetings with this new aspect of their respective eco-niches that the schools constitute, while at the same time they are not immune to the invitational character of the schools. Hence, to comprehend developmental dynamics as intertwined with a specific eco-niche implies the complementary of person and environment. We cannot ascribe the dynamics that unfold, in activities, priorities and self-understandings, solely to the person, nor to the environment, but rather we must recognize the totality of the situation in its social-material entanglement that at all times combines current and historical aspects of practice – and people – in inseparable ways. In their own ways, Anna and Lisa relate to the invitations and possibilities that the schools, and their local environments, offer, and they connect these to their ontogenetically developed sense of self and their current motive orientations. This implies an ongoing tension between 'what made sense in other or prior settings' and 'what makes sense in the new school setting', and the girls' overall sense of meaningfulness cannot be comprehended independently of the collective idealities that transcend their eco-niches, now enlarged by the high school setting. Through their participation in the various activity settings available at high school, they both contribute to and are co-shaped by the collective ideality – the objective meaning structures – that permeates the schools, and that to some extent constitutes the environment.

3

Becoming High School Students – Entering New Activity Settings

Case Study 2: Emily and Matilda

Whereas in the previous chapter I explored the eco-niches of Countryside High and Southside High and the everyday lives of Anna, Mia and Lisa, respectively, I will in this chapter explore just one high school, Westside High, and the everyday lives of Emily and Matilda, who attend the same class here.

Westside High is an inner-city school, located in the middle of Copenhagen's buzzing traffic, trendy bars and cafes. The main school building is an old majestic building in several floors. A smaller courtyard separates the main building from an adjacent ground floor building that houses music and drama facilities. The school has approximately 950 students and rejects a fair number of applicants each year as it is a very popular high school. Considering the number of students, the school is rather small in terms of physical conditions. Therefore, the classrooms and school facilities are distributed over a large area, and students have to walk up to 500 metres to some of the teaching facilities, as they are located in nearby office complexes. There is no room for school assembly at the school property, so this bi-monthly event takes place at a private sports facility close to the school. When including the distributed teaching facilities, the school presents itself as a well-equipped campus-like organ, resembling a small university. The facilities include a private cinema and brand-new teaching facilities for physics, chemistry and biology. However, some of the classrooms in the main school building are so small and narrow that there are hardly seats for all the students, and the front desk-row is so close to the teacher that it is difficult for the teacher to move around. Here students almost have to crawl over tables to leave the room, just as the teacher is at times sharing the same tablespace as the students in the front row. Other rooms are large, but serve as connecting points between other rooms, which cause quite a few disturbances, when students have to pass through in the middle of a teaching session. In general, there are very poor facilities in terms of communal areas for the students to work in, so most group work takes place within the same room. This has an advantage of the teacher being close to all the student groups at the same time; however, it also often raises the noise level, making it hard to concentrate in the room. In the basement of the school, you find the canteen and a student-driven area. This is where seniors (third-year students) prepare and sell a cheap meal once a week: a very popular happening that attracts so many students to the basement that they are stuck like sardines in a can; no one can move in or out. It also means that the food sells out very fast, so many come in vain. The same scenario plays out when there are ticket sales for the school parties.

As a physical and material location, the school does little to invite for socialization: the few communal spaces at school are usually so crowded that is it impossible to stay there. You go there for specific purposes, such as buying food or party tickets. Other than that the combination of the physical conditions and the central location of the school results in the students scattering during breaks and intermediate classes. The overall lack of communal spaces for the students implies that they distribute themselves over a larger geographical area during breaks; they go to smoke in the street (in the designates smoking area) or visit different cafes or food stalls in the neighbourhood, of which there are an abundance of options to choose from.

As students change both classroom and also class-constellations, depending on the subject, there is a large degree of movement and transitions during the school day. When one is not attending a class, there is a likelihood that one is already on the way to somewhere else, or at least standing up – as spaces to sit and hang out are limited. The campus-like structure of the high school resembles that of a university, which means that often students show up for classes and the leave the premises again right after class, leaving limited opportunity for socialization outside or between classes. These conditions afford individualism to a certain degree, as there are few spaces that invite for bigger assemblies, and everybody develops their own little routines or small groups that move around the area together. The distributed quality of the school as a concrete physical space – or overall behaviour setting in Barker and Wright's terms – conveys an invitational character of being on the move or constantly in transit. In addition to the concrete consequences in terms of how one's school is organized, this distributed quality may also, to some extent, have an impact on how the school as a practice unfolds and how the collective idealities of the school come to resonate with its students, who concurrently contribute to the reproduction of collective meaning and the overall school atmosphere.

In the following, I shall proceed with introducing Emily and Matilda, and through them I will explore the manner in which these key features of the school are integrated, reflected and actively produced, on a subjective level, in the daily life of the girls. This will allow for Westside High to unfold as a high school practice.

Emily and Matilda: Different Entrances to the Same Scene

Matilda and Emily come from different private elementary schools; Matilda attended a private school north of Copenhagen, and Emily a private school in the city, the same private elementary school at Southside High that Lisa also attended. Emily was attracted by the ambitious and strong political profile of Westside High, whereas Matilda was attracted by the school's well-renowned music line. By coincidence, they end up in the same class.

Matilda

Matilda lives with her parents and her younger brother and their dog in a big house north of Copenhagen; this is one of the most expensive housing areas in the larger Copenhagen area which implies that people who live here all pertain to a societal upper class, in terms of socioeconomic status. During the first semester of high school, Matilda and her family move to an expensive town house in the centre of Copenhagen, which means that Matilda can now bike to school, instead of taking the commuter train back and forth. She is happy about this, as it places her more centrally in Copenhagen with an easier commute and an easy access to the social life outside school. For Matilda, Westside High was the only school on her mind, though there were many schools closer to where she lived, that also had good music lines. In fact, some of the more proximal schools, where it would have been easier for her to be accepted due to geographical location, are even more renowned for their music lines than is Westside High. So, something more than just the music line must have appealed to Matilda, even though she cannot put it to words. Determined to be accepted at Westside High, she made a habit of telephoning the school every week for an extensive period of time, to push for admittance. This activity was encouraged by her parents; *'if you want something you go after it'* (Matilda's mother explains to me, when we first meet). Matilda's mother is an architect, and her father has a high-ranking job in film production; neither of them would have got to where they are today if they had just sat around and waited (in the words of Matilda's mother). This attitude seems to be a great influence on Matilda, who considers a strong personal motivation and determination key elements in getting somewhere in life.

At school, Matilda is very dedicated to her schoolwork. She often sits on the front row, and she tries to always show up prepared. She is not top of her class, but it matters to her to appear somewhat on top of her game. However, she often feels clumsy and at times says things in class that do not come out too clever. This has caught her a bit by surprise as it seems to be a new thing for her:

> At lunch, the girls start talking about the first day at school. As a way of learning the names of everyone, you had to pick something you liked that would begin with the same letter as your name, to create associations. Matilda made the mistake of picking a word that did in fact not begin with the letter M, but only sounded like it, to the great amusement of all of her classmates.[1] *'From the day on, I was the stupid blonde. I've never tried that before'*, Matilda says with a laugh.
>
> (At a different occasion, Emily shares with me that she considers Matilda 'the bimbo' of the class – however in a good way. She explains how Matilda can utter some true Britney (Spears) worthy comments, but in a cute way.)

---

[1] All the names in this book have been altered to protect the privacy of the participants; therefore, the example with the letter M does not necessarily provide the right impression, but to exemplify, it correlates with picking 'Psychology', when my name is Sofie, as to indicate that both would start with an S.

Besides her dedication to schoolwork, Matilda likes keeping up with trends on clothing, make-up and other accessories. Even though she comes from a well-off family, Matilda has to get used to attending school in the capital, and what this entails of new possibilities and new needs that suddenly arise.

> *'How can you afford eating take-away for lunch?'* I want to know, as we – again – buy our lunch at a nearby take-out place. *'We can't'*, Matilda says, and she explains how this has been a major change for her, as there was nowhere to buy anything in the proximity of her old school, whereas now there are temptations all around, and right outside school. *'I'm almost so desperate for money that I consider going trick or treating'*, one of the other girls says (as it is almost Halloween).

And yet somehow, despite not having a lot of money, the girls still frequently buy a lot of their lunches at the (overpriced) neighbourhood vendors.

Emily

Emily's background is different than Matilda's. She lives with her mother and one of her younger brothers, whereas she has another brother who lives with her father. Her parents are divorced, and have been back together, but it did not work out. Throughout the school year Emily moves a few times; in the beginning she, her mother and brother move in with her mother's boyfriend, and later they move to a place of their own as the relationship between the mother and her boyfriend ends. The home situation seems to offer little stability in terms of living arrangements, and contributes to a growing feeling of restlessness for Emily. In the beginning of the school year, she often complains about having a hard time concentrating on school. She is used to being a committed student, so her lack of concentration is stressful for her. She contemplates dropping out after the first year because of all the stress caused by the turbulence in her family life; the moving has had a burdening impact on her concentration and her commitment to her schoolwork. Dropping out is an option she keeps open to herself, like an acceptable plan B.

The home-situation often feels a bit chaotic and as if Emily is left a lot to herself. She often shows up late for class; especially during the time where she is house-sitting for her aunt in another city – this means that she has a longer train commute each way, and it is also a train connection that is infamous for its delays and frequent cancellations. However, the house sitting offers her a space of her own, at least for a few weeks.

Emily comes from an academic home: both of her parents have higher academic degrees and Emily's mother is on/off involved in both national and municipal politics. Emily as well is active in the same political environment as her mother, and it is something that she cares deeply for. The private school (Southside) that she attended before was also very political, which was one of the reasons it was hard to Emily to leave it. She appreciated the more relaxed and looser atmosphere at the private school compared to the atmosphere at Westside High where everything is new, and the rules are different – and ambition more directly goes hand in hand with competition.

Contrary to Matilda, applying to Westside High was a last-minute decision for Emily: she had visited one of her friends who attended the school and thought it could provide a good opportunity to get to know new people. When walking around the school area, Emily meets many persons she knows; her extended social network is mainly due to her involvement in student politics.

Both Emily and Matilda have chosen the music line, and therefore end up in the same class. Matilda preferably hangs out with some of the other girls in class, whereas Emily hangs out with a few of the boys and some of the other girls who also smoke. Both Emily and Matilda are happy about their class. Both of them point out how it is a well-integrated group of people and that there are no real group division among them. This is mostly due to the fact that they have been rather good at doing stuff together from the beginning, such as initiating after-school activities and hosting private parties.

As we can see, Emily and Matilda both come from private schools and from families where parents have long academic or formal artistic educational backgrounds. In different ways, an individualized lifeform is not unfamiliar to the girls: Matilda has been taught to actively pursue what she wants (e.g. telephoning the school and putting pressure on them), and Emily feels left to herself in a chaotic family life, where parents' relations change frequently, and where she is left with a lot of responsibility.

Now, let us explore the practice of Westside High a bit to further unfold how collective idealities and personal motives interweave in the various activity settings that constitute this eco-niche.

Westside High practices – Performance, Blogs and Bending the Rules

The students at Westside High mostly come from creative- or academic upper-class homes. This is, amongst other things, reflected in their appearance: most of the students are very well dressed (also flashing more expensive clothing brands and a particular style that resonates current fashion trends) and one gets the immediate impression that they come from rather well-resourced families (in terms of economy). Matilda and Emily reflect this as well, albeit in different ways. Matilda is very into fashion and keeps up with fashion trends (as presented by dominant high-street brands for that age-group). And as nearly everyone else in her class, she mainly dresses in dark grey, black, burgundy and blue colours at the moment. After starting high school, she takes an after-school job at a high-street cosmetics store to earn money for herself, as her expenses have gone up. Emily prefers to do things her own way, which is reflected in her choice of clothes as well. She usually integrates a lot of vintage clothes in her wardrobe, prefers dresses over pants, and likes to wear high heeled boots or, on occasion, stilettos to school (even in wintertime). This always results in numerous people applauding her unique style. As Matilda, she takes on an after-school job to earn some pocket money, at a downtown movie theatre.

From what appears a general preoccupation with appearance, one is left with the impression that *self-awareness* (at least in terms of appearance) seems particularly important at Westside High. An example of this is displayed by Andy, who attends Emily and Matilda's class: Andy often comes to school wearing audacious clothing items, such as big furs or other artefacts that challenge gender stereotypes. He runs an online fashion blog, and many of his classmates are often asking him to be shown on the blog. There appears to be a certain hype about him, and, in particular, about the blog that has many readers, also beyond the scope of the school. Andy's appearance is also commented on by teachers. Most of the teachers are relatively young, and many keep up a breezy tone with the students, as this excerpt shows:

> Andy enters the classroom five minutes late. Paul, the teacher, announces: '*Rockstar!*' (which is clearly a comment both about being late and about Andy's appearance). Andy is wearing a huge vintage fur coat (clearly a woman's coat), and Paul comes to Andy's table and compliments him. He wants to know where Andy got it. Andy tells him (a downtown vintage store), and Paul says that it is so refreshing to wear something and not being afraid of what others are thinking about it. Paul himself is well-dressed and wears glittery metallic blue sneakers that are hard not to notice. The conversation is friendly on the verge of flirtatious.

The meaning – and value – of appearance is reflected in the playful approach as displayed by, e.g., Andy, and it is enforced by teachers in their way of encouragingly commenting on students' appearance. Here it is clearly okay – and perhaps even invited for – to stand out and to some extent perform individuality. We see the same tendency in Emily's choice of clothing that is often very glamorous and festive. The valuing of appearance does not only impact on the activity settings at school, but also resonate in the activity orientations among the girls, as we shall see next. It often happens that there are one or two hours between classes, due to absent teachers and cancellations, or simply as a consequence of planning. Mostly Emily and Matilda spend the time doing homework or hanging out at one of the many cafes in the area, and particularly Matilda likes going to a nearby mall with some of her friends from class. The following example illustrates a typical visit to the mall:

> Matilda and three of her classmates have two intermediary hours between classes. One of them suggest going to the nearby mall, which is a ten-minute walk away. The girls quickly agree on this and we make our way there.
>
> The mall is surprisingly quiet at this time of day, and few people are browsing the stores and restaurants. The girls make their way to some couches on the second floor; they settle in and take out their computers. Apparently, only one of them has completed her homework for the upcoming French class, so the others copy her assignment, and make jokes about the potential same mistakes being evident in all copies.
>
> After completing the French homework, they pack up their stuff and agree on browsing clothing stores. One of them gets the idea of going to a particular clothing store (of a popular clothing brand that they all wear) and pick out the 'ugliest clothes' they have and try them on. The others applaud the idea and they quickly find the store. There is no one but the salesperson in the store when we

enter. She welcomes them and tells them to ask for help if needed. They politely decline, as they are 'just browsing'. The girls disperse around the store at a high pace, and each pick out a bunch of different clothing items. From the speed of their actions, one gets the idea that they are not actually picking out clothes to buy; they laugh and loudly comment on the items as they pick them out. Carrying each their selection of clothing items, they all simultaneously make their way to the fitting rooms, of which there are only two. As a consequence, the girls squeeze into the fitting rooms two and two and put on the respective clothing items. Loud laughter and comments are heard from the fitting rooms. The salesperson comes over to tell them that only one person is allowed in the fitting room at a time. The girls accommodate her directions and two of them step out, wearing their choice of 'the ugliest clothes'. Soon the other two are ready as well, and they parade in front of the large mirrors outside the fitting rooms and take turns in posing for one another, to the great delight of the others, who laugh loudly. No one else is in the store and the girls seem to pay little attention to the fact that they are in a public space, loudly ridiculing the outfits. They start taking photos with their phones, and this makes the salesperson reappear; they are not allowed to take photos of the clothes like that, the salesperson says, clearly annoyed at their behavior. The girls smile at her, and then return to the fitting rooms – albeit one at a time – where they continue to pose and take photos and make fun of themselves and each other. They tell me that the photos are for Andy's fashion blog. Soon after the girls change into their own clothes, leaving most of the clothes in piles on the fitting room stools and floor. None of the girls buy anything. We leave the store, and head to one of the mall-restaurants that has an all-you-can-eat buffet for lunch.

With our plates full, in an otherwise almost empty restaurant, they girls start talking about a girl who used to date Alfred from their class. This Wednesday she wrote him a text saying that she had no feelings for him, but only wanted to see how he would react when she broke up with him. This explains his profound sadness, that has been a topic of conversation for the last few days. The girls contemplate what they would do to this girl, even though they do not know her. Circular kicks, online bullying, and throwing eggs at her are some of their suggestions. They consider her actions a display of very poor character and they obviously care for Alfred. They then discover that someone has opened a Facebook account in Asta's name (one of the girls) and that this fake profile is liking posts at some of her friends' profiles. Asta is upset and wants to know who would do such a thing and why. The girls discuss what to do to the responsible person as revenge.

Matilda and her friends are having a good time in the clothing store, and their activity is clearly motivated by the possibility of appearing on Andy's fashion blog – and perhaps also by the incentive of simply killing time in an amusing way. As it is in the middle of the day, not many people are present at the mall and they have it mostly to themselves. This largely supports the atmosphere of playfulness and performance they create with each other: the mall, and the clothing store in particular, becomes their playground on which they can perform for each other (in playful ways). In their way of behaving in the store, they transcend the normal standard for behaviour in a given situation (looking at clothes, trying them on). Instead of looking for clothes they want (or clothes to buy), they select 'ugly' clothes and make fun of the looks obtained when wearing the clothing items. In that way, the invitational character of this specific activity setting can only be understood in connection with what is going on at the high school setting, as the girls' activities are directly motivated by Andy's fashion blog. The possibility of appearing here makes it okay to transgress the norms that otherwise apply to clothing-store-behaviour, and in that sense, the girls collectively push the limits of acceptable behaviour and do not seem to care about the opinion of the salesperson. This is somewhat contrasted by the girls' reaction to how Alfred has been treated or the person behind Asta's fake Facebook profile: here the girls quickly form an opinion about what is right and wrong, and come up with what they deem appropriate responses to such behaviours. It is highly unlikely that the girls would ever carry out *any* of the proposed revenge-actions, but it illustrates how the girls co-construct norms of behaviour. Some things are unacceptable, whereas other – in this case their own actions at the store – are. Here it seems that a situational logic supersedes general moral principles.

The performing of 'self' in terms of appearance seems to be a valued aspect of practice: by meeting fashion trends, by displaying uniqueness and by disregarding rules of behaviour (in the clothing store), which suggest that individualism is valued higher than a strong sense of community. It seems that the values at play in the classroom environment are transferred to the mall, making the mall a space of opportunities that enables these performances of self that are valued in the high school setting. In that sense, we can see how motives from one activity setting (the classroom) influence and co-create another activity setting (the girls' behaviour at the store) at a different location.

Global Ambitions

Westside High has a reputation of being elitist: a reputation that the school both tries to avoid and at the same time actively enacts. The school refers to itself as a campus and underlines the many ways in which it cooperates with universities and scientists on higher levels. It has mandatory rhetoric courses and sends students to the national debating team with both financial and practical support. As we saw in Chapter 1, we mostly hear about the possibilities of participating in different kinds of talent programmes at their introduction event, as well as model versions of various political organs (e.g. a Model European Parliament[2]). The school also boasts its own local versions of the political negotiations. 'Globalization' is a keyword at the school and a strong signifier for the school in terms of outlining their profile for comparison with other schools. At a more practical level, it is also something that all classes relate to in different ways. The purpose of this is to increase the desire – and the likelihood – of the students to study abroad after high school; they are encouraged to '*consider*

---

[2] Model European Parliament and Model United Nations are live simulation-games, where representatives meet from different nations to debate topics of mutual interest and concern, as miniature versions of the European Parliament and the United Nations Assembly.

the whole world their playground'. This, of course, presents a huge and very inviting space of opportunities and of becoming in a limitless space. At the same time, it also comes with clear expectations for students, e.g., to '*develop their global mindset*', which requires a high level of engagement as well as *a desire* to perform. In that sense, the school seems to rather openly embrace a neoliberal dynamic of having *to want* to want it: a strong motivation on the students' side is expected and almost taken for granted (Walkerdine 2006; Walkerdine & Bansel 2010). On the surface, most of the students at the school appear very comfortable with this ambitious setting: they have good conditions for participation and usually come from homes with a rather large degree of academic stimulation and general support for their individual pursuits. The transition into this particular high school setting has often not been difficult, but rather a 'natural' continuation of a self-understanding and motivation that was already in place.

Democratic Rights and Awareness

At Westside High the students are entering activity settings that invite and encourage *engagement* and *responsibility*; this is reflected in both the way the teachers relate to students, and the way the students relate to the teachers and the teaching situation. Teachers rarely interfere when students are active on social media or surfing the internet during class, and the students do not seem to care much if the teacher sees – unlike what we saw at Southside High, where computers were often confiscated due to online gaming in class. Here, everyone knows *what is expected* of them and that they are responsible for their own learning process, and ultimately their learning outcome. An example from English class is illustrative of the teacher-students dynamics:

> The students are handed back their essays, and the teacher, Ann, has compiled a document with various problematic sentences that she has handpicked from the pool of essays. The sentences are anonymized and shared with the purpose of students learning from each other's mistakes. Some of the boys in the class start laughing and loudly ridicule some of the sentences. Ditte, a girl in the class, tells them to shut up and consider the fact that someone actually wrote those sentences and might get their feelings hurt by their ridiculing behavior. Ann emphasizes the purpose of presenting them with the sentences and that she does not mean to make anybody feel stupid. Ditte then turns to Ann and starts problematizing this way of teaching, and another girl, Amalie, demands that the teacher should ask for individual permission before sharing sentences with the class. The teacher declines this demand as this would mean too much work for her, but Amalie insists; however, she infers, obtaining permission once would suffice, as then at least there would have been a democratic approach to it. Ann agrees with her and again emphasizes her original intention: to facilitate learning.
>
> A discussion develops between Ditte and Andy, who was particularly loud before; they clearly represent opposite opinions. Andy argues for the right to laugh at things that are objectively amusing, and Ditte argues against ridiculing anything. Amalie interrupts: '*I know that most people in this class are used to doing well and*

only getting good grades, but still, not necessarily everybody feels like this and if you are not as skilled as the others then it is really uncool (to be ridiculed like this)'. Again, Ann apologizes for her misunderstood intentions and asks the students to email her, if they do not want her to use sentences from their essays in the future. Class ends and while the students pack up their belongings, Ann approaches Andy and Ditte and begs them not to have a fall-out over this. Her eyes are teary. She gives Andy a hug and again wants to ensure that they are not angry at her either.

The example illustrates the dynamic between teacher and students, and how the students are quick to point out things they find to be inconsiderate and offensive. They put consistent demands on the teacher and argue with reference to democratic processes as organizing principle. This leads to a *negotiation process* of how the teacher can organize her teaching sessions, and what requirements and rights the students have in relations to this. Here it becomes evident how students are facing institutional demands in the teaching situation as an activity setting (handing in papers, meeting academic standards of, e.g., English grammar), all the while they also put demands on the teacher (who cannot solely decide the practice of the classroom), and each other (of what is acceptable behaviour in relation to demonstrating humour, of how considerate to be in relation to one another). As becomes evident in the example, it is very much a standard of what is acceptable for the group as a whole that is being debated, and there seems to be a rather well-developed awareness of rights and democratic processes that one is expected to honour.

The teacher's reaction to the students' objections largely reflects a student-teacher relation that is fairly equal and where the teacher seems aware not to become unpopular with the students or to trespass the invisible lines of an implicit democratic practice. It also reflects students who, even though they are still in their first year, are very *self-aware* and manage to react on their insecurities in very confident ways. They emerge as concurrently resourceful and demanding.

Knowledge, learning and democracy are among the defining values of the school, and these values are, in very evident ways, integrated in how the students relate to the teaching situation; with self-awareness and a readiness to point out conditions that they do not approve of. This indicates that despite a high level of individualism at the school there is also a sense of community, which we can see in the way the students negotiate the appropriateness of laughing and ridiculing in the classroom. Such behaviours must be openly regulated, and positions argued for. Good arguments get you far. The example illuminates that democratic rights, and thereby also the directedness towards creating a space for everybody, are valued and well-integrated in the teaching situation as an activity setting. If we connect this to the impressions from the introduction event, we see a high degree of consistency in what the school values on an abstract level, and what is being valued and negotiated at a concrete practical level in the classroom. One could expect that the high level of consistency in values and concrete practice contributes to an environment that is easy to navigate for the students, as long as they identify with these values. However, despite the consistency and transparency (in terms of values and expectations), school life is not always easy.

Challenges in Meeting School Standards

As is clear from examining the eco-niche of Westside High (as an institutional setting), it demands a lot from its students. Or we could say that the invitational character of the school compels for certain values and possibilities for the students that they are expected to be rather clearly directed at. There is an outspoken expectation of an alignment between the school's project of co-creating a certain kind of youth and then the motives of the individual student. The possibilities offered at the high school require the students to be engaged at a high level and to *desire* to 'make the world their playground'. This implies that the school subjectifies the students as young people wanting this for themselves, and even though the possibilities offered by the school in many ways fit well with the activities and values of Matilda and Emily, it is not necessarily unproblematic to meet the school standards, however transparent and consistent they may be. Thus, tension may be generated between the subjectifications offered in the school setting and then the girls' self-understandings. I will examine this further in this last part of the eco-niche portrait.

For Emily the high ambitions and the academic standards at the school demand a lot from her, but at the same time fall well in line with her self-understanding as committed and academically ambitious. She is used to being very active in school matters as well as academically skilled, but during the first semester she finds it hard to keep up, mostly due to her situation at home. She is often late to class because she has to get her younger brother up and ready for school. This situation on the home front is not new, and it has been stressful for a long time with her parents divorcing, her mother and the kids (including Emily) moving in with her mother's new partner, her mother moving away from the new partner and her parents getting back together. In all of this, Emily has been in a position of not having a say but at the same time being allocated a considerable amount of responsibility in relation to make the everyday life of the family run smoothly. Getting her younger brother up and ready in the morning has been part of this set-up. Emily does not mind being seen as a responsible figure in the family – as an almost-adult – and at the same time, it is demanding for her, and it makes it difficult to procure the energy needed to be as engaged as she would like to in the school context. Despite her challenges in meeting the different demands in the various activity settings that her everyday life compose of (at school, at work, at home), Emily keeps her difficulties to herself and always keeps up a façade of being in control, and not having any problems. Consequently, she sometimes finds it hard to relate to some of her classmates' problems, as she has no mental energy left to spare. She is aware that her classmates think that she has been out partying since she shows up late to class, but she prefers this image rather than to share the factual conditions of her situation.

> In French class, Emily, Christopher, and I are sitting in the back of the classroom. Emily and Christopher are both lacking in concentration; Christopher is active on Facebook, Emily is looking over his shoulder, fooling about, and laughing. A lot of the other students are also on Facebook or engaged in online gaming, while the

teacher is going through their homework assignment and handing their dictation test from last week back to them. Emily receives a 02 (E), and quickly tucks away the piece of paper in her bag.

> The teacher, Svend, says: *In case you made multiple mistakes in the dictation test, then don't go home and weep about it for days, okay?!*
> Emily: *You've ruined my life!*, she says with chuckling. Her chuckle turns into uncontrollable laughter. She shakes her head and turns around on her chair, as if she does not quite know what to do with herself: *I'm just so done right now! This fourth period completely kills you – and then French class, it's just the worst,* she says, loud enough for people around her to hear.
> Jacob, another student, asks the teacher: *Say, Svend, can't we do something to get to know one another? I mean, one only knows half of the people in this class (as we come from different classes and only meet up in French class), and we'll be spending the next two years together, so … ?*
> Svend: *I thought you guys were well acquainted from parties and such?*
> Jacob: *Not really … I was just wondering if somehow, we could make it part of class?*
> Svend: *Well, sure, we can figure something out.*

> While they are talking, Emily is chatting to a friend via Facebook Messenger, looking through her calendar and texting. She did not yet take out the text that they are about to work with, and as they others start their assignments, she continues to text, and takes out some food from her bag and starts eating. Meanwhile, on the front row, Matilda is already working on the assignment with Asta and Clara.

In French class, Emily is at the same time challenged by her lack of energy at the end of the day and the fact that she receives a very poor grade on her dictation text; she barely passed, and clearly this is not something she is proud of. While there appears to be a shift for most other students from being engaged in something else than the content of French class (Facebook, online games) to constructively contributing to the structuring of the class and actively working on their assignments, Emily has a hard time participating actively in class. In that sense, she is not responding to the institutional demands of this activity setting; she is not engaging with the text required, nor is she responding to the affordance quality of the situation at large by doing what everyone else is doing. Rather her specific social situation makes other actions more relevant: she is primarily acting on what she needs in the moment rather than what the situation (of the setting) calls for. This brings us back to the point raised by Wright et al. (1951) that despite the coercive nature of the behaviour setting, in any situation anything *can* happen, as individual actions always, in part, depend on 'the psychological habitat' of the person.

Emily is a very private person and keeping the details of her family situation to herself is also a means of self-protection; she is afraid of being judged or seen differently by her classmates. As a consequence of her situation not changing, and the tension adding up, she starts contemplating the possibility of dropping out of high school after the first year. Having this as a plan B helps her get through days where the difficulties of meeting the different demands, e.g. at school, seem insurmountable. It provides a possibility for action that she can turn to if needed, albeit it at present is merely imagined. This as well is kept to herself.

The privacy does however not exclude Emily engaging in negotiations of the class culture. As we saw in an earlier example with the negotiations of how to secure democratic processes related to classroom culture and the sharing of examples, the meaning of grades is also up for negotiation. As Emily used to attend the last years of elementary school at the private school of Southside High, she is not used to getting grades for her school assignments, as this was not a common practice there. Emily thus relates to the high level of competitiveness at Westside High by refusing to reveal her grades to the others. She is used to being able to choose whether she wanted a grade or not from her old school, so she prefers to have this option. Also, keeping her grades to herself may serve the dual purpose of also protecting herself from the assessment of others, which may be related to grades, as we shall see in this next excerpt. Keeping your grades to yourself, however, is not a common practice at Westside High: on the contrary, grades are important positioning markers among the students. An example from their midway exams in their natural science class is illustrative:

Emily's class have an end-of-semester exam in science; it is an individual oral exam that will help the teacher assess the student's knowledge before giving a standpoint grade for the semester.

Emily comes out from the exam. Right away she is asked by other students how it went, and which grade she got. *'It went quite okay',* she answers and refuses to reveal her grade even though a few of her classmates ask for this directly. As she passes through the corridors, everyone she meets asks her what grade she got, and she makes a point of not giving this information. Walking down the hallway feels like an echo tunnel of the same question lingering. Like an obstacle course that one needs to pass in order to breathe freely. Emily gives the same reply to everyone as she makes her way down the hallway: *'It went well, and I am satisfied with the grade in relation to the effort I made'.* Some of her classmates accept this answer, while others look a bit puzzled. One of her classmates, Alice, asks her why she will not reveal her grade, and Emily explains how she is against putting numbers above her own evaluation, as a matter of principle. *'There ought to be room for me to evaluate whether or not I am satisfied with the teacher's evaluation and the grade in relation to the effort I made, instead of everything being pinned on a number',* she says. It can only produce competition and the pursuit of grades; she explains to Alice. Alice applauds this idea and loudly proclaims to their fellow students that she will not share her grade either, *even* if it's a good grade (she is still waiting to take her exam).

As this example shows, there is certain meaning or understanding attached to grades; namely that they are meant to be shared or made public, when they are good, as means of *self-promotion, performance* or *positioning*. Alice's remark 'that she will not share it, *even* if it is good' reflects this point. It also implies an inbuilt assumption that Emily received a poor grade; otherwise, she would have shared it. Her attempt at making a political point about what value to ascribe to grades in relation to one's own evaluation seems to be only partially recognized.

In relation to Emily's response, there are a few things to notice. Firstly, that we do not know her grade, and in that sense it is impossible to say whether or not she is mainly looking out for herself in a self-protective manner, in relation to being seen as academically skilled. Secondly, her way of relating to the practice (or standard) of sharing grades connects with her longtime engagement in politics, in the sense that she is very aware of how positioning and power come into play. She is used to questioning rules and taking a stand on things that matter to her, and she seems rather at ease in taking up this active refusal of the common practice of sharing grades, and actively negotiating how to relate to the evaluating of self and others by numbers. Her way of handling the situation and the social demands she encounters also allows for a positioning of herself in relation to the others – and perhaps a more powerful positioning (as it becomes political) than if she had just given out her grade (good or bad). What is important to notice is the ever-present awareness of performance and positioning among the students, and how even a refusal or challenging of the pressure to perform in itself may become a performance. Taking Emily's home situation into consideration, it becomes evident how she tries to meet demands at school all the while looking out for her interest in preserving her (self)image.

Just as Emily, Matilda is challenged by the pressure to perform or keep up appearances at school, albeit she relates to it in a different way. Whereas Emily has no problem standing out and turning personal challenges into political questions or agendas, Matilda is much more preoccupied with *not* standing out. She is not a loud person, nor is she the one initiating spontaneous action, such as the trying out of ugly clothes at the mall. She prefers to be part of a group and fit the norm, even though one could argue that the norm also enables performances like Emily's; that such displays of personal stances are invited for by the school culture. This suggests that even with relatively unequivocal and transparent demands and expectations in the school setting, these may translate to or enable different possibilities for action or self-understanding in the concrete activity setting. The following excerpt demonstrates how Matilda experiences herself in the classroom setting.

> Well into the second half of the school year, Matilda contacts me asking for psychological council. We usually do not talk on the phone, so clearly this regards a different matter than me taking part in her everyday life settings. She tells me that she needs psychotherapy and that this is a conclusion that her and her parents have reached together. She asks for my recommendation of a clinical practitioner. We agree to meet up to have a conversation on the matter before I recommend someone.
>
> When we meet up, Matilda tells me about her current problem. It concerns performing academically at school, and especially in front of the class. The general discomfort Matilda used to feel when presenting at elementary school has risen to a level of discomfort that causes *symptoms of anxiety* (shaking, stuttering, fast heartrate, unclear head, sweaty palms, dry mouth, and a general sense of arousal). To Matilda, the feeling of performance pressure is immense. In her experience,

her nervousness is pulling her down, and making her perform below her level. No one in class comments on her performance in a bad way; it is her own experience of meeting neither formal, nor her own standards. The anxiety symptoms she experiences keep her from raising her hand in class as often as she would like and keep her from participating more actively in class discussions. She is not used to experiencing herself like this and it *worries* her. It challenges her self-understanding as someone capable and on top of her (academic) game. She is well aware that her academic performance as well as her level of engagement in class is being assessed by the teachers, and ultimately reflected in her annual grades.[3] Her reflection about the situation is that she needs to talk to a psychologist and receive psychological help, as, clearly, the problem is that she suffers from anxiety. And this can be alleviated through therapy, or eventually, through medication. Matilda has discussed the matter with her parents, and they agree that seeking professional help is the right way to proceed. Matilda has not shared her concerns with any of her classmates; she does not want them to know, as to her, her experience reflects a personal flaw or a problem that can be fixed individually. And, in addition, it is unthinkable to her that any of her classmates might share her experience.

Like Emily, Matilda thus experiences the performance pressure at school as a personal challenge that must be overcome. For her, the performance pressure is translated into bodily symptoms of anxiety (the pressure becomes somatic and highly individualized). However, this does not make her (or her parents) question the conditions at school, or whether or not the demands that Matilda is facing are fair or meaningful. Nor does it prone them to contact the school, a teacher or the school counsellor. Rather, with the best intentions no doubt, Matilda and her parents agree that this problem is best handled *outside* the school context, which implies that Matilda is left to doubt herself and understand her bodily sensations as an individual (and potentially psychological) problem for which she needs professional help. For Matilda the problem conceptualization is clear, and it is inconceivable that others might have similar experiences in situations with high performance pressure. In our conversation that follows, Matilda is sceptical about my presumption that she is not the only one in class experiencing nervousness the way she does, because '*everyone else seems so on top of things*'.

What follows from these accounts of how Emily and Matilda meet, experience and try to deal with the demands and standards in the high school setting is that an inherent aspect of the ambitious culture at Westside High is a high-performance pressure that students experience and may respond to differently. Attending the same class, Matilda and Emily are faced with the same demands and take part in the same local culture in class, meaning that they are both participants in local ongoing negotiations of meaning,

---

[3] In the Danish schooling system, students receive both annual grades, based on the teachers' overall assessments, and grades from final exams. However, not all subjects have final exams, and therefore (in the absence of final exams in a given subject) the annual grade may count as double, also representing an exam grade. Therefore, it may be important for students to make good impressions and excel in class throughout the year, in order to end up good grade point averages.

just as they are both subjected to, as well as co-creators of, the collective ideality that at the same time is alluring and meaningful to them and contributing to their personal challenges. The different examples illustrate how their social situations differ, and how they position themselves differently in class. Albeit participating in the same activity settings, they seem to experience slightly different spaces of possibilities, which of course reflect their different ontogenetic histories and current existential positions (Hundeide 2005). I shall return to this issue of performance pressure in Chapter 4.

Recapitulating Westside High

Spending time at Westside High left me with a strong impression of how *self-aware* the students are. At Westside High, students are aware of the reputation of the school, how this reflects on them and what standards they are expected to meet. As we recall from Chapter 1, the school motto is 'You create Westside, Westside creates you. Together, we create the future!' Therefore, they relatively readily enter the activity settings of the school accepting the subjectifications they are offered and aligning their own motives with those of the school.

At Westside High, it is as if ordinary high school is not enough; as a student, you are expected to *ask for more, want more* and *aim higher*, in an atmosphere of profound academic enthusiasm. This affords certain activity settings of performance, on various levels, e.g., Andy and his fashion blog, the girls' photoshoot at the clothing store and students' demands on the teacher to ensure their democratic rights in English class. In the same vein, talent programmes are not presented as something exceptional to participate in, but rather as an integral part of attending the school. Talent programmes are referred to by students to as 'gifts' and 'unique opportunities'. The high correlation between the values and standards embedded in the school practice, and the orientations and motives of the students mean that the expected academic enthusiasm does not appear imposed or shallow, but rather as something enticing – something you want to be part of. And all the while the invitational character of the school is alluring to students and many seem to genuinely identify with the school's projected standard student, there is, as we saw with both Emily and Matilda, a flipside to the coin in the way that students experience their potential personal inability to meet the (high) standards of performance as individualized problems that can only be dealt with in decontextualized manners. Despite their different social situations, this was the case for both Matilda and Emily. To them, trying to handle the challenges they experience *at* the school setting is inconceivable, which suggests that the school may not offer relevant help in overcoming the problems that may arise along the way. In case they do offer help and support, it is at least not deemed relevant by neither Emily nor Matilda. There is an appearance to keep up, also in relation to the school. This presents as a contrast to the way in which the school clearly supports students' endeavours to attend, e.g., the national debating team. And so, the school practice actualizes both sides of the neoliberal coin: on the one side, individual pursuit and success are encouraged, supported and celebrated, along with the responsibility for your own learning process, while, on the other side, the endless individual self-realization options come with a high degree of performance pressure and a vast experience of (self)responsibilization – the responsibility for everything that does not succeed *also* and *only* falls upon the individual (see, e.g., Rose 1996, 1999; Harvey 2005).

At the same time, there is an interesting contradiction in the way in which the school simultaneously affords competition and democratic values. The overall ambition of Westside High (of embracing its elitist reputation) is reflected in its location, the new teaching facilities, the campus structure, the discourses and the student-teacher relations. The school discourse is on '*well-defined plans of progression*', '*global citizenship*' and '*international mindsets*' that need to be developed, and students are encouraged to aim higher and pursue ambitious (individual) goals. Simultaneously, we see how democracy becomes a value in the classroom setting, continuously negotiated and enacted in the classroom among students, and among students and teachers. Practice is thus in itself contradictory despite the efforts to create transparency, which implies that students are left to handle these, often very subtle, contradictions on their own.

Among the students at Westside High, metropolitan life in the creative upper class is reflected in the everyday appearances, conversation topics and activities, and their visions of their own future lifestyle: fashionistas in class, imagining their lives with 'weed and anti-depressants' (as one of them puts it), life in big downtown apartments and lunch at neighbouring cafes. Their visions are largely supported by the geographical location of the school amidst the vast opportunities of inner-city life, projecting endless possibilities as something to be taken for granted. The professional and ambitious profile of the school acquires its human perspective through teachers who are very engaged in their jobs and who take the students seriously. This implies that the level, and general feeling, of *engagement* is dominant at school and it is hard not to be attracted to what the school has to offer: the atmosphere is compelling and clearly telling you *who* and *how* you would want to be.

4

Eco-niche Variability: The Meaning of Where Youth Life Is Lived

This chapter discusses the implications of the variability presented in the two previous chapters with an emphasis on some of the aspects that seem to differ when looking across different eco-niches. The key point in the chapter is to discuss the meaning of *where* youth life is lived and the difference it makes. This aspect of youth life is often diminished or even black-boxed in dominant discourses of youth life; youth life is generally thought to be there same regardless of where it is lived. In Denmark it is rather common to read newspaper headlines stating '*Youths in high school experience pressure, loneliness, and are bad at talking about it*', '*High school students are not pressured by a performance-culture. Many students are lazy and lack motivation*', '*Let go of the grand narrative that us students are fainting from stress*', '*High school students are just as stressed as the top twenty percent of stressed adults*'.[1] Without directly addressing the content, these headlines present abstract, decontextualized accounts of problems that young people may – or may not – be facing. This does not mean that there is no truth to the claims or that the concerns, observations or surveys on which these headlines are based are not expressing relevant youth life issues. However, the analyses or views presented in the respective articles offer little connection between young people, their experiences and the concrete environments in which they take part.

The meaning of place indicates that young people are offered different conditions and different possibilities for action depending on the location of their school. This refers to both the concrete availabilities in the environment (at, and in proximity to, the school), of the concrete architectural layout of the school and to an overall historically developed local set of objective meaning sets. Also, it indicates that there are differences in the general conditions that the high school, as part of an eco-niche, offers in terms of conditions for young people's orientation, participation and self-understanding.

---

[1] Newspaper headlines in various printed media in Denmark, years 2017–20, translated by me (Andersen 2016; Richter 2017; Boier 2019; Dalgas 2020).

Eco-niche Variability

As I introduced in Chapter 2, the human eco-niche is not something one can just point out in the environment. Rather it emerges in the dynamic movements between agency, values and concrete possibilities for action, enacted by persons in their concrete environmental settings. In the previous chapters, I have explored and portrayed different ecological niches, focusing on this very interplay between high schools and the young people who attend them. These explorations have established an impression of a considerable variability; not only in the daily lives of young people, but also in the way the high school practice unfolds and possibilities for action (and in the bigger picture, *for life*) are co-constructed by the young people and the school.

As the previous chapters illustrated, high schools contain (and create) networks or systems of affordances that invite for rather different ways of being-a-high-school-student, reflecting different versions of youth life. This means that high schools are not uniform institutional settings for education, but rather specific and concrete institutional settings that each have their own ways of conditioning and enabling youth life, as well as subjectifying students. Consequently, to comprehend the developmental dynamics that unfold in the lives of young people, we need to consider them concretely, acknowledging and incorporating the meaning of their situated embeddedness in concrete time and concrete places. The significance and meaning of historical time and place in relation to developmental trajectories have already been pointed out by Elder (1974, 1998, 2001), and this chapter thus builds on insights previously voiced in his work. In continuation, I here intend to further emphasize the geographical location and the physical environment as aspects of importance in our comprehension of developmental dynamics.

As an educational institution high school reflects general societal practices, values and discourses (e.g. in carrying out political agendas or in the historically developed, societal meanings attached to high school as an institution). This is what makes high school a recognizable institutional setting across the country as well as over time. At the same time, the manner in which a particular high school *integrates* and *reflects* these societal values varies from school to school. Not necessarily on an immediate and general level, but as the particular high school practice unfolds, it becomes evident that high schools need to be understood in a *situated* and *local* manner. Therefore, the possibilities that the high schools create for its students, qua the conditions it offers, vary – and so does the manner in which the schools subjectify the students along with the space of opportunities that is made available. As we recall from Chapter 2, Wright et al. (1951) demonstrated how behaviour settings were not in themselves determining behaviour in the sense that they would prevent certain behaviour patterns from occurring. However, behaviour settings tend to bring about certain behaviours more than others. This implies that the variations, albeit perhaps only at the level of slight nuances, that occur between the different overall behaviour settings that the high schools constitute, in themselves constitute significant differences in the developmental spaces that young people are invited into. In any high school setting, anything *can* happen; however, the invitational character and the specific, historically developed collective ideality of the school are a considerable force to be reckoned with, in terms of individual development. High school information and welcome folders contain a lot of useful information about practical matters, as well as about what is common practice and social values. However, these are the closest thing to a user's manual, and they do not contain that which is hard to put into words; that which is there but not directly point-out-able. In that sense, young people are left to make sense of their new environment, its implicit taken-for-grantedness, and its (often contradictory) invitations to think oneself and the world on their own – or with one another.

This chapter is thus devoted to a more systematic exploration and discussion of the manner in which *variability* occurs and is created in the high school setting. To do so, I will briefly summarize some of the variations that stood forth when exploring the different eco-niches. Table 4.1 presents an overview:

Table 4.1 Eco-niche variations

Countryside High	Westside High	Southside High
• Proximity principle • Sense of community • Integration in local life • Close relationships • Openness • Ambiguous subjectification	• Global ambitions • Engaged enthusiasm • Self-awareness and performance • Distributedness • Individualized problems	• Basic democracy and political engagement • Community vs. being different • Transcending norms • Alternative normativity • Freedom from categories and control

Table 4.1 highlights some of the aspects that characterize the variations between three of the high schools. With its profound integration in the local community, Countryside High is characterized by proximity and a strong sense of community. This entails close relationships, transparency and a general openness, but also ambiguous subjectifications in practice. Westside High, on the contrary, is characterized by an explicit orientation towards a global scene and by a general availability of opportunities connected to life in a big city, a high degree of self-awareness and pressure to perform, and clear demands and expectations for ambitions and engaged enthusiasm, resulting in an individualized responsibility and the manifestation of individualized problems. Finally, Southside High encompasses a tension between a strong sense of community and mutual care, and then the need to be different or stand out. This resonates the need to be free of categories and control, contributing to an atmosphere of transcending norms, grounded in a high political awareness and engagement. Evidently, these differences are neither exclusive, nor universal, but they represent tendencies that manifest over time, as variations in the high school practice as an institutional setting. In the remains of the chapter, I shall discuss these variations in relation to the following themes: the meaning of place, performance and self-awareness, and finally societal conditions and contradictions in practice, with the intention of teasing out the difference that these variations constitute in relation to development.

The Meaning of Place

High school as a social institution is not an abstract entity; it is a collective of activity settings that are part of a concrete eco-niche, which implies that it *contains*, *produces* and *reproduces* its own collective idealities. On a supra-individual level, it affords a certain range of subjectivities and orientations from its participants: it enables and subjectifies subjectivity in specific ways that vary from high school to high school. At the same time, the (specific) high school becomes the concrete conditional frame for various activity settings that its participants orchestrate and set in motion, which brings about their agentive subjectivity and their values. Therefore, high school cannot be sufficiently comprehended as an abstract entity but must rather be understood as a *specific way of conducting high school*. In that sense, the meaning of place relates to more than locality and geography, and I will look at it in relation to two different and yet often correlating aspects: (1) how location matters in terms of creating availabilities, and enabling and constraining possibilities, and (2) how place relates to variations in objective meaning sets.

Variations in Conditions and Availabilities: A Matter of Location

From the explorations of the three high schools, and the young people who attend them, it is obvious that the geographical location of the school has concrete implications for the way high school life – and youth life connected with high school – unfolds. A considerable aspect of this variability relates to differences in environmental availabilities. Environmental availabilities can be broken further down into a matter of distance and directedness. I shall discuss them in this order.

As we recall from the previous chapters, there was a great variation in the location of the schools in relation to other activity settings in the everyday lives of the young people in the study: the activity settings (besides) high school in which the young people were engaged were dispersed geographically, which implies that distance is a factor to be considered. To some of the girls, Emily, Matilda and Lisa, most settings in their eco-niche were placed very close to each other, indicating that high school life was closely connected to other activities such as going to the mall or sitting in cafes – even during the school day. These were readily available activity settings, each with their invitational character, presenting ever-present possibilities for action. In their daily life, neither Emily, Matilda, nor Lisa, can move between their home- and school setting without passing these other activity settings, which makes them an integral part of the space of orientation that they move in and relate to (in terms of possibilities for actions). For Anna and Mia, at Countryside High, the opposite is the case: there is a considerable distance between home and high school, and areas where one can pursue activities such as shopping and going to restaurants (in the bigger city). These variations have an impact in the way the girls structure their daily life, and on the possibility for spontaneous activities to arise. Examples of this are when Anna chooses not to attend the school café, because it involves waiting at school for several hours for the café to start. And it is unthinkable to go home only to return to school later; the transportation time – even though it is not insurmountable in itself on an objective level – presents a barrier between home and school as two distinct activity settings that are separated by both (transportation)time and location. There may be other reasons for not attending the café (that I shall return to in Chapter 6), but the transportation-time-location divide constitutes a condition that, together with Anna's orientations and priorities, co-constructs a non-participation outcome. Another example is how Matilda and her friends spend an intermediate class going to the mall (an opportunity that only arises due to the close proximity of the mall), and when Mia has to spend the afternoon at Anna's place before work, because she does not have time to go home between school and work (reflecting the concrete meaning of greater distances between activity settings). Mia lives even further away from high school than Anna and she is therefore more dependent on structuring her daily life in ways that consider her schedule for the entire day, including if she has afterschool work. As we saw in the eco-niche portrait of Countryside High, the local busses are at best timed with the hours of the school, but also only run once an hour (and at some hours with even lower frequency), which implies that structuring and prioritizing one's day according to bus schedules is a necessity and a concrete condition. A condition related to living in the countryside and thus of geographical place and location. Hence, the distance-aspect of 'place' refers to the concrete implications of having (or not having) to move between places in order to pursue different activities; it often becomes a constraining condition for Anna and Mia (who rely on infrequent public transportation for moving around), and it becomes an enabling condition for Emily, Matilda and Lisa, who can move freely (on bike or foot, or by various and frequent means of public transport) to the nearby café/park bench/mall/restaurant, etc. However, which availabilities become more interesting or relevant is connected to the way in which they relate to the directedness of the young people.

If we recall from the initial descriptions of the high schools and their surroundings, Countryside High was surrounded by fields, a kindergarten and an elementary school, whereas both Westside High and Southside High were placed in central Copenhagen with myriads of cafes, shops, multi-ethnicity and diversity, and the neon signs of large corporations, various displays of wealth and consumerism alongside homeless people, etc. The different settings that exist in the area of the high schools (and the homes of the girls, for that matter) afford certain possibilities and present concrete availabilities for the girls. The settings invite the girls to make use of them; in Copenhagen the high schools are surrounded by big colourful signs and advertisements telling you what you cannot or should not want to live without, by delicious-looking food in one window and beautiful clothes in another; a myriad of opportunities to make use of. If you attend Countryside High, you have to travel to the bigger city to find the same opportunities. This takes time – and money for the train or bus ticket. The smaller town in which the school is located does have stores, but these are more targeted at household needs (grocery stores, bakery, hardware store, flower vendor), and/or a more adult target group (yarn store, jewellery store, watchmaker, etc.). When you leave the high school building (of Countryside High), you will hear children laughing, playing, screaming or needing help to ride their bike. And close to your home, you find the local sports hall where you practise Zumba with your mother (as there only is one class to choose from, running once a week).

I would argue that there is a connection between what is available to me in my local environment, and the directedness I develop towards the world. This indicates that intentionality is an ecological concept in that it contains a simultaneity of an 'inner' and 'outer' directedness, or what Bertelsen (2003) refers to as *intentio* and *intentum* – a point I will unfold in Chapter 7. This implies that the availabilities of the environment become integrated in the directedness of the young people, as intentums; *what they are directed towards*. The developmental dynamics that unfold over time suggest that the availabilities of the environment feed into the dynamic of ever-evolving subjectivity. Subjectivity is not a constant, and despite a young person's, at times, strong stance, and sense of direction when they enter high school, they are not immovable or immune to the affordances of their concrete environment. A point I shall explore further in Chapters 6 and 7. It is the concrete activity settings, in which the young person takes part, that in the longer run subjectifies the person and enables new modes of existence, participation and self-understanding, as a concrete and embodied reciprocity between person and environment. Activity settings that are always also co-constructed by young people's participation and meaning making processes. However, there is a difference in the way one becomes subjectified by participating in a kindergarten practice, a church choir practice, a shopping practice, a café practice and so forth. Who these different activity settings or practices allow you to become comes with great variation and cannot be understood apart from the person's unique social situation (Hedegaard 2012). Young people are concurrently participating in several different settings and practices that influence their directedness and sense of self, not to mention their way of continuously ascribing – and negotiating – meaning to the world. This often results in complex patterns of processes of being and becoming, or as I shall argue later of 'subjectified subjectivity', and it is through these complex patterns and processes that the young people develop.

'Place' as Reflecting Objective Meaning Sets

As has been briefly outlined, *place* refers to more than geographical location and availability. It also refers to the locally developed objective meaning sets that have been created historically. When we gaze upon the different activity settings that stand forth in the daily life of the girls, there are some notable differences, just as there are of course similarities. If we look at Anna and Mia, their everyday life is to a large degree centred on 'home' and 'family' and activities in the local community (where everybody knows everybody). This correlates highly with the values found at Countryside High, and I will not call this a coincidence. In the same way, there is a correlation between the way in which Emily, Matilda and Lisa value individualism and the way in which this is embedded in big city life. These correlations are not just resulting from brief encounters between a given high school and particular persons. On the contrary, they reflect how a high school practice has developed in a specific way over time, as a result of the school's physical location in society, as well as the manner in which all the persons who have attended the school over time have reproduced, and thus refined, specific meaning sets. In the same way, the girls have been born into the world in a particular location in society, by parents with specific meaning sets who have co-constructed particular developmental conditions for them. Now, when the girls attend high school, and experience larger degrees of personal freedom (that comes with age), their ways of engaging with the activity settings in their environment will reflect the objective meaning sets through which they have developed their personal sense. This resonates with the historical and dialectical co-constructive processes between child and world, as addressed by Wartofsky (1983), and reminds us how some transitions, as, e.g., starting high school, may also to a large extent be experienced as continuations and something that one has prepared for, for a long time (see also Winther-Lindqvist 2019).

To sum up, the differences in how, for instance, proximity and globality are valued at different schools (and by the girls) reflect historically developed meaning sets that over time have become objective meaning ('this is natural to us'), and it thus reflects a collective ideality that characterizes a certain environmental setting – and constitutes an eco-niche. Collective idealities vary across different eco-niches, implying that some of the taken-for-grantedness in one place is not at all taken for granted at another, if even considered an option. This inevitably impacts which space of opportunities that presents itself to students, and how students engage in co-constructing this space in an ongoing manner. In that sense, such variations do not suddenly 'fall upon' or appear to young people when they enter high school but are more so continuations and perhaps even magnifications of already existing values in given eco-niches. The meaning of place thus points to both concrete availabilities in the environment, through which the young people can develop their subjectivity and sense of self, and that will shape their intentionality in terms of instating concrete possibilities to be directed towards. At the same time, 'place' refers to the particular objective meaning sets that have been developed historically, reflecting how value is (and has historically been) ascribed to practice in situated manners.

Performance and Self-awareness

The differences in availabilities, which I have just discussed, influence the range of opportunities for young people to define themselves. And it appears from the previous section that *place* matters in relation to establishing these differences. Now I will turn to the way these opportunities are subjectively handled by the young people and discuss the variations that occur.

If we start with Countryside High, and Anna and Mia, I have already established that the range of opportunities in their everyday lives is considerably narrower (in a practical sense; not in principle) than the ones found in Copenhagen. However, as Anna and Mia's directedness is adapted to this (not in a passive sense), it is not experienced as a limitation. The proximity in the close-knit community of their everyday lives indicates that one is much more easily recognized in a small-town environment; 'everybody knows everybody'. This may imply a certain level of social control, which means that one's behaviour is socially binding in a different way than within the anonymity and plurality of the big city. Social control is of course not limited to a rural setting but is connected to different values in the eco-niche. Obviously, there are both advantages and disadvantages brought on by the close-knit community feeling of the small town. One the one hand, the proximity in everyday life provides for a sense of security and close networks. There is large degree of connectivity with each other's lives, as people are (to a larger extent than in the city) exposed to each other. People make up each other's conditions in more concrete and direct ways. This affords mutual caring, which is exemplified, e.g., when Anna keeps an eye on how much Mia eats for lunch (which I will return to in the next chapter). And it affords a shared sense of responsibility which comes out in the way the students at Countryside High wear slippers indoor at times (this also implies that it is very unlikely that Anna and Mia would perform the same scenario at the clothing store as Matilda and her friends in Copenhagen). On the other hand, it is exactly the same mechanism that provides for the element of social control that the young people exert on each other; here it is more about fitting in than standing out. This means that there are fewer sub-cultures to choose from and participate in, and less variability in the local environment. It indicates that the young people in the rural areas are less free to define themselves, compared to young people in big cities. And then again, the security brought on by the close-knit community enables a larger degree of exploration and playfulness with each other, as joint activities (e.g. when the girls discuss things that matter to them openly, or when Anna is not afraid to reveal that she reads Billedbladet (a Danish tabloid) or does not care what she wears). This provides the girls with a degree of freedom 'to be' that may be hard to find in the bigger cities.

When we look at the eco-niches that unfold around the high schools in the city, it is not so much their specific location within the city that counts, but rather the fact that they are located within a metropolis. The city creates an abundance and a plurality of opportunities for action that enables young people to define themselves in rather free and playful ways. The anonymity of the city supports a relatively careless attitude that, along with a consumption culture, affords for the individual to perform her- or himself more deliberately. And not only does big city life afford this; I would go so far as to say that it also adds a certain pressure to the individual to comply with these invitations.

The Need to Stand Out

At both Southside High and Westside High, performance culture is outspoken, albeit connected to different standards. At Westside High, standards are primarily related to academic ambitions and performance, as well as appearances. It is reflected in the fixation on grades, the expectations to engage with extracurricular activities (such as National Debating team; political youth parties, etc.), and the way in which Andy's fashion blog affords for Matilda and her friends to do a spontaneous photoshoot in the clothing store. At Southside High, standards relate to being different, to academic performance and to being critical (to rules, normativity, the law and other societal structures). This implies that in both places academic achievement is valued, just as appearance is an important identity marker, albeit in very different ways (fashion blogs and designer clothes at Westside High vs. 'Do-It-Yourself' piercings, dreadlocks and so forth at Southside High). To Lisa, standing out from the crowd is so important that she actively pursues this in many of her activities, just as she makes an effort of not fitting into any categories (by combining often contradictory practices and activities in seemingly unproblematic ways). However, it is not so much the similarities between the two eco-niches that are interesting, but rather a significant difference that appears in terms of standing out, in relation to *performing normativity*. If we consider Emily and Matilda, they both go out of their way to keep up appearances and not let anyone see the difficulties that they each are struggling with. I shall address this shortly. By contrast, for Lisa, the less 'normal' you are, the better. This implies that all matters that, in a mainstream normative context, would be considered potentially stigmatizing become very important parts of a narrative to Lisa (and her friends for that matter). The need to stand out is thus practised through the open conversations about psychiatric disorders (what diagnosis Lisa and her friends have, or have had), engaging in excessive drinking on a daily basis (and being open about it) and loud sex (even when you know your parents can hear). *Standing out* has value in itself and depending on the eco-niche there are different standards in play in regard to 'standing out'; standing out is thus not just a random thing but relates directly to the values found in a given eco-niche.

The Downside of the Pressure

The pressure of performance – and standing out – has a downside. This downside is evident at Westside High where both Matilda and Emily struggle to meet performance demands. Albeit one could argue that their struggles relate to two very different issues, the similarities are still worth considering. In addition, it would be naïve to assume that young people will not experience any kind of struggle during their time in high school. What correlates between the struggles of Matilda and Emily are (1) that they both experience their problems as a problem of not meeting performance standards, and (2) that they handle their struggles as individualized problems.

At Westside High demands on students are explicit and high, and school standards afford for students to be on top of things, both academically and personally. The elitist reputation of the school translates to the students as being among the '*best and the brightest*', which has an obliging character. This subjectification of students is appealing to meet; however, it is equally difficult to handle when one fails to meet it, for various reasons. To Emily, the problems arise in the intersection of her home conditions and the demands she faces at school, where she experiences not being able to meet academic standards – this presents a challenge to her self-understanding as someone being capable and skilled. To Matilda, the problem consists of the anxiety symptoms she experiences in class, as a result of being afraid of not meeting the standards for performance. The girls' problems are thus on two different levels (an experience of not meeting performance standards, and a fear of not meeting performance standards), yet they both relate to performance standards that appear unquestionable. And in their silent and individualized ways of dealing with these challenges, Emily and Matilda actually reproduce, and thus enforce, the very same performance standards that they are challenged by.

We recall from the introduction events that at Westside high, unlike at the other schools, there was no talk of study counsellors or the possibility of facing struggles (of any kind) during your time at school. On the contrary, there was an explicit request for potential students to carefully consider if they would fit in. In other words, a clear emphasis on what was expected, leaving little or no room for personal struggle or the experience of difficulties. And though both girls do share their concerns with others (Emily with a friend outside school, and Matilda with her parents), their way of considering these experienced challenges as something relating solely to themselves co-creates a predicament where the girls eventually restrict their range of perceived possibilities for actions (by avoiding certain situations), or they limit themselves from participation, all the while the performance culture, and the high standards, at the school is kept intact. This means that the subjectification of the students from the school's side is not challenged, and is not actively negotiated, but rather adapted to or taken over. This implies that if one does not manage to develop in accordance with what the school affords, it will be experienced as a personal problem (that one will need professional help to handle, outside the realm of the school, or will handle by simply dropping out).

Obviously, the youth life afforded at the three high schools comes with great variations, also in the way the students experience and realize demands related to performance. These variations cannot be fully explained or comprehended by merely regarding high school as a (universal) institutional setting. Clearly, the schools offer different collective idealities to comply with (e.g. the differences in terms of performance), which points to the fact that variations do not rely on geographical aspects (such as urban/rural) alone. Though many activity settings may be similar across the schools, they are infused with different collective idealities and values that in turn impact the invitational character of said activity settings, the spaces of possibilities they offer as well as the explicit and implicit demands and expectations, *and* are continuously actively met, negotiated and (re)produced by current students. The performance culture, with its variability, is therefore not to be comprehended as enforced upon the students, but rather as dynamic and concrete relations between persons and their respective environments, leaving students room for interpretation and personal meaning making. However – and here I will return to one of Barker and Wright's most significant findings – (behaviour) settings are 'coercive' in the sense that they tend to bring about a certain behaviour (see Wright et al. 1951), and hence, the collective idealities of the schools may come across as rather persistent invitations to consider oneself in specific ways. In the case of the inner-city schools, it is hard not to notice a certain correlation between the school's explicit values and demands, the performance culture, the (motive) orientations of the girls and the personal challenges they are facing in the light of the pressure they experience to perform in certain ways.

Societal Conditions and Ambiguous Subjectification

In this last part of the chapter, I will explore how the high school practice is embedded in societal demands and unfold the variability that results from the different ways in which schools handle these demands. I will start by outlining what I find to be the societal demands that high school must adhere to, and then proceed to examine how the different ways of integrating demands produce ambiguous subjectification processes – that may contribute to a diversity of tensions that students may, or may not, perceive in their daily life, but that exist either way.

High School as a Normative and Formative Project

As a societal institution for education, high school is subjected to a political system that generates laws and legislation regarding education and educational goals. This means that high school, as an institutional setting, has to integrate political strategies, usually formulated as high school reforms. The political project of high school has historically been a formative project, providing an educational steppingstone (and connection) between elementary school and university. It was thought as a setting for general formative education. With the high school reform of 2005 (the reform that was operative when the research project was carried out), high schools were increasingly expected to prepare students to pursue academic careers at university. Among other things, this could be seen in the transition from a dual-lined high school structure (natural science vs. linguistic/humanistic lines) to a multiple-lined structure, with several parallel academic lines. This had the purpose of streamlining university admittance, to ease (and speed up) the high school-university transition. This implied that students had to make choices relating to their (expected) later studies at the university, whereas with the earlier high school structure this choice was (to a larger degree) left for *after* high school. As I see it, this brought university into the high school in new ways. With this new structure, and an increased focus on university life, high schools increasingly became a project of individualization (the normative project). The new normativity that arose with the high school reform reflects, in my opinion, a pursuit of having students 'making projects of themselves', based on neoliberal strategies (Rose 1999; Harvey 2005; Walkerdine 2006; Klitmøller & Sommer 2015). With this I refer to the neoliberal governing strategies that were first implemented politically by Reagan and Thatcher in the 1980s, and later were also integrated in a Danish context. The neoliberal project entails that the individual needs to be able to rely on her-/himself, which indicates the relevance of considering oneself a product that needs to increase its value. This emphasizes individual governmentality and an economical rationality as basic societal principles. Consequently, the directedness towards a larger community is challenged or put under pressure, as less value is ascribed to the community than to the individual alone (Bertelsen 1994; Rose 1999; Minken 2002). This implies that the individual can rely only on her-/himself ('I am only responsible for myself'), which in turn means that whatever problems I may experience are my own fault (or my own problem to deal with) (Furlong & Cartmel 1997; Willig & Østergaard 2005; Harvey 2007; Borup & Pedersen 2010, see also Dean 2010).

If we translate this to conditions for young people in a high school setting, it means that they are expected to be much more determined in relation to their pursuits of career, so that they can make a qualified choice of academic line already when they start high school (to waste as little time as possible after high school). In addition, what high school offers is, in itself, no longer enough; talent programmes have become an integral part of all high school offers, however in very different ways. Political demands on young people (such as fast progression from one educational system to the next) are integrated in various ways in the high schools, which may produce tensions and challenges in the manner in which the school subjectifies its students; this largely depends on the self-understanding and historical and social identity of a particular school.

Transparencies, Contradictions, and Ambiguous Institutional Spaces for Becoming

As I described in the portrait of Westside High, it is very clear to students what is expected from them. This is mainly due to the fact that the school is very straightforward about the demands that are placed on the students. However, it also relates to the manner in which the school has overcome the potential tensions between political agendas and its own way of practising high school: the school has fully integrated political agendas in the school's self-understanding. This results in a high school practice that is relatively transparent in terms of expectations and demands from the school's side. In this case, it implies that the school to a relatively large extent reflects the general political current (a neoliberal governing strategy) of pressure on the individual in terms of excelling and performing the self (as something to enhance). Students are openly invited into an atmosphere where this way of performing 'self' is seen as natural and is expected. The good thing about this is the high level of clarity for the students, because with their choice of this school they readily abide to this way of perceiving themselves. The clarity implies that there are no obvious tensions between societal or political demands and high school life as such; the elitist identity of the school is very clear and straightforward and talent programmes are a natural part of school life. In a sense, some of the contradictions have been eradicated.

The downside (because there is a downside!) is that students have embraced this societal form (and standard) to the extent where they can only perceive problems as 'their own'. This is, e.g., the case when Matilda's solution to the problem she experiences is to label it with a psychiatric diagnosis (anxiety) and seek out psychological help. In many ways, this can be seen as a display of agency from Matilda; that she acts on the problem she experiences, takes herself seriously and seeks out help. However, it is an agency enacted within, and with the aid of, a neoliberal strategy, which brought with it a strong emphasis on *psy-management* (referring to the need for different kinds of psy-professionals, such as psychologists, psychiatrists, to handle one's problems; again, on an individual level) (Rose 1999; Brinkmann 2010; Rose 2010; Svendsen 2010). Thus, problems that, in many ways, are created in relation to the pressure and the demands experienced by the individual (and the difficulty of meeting standards) become individualized and perceived as such, by students, by parents and by the school. In line with a neoliberal strategy, the problem belongs to the individual and the individual needs to take responsibility, to manage and to make sense of the problems as well.

I would argue that the ambiguity in this case exists in the *transparency* of the school; by fully integrating a neoliberal strategy along with societal demands, the school presents *no* tensions to the young people. Instead, the tensions are passed on directly to the individual, as increased pressure to perform, and in the case where this is difficult it can only be ascribed to the individual her-/himself. And as the young people in this project belong to a generation who have been brought up with these neoliberal strategies, it is even more difficult for them to conceive of their problems as more complex and perhaps linked to concrete conditions in their institutional settings. If we include Lisa from Southside High, we can see how she represents similar movements;

she has embraced the notion of ultimate individual freedom and experiences a strong need to be different and unique at all costs (which corresponds with the values of her school of being 'alternative').

At other schools, as we saw at Countryside High and at Southside High, the ambiguities exist in the *contradictions*. At Countryside High the general openness and transparency that characterize the atmosphere are contradicted by the way in which teachers consider students with a humanistic profile (specifically the Social Science, English, Psychology profile) academically weaker, and, presumably, act accordingly, perhaps contributing to this expected outcome. The invitations to think and choose freely are not transparent or substantiated when, in practice, other logics reign. And specifically, this becomes problematic when such logics, or idealities, are characterized by 'nothingness'; they are nowhere specific to be perceived, and yet they are present and have an influence on the social interplays at school. Ultimately, this means that students are left to make sense of such contradictions on their own, and perhaps even blindfolded, metaphorically speaking, as that which they may perceive as tensions can be hard to validate or even to verbalize – it is there but not there at the same time.

At Southside High, contradictions are evident in the way in which the students, in their quest for transgressing norms, to some extent reproduce them uncritically. As Lisa, who has integrated formal grades as means of self-evaluation and self-governing, all the while she in terms of values, largely rejects their meaning, as does the school. The outspoken quest for uniqueness and standing out in practice implies that part of what one chooses to do is largely defined by others, as one is inclined to choose that which others do not, even though it may not in itself be meaningful or consistent. As for instance when Lisa refuses to keep track of social events in the class community on Facebook, albeit she has an intention of participating and has an active Facebook account (that she only checks for important things). Such contradictions are not necessarily constituted by intersections of societal demands and individual interests, but they are largely driven by societal standards and the way in which these are integrated in more or less explicit and reflected manners. No doubt that Lisa would argue against being governed by neoliberal strategies that she on a political level opposes, and yet, in practice, we see how self-governing strategies and -technologies form an integral part of her lifeworld. At the same time, the school practice in itself contains some interesting contradictions that afford student's self-awareness as 'students' in confusing manners: on the one hand it abides by a basic democracy, empowering everyone with equal votes and thus subjectifies students as 'adults' in effect (as they have the same rights to exert their influence on the wholeness), and on the other hand we see how teachers to various extents employ rather undemocratic strategies in order to ensure students' learning (e.g. by yelling at them or confiscating their computers), positioning them as someone incapable of looking out for their own (learning) interests. Here one could argue that societal demands for the schools to succeed in producing skilled students also play a part in how school is enacted, perhaps coinciding with overall values of democratically establishing the values and doings of practice together. In that sense, there is no 'setting aside' of societal demands.

A Multitude of Ambiguities

In this part, I have given a few examples of the ambiguity connected with societal demands in high school. There are many more, e.g., relating to the implementation of health profiles, which I will explore in the next chapter. The examples emphasize that the manner in which high school implements societal demands creates different kinds of challenges for the young people. In the examples I have included, I have specifically focused on the individualization tendencies that correlate with a neoliberal governing strategy. The neoliberal tendencies appear to be more ambiguous in terms of implementation in the rural areas, compared to schools in the capital, and one could speculate that this has to do with a geographical aspect in the sense that implementation of new (political) initiatives usually begins in the bigger metropolis (see also Klitmøller & Sommer 2015).

At Countryside High, where societal demands are implemented in what appears to be a less considered and direct way, the challenges it creates for the students relate first and foremost to various contradictions (between clear messages and practice, and, as we shall see in the next chapter, between individualized health focus and community). This implies that the ways in which the students are subjectified from the school's side are *unclear*. These contradictions, and the accompanying uncertainty, are largely avoided at Westside High, where expectations are clear. However, this implies that failure to meet expectations translates to an individual problem with little possibility of generalizing, contextualizing or 'communalizing'.

What is worth paying attention to is how the manner of performing 'high school' (from an institutional perspective), and the way in which individualized tendencies are implemented in the high school practice, creates different kinds of potential tensions or challenges for the young people to navigate in. This is the case regardless of the extent to which the school has fully integrated political agendas or not; however, the character of the tensions, pressure or challenges for the young people varies according to this integration, and to the school's manner of valuing and ascribing meaning to it. And if we consider this in relation to the increasing numbers of young people, who experience mental health problems, such as depression, anxiety and stress, then one must speculate and question, whether the (often-individualized) manners in which such problems are dealt with (with medicine or individual therapy) actually correlate with the nature of the problems, as these did not come about in placeless, societal or historical vacuums.

The Meaning of *Where* Youth Life Is Lived

Part of the motivation for this book connects with a desire to challenge the preconception of 'youth' and 'high school life' as universal entities that are 'the same' regardless of where we encounter them. In the book so far, I have explored concrete lives of young people, in particular high school settings; based on ecological notions of high school as part of (and constituting) different eco-niches, and always connected to the activities and directedness of the individuals who inhabit these niches and participate in the particular school practice. From the analysis of various ways of conducting high school life, it becomes clear that young people actively relate to the standards they encounter at high school – be they standards of academic performance, of the use of Facebook or the meaning of grades, just to mention some. This implies that young people are relating to – or perhaps trying to resist – standards as idealities; as something that is concurrently present and not present, in terms of the inability to point them out. Lisa, for instance, spends a lot of energy opposing the standards of 'social-organization-through-Facebook'; however, when she claims that Facebook is a stress factor, what she does not realize is how also opposing Facebook as a standard is perhaps an even bigger stress factor.

What is striking in terms of youth development is how young people, regardless of where in the country they are located, experience and consider their high school conditions as 'natural'. At the same time, we can see from the outside, how high school conditions are in no way 'natural', but instead, and on the contrary, are highly local, cultural, historical and to some extent geographical.

I propose that these variations are best understood as different eco-niches, which allows us to understand the collective creative processes that lie behind the concrete and local ways of practising high school – and behind the way in which meaning differs across the different high schools. What I have tried to demonstrate so far is how differences in these collective idealities are co-created and maintained, produced and reproduced, while understood as 'natural' (they are (most often) not questioned by the students). The differences cannot be explained merely as the high school's way of practising high school, nor as reflecting the actions of individuals (the young people), but rather they (the differences) must be comprehended in their dialectical and historical context, where both high schools and young people have co-created (and concurrently co-create) themselves and each other – thereby reflecting locally anchored and mutual processes of becoming. This in turn supports the inseparability of person and environment as proposed by Vygotsky (1994; Leontjev 2005) as well as ecological thinkers, such as Barker and Wright and Gibson, and expands it in the sense of nuancing the individual contribution that in Barker and Wright's writings remained relatively unexplored as the 'psychological habitat of the person'. By looking at how young people in various high school settings are engaged in concrete activity settings, pursuing personal motives and trying to make sense of the world and themselves, we are able to better comprehend variations in youth life, as something that is deeply embedded in their concrete environment, and thus not solely a matter of individual differences, albeit these are not excluded as influential.

When perceiving high schools as expressions and enactments of different eco-niches, we see how high school is practised differently, thus creating different possibilities for action and different developmental conditions for young people. This does not imply that differences in high school practices determine youth development, nor young people's self-understanding, albeit at the same time the influence of ways of practising high school needs to be recognized as part of the person-environment dynamic. In that way, high school practice presents a particular conditional setting for young people, containing challenges and tensions that largely reflect this particular high school's way of integrating or relating to societal demands (also as a historical becoming). This in turn puts a high demand on high schools in terms of reflecting upon the way in which they conduct and practise high school – and in which way they, for their part, create an ecological setting, containing activity settings with specific conditions for activities and self-realization options for young people. Eco-niches are, of course, constituted by more than just high school, and the way in which high school is co-constructed as a space for youth development therefore coincides with the other activity settings in which young people participate. In that way, high school is not unaffected by the availabilities in the local environment (close to the school) as these are the settings that young people will most likely step in and out of while participating in the high school practice. Therefore, what these environmental availabilities invite young people to become – or subjectify young people as – might also play a role in how young people participate in the high school setting, and what subjectivities or self-understandings they develop.

To sum up the relevance of the eco-niche as an analytical concept in relation to studying dynamics of youth development, it is evident that the eco-niche can account for some of the variability present in environmental conditions for youth life across different geographical locations. I would suggest for this to be a relevant aspect to consider (in relation to understanding developmental processes in youth) as it entails a profound comprehension of the complex, interacting, reciprocal aspects of the everyday lives of young people, and as such offer an alternative or a supplement to often-applied analytical factors such as socio-economic status, drop-out rates, grade point averages, etc. The eco-niche portraits illustrate how young people are invited to 'become' in specific and yet dissimilar ways, and how they are subjectified as high school students, and as many other positions, roles or qualities, depending on the availabilities of their respective eco-niches (e.g. as responsible gymnastics trainer, as baby sitter, as junior politician, as someone on top of fashion, as someone different, as someone who can do what she wants, as a beer-drinker, a choir-singer). As such, I propose that the eco-niche, as a concept, may be a productive unit of analysis for comprehending the meaning of *where* youth life is lived. As analytical unit, the eco-niche connects historically developed collective idealities with people's concrete engagements in practice, their activities and understanding of themselves and their environment. This may assist us in our pursuit of comprehending developmental dynamics by operationalizing and foregrounding the environment, as part of the person-environment dialectics. Exploring young people's life-worlds as part of eco-niche portraits enables the concurrent analysis of individual motive orientation, meaning and participation as inseparable from the concrete activity settings, collective idealities and spaces of possibilities in relation to which these occur and are shaped. It offers a way to broaden the analytical lens and to comprehend material, institutional and societal aspects as intertwined with individual orientations, participation and meaning making. In so doing, we are able to grasp variability on the level of the environment and how this contributes to the variability found on the level of the individual. Not in determinant sense, but as qualities of the environment that contribute to the invitational character that young people inevitably relate to. And, as we have seen so far, co-constitute various kinds of ambiguities that young people are left to handle or make sense of.

5

Standardizing the Body? – Negotiating the Meaning of Health

Understanding the complexities of developmental dynamics requires an integration of multiple interacting aspects of everyday life; some pertain to individual biology, some to the interactions with family and social others, and others to the invitational character of the environment and the space of opportunities that it provides. In addition, societal norms and values play a part – more or less overtly – just as political agendas shape the institutional settings in which our everyday lives unfold. In a more sociological perspective, our analytical gaze would enhance such broader societal and political aspects, and these aspects tend to either play the dominant part in the analysis or hardly any. This contributes to the misconception that we can easily isolate such factors and analyse them separately from the social, interpersonal dynamics that unfold in everyday life settings, where people try to make sense of their lifeworld and (co)-construct a meaningful life by attempting to realize various life projects, such as finishing high school. Hence, to understand how political agendas or societal standards play a part in the lives of young people in a high school setting, we need to look into how said standards are introduced, attributed with meaning, integrated, challenged and altered by young people; not (necessarily) deliberately, but as part of manoeuvring a specific life situation that contains multiple invitations, demands and opportunities that all need to be dealt with by the individual, who is also – all the time – pursuing already established motives (that are concurrently being altered and adjusted) while trying to preserve a sense of self. When young people start high school, they are not, as I briefly hinted in the introduction, empty vessels that the school as a societal institution can sculpt at will, as earlier notions of youth seem to suggest. Rather we need to acknowledge that their subjectivity and self-understanding are already shaped by their (ontogenetic) participation in numerous institutional settings and interpersonal dynamics. They have encountered a multitude of subjectifications and demands that they have appropriated to various degrees, just as their current motive structure must be comprehended in its ontogenetic and historical entirety.

What I will therefore explore in this chapter is the intersection of a politically motivated standard relating to health promotion (materialized by a health profile), and the interpersonal dynamics that unfold among a group of girls related to their use of, and preoccupation with, health, bodies and the ambiguities that arise in this interplay. What evolves around this interplay relating to standards of health provides an interesting example of how the (social) meaning of introduced (politically motivated) standards is negotiated. The standard in question is represented by a health profile that students are required to complete twice a year during their time at high school. The implied expectation is that awareness of personal health will affect young people's behaviour in certain ways (towards an optimal health status). However, what we see over the course of the school year is how the content of the health profile is negotiated and acquires its own life, so to speak. This implies that the well-intended political incentives of drawing young people's attention to health issues by introducing mandatory health monitoring cannot be regarded as providing a predictable outcome or effect. Rather, it demonstrates how meaning is continuously negotiated socially, and various aspects of everyday life are interwoven in unpredictable manners. Therefore, we need to acknowledge the way in which young people actively make sense of the standards they encounter, including how they alter, or even pervert them. It exemplifies how politically motivated demands, as embedded in institutional practices, cannot be understood as directly influencing young people in a narrow and uniform sense (as determinism), but rather how these demands are met differently, depending on personal motives, and the social setting in which they are introduced; it thus becomes a contextualization of standards of health and bodily normativity. At the same time, it illustrates how young people's development is always situated and hence framed by the specific institutional context and the conditions that this context implies. In part, the chapter picks up where the last chapter left off, by exploring in detail how there may be contradictions between societal and political interests in relation to the education of young people, and then how such interests are met and integrated in the concrete everyday life practices of young people. To explore these dynamic interplays of standards and the social negotiation of meaning, we shall return to Countryside High, to Anna and Mia and their group of friends, as this is the only school in the study at which this specific health promoting technology, the health profile, is at play.

Monitoring Yourself – and Each Other

As we saw in Chapter 2, there is a relatively strong sense of group belonging and community at Countryside High, at least this is the impression one gets from taking part in Anna and Mia's everyday life at school. The girls and their close friends are very engaged in each other's lives, and this becomes particularly evident in the way they relate to food, calories and health. In addition, comments on everything from clothes, to class assignments, to yesterday's TV show regularly fly through the air leaving an impression of a rather relaxed and open culture of talking about everything. The awareness and preoccupation with healthy food arise during the first months of high school and coincide with – if not initiated by – a mandatory monitoring of health as part of gym class – a health profile. Here students are to complete a series of tests twice a year throughout their time at high school in order to monitor their health and physical development. The health focus in gym class is part of a bigger Danish online system that generates statistics, etc., for different schools, companies and so forth, in the hope of increasing general health and health awareness among students and employees. The initiative is a project funded and run by a private Danish foundation (Rockwoolfonden), aimed at increasing welfare and developing welfare solutions. Not all schools in Denmark take part, but many do, and the names of the schools are listed on the web page, allowing for school comparisons. The individual health profiles are generated on the basis on various tests (BMI, running tests, muscle strength test, etc.) that students complete along with an elaborate questionnaire. After completing the tests, the students log their results into the online database which then allows them to not only monitor their own results (as numbers and graphs), but also see the result for their entire class (as a unit) as well as the results from other classes and schools in the country, for comparison. When you open the web page, the title and motto read '*The Health Profile – You are what you measure*'.

One day, right after the health profiles are first introduced and the girls have done the first run of tests, they start comparing their results over lunch. Anna happily shares her results, even though they were not all particularly good. Mia, on the other hand, seems to try to avoid the conversation. The following scenario plays out:

The girls start talking about the health-profile that they filled out during gym-class the day before. Simultaneously they start commenting on the results from the test, as well as comparing their results with one another. The results came in shape of differently coloured curves and graphs that they could access individually, online.

'*I had a high curve on that parameter …*', one says, and another adds: '*mine was red* (indicating a not 'optimal' health condition), *ha ha …* (laughing)'. They also discuss the questions in the test and found some of them rather difficult to answer.

Anna: '*My results were way beyond the curve … !* (pause) *Did you fill out yours, Mia?*' Mia answers in an avoidant tone: '*No …* (she hesitates a bit), *but there were several things, I couldn't really answer, so …*'. She looks away and continues to fumble with something in her backpack.

I ask about the health test. Anna explains that it was introduced as a mandatory part of gym class yesterday and consisted of a so-called beep-test (a running-test), along with measures of height, weight, BMI, muscle strength etc. Then there were also a lot of questions to answer. It resulted in a profile on the computer. They have to complete it twice a year throughout high school, so that it is possible to follow their development in gym-class. One of the other girls adds that you will receive good marks in gym-class, if your profile results improve during your time at high school – because the teachers can monitor the development as well. Anna nods and confirms this information.

Everybody except Mia starts to eat their lunch. Anna is about to take a bite of her sandwich, but puts it down and, in a commanding tone, says to Mia: '*You have to remember to eat!*' while directingly pointing two fingers at her. '*Yeah, right, whatever …* ' Mia replies, obviously not wanting to make a conversation of it. Anna continues: '*You are losing too much weight! … You used to eat a whole lot more, when we were in elementary school and now you eat hardly anything!*' Mia does not object. She just shrugs and turns to me and says with a little smile: '*Anna is like a mother to all of us …* ' Anna shakes her head, looking annoyed, but says nothing.

Over the next few months an increased awareness about calories and 'healthy' versus 'unhealthy' food arises among the group of girls that Anna and Mia are part of. In the beginning, it appears to be more of a focus for Mia than Anna:

> After having finished our lunch, we make our way to the arts room on the basement floor. Anna and Sandra pass by the canteen on the way to pick up a granola bar each, and Mia loudly declares that she refuses to eat 'something like that': *'You will soon stink of banana'*, she says, referencing the banana-chocolate version of granola bars that the girls have bought. She takes Anna's granola bar and starts inspecting the calories content written on the package. Anna grabs it again: *'I really don't care ... I really feel like eating this kind of chocolaty bar'*, she says and starts eating it.

Here the emphasis is not directly on the (un)healthy aspect of the granola bar, but more so on the synthetic banana scent that comes with it. Soon, however, Anna is increasingly preoccupied with 'healthy foods' and she starts eating dietary products that she primarily gets from her mother (who wants to lose weight herself). Calorie content becomes a frequent topic of conversation among the girls at school, and even the taste experience of various food products is evaluated based on their health-factor. Evidently *health as a standard* is a new shared focus of attention for the girls that is co-constructed in the interaction between the girls (and their families) and a deliberate standard introduced by high school through health profiles and tests. However, it not only affects the girls' ways of evaluating their own bodies and the food they eat but also influences how they evaluate each other (in terms of actions, bodies and choices of food) and what becomes integrated high school practices among them as a group (e.g. comparing calories in food).

> In the main recess we place ourselves in the canteen. Most of the girls eat variations of pasta salad that they brought along from home. Mia is eating a small yoghurt. Sandra joins us. She enthusiastically starts telling us about a new guy in her class, David, that she finds super funny. Apparently, he was expelled from his second year at another high school due to too much absence. *'His arms are extremely freckled, but interestingly enough he has no freckles in his face,'* Sandra says smiling and the other girls listen attentively. Mia smiles along and seems preoccupied by Sandra's news. One of the other girls buds in: *'Oh, I know him. I used to go to elementary school with him – he is super annoying!'* Sandra does not pay attention to this remark and continues: *'Well, he wasn't thriving at the other school and apparently, he was bullied by a teacher there.'* This information is followed by a collective silence as to take in the added dramatic twist to the story. Anna takes out a small package of cookies from Weight Watchers (a dietary brand) and starts eating them, all the while the girls start commenting on their arts teacher for being particularly grumpy at the moment. Some give their best impersonations of her and the others laugh. *'How was the soda, you just had, Mia?,'* Sandra wants to know and Mia answers: *'Well, it tasted alright, but very healthy ... and not really like a proper soda, you know.'* *'Oh well, at least it was healthy,'* Sandra adds. *'Yeah, I just brought these, and*

they're so delicious even though they are healthy,' Anna proclaims while pointing towards her cookies. '*I really dig them!,*' she adds. '*The only sweets that are tasty, are Nupo-sweets*[1]*,*' Sandra says and Anna comments: '*Nupo-sweets ... !,*' as an act of affirmation. The conversation moves into the topic of the upcoming school dance related to gym class, and the discussion relates to whether to show up wearing a dress or casual sportswear. Apparently, the teachers have encouraged them to show up wearing dresses and high heels, but they have also made it clear that this attire is not mandatory. There are mixed opinions among the girls on the matter.

(the next day)

We proceed to math class, where they will have a different teacher than they are used to today, Rasmus. He will run a statistics course with them. Sandra, Caroline, and Anna are all playing Candy Crush on their computers. Rasmus asks everyone to shut down their computers and pay attention, however Anna only closes hers a little, so that she can continue to play. Five minutes later she also closes her computer, and instead takes out her phone and starts looking at it. She closes her eyes, as if sleeping briefly, then looks at me and smiles, and says: '*But it is so incredibly boring!*' She then fetches a small package from her bag; it is a cookie-like biscuit. She starts eating it. Then she eats another. It is the same Weight Watchers cookies that she has brought to school before; the chocolate cookies that she really likes. She shows me the wrapping and says: '*This is one hell of a healthy snack!*' This makes Mia laugh, and in response Anna says (to Mia): '*Hey, I mean, she* (with reference to me) *should know what we're eating, and this is healthy, so..!*' Anna and Mia both have a hard time concentrating on the inputs from the teacher, and they instead end up discussing whether or not various food items contain 10 grams (of fat) too much or not. The conversation turns in to amicable mutual teasing, and although they both laugh, their laughter is not loud enough to attract the teacher's attention.

In the next break, I ask Anna about the cookies:

Me: *So what's the deal with those Weight Watcher cookies you were eating in class?*
Anna: *Actually, I was gonna save them for Social Science class, but they tasted so good that I just had to eat both right away ... and then I found out that they were also healthy.* She puts up a big smile, genuinely happy about this new awareness.
Me: *So do you eat them because they taste good or because they're healthy?*
Anna: *Both. It's my mom who buys them, cause she's on some kind of diet ... and then she tells my brother and me how many we can have a day. And I don't eat any when I come home from school. Well, I have eaten them now, so ... and my brother, you know, he can eat like five packages easily, if no one tells him not to!* She rolls her eyes and laughs.

---

[1] Nupo is a weight loss brand offering mostly various powders for dietary shakes, but also various other food items, such as sweets.

The focus on health is not a main concern for the girls and it does not present as a uniform understanding or value. However, it sneaks into the conversation here and there and we see how they shift from discussing the new boy in class to evaluating a healthier choice of soda and praising weight-loss-intended sweets (the Nupo sweets). We can see how many of the girls seem to have their own health priorities, where some care more or less about the health factor (in relation to, e.g., taste). Anna's prioritizing of 'eating what she feels like' (the granola bar) has shifted into a more calorie-aware eating preference, albeit she still values the taste experience a lot. Food – and the health-food factor – becomes a recurring topic that is debated and evaluated together in the group of girls along with other aspects of high school life, such as social relations and what to think of the various demands they are facing. This implies that the meaning or value of, e.g., health is not set in stone, but is something moveable and negotiable among the girls. However, the negotiation is not merely among the girls in an isolated manner but must be understood in relation to, and entangled with, the demands from the school's side (e.g. in the shape of introducing an array of mandatory health measurements in gym class), the materiality or invitational character of the dietary products (e.g. the delicious-looking cookies that Anna gets from her mom), and of course a general cultural focus on health, and perhaps on weight and body image in particular. What is interesting though is to see how the girls' increased focus on health does not necessarily correlate with the intent of the health profiles, in the sense that the girls become preoccupied with dietary products, rather than an overall healthy lifestyle. None of them are overweight and in the target group for dietary products. This implies that the demands conveyed via the emphasis on health in the health profile are met and negotiated selectively by the girls. The perceived demand from the school on improving your results on the health profile in order to get good grades in gym contributes to this increasing shared preoccupation with food, however in the girls' own way and not as a clear dictation from the school or the health profile per se. If we are to follow Anna's rationale, one can eat more of the foods that taste good, as long as these are low-calorie products, which implies the dietary products that she is in no way the target group for. In that way, the attention of the girls is slightly pushed towards a dietary regime (e.g. by suddenly selecting Nupo-sweets over regular sweets), which includes a specific take on health that perhaps does not correlate with the health promotion intended in gym class.

Despite the increased focus on calories, the girls hold on to previously established food-related practices that do not fit well with their new dietary regime. Anna and Mia share a joint activity that involves going to a nearby big city and eating at Jensen's Bøfhus (a Danish steak-restaurant chain) for lunch. They go there often, so Mia knows the menu by heart (and prefers a big plate of chicken nachos). They often combine this lunch-practice with going to different clothing stores, where Mia likes to shop. Anna rarely buys anything. To afford this activity, Mia works a lot at a local supermarket. It used to be in the town she lived in, but since she and her mother and brother moved to another town just before starting high school, it means she has a considerable amount of transportation time to get to and from work. She spends a lot of the money she earns on clothes; however, her mother is not too happy about this, so she tries to sneak it in and keep it a bit of a secret.

The concurrent occurrence of the calorie fixations and the restaurant visits demonstrate that the girls are very engaged in each other's lives. And that their relation can contain both calorie comparisons and chicken nachos-sessions at their favourite restaurant. This illustrates how standards and practices seldom exist on their own, but more often as deeply *entangled* with one another, contributing to complex spaces of possibilities across different activity settings, often containing contradictory practices. And also, that what makes sense in a school setting may be less meaningful in another setting that has its own activities and repeated behaviour patterns and routines (shopping, eating nachos at the steak house). And finally, we see how the shared preoccupation with 'healthy foods' and calories among the girls is intermingled with a practice of mutual care. Monitoring oneself and the other goes hand in hand with caring for one another, and Anna's expression of concern with Mia's eating habits cannot solely be ascribed to the introduction of the health profile the day before but must be comprehended as temporally extended through Anna and Mia's relation that dates back to elementary school. In that regard, the introduction of explicit standards, such as the normative health standards in the health profile, may serve to reinforce concerns, tensions or perhaps even competition that were already present.

Ambiguous Standards of Normality

The health profiles present a very concrete and tangible initiative in line with political incentives to promote (bodily) health in a general sense, and to prevent that young people develop mental health issues; in recent years, the frequency of the national well-being surveys has increased, and numerous initiatives have been set in motion, offering easy access to professional counselling, meditation programmes to prevent (or cope with) stress, etc. (see, e.g., Nielsen & Lagermann 2017). These initiatives are organized on local, municipal and national levels. The health profiles can be seen as part of a general political interest in health promotion, in a broad sense, based on the philosophy that increased awareness (automatically) leads to increased health. It falls in line with neoliberal governing strategies of making people responsible for their own life situation by giving them the tools and technologies to self-monitor and self-improve (in line with, e.g. Dean's thoughts on conduct of conduct (see Dean 2010), see also Turkle (1984), as well as Schraube (2013) in relation to the use of technologies specifically). Such rationales (of the potentially causal relation between knowledge, tools and actions) are easy to adopt, assuming that the awareness instated by the mandatory health tests in gym class will (automatically) lead to and encourage students to be more mindful and responsible about their own health situation: that it will automatically play into their motive hierarchy. As we saw from Anna, Mia and their group of friends, this seems to be only partially the case, as health becomes a topic of interest as well as something that is continuously present as a standard to negotiate, albeit not necessarily in the way it was intended.

As societal, or socio-material, beings, we live our lives in, with and through artefacts, and in this process, we change not only artefacts but also ourselves[2] (Wartofsky 1979, 1983). Hence, to assume that the artefacts or standards work only as intended or as one-way determinants, which in the case of the health profile would imply that its effects in the world would consist of nothing but a normative standard of health that all students would understand and act on in a uniform sense, would be an illusion. Indeed, artefacts, such as the health profile that procures normative ideas and ideals of what health ought to 'look' like in a numerical sense – hence presenting a certain standard – are powerful in the sense of co-constituting subjectivity (sensu Wartofsky 1983). They not only influence individual action (in the manner of direct perception-action), but also potentially co-shape motives and intentions, as well as interpersonal dynamics. And yet, artefacts cannot claim singularity in terms of dictating meaning; rather, as goes for everything else in the environment, artefacts are encountered, engaged with, and used in personal, intersubjective and situated ways. They are met by subjects, who are *always* in the process of doing something, going somewhere, becoming someone (or remaining the same), and whose actions, directions, and self-understandings are at the same time *always* co-shaped by artefacts.

What follows from the intersubjective interplays of Anna, Mia and their friends at school is how the awareness of health – that was perhaps instated, and perhaps just supported or encouraged by the health profile – does not exist as detached from the dynamics of their friendship, their mutual care and concerns, nor from parental guidance, the availability of (food) products, personal taste preferences, etc. Hence, rather than directly subjectifying the girls in a uniform sense, the interplays between the girls and the health profile suggest an immanent dialectical relation where undoubtedly, the girls' everyday life practice, their interplays and their self-understandings are not unaffected by the inscribed intentions of the artefact while, at the same time, the girls collectively negotiate and alter the meaning of it, by integrating it into their shared life worlds. As such, the health profile becomes a potentially powerful (yet, not determinant) factor in establishing standards in relation to (bodily) normality, as it feeds into ongoing and multileveled negotiations of who and how to be. And as we already know, the questions of 'who' and 'how' are not easily answered, nor unambiguous in their constitution.

If we return to the high school practice at Countryside High, ambiguities in relation to the health profile are further accentuated by the fact that 'health' in itself is not necessarily an unequivocal standard, despite the fact that numbers and online graphs seem to suggest otherwise. This is illustrated in gym class, where the demarcation lines

---

[2] Here, I address the health profile as an artefact, sensu Wartofsky, to be understood (historically) as saturated with (political) intention. Other researchers such as Turkle (1984) and Schraube (2013) explore life with technologies more specifically, and as an integral part of the human lifeworld. As Turkle writes: '*Technology catalyzes changes, not only in what we do but in how we think. It changes people's awareness of themselves, of one another, of their relationship with the world ...* ' (Turkle 2005, 18f, cited in Schraube 2013:14).

between 'a healthy/normal' and 'an unhealthy/abnormal' body suddenly become a topic of controversy among the teachers:

> I have joined Anna and Mia for gym class, but as I was not prepared (I did not bring a change of clothes), I am now hanging out with the five gym teachers, while the students are out running. Today, there is a run for all the first-year students, so they are all attending the same class, and are therefore under the instruction of five teachers. In this run, students have to complete a 2,5km lap as many times as possible, with a minimum of two laps. The teachers are noting down the numbers of laps the individual student completes. The classes are competing on class-level, so the scores are added up for each class.
>
> One of the teachers tells me that around 15 students – 10% of the students – are not out running based on a ton of different excuses that none of the teachers believe. Some students are out on the run wearing their regular clothes even though it is clearly stated on the doors of the sports hall that one is to show up in appropriate sportswear even though one is not participating. A girl takes a minor fall while out running, and hurts her leg. As she scraped her knee, there is a tiny bit of blood and three of her friends willingly insist on carrying her back to school. One of the teachers take over so that the three other students cannot (according to the teachers) use this as an excuse not to participate in the run; the students are debating this, but eventually return to the run.
>
> I take the opportunity to ask Teacher A about the health profiles that I heard about last week. She explains to me that it is various kinds of measurements that the students tab into an online web page and that they will complete these tests twice a year throughout high school. The results are *not* visible or accessible to the teachers, so the profiles are completely private; they have the sole purpose of raising students' awareness of their own health situation. I tell her that the students seem to think that they are evaluated and graded on the basis on their improvement on this profile. She laughs and so do the other teachers next to us; she tells me, that they all (the teachers) know about this and that they have no intention of changing this assumption among the students, not right now at least. It is only great, if this false assumption serves as a motivator for students, she says. The teachers start talking about how there are huge variations between classes in terms of motivation and enthusiasm for gym class: one class has a specific sports profile and are highly engaged, whereas for other classes there is a tendency towards a norm of not participating at all, which clearly annoy the teachers, and which explains their general mistrust in students' reasons for not participating.
>
> While we are talking, students come up for a mark for each round they complete. It is clear that the engagement varies. Anna runs alone and finishes three laps, while Mia run with Sandra and they only finish two. A girl from Anna and Mia's class, Vicky, returns from her second lap, and Teacher C encouragingly says that she should be able to make another round, if she pushes it a bit. Vicky seems hesitant whether to run another lap or hit the showers, leaning towards the latter. Teacher A, who is clearly more of an authority than Teacher C, interrupts saying (in a decisive tone) that Vicky should definitely hit the showers. Vicky

leaves for the showers. When Vicky is well out of sight, the following conversation takes place:

Teacher A: (in a very harsh tone) *Under no circumstances, Vicky should have been running an extra round. Have you even looked at her and how skinny she is?*
Teacher C: *I have. But some people are just built that way.*
Teacher A: *Yes, but that is not the case with this one. … She is ill! … She should not be running at all!*
The conversation dies out.

Vicky does appear noticeably skinny and from attending the class on a regular basis, one is left with the impression that she is not doing well. She consistently turns up late for class, and usually comes in with red and swollen knuckles (apparently from self-induced vomiting, one of the girls tells me). No one comments on this, and the rest of the students in class seem to avoid her, both socially and in relation to group work. She often spends her time in class browsing various food related web sites and generally sticks to herself. When asked about her, Anna and Mia say that 'she is weird'. Two weeks after the gym class with the run, Vicky is admitted to a psychiatric hospital to be treated for an eating disorder. I later learn that when she returns to school a few months later, she switches to another class, the sports profile class.

One cannot draw causal relations between the health profile, the school's focus on health promotion and the eating disorder that Vicky seems to be struggling with. Nor can we disregard the fact that the demands instated by the school co-construct a focus on health, by the use of self-monitoring technologies. It is thought-provoking how the gym teachers assess Vicky so differently, and they clearly abide to very different notions of what 'healthy' looks like or how it manifests. The distinction between encouragement and discouragement – between seeing health and successful performance versus seeing potential illness and a student (and a body) that needs to be cared for by *not* pushing the physical limits – is considerable, and it demonstrates an ambiguity in the school's way of conceptualizing health, which blurs the context for the health profiles in terms of what is idealized and promoted. Gym class is thus an activity setting with inbuilt ambiguous demands relating to health.

Students' motives for participating must be understood in relation to this ambiguity, as well as their personal directedness that extends beyond gym class and the school setting. For instance, Anna's motivation for doing well in gym class relates to her engagement in gymnastics outside school; on our way back from gym class, she tells me how she will be earning more (money) from teaching gymnastics this year, as the other coaches can see the level of responsibility she is taking and that she is a reliable participant. If she could do gymnastics all the time, she would. Her engagement in the run at school was not about earning points for her class, but rather about demonstrating her engagement in gymnastics and sports in general. And just as students have multiple motives that weave in and out of each other, and across different activity settings, there may also be several motives at play for the teachers, who seem to have a general impression that students are reluctant to engage in gym class, which (1) is a cause of irritation and perhaps frustration for teachers, and (2) that tends to justify teachers' awareness of the misconceptions that flourish among students, e.g., relating to the structural conditions for grading in gym class (do grades depend on improvements on the health profile or not?). These misalignments between teachers' and students' motives and knowledge of the actual conditions may contribute to even more ambiguity in gym class as an activity setting – an ambiguity left for students to make sense of.

You Are What You Measure

As we recall from the eco-niche portrait of Countryside High, some ambiguities arose in the school's way of subjectifying students. This became evident in the contradictory ways that students were invited to choose their academic lines freely (according to interests), all the while being evaluated and categorized by teachers on the basis of their choice. Another ambiguity related to the school's attempt at integrating students with Asperger Syndrome and the way the girls categorized these students as fundamentally different from themselves, as a way of simultaneously caring for the needs of the students with Asperger and looking out for their own interest in using the common space area. As becomes clear from the examples with the health profiles, these are cause of additional ambiguities that students are left to handle or try to make sense of.

Regarding the health profile as an institutional tool, it is meant as a way of increasing awareness of health and different health factors. The way the health profile is used in the school implies that it is simultaneously working as a self-monitoring technology, and as a monitoring tool on an institutional level (the students *think* they are being evaluated by the teachers and therefore (might) perform in relation to motives of improving their grades).

As mentioned earlier, the health profiles are part of national project. The motivation behind introducing health profiles is (evidently) the idea that *awareness of health* creates better conditions for being healthy – and for choosing and doing the 'right thing'. It is a health-promoting initiative aimed at shaping students' motives. Despite the fact that such an initiative is hard to dispute, in terms of its potential long-term societal value, its influence is not limited to individuals on an intra-individual level ('I relate to myself through numbers'). What becomes evident over time is how the numbers – and the increased awareness they bring about – entail an increased awareness of 'healthy' versus 'unhealthy' among the group of girls that Anna and Mia are part of, and it therefore also has implications on an intersubjective level. The girls thus develop their subjectivities reflecting these new health standards and the subjectifications or self-understandings they offer, via numbers and coloured curves in the database. The numbers become ways of *comparing* with one another and *keeping an eye on each other*; and in the wake of this, food consumption, as well as enjoying food, becomes entangled with knowledge of health value (based on the content of calories). In that sense the health profiles are efficient, in that they do accentuate an awareness that, in their absence, might have been less outspoken. However, what is also illustrated by the interplay between Anna, Mia and their friends is how the health awareness is not solely a personal relating-to-self-and-body, but an integral part of relating to (food) objects, self and others, inseparable from other dynamics of everyday life.

At the same time, 'health' is not a self-evident matter, and even among the gym teachers at Countryside High there are significant differences in what they consider a healthy or even 'normal' body. This suggests that the standard of health presented in the health profiles is taken at face value and considered unequivocal, albeit there appears to be a large variation in how health is viewed, assessed and practised in everyday life settings. However, these variations – or this unclarity – do not seem to become an explicit focus from the school's side. Followingly, an ambiguous and possibly contradictory space of possibilities in relation to health, and the demands associated with it, is co-constructed, and we see how girls from the same class connect with various aspects of these demands and possibilities in very different ways.

If we dwell on the ambiguity concerning health for a minute, it consists of several aspects: *firstly*, in the entangled manner in which health profiles are introduced (as partly self-monitoring-, and partly institutional monitoring tools for teachers to make use of); *secondly*, how a precipitated reference to 'health' means that instead of only supporting long-term awareness of health (as intended), the health profiles also introduce potentially problematic ways of relating to food (primarily in terms of calories); and *thirdly*, ambiguous ways of relating to each other (the girls increasingly focus on calories as a joint practice of monitoring self and the other, and it inflicts on their internal dynamics, e.g. between Anna and Mia). *Finally*, it becomes ambiguous in the sense that the individualistic approach brought on by the health profiles does somehow appear dissonant vis-a-vis the strong sense of community in the school atmosphere, and the students are left to handle and make sense of these *potential contradictions* by themselves.

On a meta-level, this may reflect a general societal tendency, where health standards are promoted in a variety of settings and where being successful is often equated with being fit and healthy (in a particular way, associated with exerting or demonstrating bodily control). This, again, may reflect a neoliberal individualization tendency, where one is to optimize one's own value; also, as a body. I would problematize that instead of aiding young people to establish and maintain a balanced approach to a healthy body, the health profile seems to push towards body images that may be distorted more than natural (and healthy). Introducing a motto of '*You are what you measure*' and coupling it to academic assessment (as part of a class that is graded) carry the risk of installing an unreflective valuing of numerical self-assessment; be it of grades, weight, BMI or other measures. This motto – that is not chosen by the school, but an integral part of the programme employed by the school – presents a strong invitation for students to continuously assess themselves by means of numbers. The girls' references to the curves on the online platform suggest a certain affordance quality from the design of the profile. And as an artefact, it does not divert considerably from other health-directed technologies of everyday life, such as exercise apps, or inbuilt pedometers in smart phones that a majority of young people are most likely familiar with and not necessarily sceptical about. Therefore, my intention is not to exoticize or even criticize it, because on its own it is neither fish nor fowl. Rather, what is interesting from a developmental perspective is the manner in which the health profile comes to work as entangled with relational dynamics, personal motives, institutional performance demands and potential insecurities (of who and how to be); this is where it acquires its subjectifying power or its meaning, and where we can reflect upon its effects, even if these are only indirect or partial. And here, I would argue, that the high school, as an educational setting, constitutes an obvious space of possibilities for facilitating and supporting critical reflection about such self-monitoring tools and technologies, concerning their meaning and implicit power. Not for the sake of criticism, but as an acknowledgement of the societal realities in which young people are developing. From the interplays between the girls, as well as the teachers' considerations about how the health profile is perceived by students, we are left with the impression that students are expected to make sense of the profile on their own. And that it is expected to automatically work as intended. However, what is also illustrated is that the health profile does not only materialize the intended, but also unexpected actions, reflections and intersubjective interplays.

The ability to critically reflect upon the means (e.g. the meaning of graphs, curves and numerical values) by which they assess and think of themselves, I suggest to be of importance for young people, seeing that the self-governance that is expected from them (in relation to health) is taking place in a rather ambiguous space of opportunities. Here students may just as well abide to the implied civilization process (instated by the health profile) or to its negation, by perverting or distorting the notion of health. Gilliam and Gulløv (2012) raise this point in relation to teaching, outlining a paradox inherent in civilization processes: '*The paradox is thus that those who are preoccupied with civilizing or integrating, simultaneously mark an array of behaviours, social categories, and specific persons as problematic. They therefore risk, in the same motion, to stigmatize and exclude a part of the persons they were intending to civilize and recruit into their own civilizing category*' (Gilliam & Gulløv 2012:36, my translation). They stress how civilizing institutions, such as schools in a broad sense, may succeed with the promotion of certain behaviours or ways of being in the world, but that they also, concurrently, contain (and promote) the germ seed or possibility for the opposite (ibid.). Considering the high school an institutional setting with a certain and more or less explicit civilization project, it offers multiple activity settings that in different ways convey institutional and societal demands. However, students are not passively accepting, taking over, or assimilating to these demands in a 1:1 manner; they negotiate their meaning collectively and they work to make different demands fit their currents motives that often extend beyond the high school arena. The civilizing aspect of the health profile is at the same time a demand that students are required to meet as part of gym class, and an invitation to think of oneself in specific ways. But as we see from the data excerpts, the girls only pick up on *some* aspects of intended civilization project and integrate them with their ongoing and collective meaning-making dynamics, as part of their conduct of everyday life. This implies that the built-in assumption that increased awareness automatically leads to better health is challenged, as there is no direct reading and 'taking-over' of the meaning of health and numbers. And one must, with reference to Gilliam and Gulløv, recognize that any civilization project also concurrently contains the germ seed for its own negation. In this case, one could argue that the self-control and strict regime displayed by Vicky may also be encouraged by the health profile's invitation to consider oneself via numbers, even though this, in Vicky's case, becomes distorted (both in relation to general measurements of 'normal bodily health', as represented by the BMI-measurements, but also in recognition of Vicky's situation having little to do with the health profiles in themselves). However, introducing universal and normative standards for health always comes with an implicit pointing out of those who do not fit such norms, and as such the health profiles may also contribute to the magnifying of tensions, insecurities and differences between students – as displayed in Anna and Mia's way of relating to Vicky – rather than contribute to increased understanding and mutual care (see also Kofoed & Søndergaard 2009).

Hence, the point I wish to make here is twofold: firstly, young people do not deal with the various aspects of their everyday life in compartmentalized manners. Rather, they selectively pick up on information and invitations to act in their environment (cf. Gibson 1986), and they make sense of this with one another in entangled (and unpredictable) ways. Everyday life dynamics have a way of overriding the unambiguousness with which the health profile was intended, which in turn questions the transferability of the intentions of the health profile and emphasizes the need to recognize how such artefacts or technologies are not adopted in uniform or unequivocal manners. And secondly, that societal standards of what constitutes 'normal' – or what 'normal' looks like – needs to be approached and handled with caution, and perhaps high school, as a societally structured setting for youth life, is a potent setting for more actively exploring, questioning and debating that which often presents as unambiguous categories, such as (bodily or mental) health. The manner in which an awareness of 'health' acquires its own life among the girls illustrates how young people continuously engage (with the world and one another) to make sense of the standards, norms and expectations they constantly encounter, and how technologies exist and come to matter, intimately interwoven into the fabrics of everyday life. Here high school, as a societal institution, has the potential to support critical reflection and the expansion of norms, rather than contributing to a reproduction of – perhaps – unreflective and decontextualized standards.

6

Exploring Subjective Processes of Transformation

In this chapter, we dive further into the subjective aspects of relating to the standards of youth life that are encountered in the high school setting, and how relating to these standards co-create development on a subjective level, in relation to not only participation but also self-understanding. Here we return to Anna, and we follow her closely to see how her understanding of herself changes over the school year, and more specifically in relation to drinking beer, as representing a standard of social participation. What is interesting is that we may readily interpret Anna's development in relation to beer-drinking and meeting standards of social participation as a case of simple socialization, where norms are gradually appropriated and internalized. However, what becomes evident over the course of the school year is that the changes that occur are not limited to Anna, but also to the ways in which the others in her class participate as well as the very meaning of the standard of social participation itself.

This allows for an understanding of youth development as a dynamic relation – a dialectical process of meeting societal standards and negotiating their meaning while acting on personal motives. This points to a theoretical proposition of a dialectical-ecological model of youth development to better grasp the subjective processes of transformation in relation to 'self'.

As I already touched upon in Chapter 1, standards are an integral part of people's everyday lives. Any person lives with, and lives by, standards, as these are deeply enmeshed into the fabric of everyday life. Standards, however, are not uni-dimensional, uni-directional determinant conditions that people are passively exposed or subjected to; rather, they are continuously co-created and re-created in people's conduct of everyday life, as they take part in multiple and various practices. At the same time, we need to recognize how they come to influence that very same everyday living by making some actions more likely than others, some choices more desirable, and hence how they may ultimately work to standardize subjectivity across time, contexts and practices (see Busch 2011; Nissen 2014; Pedersen & Bang 2016a, 2016b, 2016c).

This chapter is a reprint and an elaboration of a joint publication by Jytte Bang and me (see Pedersen & Bang 2016a), and it reflects collaborative work concerning the theoretical propositions and analysis. It was originally published in Integrative Psychological & Behavioral Science in 2016 and is reprinted with the permission of Springer Nature. For this publication, it has been slightly altered and the analysis has been expanded.

Part of developing a 'fully dialectical view of human development is the difficult challenge of theorizing individual processes' (Stetsenko & Arievitch 2004; Stetsenko 2013) because by doing so we often resort to dualistic understandings of the individual mind as something inherently different from the social world, as if 'the individual' makes it somewhat closer to an entirely biological matter, and ipso facto 'not social' (Stetsenko 2013). Furthermore, we often tend to either foreground the individual *or* the context (as structures, standards, surroundings, social others, etc.), and background the other in attempting to grasp developmental dynamics. And perhaps we sometimes fail to grasp the dialectical interconnectedness of individual and environment (to use a broader term). This problem has, among others, been specifically addressed by Rogoff (2003), who problematizes how developmental theory in general tends to employ what we might term an 'individualizing' gaze, where relations between the person and social others, material or cultural objects or broader societal structures are depicted as causal relations or one-way determinants. When trying to grasp developmental dynamics, we therefore on the one hand need to understand the power and influence of said standards, while, on the other hand, avoid the dissolution of subjectivity. And, addressed reversely, we need a point of departure in the subjectivity, intentionality and agency of the subject, without losing sight of the intimate connections to relational, material, cultural and societal context (see also Vygotsky 1978).

The fact that persons live with and live by standards makes it important to address standardization processes at the level of the person, when theorizing about youth development. As was clearly illustrated by the various introduction events at the different high schools, powerful standards are at play that place demands and expectations on young people on how to take part in high school life, and on how to understand themselves in relation to 'being-a-high-school-student'. This means that even before they start high school, notions of how one ought to be as a high school student are introduced. From this it is a fair assumption that standards have an important influence on the development of young people, but also, young people meet standards from different perspectives and with different backgrounds and resources. Albeit Anna and Mia attend the same class at Countryside High, they are not the same, and they meet the standards that are conveyed at their high school from their unique positions, or with reference to Hedegaard (2012), in their unique social situations. They may take part in the same activity settings and meet the same standards or invitations to participate; however, they do so with different motive hierarchies, and drawing on different ontogenetic life-courses.

This implies that studying the influence of standards on youth development means studying the relationship between subjectivity and subjectification. Between being and potentially becoming, and as an ongoing and ever-present tension. Before we dive into Anna's development over the course of the school year to follow her micro-genetic (developmental) movements over time, I will first dwell on the subjectivity-subjectification relationship. 'Subjectivity' refers to the experienced first-person-givenness of a person (Zahavi 2008; Schraube 2010, 2013); it has to do with the experience of the self as a source of experiences, intentions, orientations, actions and change. During the life-course, subjectivity, as a feeling of 'me' as a person, may change over time in accordance with the person's life narratives, and in relation to new ways of participating and relating to the world. In subjectivity, there is the freedom to make choices, to resist and to make changes; in other words, 'subjectivity' grasps the principled autonomy in any living organism, including humans. 'Subjectification', on the other hand, is the process through which a person meets standards (in line with Foucault's (1995) notion of the discursive production of subject positions, as means of regulation (see also Walkerdine 2006:241); it is the process of negotiating and appropriating standards, hence installing them so that they furnish a person's subjectivity (which, importantly, is not erased in the process of subjectification) and thereby influence the direction of a person's feelings of personal freedom and of action possibilities. As Rose says:

> [...] *modern forms of subjectivity, contemporary conceptions of agency and will, the present-day ethics of freedom itself – are not antithetical to power and technique but actually the resultant of specific configurations of power [...]. One cannot counterpose subjectivity to power, because subjectification occurs in the element of power; one cannot counterpose freedom to technology, because what we have come to understand as our freedom is the mobile outcome of a multitude of human technologies.*
>
> (Rose 1999:54f)

To overcome the aforementioned challenge of grasping developmental dynamics processually and in a non-reductive manner, I – building on my work with Jytte Bang (see Pedersen & Bang 2016a) – propose to conceptualize subjectivity and subjectification in synthetic terms to comprehend the person-environment (reciprocity) dynamics, from the perspective of the person. The person, one might propose, becomes a *subjectivity-subjectification synthesis* over time; this happens through ongoing changes and stabilizations.

Subjectivity is multidimensional in that it refers both to the experience, the directedness, engagement and the action potentials of a person, and to actions initiated by a person. In this manner, the term acknowledges that these dimensions belong to a person. However, to insist on the dialectical constitution of subjectivity, and to avoid a reductionism to potential 'subjectivism', rather than operate with 'subjectivity' alone, I propose to think of subjectivity as *subjectified subjectivity*, as conceptualized by Pedersen and Bang (2016a). Here, 'subjectification' indicates that subjectivity, as essential as it is to any person, over time, furnishes itself on the basis of available standards, or broadly speaking through the various invitations to think of – and act – oneself in particular ways that the person has encountered through the life-course (see also Foucault 1982, 1995). In this light, standards play their role in youth development through the ways in which they are negotiated and appropriated as subjectified subjectivity. Of course, such personal processes are not private in an individual sense. It is well-known that discrepancies between standards and the particular lives of persons, given their conditions and ways of living, can have notable social and personal consequences, such as bullying, social isolation, the establishment of marginalized peer groups, development of mental problems and so forth (e.g. Kofoed & Søndergaard 2009). Standards are integrated into our concrete everyday life conditions; often so implicit that they go unnoticed (as invitations or constraints, expectations and possibilities). The change of standards at a personal level may go unnoticed as well; what changes is the *sense* that standards make over time. However, when observed 'from the outside', standards often appear immutable and rather consistent, and we tend to suggest that change only occurs on the personal level, as development. That is why the comprehension of developmental dynamics on a personal level implies an analytical awareness of how also standards change over time, and how these processes of change are intertwined. Hence, the analysis presented in this chapter concerns both the personal development of Anna and the development of a dominant standard in her high school class: here it will be unfolded as a subjectivity-subjectification synthesis. Especially, the analysis will focus on how this synthesis undergoes changes over time; how the feeling of being that particular person, with those sets of experienced meanings, changes, while coming to know about – and taking part in – high school life. Paraphrasing Wartofsky (1983:198), 'young people are what school architecture, age regulations and living spaces in the current ecology and economy of families constitute the life-worlds of young people *as*'.

Societal Ecological Existence

Following the notions outlined above, youth is not an abstract category and should not be viewed merely as exposed to or shaped by socialization or subjectification, as has otherwise been dominant historical narratives, following, e.g., Lesko 2001. Young people co-construct their everyday lives and themselves, and they relate actively to what they meet as well as actively deal with challenges and issues that arise. They actively conduct their everyday lives, which implies working actively to create meaning, also across contexts (Dreier 2011, 2016). Often, environmental novelty (such as starting high school) takes the form of challenges which may be thought of in existential terms: being thrown into uncertainty is a defining characteristic of existential being. Valsiner (2014) touches upon the issue of uncertainty when he points out that:

> '*Being social*' *is not equal to* '*participating in the social context*' *(or* '*joining society*')*; rather, it is a person-centered, calculated, goals-oriented movement through the social field with all of its constraints and affordances.*
>
> (Valsiner 2014:16ff)

We could thus argue that such uncertainties are essential to development; this implies that developing means dealing with existential matter with regard to changing specific conditions of life. Contrary to textbook views, which focus on 'kinds' of development (cognitive, emotional, physical, gender, etc.) or on specific skills, development is here understood as the transformations that happen with regard to the value-laden engagement in the individual-environment reciprocity that, through these processes, undergoes changes over time. This view correlates with the work of, e.g., Lewin (1935) and his conceptualization of the life-space, and also with Stetsenko (2012, 2013) who emphasizes the social and collective nature of subjectivity (subjectivity as an outcome of collective activities). In their everyday lives, persons take part in processes which turn out to be transformative and newness appears along the way. This makes developmental transformation and the appearance of newness part of the ways in which a person meets and responds to existential challenges.

Therefore, to be able to really investigate and understand development, as the emergence of newness in a person's life, it must be studied as pragmatic solutions to existential challenges in the particular person's life. One must focus on how, and in which contexts, persons deal with uncertainty (Valsiner 2014) and how situations may embed future possibilities (Hundeide 2005). There are 'dramas' of everyday life which may be important inspirations for developmental transformations to occur. The everyday life of young people consists of ongoing situations with existential qualities. To put it more precisely, there is no non-existential situation – a situation in which a person takes part always has existential qualities, where a person actively relates to an experience of self in relation to the possibilities, invitations and demands of the situation. There is always a core dimension of importance; there is no such thing as a neutral situation indifferent to values in a person's life. Therefore, we must study developmental changes from the person's subjectified subjectivity perspective; that is, from the perspective of the person's everyday existence, where subjectivity cannot be understood apart from the environment, and hence subjectification. What we think of as developmental paths is nothing but the visible and contemporary 'signs' of ongoing existential dealing with the ongoing challenges in life; the appropriation and negotiation of meaning and standards. Such paths may change slowly or rapidly and influence the future of the person's life in different ways. As is well known, a 'path' is not a life insurance or a destiny; it is a contemporary point of existence and point of departure in a person's life, a place from which new possibilities inspire, new challenges are met and new struggles are fought[1]. If we connect this to the writings of Elder (1998), we can only retrospectively understand the existential significance of each choice in our life course; however, we must recognize how not only our choices, but also the historical, temporal and relational factors in relation to which these choices are made, have an impact of the development of our individual life course or 'developmental path'.

Methodological and empirical consequences follow this way of approaching developmental processes. We need to find a way to analyse the connecting points between (1) the existential challenges experienced by a person (where and how the person is being 'thrown' into uncertainty), and (2) the societal perspective (in the shape of, e.g., concrete standards). When regarding Anna's development over the course of the first year in high school, there is a particular aspect that stands out as invoking some form of existential uncertainty for her; it relates to the concrete, and rather dominant, standard of drinking beer and taking part in beer-drinking-socializing. This analytical focus-point addresses a theme that is inescapable in Danish youth culture and especially relevant to high school students: the role of alcohol. Following the above-mentioned connecting points, this chapter presents an analysis of the interrelatedness of (1) the existential challenges experienced by Anna,

---

[1] A similar comprehension has been illustrated by Hundeide (2005), in his writings about socio-cultural tracks of development.

and (2) the societal perspective on alcohol (beer, in this particular case), and finally (3) how the local standard of beer-drinking-socializing in Anna's class also changes over time. By approaching 'beer' as an artefact and how Anna approaches the alcohol culture over time by increasingly becoming a consumer of beer, the specific empirical analysis exemplifies how subjectivity and subjectification interrelate and give rise to self-development.

The Issue of the Person-Environment Reciprocity: Subjectivity/Subjectification and the Affording of Standards

In order to shed light on the major transactional relationships between the person and the environment – which is foundational to an ecological theory of developmental change – I will present a general model of self-development and its theoretical ground, as it has been developed by Jytte Bang and myself (see Pedersen & Bang 2016a). In order to point out the complexities which characterize an ecological analysis of development, a closer look at the transactional, that is, dialectical, character of the person's relationship with the environment is crucial. For this purpose, two concepts will be proposed: (1) the subjectivity-subjectification dialectics, and (2) the affording of standards.

(1) Subjectivity-subjectification dialectics
From an ecological point of view, studying developmental change by focusing on the subjectivity-subjectification dialectics requires an analysis of what a person 'meets' and relates to. The study of the person as *a subject* is made complex by the fact that subjectivity is always-already a position of a subject in the world; and subjectification is always-already the way in which subjectivity is furnished *by* the subjective person. The point is that due to this dialectic, one both *should* and *should not* draw a line between 'subjectivity' and 'subjectification'. One should draw a line because subjectivity is acknowledged as phenomenological first-person-givenness (Zahavi 2008), which is essential, and subjectification is the 'installed' societal discourses and practices (sensu, e.g., Foucault 1995). Simultaneously, one should not draw a line because the phenomenological first-person-givenness is always furnished and because subjectification is no mechanical process of installing discourses and practices into the person – there are choices to make and perspectives to develop. Because of this dialectical character of subjectivity and subjectification, the experiential, sense-making, first-person-givenness of the person is always-already ecological. In other words, an ecological model for self-development must also be a dialectical model, and vice versa. It must grasp the dialectical movements of change of the sense-making experiential person, which take place over time; and it must theorize how such self-development becomes a synthesis – how a person becomes a synthesis of subjectivity and subjectification. This point makes an ecological analysis of self-development more complex compared to the fundamental ecological idea of person-environment relationship. Hence, an ecologically grounded perspective that focuses precisely on the

person/environment *transaction* is proposed, implying the change of both dialectical and synthetic manners.

(2) The affording of standards
To enable the understanding of the human environment as a societal environment, organized through institutions and activity settings, the concept of the 'affording of standards' is suggested as a productive elaboration of Gibson's notion of affordances (see Pedersen & Bang 2016b)[2], as I also outlined in the introductory chapter. The concept of affording of standards draws on both Gibson's ecological psychology and his notion of affordances (see Gibson 1986), as well as on the cultural-historical activity theory and its conceiving of the societal nature of humans (see, e.g., Wartofsky 1979; Leontjev 2002; Hedegaard, Fleer, Bang & Hviid 2008; Stetsenko & Arievitch 2004, 2010). Affording of standards refers to the point that a person meets and deals with society through a great variation of standards, which guide collective practices as well as persons' sense-making and development. By emphasizing *practice*, the intent is to underline the fact that the environments in which humans are embedded and participate are not reducible to physical 'immediacy', such as perceivable things or persons cut off from history, politics or other people's agendas and projects (also in line with Vygotsky 1994; Leontjev 2005). Instead, our lives are lived in concrete practices, shaped by historical interests and movements, political agendas and other people's participation over time – as well as our own. Practices are considered as the human form of environment which includes humanly produced artefacts, standards, norms, etc. Practices offer both certain possibilities and constraints that we do not necessarily ponder as such. How possibilities and constraints work can be approached by both extending and applying Gibson's notion of affordance. Gibson (1986) thought of affordance as a way to instate reciprocity and mutuality in the individual-environment relation. Inspired by both early gestalt thinkers, such as Lewin and Koffkaand behaviourism, Gibson wanted to create a psychology devoid of mentalism and with the aim of *'establishing predictable functional relations between environmental conditions and behavior'* (Heft 2001:106-7). To properly understand the dynamics of life in a social and ecological world, Gibson called for a term that can adequately describe what our surroundings (including other social beings) offer us and how we perceive these offerings; with the intent of creating a genuinely reciprocal understanding of the individual-environment relation (Gibson 1986). One could argue that Gibson's notion of affordance is, in fact, a dialectical construction albeit Gibson does not refer to it as such. The notion of affordance is appealing as a way to draw attention to the environmental factors that invites in a certain direction with regards to action. However, Gibson's notion of affordances needs to be extended when dealing with human societal life. For that aim, one could argue that the concept employs a somewhat undifferentiated notion of human activity and thus mostly relates to the operational aspect of human activity (in a Leontjevian

---

[2] The further development of Gibson's notion of affordances draws extensively on the work of particularly Bærentsen and Trettvik 2002; Costall 1995, 2004; Costall and Richards 2013, as well as Heft 1989, 2001, 2007, 2014.

sense[3]), as it focuses primarily on the direct relations between bodily features of the person and concrete environmental possibilities (for this discussion, see Bærentsen and Trettvik 2002). In addition, everything that is not direct perception, such as cultural or societal qualities, is cast aside as being of second-hand importance. Gibson basically portrays an environment that is immediate and material. And although one can readily acknowledge this focus, it makes it hard for him to grasp the world beyond this scope, for example, the environmental matter with regard to existential challenges, or how subjectified subjectivity processes add to the human environments, human activities and human development.

The human world does not exist in a vacuum; it is imbued with artefacts, possibilities, constraints and meanings, created by others across generations. Inspired by Costall and Richards (2013), it is therefore more on point to use the term of affording rather than keeping Gibson's term of affordance. This relates to the fact that the invitational qualities of the environment are not just perceivable to an exploring observer; they are also – as this book seeks to explore –negotiated and (re)created by the participants in concrete societal practices. This implies that the invitational character of the environment may also change over time, as new meanings are attributed or constructed, and new orientations arise. Hence by changing the noun *affordance* into the gerund *affording*, we are better able to embrace a processual perspective in the person-environment transactions. It allows us to better integrate the fact that persons actively co-create their own world, and thereby themselves, by participating in activity settings.

Aufhebung and the Development of Self – A Dialectical Ecology

It follows from the conceptual argumentation that to study and to conceive self-development, one needs to realize that the standards that co-constitute human everyday lives are met *as* the environment by persons; those standards inhabit values which become part of a person's negotiations with and within his/her societal practices. This implies that a person's development of self is continuously and actively being shaped by the person who participates in relevant practices; thus, a person's development of self is continuously connected to historical and social standards. As Wartofsky says:

> […] *the objects and practices and institutional facts of my particular lifeworld – all of them artifacts, even where these are transformations or utilizations of nature – obviously constitute me as the concrete, historically particular individual that I am. I am thus constituted by what I do and say – the artifacts, language, forms of action, rules, and social structures, all of which characterize the manner and means of my doing and saying or the modes in which I am who I am.*
>
> (Wartofsky 1983:197)

---

[3] This also connects to the criticism that Leontjev (2005) extends towards Vygotsky in relation to his proposition of comprehending the environment by analytically focusing on the child's emotional experience; here Leontjev argues for the need of analytically anchoring such comprehension in the study of activities (as concrete person-environment relations).

A dialectical notion of the development of self implies that the poles of 'subjectified subjectivity' and 'affording of standards' are dialectically interrelated; they co-constitute each other, in that persons shape, and are shaped by, their societal environments. Of course, these processes, of the development of self, take place in historical time (much emphasized by Wartofsky 1983 and Elder 1974, 1998; see also Lesko 2001), both regarding the person's life history and regarding the history of societal practices and standards. A person's development of self synthesizes these intertwined co-constitutions. Hegel (1807/1979) used the term 'Aufhebung', which refers to the transformation of dialectical relations into new 'forms' (of person-environment reciprocities); it is such processes of Aufhebung that give rise to the ongoing synthesizing of the developing self. Others within a cultural-historical framework refer to the same need for dialectic models (with Aufhebung qualities); e.g. Stetsenko (2013) who argues that cultural-historical activity theory supersedes theories of dialogical ontology, despite their vast similarities:

> *The term 'superseding' used in a dialectical sense, denotes a conceptual move that does not eliminate a given phenomenon or its properties but instead, lifts them up and includes them, albeit in a subordinate role, into a new systemic whole comprised, in this case, by human collaborative practices. That is, these practices are fully dialogical and relational, yet what makes them what they are, their formative feature and character cannot be reduced to dialogicality only. Instead their formative feature has to do with people collectively and materially producing the conditions of their existence, while along the way necessarily interacting, dialoging, relating, as well as and coming to develop specifically human psychological processes, agency, and subjectivity.*
> (Stetsenko 2013:12–13)

In my reading of Stetsenko, she is referring to the exact same dialogical relation that Bang and I (Pedersen & Bang 2016a) are trying to establish, though referring to it as 'superseding' instead of 'Aufhebung'. So, to return to our initial problem focus – that is, how to understand the development of self among youth (with 'Aufhebung' and the synthetic processes in mind) – it is clear that we need to propose a model of development that transcends not only abstract categories of youth, on the one hand, but also individual(istic) perspectives, on the other hand. Abstractionism and individualism should both be avoided.

A more productive (dialectical-ecological) contribution to understanding development as subjectified subjectivity needs to study the interwoven 'layers' of person-environment reciprocity. The model that will be proposed relates to a long-standing tradition within developmental research that aims at establishing a wholeness approach to the study and conceptualization of developmental phenomena (Hedegaard et al 2008; Hedegaard 2009, 2012). Wholeness refers to a global yet differentiated field of mutual reciprocities (dialectics) between a person and that person's environment (ecological) in terms of materiality, ideas, self-relationship, relations to other persons, etc. (Bang 2009b). The newness in this contribution lies in insisting on a dialectical and ecological comprehension: that ecological always-already must mean dialectical and vice versa. This opens constructively to the analysis of the variabilities and differentiations of developmental potentialities in the lives of young people. The figure below is sensitive to the developmental dynamics on a micro-genetic level exactly by enabling a multi-layered wholeness analysis.

The dialectical-ecological model of subjectified subjectivity

Figure 6.1 depicts the interwoven dimensions; it is a dialectical-ecological model of how subjectified subjectivity emerges. The emergence can be understood by a 'layered' analysis which aims at illustrating its dialectical and synthetic character. In other words, the figure depicts subjectified subjectivity as Aufhebung (ongoing dialectics and synthesis):

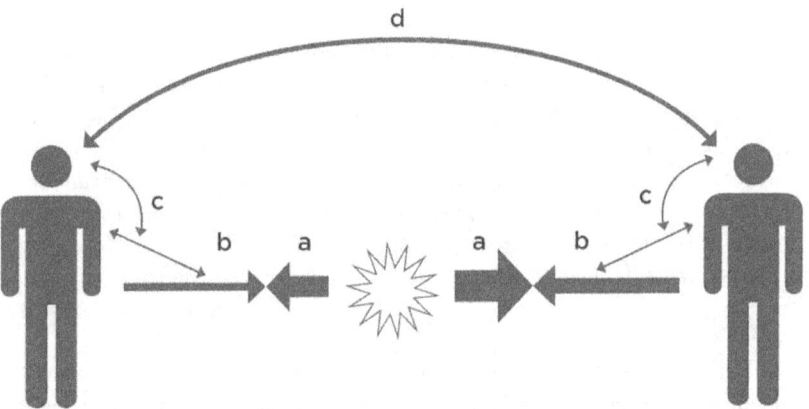

Figure 6.1 The dialectical-ecological model of subjectified subjectivity (Pedersen & Bang 2016a).

a) The basic person-environment reciprocity (perceiving and acting) is both the source for, and an outcome of, subjectified subjectivity. The perceiving-acting dynamic is worldly (practical-social and object-oriented).
b) Each person always-already co-experiences the self while participating in ongoing and changing person-environment reciprocities; these co-experiences of the self influence and co-produce the dynamics of the basic reciprocities.
c) Each person also always-already co-experiences the existential dimensions of the self while taking part in a) and b) processes. This implies that each person takes part in meaning-making processes which concern the person beyond the specific activity; and these meaning-making processes feed into the ongoing and changing person environment dialectics.
d) The persons 'negotiate' both the basic person-environment reciprocity and the meaning-making processes; hence personal interaction contributes to the other 'layers'.

In that sense, Figure 6.1 illustrates that both social standards and subjectified subjectivity emerge out of the same dialectical-ecological processes.

Let us begin by looking at the figure as 'layered' and subsequently, with regard to synthetic possibilities of the 'layers' as Aufgehoben. Beginning with the bottom layer (a), it depicts the basic inter-relationship of a person with her or his environment. Here 'environment' refers to more than what is physically present and surrounds the person in a material sense; rather, it refers to the human environment in a very broad sense which includes all that is historically constituted along the way of human history. Specifically, this includes standards and the ways in which they present themselves (as invitations or affordings) to a person. Therefore, even though this basic 'layer' may look like the immediate physical, surrounding environment, this would be a problematic reduction. Rather, it is immediate in a broader three-dimensional sense: (1) in the behavioural sense (action): when something in the environment, and concerning the person, is present in a perceivable way and can be looked at, touched, smelled, etc.; wherefore it is possible to initiate practical activities upon the beforehand environment or to respond to stimuli from the environment. This is the immediate perceptual quality that we find in Gibson's notion of affordances; (2) in the intentional sense, which means that the person is to be understood as a subject with intentional agency. The person may initiate openminded and interested exploratory and investigative activities; and (3) since the process is also dia(multi)logical (Hermans 2001), each of them feeds into the immediateness from personal life-worlds. Taking these dimensions into consideration, it implies that the basic ecological 'layer' (a) *always-already* synthesizes the whole 'layered' dialectics; these dialectics become Aufgehoben into a reality of the environment and are not just as a fact of consciousness added to the basic ecological 'layer': immediate and mediate implies a synthesis, it is always-already Aufgehoben.

In order to understand how these synthetic processes contribute to subjectified subjectivity processes, let us turn toward 'layer' b. The layer b analysis suggests that a person, being an intentional agent, relates to the basic inter-relationship in manners that, over time, transform this person-environment relationship into the person's lifeworld. The person deals with the standards of everyday life in subjective manners which includes negotiation, appropriation, resistance, etc., as we shall see later in this chapter. These are the processes – of negotiation, appropriation and so on – that are referred to as the 'affording of standards'; here the gerund 'affording' is preferred to the noun 'affordance' with the intent of stressing that a person is in a 'dialogue' with the standards (and the environment at large) and actively relate to them in their conduct of everyday life.

This dialogical character of how a person relates to the environmental standards has two interconnected implications. Firstly, it means that 'layer' (a) becomes modified during the life-course of a person. It undergoes changes along with whatever experiences and novelties that appear in a person's life. Secondly, since the person is an intentional agent, she/he always-already relates to herself/himself as an agent and co-experiences herself /himself as such while experiencing her/his environmental relationship and dialogues with the standards. She/he not only initiates activities or responds to information, but also co-experiences those activities with regard to personal relevance; while doing so, she/he co-experiences herself/himself as the agent she/he is. In other words, anything that goes on at (a) also implies activities at (b): being an agent participating in activities means experiencing oneself being involved with participation, as well as co-experiencing oneself as an agent involved with participation. 'Layer' (c) implies that any activity always is being experienced (and sometimes reflected) within the frame of overall experienced relevance of participation for a person's lifeworld. Value and emotionality co-contribute to the whole process. Hence, 'layer' (c) relates to (a) and (b) in ways similar to how (b) relates to (a) and their interwoven character, that is, their ongoing differences and ongoing synthesis.

The relevance of the model for processes of subjectified subjectivity is this: a person is both different from and initiates her/his relationship with her/his environment in subjective manners; and she/he deals with environmental affordances in the form of standards, which come to furnish that same subjectivity. In this sense, a person becomes a synthesis which continuously creates new openings and contradictions[4], all of which fuel the process. A person is – always – the wholeness of these interwoven relationships: a person relates (c) to the fact that she/he relates (b) to her/his basic relatedness (a). In this manner, a person necessarily is an existential being in that she/he deals with basic (societal and historical) conditions of life in personal ways. As this chapter, as well as the next, will explore more in depth, the young people in high school are continuously dealing with the (often contradictory) standards they meet all the while they are looking out for their own interests, motives or life projects. It is exactly in this active and simultaneous relating to the different existential 'layers' that existential aspects change over time; the young people are continuously becoming 'someone else', while remaining 'the same'.

Certain conditions of life, of proper ways to do things, of naturalized moral and ethical standards, etc., are part of the world that becomes her/his lifeworld. None of these are set in stone, but as we have already established, some of them may appear rather immutable or consistent. It is my assumption in this book that a certain portion of such standards is tied to institutional spaces (e.g. as values, demands, and im- and explicit rules), which is why we can expect that young people who start high school encounter a myriad of invitations and expectations of how 'to be' and hence are forced to relate rather explicitly to the possibilities and possible contradictions that these invitations and expectations entail. And that aspects of these new conditions will become part of the lifeworld over time, by processes of subjectivity-subjectification synthesis. The essential point is that in these dialectical processes of difference and synthesis – between relating to novelty and working to preserve status quo (e.g. in self-understanding) – a person's development of self is a dynamic, variable and synthetic process which always rests on the ecological nature of her/his worldliness. In these processes, the developing self becomes both more subjective and more subjectified at the same time. 'Layer' (d) depicts the fact that these processes of subjectified subjectivity are largely negotiated with others; a person negotiates meaning and standards of 'ways of relating' with others, as a participant and co-creator of her/his own societal lifeworld (and hence of the societal lifeworld of others).

---

[4] The understanding of contradictions as an inevitable part of the developmental process is deeply rooted in the cultural-activity theoretical tradition. Here it draws reference to the work of, e.g., Riegel (1975), Vygotsky (1978, 1998) and Hedegaard (2003, 2009, 2012), just as we find it a central understanding in the critical theoretical further developments of activity theory. See, e.g., Højholt and Kousholt (2020), Højholt (2020) for an elaboration on contradictions and conflictuality in children's lives in particular, and Axel (2011) who proposes the term 'conflictual cooperation' to refer to the way that contradictions are built into our everyday lives across contexts as a foundational condition.

The Subtle Transformation of Anna over the Course of the School Year

One of the questions I was most often confronted with during my time the high schools – both from colleagues and from high school students, their teachers and parents – was this: 'which standards are you studying?' And my answers remained, to the surprise of many, as follows: 'I don't know'. And there was a point to this, namely, that I did not preselect particular standards of interest, but had a methodological principle of remaining open to that which came to be of importance to the young people whom I was participating with; what would stand out as standards over time, in the sense of what would actually have a 'standardizing' effect on them and their way of participating and/or relating to themselves? This could only be studied in situ and – perhaps – best understood retrospectively. In the case of Anna, one such standard particularly stood out in relation to a change perceived by herself (and me, for that matter); a standard relating to a certain kind of social participation, of partying and drinking alcohol. From the impressions we were left with from the introduction events at the different schools (in Chapter 1), clearly, said standard appears rather dominant and influential in the lives of (new) high school students; however, it was not a preselected focus of interest per se. The standard of a specific kind of 'social participation' relates to an outspoken drinking culture among young people in Denmark, a culture that is socially accepted (and legal), and which has come to work as a general societal standard of youth life (transcending both generations and geographical locations, as well as socio-economic status)[5]. Following this, it is important to emphasize that the social participation related to beer-drinking has not been selected as a central standard to analyse for its stereotypic properties but rather because it emerged over the course of the first schoolyear as something meaningful – and something that changed its meaning – to

---

[5] In the 1990s several large-scale international surveys, the so-called ESPAD surveys (Hibell et al. 1997), revealed that Danish youth were among the top in Europe in alcohol consumption, which provoked an array of surveys and research projects in Denmark focusing on alcohol consumption, alcohol culture and potential preventive measures in Danish youth culture (see, e.g., Beck 2007; Elmeland & Kolind 2012; Frederiksen et al. 2012 for more recent research on the topic). Beck (2006, 2007) examined the way in which student culture (in high school) in relation to alcohol is developed and which mechanisms can be identified that create variations in student culture. In his study, he drew on Ziehe's notions of subjectification and potentiation, respectively. Subjectification is (here) understood as the process of becoming, in which an individual seeks out situations that are experienced as 'warm' or inviting, as opposed to 'cold' or hostile, the latter creating a sense of insecurity. This could readily be understood as different affordance qualities, if we were to describe the dynamic in ecological terms. Potentiation, on the other hand, is the process of seeking out *'intensity and dynamic instead of deep belonging'* (Beck 2007:14, my translation). On the basis of his data material, Beck proposes that there is a tendency towards girls applying a strategy of subjectification, while boys employ of strategy of potentiation (in relation to alcohol and alcohol culture) (ibid.). In addition, Beck reports that the concrete location of the high school (in terms of urbanization) has an impact on the way in which an alcohol culture unfolds within the high school culture, e.g., that going out/drinking on weekdays is more common in cities than in rural areas, simply because of availability. He adds that not only consumption but also norms in relation to alcohol vary from school to school (and relate to rural vs. city location). Beck concludes by pointing out that the excessive alcohol culture among Danish youth must also be seen in relation to *history*; that cultural liberation and the social informality in societal institutions play their part along with a teacher's generation largely dominated (still) by persons who participated in the youth revolt in 1968 (and who are therefore not likely to set rules or boundaries for the students) (ibid.).

Anna over time. It thus demonstrates the variability allowed for in Figure 6.1: beer and beer-drinking serve as environmental possibilities that Anna negotiates (in terms of meaning) with social others around her, and over time these negotiation (and participation) processes come to alter the way in which Anna sees (and experiences) herself and her environment, and thus who Anna is.

The extended timeframe of my participation in Anna's lifeworld made it possible to study the subtleties of the developmental dynamics that were taking place. This does not mean that we do not get a feeling of something changing along the way (according to Vygotsky's genetic method (Vygotsky 1978; Wertsch 1985)), but we cannot say exactly what it will change and how specific changes relate to the overall ontogenetic development in terms of changes of the lifeworld. The analysis that follows will reflect this by having different points of interest, structured chronologically, aiming to show concrete micro-genetic negotiation processes and changes in Anna's self-understanding, her directedness and her way of participating. By following Anna's approach to beer-drinking (and the alcohol culture 'behind' that theme) over some time, it becomes possible to see how Anna's approach to beer-drinking changes and also, how Anna comes to view herself differently. In this manner, Anna serves as a case example of how the presence of beer (as an artefact) and beer-drinking (as a common practice among high school students) influences the development of her subjectivity. Or more precisely how Anna (herself) contributes to her own processes of subjectified subjectivity, by dealing with the affordance of beer and a beer drinking practice as high school standards.

'I Actually Don't Like Beer'

Anna's active relating to beer and social practices involving beer-drinking first becomes noticeable to me in October, which is around two months into the school year (that starts in August). It is a Thursday morning and as we are waiting for classes to start, Anna is going over her schedule for the next two days.

> Anna: *Yeah, so tomorrow is a really interesting day, right!?* (She says in an ironic tone). *Look! Math, natural science and physics ... but at least there is the student bar afterwards, so it looks like I will also be home late tomorrow.*
> Me: *The student bar ... do people get drunk there or..?* (asked in a slightly teasing tone)
> Anna: *Hm.. yeah..* (Anna curls up on the couch as to make herself smaller and continues in a low voice) ... *not really, cause I actually don't like beer!* (She smiles a bit and makes a funny face, indicating that this is not information to be shared with people around us)
> Me: *Oh, I see.*

It is not so much the fact that Anna tells me that she does not like (and hence, implying that she does not drink) beer that stands out to me, but more the way she says it and the contradictory way in which she promotes the student bar, but at the same time reveals her dislike of beer – and that this is information meant to be kept between the two of us.

The next day Anna's classes end two hours before the student bar opens and she therefore decides to not attend the student bar after all. She does not want to wait at the school for the bar-activity to start, and on the other hand she does not have the energy to return to school, once she has gone home. There is both bus- and train connections to school, but these run with a low frequency and offer little flexibility in terms of timing.

On our way home from school, Anna shares information she just got from Mia:

Anna: *We just found out – just now – Mia told me, that tonight most of the other girls are going to Carla's place* (another girl from the class) *to have a party. In the beginning she* (Carla) *was very into that ... (...) when we had that sleep-over at school, Carla said, as we were all eating, that she had thought about throwing a party at her place, because she had lots of space and stuff, but now you sense it clearly that the party is only for them, because now they are hanging out together. The rest of us are not even invited; none of us, neither girls nor boys.*
Me: *Okay, so it's only for a small group of people. How did Mia find out about it?*
Anna: *Well, I don't know, maybe she overheard it or something. Because it is not like they are hiding it, you know. They are not. I mean, they don't have to or anything, but it's more that in some way they are trying to, you know ... but it's not like I care anyways, I have other plans today, so ... But sometimes it would just have been nice to have been invited, you know!*

Here we get a first glimpse of Anna's relation to (and experience of) beer but also of social groupings in the class, which she is concerned with. Apparently, there is a 'we' and a 'they' when it comes to social participation, and it appears that at least part of what defines this 'we' and 'they' is related to the meaningfulness (or lack thereof) of beer-drinking and partying.

From Anna's comment about beer, we learn that her relation to beer as an 'object' is shaped by the fact that she does not like the taste and therefore she tries to avoid it. Gibson (1986) might suggest that the beer affords drinking because of its fluid consistency and the shape of the beer bottle that fits the hand, along with the shaping of the bottle opening to fit the lips. However, in Anna's case, it is more adequate to talk about afford*ing* of beer as a standard. Beer does not afford drinking to Anna because Anna does not like beer, and therefore she negotiates what the beer affords as well as the standard of drinking beer. We may connect the background for this directedness, or lack of directedness (towards beer), to Anna's lifeworld prior to starting high school. Here her time was mostly consumed by school, gymnastics, babysitting, hanging out with family and with her girlfriends. Partying and drinking were far from being in focus in her lifeworld, let alone a practice. However, she seems to be fully aware that as a high school student, one is supposed to drink beer, if not on a daily basis, then often. Social capital (Bourdieu 1986/2011) grows out of that. For that reason, she is secretive about her not liking beer and she does not go out of her way to participate in the monthly Friday bar at the school; albeit she chooses to argue for her choice of going home as a merely practical matter. At this point in time, it is difficult to assess whether practicalities are the main reason or merely a convenience that allows her to argue for her choice of going home, without 'losing face', so to speak. What is illustrated here, however, is how Anna intentionally (subjectively) deals with the constraints and the expectations embedded into lives of high school students.

However, as is evident from Anna's account of 'the others' attending a private party at Clara's place, beer as an artefact connects to the social practice in the high school class, and so beer – over time – comes to play a role in Anna's transition from a schoolgirl to a high school student. Being an artefact, the beer is both a material and a cultural object to which certain meanings are attributed within (different) social settings. Anna's relationship with beer inescapably has to deal with the affording of beer as a social standard. As time passes, she can no longer keep up her tendency to ignore and/or avoid beer drinking. For many of Anna's classmates (and in youth culture in general), beer-drinking is a natural part of the parties and/or social gatherings, signifying fun, adulthood (as opposed to childhood), letting loose; a way of being social. It may be a way of being 'cool' and to be seen as someone having left childhood behind for good. It is also a practice that, for some, if not many, is already well-established before starting high school. In this regard, it is noticeable that young Danish people consume more alcohol than young people in most other European and North American countries (Vinther-Larsen 2011), which indicates that beer-drinking is a strong cultural feature, signifying youth life. This is perhaps what we can detect in Anna's contradictory communication about beer (and the student bar); there is a potential conflict for Anna, between her direct relation to the beer as an artefact ('I do not like beer') and her relating to herself as someone relating to the social affording of beer ('I know I *ought* to like beer'). She thus deals with the conflict between her own subjective preferences and her adaptation to social expectations by being aware that this ('not liking beer') is not something to boast about in public, but rather keep to oneself, and it surprises her that she is already 'grouped' in a socially exclusive way by other students who only invite selected classmates for a party (and not Anna). The ones who *are* invited to the party have, to a larger extent than Anna, managed to integrate beer-drinking as practice, and thereby respond to this high school standard more readily. For Anna this reveals contradictory standards of social participation in class ('it is okay for others to have parties and not invite everyone' but 'you should invite everyone').

At the same time, Anna experiences a conflict between what the beer affords as a thing ('don't like it') and what it affords as a social practice ('ought to like it'). This conflict is somewhat accelerated when Anna learns that beer-drinking as a standard practice is starting to influence and partly organize social life in her class, in an excluding way in Anna's case. It is the social practice built up around participating in concrete social settings (where beers can be more or less present) that at the same time invites and constrains Anna's lifeworld and thus sets concrete ecological conditions for Anna to understand herself within.

'One Could Have One Beer Probably'

A few months later, in February, it becomes clear that something in Anna's way of relating to beers – and to herself – is changing. We are sitting in class, during a break, and Maria (a classmate) comes over to talk to Anna about the PowerPoint presentation that they are making for Monday's introductory session for potential new students, who will be visiting the school.

> Maria: *So I wonder what is important for us to remember to include (in the presentation)?*
> Mia (sitting next to Anna) comments: *Just remember to mention beer drinking, then everybody knows what school is about!* she says and smiles.
> Anna: *Definitely! That's what it's all about!*

This conversation and Anna's (as well as Mia's, potentially) comment reveal a potential ironic distance to the significance of the beer culture in high school, that 'this' is what it is all about. However, and at the same time, the culture is also reproduced; the girls' comments convey a potential acknowledgement and disappointment at the same time; however to an outsider, this would not necessarily come across.

That we are perhaps closer to acknowledgement than disappointment becomes clear later that same day, when I go to hang out at the mall with Anna and her grandmother, who lives nearby the mall in the closest bigger city. As we recall from Chapter 2, Anna has a close relationship with her grandmother and likes to spend time with her. The mall hangout is a usual way for them to have a good time; they browse specific favourite stores for good offers on DVDs or clothes and catch up on everyday life. After taking a tour of the mall, we sit down for pizza slices at one of the restaurants. While we are eating, Anna tells us (her grandmother and me) that she will be attending a Rasmus Seebach concert (a Danish pop singer-song writer) soon, which she is rather excited about. It is important for her to underline that she comes to the concert to hear the music, not to drink. She explains:

> *I mean, one could have one beer probably, but if I get drunk, I won't be able to remember anything.*
> Her grandmother nods and mumbles but seems rather indifferent.

These two episodes (from the same day) illustrate a change in Anna's way of relating to both beer and herself (layers (a) and (c)). In the preparation of the presentation for new students, Anna readily agrees with her close friends, that beer-drinking is an essential part of (successful) high school life. Whether or not this is how she feels or merely what she has learned to say is difficult to establish and from that data excerpt alone we cannot say for sure in which ways and to what extent her approach to beer has changed. However, there seems to be a change in the way she relates to herself as someone drinking (or not drinking) beers. From somewhat avoidant behaviour to openly acknowledging the importance of beers for social high school life, Anna seems to gradually adapt to the practice she meets, and she gradually integrates this practice into her self-understanding and self-presentation. That her approach to beer is changing is also evident when Anna later tells her grandmother, with whom she is very close, that she will be attending a concert: 'beer drinking is not the reason for going, but still, something she might do'. So, from something being avoided because Anna does not like beer, it is now something to be experimented with, along with a new self-understanding that she is probing with a trusted older person, who knows her well. She takes a potential self-understanding (self-relation), created in another social setting (high school) into the social setting with her grandmother and thus tries to integrate the potential 'new' Anna ('someone who can drink a beer') with the 'old' ('I don't like beer'). Anna's challenge in this situation seems to be her own understanding of the object beer ('beers equal drunkenness') and her self-understanding ('I do not get drunk') and how to combine these. This reveals a potential new meaning to us on her statement of 'not liking beer' back in October; it may very well be that Anna did not like the taste of beer, but it is equally possible that she did not like the potential drunkenness (and loss of control). From Anna's own reflection, it is evident that she has little direct experience with beer, since she equates drinking more than one beer with drunkenness to the extent of memory loss. Also, experiencing the concert is more important to her than drinking; however, the concert situation serves as an ideal opportunity to experiment with beer.

Anna's understanding of beer, as something which indicates getting drunk, being forgetful and losing control, is a challenge to her. She seems to have a hard time integrating these 'values' or forms of appearance (and experience of self) into her self-understanding. Changes like this pose an existential challenge for Anna, because other of her classmates clearly relate to beer differently than her and have taken on a practice of organizing social life around alcohol. Hence, Anna finds herself excluded from this practice since she has not participated in the social space that is created, e.g., at the student bar. From the impressions we are left with on this day, it seems that Anna is starting a more active and direct negotiation of standards, partly with herself and partly with others; however, first and foremost with herself, using her grandmother as a kind of validator. In the meeting with her grandmother, she is probingly telling her grandmother about her thoughts on beer drinking, even though her grandmother does not ask, and the topic is not a natural part of the conversation. A possible interpretation of this is Anna's way of trying to integrate beer into her self-understanding; 'I am someone who can drink a beer without losing control'. Over the next few months, a lot of things seem to happen with regard to Anna's self-understanding, her ways of relating to beer and to the standards of sociality in the class.

'Weekends Are Just More Booked Now'

In June, the schoolyear is coming to an end and it is time for exams and annual tests. Anna has an annual test in history, and this is the last test before summer vacation starts. I accompany Anna to the test, and when the test is over, we are hanging out outside the examination room and small talk with some of the other students we meet. Carla from Anna's class, who also just finished her test, is sitting with us. She is clearly relieved and happy that exams and tests are over for this year.

> Carla gets up and gets ready to leave. She packs her belongings.
> Carla: *So, when will we all see each other again?* she asks and continues: *Cause I am not throwing another party, you know!*

No one knows, and Anna and a few others who are partly part of the conversation shrug. Carla hugs Anna and a few others goodbye and leaves.

I ask Anna what happened at the party since Carla will not host another one – and has a need to make a statement about it. Anna tells me that many got extremely drunk at the party and acted stupid and played 'kissing games'. They behaved like they were back in fifth grade, she says.

Next day as I am walking back from a shopping trip with Anna and Mia, we start to talk about changes in the past year.

> Me: *So as I recall from earlier in the year, your class was a bit … I don't know if 'divided' is the right word, but there were some factions, especially among the girls … ?*
> Anna: *There still is but … uhm …* (Mia interrupts)
> Mia: *It has improved a lot after the party.*
> Anna: *Yeah, after David's* (a boy from class) *18th[6] birthday party, we have become more joined as a group* (in the class) *… but it is funny that it happened after his party actually ….*
> Me: *Oh okay, when was that?*
> Anna: *About a month ago or something; not long anyways ….*
> Me: *Okay, so what happened at that party?*
> Anna: *Well … I don't think I feel that something has changed really* (as in 'I have changed'), *but probably if you ask my mom, she will think so. Because there was one day where I told her that I didn't think that I had changed* (since I started high school), *but she thought I had, but I just don't notice it myself. It was not like everything has changed, she said – because I asked her ….*
> Mia: *I also think that my mom thinks that I have changed a lot; especially when it comes to attending a lot of things and all the time being up to something and stuff. I think it is mostly that … I mean before, with my class and all, it was quieter but now there are a lot of parties and work and* (social) *things to do all the time.*
> Anna: *yeah, the parties especially … I mean the weekends are just more booked now, because there are a lot of 18th birthday parties, and then some are throwing parties for our class, and then there are parties at the school and stuff. And I didn't use to go to parties before really, so that has changed a lot – that I am now going to parties and drinking more than I did at the beginning, because now I attend the parties, so … it's like that.* (she pauses) *But about David's party, I mean, we arrived at the party that he was hosting with two other friends, and we just kind of sat there as a class and we did a lot of stuff together, because we didn't want to split up – it was really awesome! … And then when we came to school the Monday after the party, then everybody was just talking about the party and the ones who didn't attend the party were like: 'what are we gonna talk about?'. So, everybody was going on about the party, so if you didn't attend you were actually really outside* (of the group).

[6] In Denmark, the age of eighteen marks the full legal transition to adulthood and is thus (most often) the cause for a big celebration.

As this conversation shows, a lot has changed for Anna since she started high school; a fact that she does not reflect about in daily life, and at the same time is aware about when invited to reflect upon it. First and foremost, Anna has started participating in the social practices at school that involve beer-drinking and partying and she is starting to make this an integral part of her self-understanding as well. It is difficult for her to separate her own new drinking-practices from the fact that she now – more naturally – takes part in the social practices in class relating to partying. These aspects appear interconnected.

Simultaneously, there has been a change in the way the social practice of partying and beer-drinking is organized and practised in Anna's class, and it appears that the former tendency towards internal factions (among the girls) is no longer so outspoken. From Anna and Mia's account, it follows that this change, in collective social practice, has come about through a number of bigger birthday parties, where (ideally) the whole class has been involved and through which people have developed an increased feeling of group belonging with each other, implying collectively shared standards for participation (reflecting a shared collective ideality). In addition, there has been a party at Carla's place – where everyone was apparently invited – where some got really drunk and acted childish and irresponsible (e.g. by playing kissing games). Carla especially was not pleased with this, which reveals an ambivalence towards beer-drinking that does not only 'exist' for Anna. It points to the fact that the practice of beer-drinking – and what is appropriate behaviour in this connection – is a dynamic relation that is constantly being re-negotiated in practice (e.g. at Carla's party, where some 'crossed a line' and were acting 'too drunk and childish'). From what happened at Carla's party we learn that, within Anna's class, ideally one joins a social practice of beer drinking, albeit without 'acting childish' and 'playing kissing games'. And from Carla's comment about the party, we get the impression that something may also have changed in the way Carla feels about parties and what status they have socially (in comparison to the beginning of the year, where she would have been less likely to critically reflect about 'the right way to party' with Anna). Beer-drinking is therefore not about just drinking beers and getting drunk; preferably it is about drinking beers 'the right way'; getting drunk, but not too drunk. The standards of 'the right way to drink beers and behave at a party' are best understood as an ongoing negotiation process between the (concrete) participants (here: Anna and her classmates). It reflects a collectively developed meaningfulness of 'doing youth' that at the same time adheres to dominant standards of youth life that transcends everyday life at Countryside High, but at the same time cannot be understood apart from the collective ideality that is at play in this specific eco-niche.

To Anna and Mia, the party that really made a difference was the birthday party of one of the boys from the class (David), where a new feeling of group belonging for them as a class emerged – and where shared standards for social participation were negotiated in a noticeable way (and as such came to mark a shared reference point among the participants in relation to acceptable ways of participating). And perhaps this was most evidently felt the Monday after at school, where the party was the sole topic of conversation, meaning that you were extremely outside the group if you did not attend the party; again, something that reproduces the importance of the standard, all the while solidifying it in its new collective meaning. Anna has an awareness of this potential outsider position, but in comparison with October, she is now an 'insider'; one who attended the party. And one can speculate that this is what makes her aware of the potential outsider position; it is one that she recognizes from earlier in the school year. Over the course of the first school year, Anna has thus moved from a position 'on the side' of the dominant social group to a full participant, all the while the way of defining the dominant group has changed into something else than it was in the beginning. Therefore, it would be insufficient to say that Anna has merely adapted to the norms of the dominant group, as would be a more classical socialization view of Anna's developmental process. Instead, it is meaningful to consider this process as the concurrent (1) negotiating of standards (for social relations, for the meaning and importance of beer drinking, etc.), and (2) participants' (e.g. Anna's, Mia's, and Clara's) relating to their own ways of relating to beer, which again comprises both self-understandings and concrete meanings tied to the objects, as well as social and existential situations that the participants encounter and experience. Hence, the totality of the developmental situation cannot be reduced to Anna's 'socialization' process alone.

Anna's Development of Self – A Dialectical-Ecological Analysis

To sum up, during a period of about ten months – roughly the first high school year – Anna's approach to beer and to beer-drinking changes from (1) ignoring and avoiding it in September, over (2) probing it and negotiating it carefully and with awareness of the extremes in February (from what we could readily term an 'outsider' or 'newcomer' position), to (3) actively drinking it in many social settings towards June. Similarly, the ways in which she talks about beer go from (1) '*I actually don't like beer!*' in September, over (2) '(beer drinking) *Definitely! That's what it's all about!*' and '*I mean, on could have one beer probably, but if I get drunk, I won't be able to remember anything,*' in February, to (3) '[…] *I didn't use to go to parties before really, so that has changed a lot – that I am now going to parties and drinking more than I did at the beginning, because now I attend the parties,*' in June. It is now time to discuss how these changes in Anna's approach to beer and to beer-drinking can be understood with regard to the interrelationship of standards and the development of self; that is, the 'subjectified subjectivity' perspective outlined earlier in this chapter. If we return to Figure 6.1, the argument is that beer as an artefact, combined with beer drinking as a social practice, constitutes an urgent part of Anna's new environment as a high school student; and that Anna, as a person, experiences the urgency to deal with these new environmental realities. In this respect, the analysis serves to illustrate both how young people deal with high school life specifically; how their experienced subjectivity takes shape and becomes subjectified by dealing with environmental affordances; and how subjectified subjectivity emerges ecologically in a person's life in a larger scale.

When analysing the changes with reference to Figure 6.1, it becomes possible to grasp how the interwoven and dynamic character of the 'layers' over time leads to new realities for Anna, both with regard to her environmental activities (in what she takes part), to what appears as meaningful and valued to her (what does she allow herself to do), and to herself (who 'is' Anna). If we analyse Anna's changes over time, we find that the 'layers' (a) and (d) are interwoven sources for the change. Beer (and alcohol in general) is a very important and present artefact to high school students in a Danish context (see also, e.g., Beck 2006, 2007; Elmeland & Kolind 2012; Frederiksen et al. 2012). The presence of beer and of the practices built up around partying and beer-drinking prompts Anna to deal with herself in new ways. This is inescapable since *not* dealing with beer-drinking may have unintended consequences, such as facing issues of social marginalization with regard to activities related to her high school life – as was already experienced by Anna in the beginning of the school year. The point is not that this (social marginalization) will necessarily happen, many other things influence Anna's life in high school, only that the invitational character of standards (which implies actively relating to them) seems a must. Whereas 'layer' (a) represents the environmental presence of beer and beer-drinking as a practice, 'layer' (d) represents the mutual negotiations going on among Anna and her high school friends concerning 'who am I' and 'who am I becoming'. Such negotiations take the form of who decides to join which parties, and who stays away; who would like to be included and who actually is included. By taking part in shared activity settings, each with their subjectivity and with their unique social situation, young people co-create shared meaningfulness of the standards that at the same time co-construct their sense of self.

Over time, the ongoing dialectics of these 'layers' implies that what counts as ecological realities (a) for Anna changes along with the changes of herself as a participating (b) person (c). The environmental presence of beer and of beer-drinking practices changes with regard to their (negotiated) invitational character (their affording). These changes of Anna's life world (concerning beer-drinking as a social standard) come along as Anna moves from being quite inexperienced with the 'tools' needed for partying to becoming a somewhat skilled participant in a party practice. By appropriating the environmental 'tools' (beer as an artefacts and beer drinking as a practice), Anna ensures for herself a safe social position much needed as a high school student. Hence, she also ensures for herself a future position in class and at the school which, again, may influence her future educational possibilities due to the social skills that she appropriates. The practice that invites and constrains Anna's behaviour, her motive orientation and her ways of relating to herself and to others is at all times the carrier of Anna's agency, both behavioural and intentional. In other words, she is the subjective carrier of subjectification by way of social standards of high school life. Anna does not seem to let go of her ideals nor of who she feels like being as a person. On the contrary, she seems quite aware of her need to find pragmatic solutions and to find her way through the alcohol culture, in a way where she 'recognizes' herself. 'Layer' (b) and (c) reflects that Anna does spend time experiencing herself as a participant (b) and dealing with the challenges that this process offers her; and she also spends time experiencing herself as a person (c), who participates in inescapable relations and activities. In this manner, her subjectivity becomes subjectified through environmental artefacts, practices and standards; but her subjectivity is not *reduced* to subjectification. For example, when Anna in February thinks that drinking a beer is okay but getting drunk and being forgetful is not, she negotiates herself as a person and she reaches conclusions about herself. In this manner, Anna both consolidates values that she feels are hers as a person, and she includes new values by guiding herself through the environmental realities. She seems to know that she must adapt to some standards since refusing to do so or being avoidant may cause her to live her life on the edge of high school activities; hence, ignoring the standards may lead to an unfortunate social position which, in the worst case, may lead to unfortunate future educational possibilities (due to social marginalization). Anna is, so to speak, a person who must change according to the timing of high school life. But, at the same time, she must remain the same person to not end up as a caricature of a high school student.

All of these dynamics are what constitute subjectified subjectivity over time, as dialectical and synthetic processes. This implies that Anna, as a person, does not simply replace one set of activities, motives, beliefs and self-understanding with another. Rather, she constantly negotiates herself with herself, and her self-development takes place as she is able to both relate to herself from a first-person perspective and experience herself as a subjective agent; and able, from a third-person perspective, to experience herself as others might see her. These processes are *dialogical* (Hermans 2001) but also, they are *ecological*. Once Anna begins to experience herself in new ways by dealing with her environment and the environmental standards, she becomes another agent in the world: she decides to do things that she did not do before; she seeks out new relationships and new social activities, etc. In this manner, Anna herself becomes a new environmental fact to others, and in the way in which they respond to her, she influences both her environment and herself; in this case, she adds actively to sustaining a culture among high school students of partying and drinking beer. These processes are ongoing and dialectical; this implies that they may take other directions with other persons and with other/new environmental realities (which are manifold). This is Anna's life in her 'niche' and in relation to her ecological realities. As a person, she becomes a synthesis of the process and of her personal development in her unique circumstances, with her ontogenetic background and visions for the future. Based on the same ecological and dynamic model for understanding the development of self, one may find other unique developmental possibilities in other young people.

Diversities of the Development of Self

To unfold this point, let us take a brief look at Carla. Evidently Carla's way into high school life differs from Anna's, and so (apparently) do her priorities, and (I propose) most likely her self-understanding[7]. In the beginning of the school year, Carla initiates a social gathering that excludes a lot of the people in the class. She belongs to a group of girls in the class who wear a lot of make-up, talk about guys and partying and who, from an outside perspective, appear a lot more engaged with an 'adult life agenda' than the group of girls that Anna hangs out with. Carla remains very oriented towards the social life at school and has had the whole class over for a party which has seemingly

---

[7] We do not have a first-person-account from Carla, so the analysis is based solely on observations and second-hand accounts (through Anna).

caused her to change her way of inviting for – and reproducing – a practice of partying and beer-drinking. Other classmates' way of behaving at the party was at the same time childish and offensive to Carla. This brought about a new orientation for her in relation to her classmates *and* the practice of beer-drinking. From Carla's remarks in June ('when will we all see each other again?' and 'I am not throwing another party') it becomes clear that Carla has maintained her directedness and engagement with the social practice of partying, as something meaningful (and something that needs to be organized). Yet simultaneously, her remarks reflect a change as well – a change in layer (a) (her way of relating to the practice of partying), and the layer (d) (her way of actively negotiating the standard of *how* to party. When we compare (or contrast) Carla's actions in June with her actions in October, where she selectively invited girls from the class for a party, a change in her way of relating to – and engaging in – the practice of partying (and beer-drinking) is evident. This implies that the way in which Carla has been subjectified by others, in the high school practice, has changed her sense of herself as someone who practises beer-drinking in a specific way (with specific persons). Her subjectified subjectivity at the end of the school year (June) demonstrates a different openness and orientation towards the class as a joint group (compared to earlier in the school year). This change in (a) Carla's way of relating to the social practice of beer-drinking, and (b) her experience of herself as a participant, is connected to the ongoing negotiation process (d), where Carla, just as Anna, is influenced by what others (and each other) contribute with in terms of establishing, challenging, appropriating and negotiating standards of, e.g., a joint social practice of beer-drinking (and parties) in high school. This reflects how change does not only happen to, and with, Anna, but also to, and with, Carla, concurrently; and that these changes are interrelated processes of becoming high school students, as participants in a joint social practice that is continuously evolving. Even though the girls participate in the same activity settings, e.g., at school, or at a party, they do so with different social situations (Hedegaard 2012), reflecting distinctive ontogenetic histories and motive orientations, that over time, seem to overlap in relation to the meaning and practice (the how-to) of social life outside school hours. The reason for briefly bringing Carla into the analysis is to better demonstrate how these processes of change – in relation to self, other, artefacts and standards – are best understood as 'aufgehoben' relations. This, in turn, emphasizes the continuous, yet unvoiced, social negotiation and (re)production of collective ideality in relation to concrete practices pertaining to high school life.

Interrelated Collective Negotiations of Meaning

Though we might be left with the impression that the only standard of importance in Anna's class relates to social participation and the practice of beer-drinking and partying, this is far from the case. As we saw in an earlier chapter, other ongoing negotiations among Anna and her close girlfriends concern, e.g., how to understand oneself in the light of discussions and practices related to eating and (healthy) food;

a concern partly fuelled by, and connected to, the high school's use of a health test in gym class that also installed numerical values as means of self-assessment. And there are numerous standards at play, of which some are more outspoken and persistent than others. The ones I include here have been selected as they appear to be of importance or significance to the specific young people who took part in research project, here Anna. And what becomes evident when taking part in practice is the way in which a multitude of standards co-exist, intertwine and are negotiated in ongoing flows of conversation and activities. Diving into practice, it is possible to deepen our understanding of the complex developmental dynamics that unfold among the young people, and how the way in which collective meaning is co-constructed relates to multiple aspects of practice in interwoven manners. The co-construction and ongoing negotiation of meaning relating to the standard of social participation (in this case beer-drinking and partying) co-exist with – and is closely connected to – the negotiation of the meaning of other standardizing aspects of practice; I will here draw in the example of grades, as it was – actually – part of the conversation from June that was outlined above. As we recall from the excerpts presented above, the conversation between Anna and Carla in June took place after the annual test in history. Now let us contextualize this conversation a bit:

As Anna and I arrive at the school, it is fairly quiet. You can sense the deep concentration, and the atmosphere vividly brings back the bodily sensation of pre-examination jitters that I recognize from my own time in high school; part excitement and part profound nervousness. We find the right room and take a seat in the couches outside. While we wait, a boy from Anna's class, Rasmus, exits the examination room. He exhales loudly, as from relief, and walks around restlessly while waiting to be called back in for his grade. Finally, the door opens, and he is let back in. Anna looks impatiently at the door, while we wait for his return. He comes over and sits down; he got a 4 (equivalent of a D[8]), for which he is rather satisfied, he says, although he does not appear to be in terms of his body language. The next person to enter the exam room is Beatrice – Anna will be next.

Anna says that she will be contented with the grade 7 (a C). We wait.

Beatrice gets a 12 (an A) and is very happy. She is one big smile and loudly shares her grade with everyone around, including the fact that she has received nothing but 12 in all of her exams and tests this year. She calls her mother to share the news. Anna is up next, and she is fairly relaxed about it.

When Anna reappears from the exam room, it is difficult for her to assess how it went (while waiting for the grade). Meanwhile, Carla has arrived.
Carla: *But of course, you'll get a 12!* (she says to Anna)
Anna: *Ah, I'm not sure about that, but it went okay. I mean, it's more like a dialogue. Like in class, really ...* (she says while smiling).

---

[8] The grade 4 in the Danish grading system translates to a D in the British/European system.

Beatrice: *Yeah, it's kinda like in class*
Anna: *... rather down to earth, really* (she says whole taking a seat in the couch)

Anna is called back in to get her grade. She is gone for a while, which Carla, who's up next, does not fail to notice, a bit anxiously:

Carla: *Oh, what's taking them so long?!*
Beatrice: *It's probably alright ... they take the time to explain the grade and give you feedback, so ...* (she says reassuringly).
Anna reappears and Carla immediately asks: *Did you get a 12?*
Anna raises her arms and makes a dismantling gesture: *I officially have summer holidays now. It's like that ... No need to cheer! ... I got a 4!*, she says clearly disappointed and somewhat surprised, as if she is still processing the result herself.
Carla: *But hey, that's not bad! Congratulations!* (she says in a very direct tone)
Anna: *It's quite alright. They said I wasn't thorough enough with my sources and stuff ...* (she explains, still with the surprise resonating in her tone of voice, as if she is mostly trying to make sense of it herself, while telling the others).
Anna walks a bit down the corridor to call her mother (without disturbing), and from her body language and tone of voice with her mother, she is clearly disappointed of the grade. Meanwhile, Carla enters the exam room.

A little while later, Carla is done with the exam. '*It went fucking bad! No doubt I will get a 2 (which means that you just pass (an E). It just didn't fly ...,* ' she proclaims, before she re-enters the exam room for her grade. A few minutes later, she exists, arms in the air and clearly relieved: '*I got a fucking 4 and now I am on summer break, and it is absolutely awesome!*'

Beatrice, Carla, and Anna sit around for a little while and talk about the exam situation and their impressions of the teacher and external examiner. '*But mine was a clear-cut 4, and not a 'weak' 4, and I'm really happy about that,*' Carla says. '*I don't know about my 4, but fuck it, it doesn't matter. Now it's the summer holidays,*' Anna says.

'*Are you satisfied with grade?,*' Carla asks in a caricature voice, imitating her father. '*Will he ask you that?,*' Anna asks. '*Yes, he did after the English test as well ... because I used to only get 12 (A) or 10 (B+) in elementary school, and now I got a 4 in English,*' Carla says and continues, again imitating her father: '*But are you really satisfied with a 4?*' '*Yes, dad, I am,*' she says, pretending to answer as herself. '*He just doesn't get it,*' she says and looks a little lost. '*I'm considering whether or not to write my sister* (about my grade),' Beatrice says and continues: '*but she has a way of getting annoyed with me when I get good grades, and I don't really know why ... ?*' '*How odd!*' Carla says with a puzzled face. '*And what about your mom, Beatrice?*' Anna asks, indicating that Beatrice might want to call her mother. '*Yeah, my mom was like: 'Can't you for once get a 4, just to try it, so you know how it feels?*'' Beatrice imitates her mother. '*Really?!*' Carla says, with a surprised look.

Evidently, the girls are not only negotiating social participation as standard, but concurrently the meaning of grades and how to relate to them. From their conversation, we see how grades are not uniform signifiers of academic achievement or skills, but rather enmeshed with parental expectations, potential sibling rivalry, social dynamics of positions and hierarchies in the class, as well as expectations to oneself (and thus the stabilization or confirmation of self-understanding, across time and different educational settings). The grade 4 can mean various things to various persons (at various times): it is a disappointment to Anna (who is expected, and expecting, to get something higher), but a relief to Carla, who is expecting a lower grade. It can also be 'a clear-cut 4', which is better than a 'weak 4', which is something to consider afterwards without necessarily knowing. Also, we might speculate, bringing up 'a clear-cut 4' may both serve as means of positioning vis-à-vis others (who also got a 4), just as it might serve as a way to make the grade seem better than it is (as part of making sense of it). From Carla and Anna's exchange about receiving the grade 4, we get the impression that Anna's disappointment is somewhat diminished after Carla's reaction which is relief and a focus on the summer holidays as the most important. From their respective – and distinctive – ways of relating to the grade as an environmental feature (a), they co-experience themselves (b), their own experiencing (c) and the other, while negotiating the meaning of the grade (d). Their interplay illustrates how their different social situations play into the variations in their initial reactions (and experiences of both the grade and their own reactions), despite the fact that the grade, on paper, means the same.

An additional feature that comes to play a part in their ongoing negotiations of meaning (and possible self-understandings in the light of their grades) relates to what we could call an 'absent present' in this situation (see von Uexküll 1982; Bang 2009a): the expectations and opinions of their families. Anna, Carla and Beatrice are, very directly, drawing reference to their family members in their joint process of making sense of the grades and their meaning, in the light of the current situation (that they now have summer break). Anna and Beatrice call their mothers right away to share their grades, and both Carla and Beatrice draw their expectations of the family members' reactions into the conversation, as imitations. This opens to a doubleness for both Carla and Beatrice. Although Carla was relieved of her grade when she originally got it, her expectation of her father's reaction allows, and perhaps calls for, other reflections about herself and who she is becoming. Or we could say that she is relating to herself (level c) on a more existential level than just that of experiencing the grade. Or, in this case, experiencing the grade and herself receiving it (levels a and b) cannot be separated from an expected third-person perspective on her (from her father); and here we sense a critical stance, a potential disappointment or perhaps a worry of the direction that her grades are taking.

For Beatrice, it is hard to sense a disappointment, as she received the highest possible grade; however, she brings forward how her mother manages to problematize her consistently good grades and encourage to get a lower grade for a change. Also, Beatrice hesitates to share the news with her sister, as her sister tends to get angry with her when she gets a good grade, and although Beatrice does not know why this is the case, one could speculate that sibling rivalry or some sort of jealousy was at play.

Beatrice's references to her family could serve in two distinct, but perhaps interrelated, ways in the given situation: (1) it could be a way for Beatrice to tone down her good grade and approximate the feelings of Carla and Anna, which would be a directedness towards the collective meaning, and (2) as a nuancing of how good grades are not always unequivocally joyful and easy to receive. As we do not have first-person-accounts from neither Carla nor Beatrice, we can only speculate of their feelings and motives in the situation. However, what becomes evident is how the girls actively and collectively engage in meaning-making processes regarding the grades and how these processes, or negotiations, relate both to their self-understandings and to their close relations that are not present in the situation (their families, and the standards or values in the families). This again reflects the openness that characterizes Countryside High as a school and demonstrates how openly disappointments and complex feelings are shared with one another, even though the three girls are not necessarily the closest of friends.

Interconnected Subjective and Collective Processes of Transformation

The argument that has been presented in this chapter concerns the need to think along the lines of dialectical movements and relations between people, artefacts, places and meanings, in order to comprehend the developmental processes on an individual level. Most often developmental changes on an individual level are understood primarily in individual ways; as something occurring *within* an individual. However, comprehending the ways in which change is brought about as processes of Aufhebung, or as subjectified subjectivity – as synthetic interplays of self, others and the environment – seems far more productive, and as a way to regard individual development from a wholeness perspective.

The chapter accentuated Anna's development over the course of the school year, in relation to a particular standard of social participation and beer-drinking, and we saw how Anna, as well as the standard she was relating to, changed over time, as micro-genetic movements and negotiations with herself and others. Following the analysis, we cannot conclude that Anna's development is comprehensible as *adaptation* to standards set forth by, e.g., Carla, since Carla's way of relating to the social practice of beer-drinking and parties (and herself) is also changing (in relation to, e.g., Anna's way of relating and participating) over the course of time. In that sense, the developmental 'situation' consists of numerous people's simultaneous co-construction of social spaces of participation and ways of relating and can be seen as a result of an ongoing process of negotiation of standards among young people. To take it a step further, the standards are not being negotiated apart from other co-existing standards (as we saw in relation to the meaning of grades), but rather closely connected to and interwoven into the very same practices, and even as part of the same conversations. Nor are they only being negotiated locally among the girls, in the concrete situations presented in this chapter, but also with people in other places, as we, e.g., saw with Anna's grandmother, just as other people's standards are drawn into the negotiations among the girls in their shared attempts at meaning-making (as we saw with the references to, e.g., Beatrice's sister and Carla's father). Hence, negotiations are not delimited by space-time constrictions, but seem to move dynamically across activity settings, relational contexts and institutional practices. Furthermore, bigger cultural and structural levels also play a part in the sense- and meaning-making processes that take place, since beer (and beer-related practices) or grades (as artefacts) are already imbued with societal meaning and expectation, which is historically and societally created and reproduced (e.g. beer-drinking is an integrated and legitimate part of high school life, as teachers sell beers to the students at high school parties, and the meaning of grades is continuously emphasized, also formally, as they determine possibilities to enter other educational settings, such as university).

In terms of the invitational (negotiated) character of standards – the affordings of standards – both Anna and Carla change their motive orientations, or their motive hierarchies, and themselves, throughout the school year, and thus at the same time respond to standards, and actively negotiate and (re)produce them. Or we could say that standards, through their embeddedness in the high school practice, afford certain 'behaviour' from the young people, as a way of becoming high school students, while the young people are continuously co-creating the practice themselves (including standards). This in turn underlines why a wholeness approach to developmental processes is necessary and needs to encompass the complexities of people in their concrete and situated existential life-worlds, inseparable from concrete social, material and historical meanings. The proposition here is that a model of dialectical-ecological analysis (Pedersen & Bang 2016a) may assist us in such endeavours, and that it has the potential to comprehend developmental processes of self, in ways that insist on seeing the individual as a person-environment synthesis; as *subjectified subjectivity*.

Note:

I am deeply thankful to Associate Professor Jytte Bang for co-developing the theoretical propositions and analysis presented in this chapter with me. See original work published in *Integrative Psychological and Behavioral Science* (Pedersen & Bang 2016a).

7

Negotiating Self within a Multitude of Invitations and Possibilities

In the high school setting, young people encounter a myriad of standards, inviting them to behave in certain ways, prioritize some activities over others, adopt specific values or participate in specific ways. In other words, the high school setting presents standards of how one *ought* to be, to its students. As we saw in Chapter 1, some of these standards are discursively very dominant, e.g., that one must party every weekend, and/or be an academic achiever. There is a tendency to assume that when starting high school, young people become 'high school students' in a universal sense, which entails a potential negligence of the variations in the ontogenetic history, self-understanding and directedness. Discourses on high school students often appear to assume that all students have the same preconditions and orientations when starting high school, providing them with the same possibilities for meeting (and adapting to) new standards.

However, standards are seldom fixed entities that are merely taken over and enacted by persons. On the contrary, in order for, as an example, beer-drinking and participating in beer-drinking practices to become (and continuously to be reproduced as) a standard, it requires that young people should continuously recognize *that* standard as meaningful; and for this to happen, the meaningfulness of the standard needs to have a connection to other aspects of the individual person's life. This implies that for us to conceive of a notion of standards, we need to include a *subjective* level: the meaningfulness of standards (as any other feature of the environment) to any given person depends on the subjectivity and how she/he has been subjectified in the course of ontogenetic development. This subjective aspect of standards further implies that the manner in which (and the extent to which) meaning is added to and deducted from standards in the daily lives of young people not only relates to, but is highly dependent on, the concrete persons who engage in these negotiation processes. Therefore, the way in which young people relate to standards is by no means arbitrary, but is rather embedded in and influenced by the ontogenetic history as well as the intentionality of the person.

In the previous chapter the influence of environmental standards on the development of self was explored, with a specific focus on standards regarding beer-drinking as a social practice connected to youth life in high school. In the chapter a dialectical-ecological model of subjectified subjectivity was proposed, and it was argued how a concept of subjectified subjectivity could account for the inbuilt dialectics in subjectivity; at the same time a subjective experience of being-me-in-the-world, all the while reflecting the way the person is subjectified by her/his surroundings, e.g., as a high school student, a daughter, a gymnastics teacher. In the previous chapter it was explored how Anna's self-understanding changed in relation to beer and the practice of beer-drinking, throughout her first year at high school. Thus, focus was primarily on the dynamic relation between Anna, beer (as artefact), and the social practice connected to beer-drinking.

As I have explored so far, a youth life environment (e.g. at high school) is full of various degrees of invitations and demands, affordances and possibilities. However, I will argue that young people do not perceive all these invitations and demands equally, just as not all standards are 'appropriated' or approximated by the person. Instead, I will propose that young people *navigate* their way through the social space of high school; not in structureless ways, but rather based on their ontogenetic history and thus their self-understanding and directed at something – hence a navigation constituted by a concurrent backwards- and forwards directedness; by past experiences of self and world, and by hope, wishes and concrete goals for the future. This implies that what become meaningful invitations (to be acted on) in a high school setting are co-dependent on the ontological history; and not only on the strength with which a certain invitation or demand is presented in the environment. At the same time, the ontological history and the self-understanding are also dynamic; they continuously change over time.

Let us return to the model:

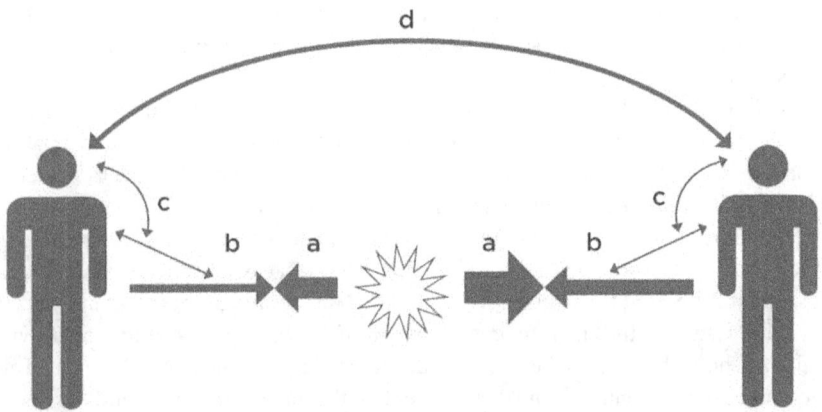

Figure 7.1 The dialectical-ecological model of subjectified subjectivity (Pedersen & Bang 2016a).

a) The basic person-environment (perceiving and acting) is both the source for, and an outcome of, subjectified subjectivity. The perceiving-acting dynamics are wordly (practical, social and object-related).
b) Each person always-already co-experiences the self, participating in ongoing and changing person-environment reciprocities – and these co-experiences of selves influence and co-produce the dynamics of the basic reciprocities.

c) Each person also always-already co-experiences the self-relating to the object – Existential-societal dimension.
d) The persons 'negotiate' the meaningfulness of an a, c, c synthesis as part of the synthesis. A negotiation of standards.

In Figure 7.1, we see the totality of the situation, where a person is constantly relating to both artefacts, social others and her/himself, in the sense of experiencing her/himself as 'an experiencing person'. At the same time, we see how the person is engaged in a constant exchange and negotiation process with other persons in the environment, about meaningfulness and standards, and in that process constantly engage in the (re)production of societal conditions (for her/himself and others) (see also Pedersen & Bang 2016a).

In this chapter, I will focus on how a person's self-understanding becomes an important navigation tool in the high school setting or, in relation to the model (see Figure 7.2), how subjectivity influences the meaning of standards, and of the subjectification processes that occur. Here, we could say, with a reference to Vygotsky's (1994) point about the environment always being a specific relation between person and her/his environment, that the ambition in this chapter is to explore the meaning ascribed to the environment from the perspective of the individual. Hence analytically placing a magnifying glass on 'the personal side' of the person-environment dialectic. To approximate subjectivity even further (than in the previous chapter), the aim of this chapter is thus to explore and unfold the manner in which these negotiation processes (of meaning) occur, as *mediated by subjectivity*. I will argue that the dynamics of standards are inseparably connected to the way in which concrete persons engage with artefacts and each other in their everyday lives; based on their (constantly evolving) self-understanding.

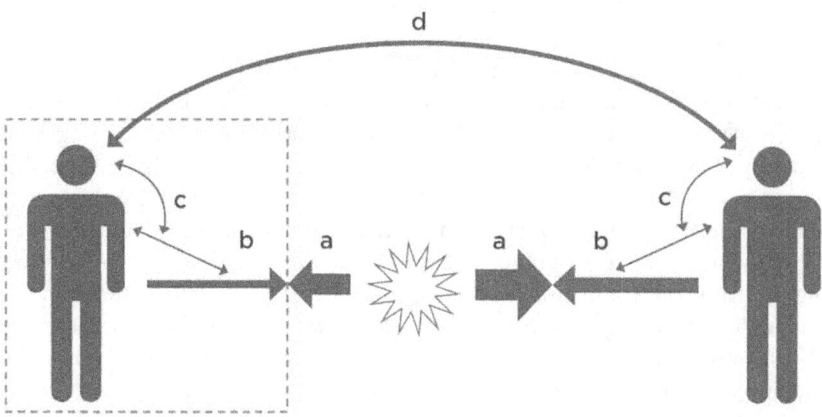

Figure 7.2 The dialectical-ecological model of subjectified subjectivity (Pedersen & Bang 2016a). Analytical emphasis on the 'personal side' of the person-environment dialectic.

The chapter explores the lifeworld of Peter, with an emphasis on his navigating through the standards he encounters in the high school setting, and the numerous ways in which he engages in negotiation processes along the way. To analytically unfold Peter's developmental dynamics further on a subjective level, I will consider how 'self' may also carry affordance quality, and how we may notice developmental change as small dynamic alterations in a person's directedness.

The Affordance Quality of Self

Critically inspected, the dialectical-ecological model of subjectified subjectivity could assume that the person has just 'landed' in the situation that the model depicts. This is of course not the case, and it needs to be specified how the ontogenetic and socially embedded character of a person's lifeworld influences the model. As we recall from the introductory chapter, one of Elder's four principles is that of 'human agency'. According to Elder (1998), human agency refers to the fact that individuals construct their life-course through the choices and actions they take within the constraints of history and social circumstances. This, for once, implies integrating a focus on the active participation of the individual in our understanding of (a) the developmental processes of the individual and (b) the development of practice as a continuous and dialectical relation. Also, it implies regarding developmental processes as dynamic auto-generative processes (see also Engelsted 1983, 1989), which challenges the widespread understanding of development as something that occurs 'on its own' mainly due to biological, and more specifically (in the case of young people), hormonal changes in the body, or, as the consequence of an appropriation of norms, as socialization (as an automatism). An emphasis on subjectivity implies human agency as well as regarding the person a *historical becoming*, who is *always* conducting her/his life, dealing with particular conditions and pursuing various and changing motives, and by doing so transforming the environment.

If we look at the person on a subjective level, Bang (2009b) proposes three different aspects of the human lifeworld to have affordance quality: (1) the environment – or artefact aspect (in accordance with Gibson), (2) an aspect of 'social others' and (3) one of 'self'. She suggests that these three aspects in combination account for the activity setting of the child at school, and hence she promotes an ecological comprehension of the child's developmental situation that, indirectly, stands opposed to more traditional accounts of developmental (solely emphasizing strictly individual aspects, or the effect of socializing efforts on the child, reducing development into a question of adaptation). In her analysis of the activity setting, Bang first examines how concrete artefacts enable and promote specific activities in the classroom setting. The artefacts and the way they are used in the classroom represent reifications of cultural understandings of how learning is facilitated and occurs and can be seen as a result of historical developments within the school practice.

Therefore, an artefact in a classroom not only affords, for instance, write-on-ability (the whiteboard) or point-to-ability (a world map), but at the same time ways in which children and teachers are expected to engage with the artefacts (and each other) in the given practice, all the while representing cultural values and norms (of what is taking place in a classroom setting and what one is expected to learn). In several places in Gibson's 1986 publication, where he introduces affordances, 'social others' are seen as a great source of affordances, however without further elaboration (for *how*) (see also Pedersen & Bang 2016b). According to Bang (2009b:172): *'the child learns about "who am I" in the relation to social others in the particular institutional setting.'* Through the child's participation in practice, Bang argues, the child learns about – as well as negotiates – her position in relation to others all the while she experiences it. Over time, this forms more generalized experiences of 'who am I' in relation to others. This implies that a generalized experience of 'who I am' is continuously negotiated as part of the social interactions in which a person participates, as we also saw with Anna's development. And it further indicates how a person's self-understanding is concurrently mediated by artefacts, social others and the up-until-now developed self-understanding. As Bang (2009b:175) writes:

> *In this sense, the child is not only the centre of agency, she also experiences her agency (first-person perspective) from the side of the possible and available cultural positions (third-person perspective) during the interactions with social others. One might say, therefore, that the child also inhabits an agent position in relation to herself.*

Hence, self-understanding reflects a collected knowledge of 'who I am' in relation to social others, to artefacts and practices: with specific capabilities, preferences and a collected history of actions and action potentials. This influences the manner in which a person perceives the world, and concrete social spaces, as possibilities for action, and it influences the intentionality that is developed; the general directedness of the person.[1] As we shall see in this chapter, self-understanding becomes an important navigation tool for Peter in relation to how standards are met (and managed) in the high school setting, and in that sense, one could argue that there is a certain affordance quality to self-understanding.

---

[1] A similar comprehension is proposed by Hundeide (2005), who considers the person to always be in an existential position from where the action possibilities are perceived concretely on the basis of previous experiences and knowing oneself as an agent.

Intentionality as a Dynamic Ecological Relation

Through participation with others, the person is introduced to the general expectations and values present in a given activity setting; however, an analysis limited to the possible agent-positions in an activity setting carries the risk of remaining slightly functional and would, as such, not differ much from a Gibsonian analysis, as we would still be missing a comprehension of the person as an intentional agent. Hence, to better comprehend the manner in which agency is enacted, we need to connect it with the *directedness* of the person; the intentionality and motive-orientation.

Activities are never without direction, never unmotivated (Leontjev 2002; Minken 2002; Aboulafia, Hansen & Bang 2003). As we have already seen, young people in high school continuously try to align the demands they are facing with their own motives, be it of short- or long-term perspective. At times this implies developing new motives, restructuring one's motive hierarchy, or negotiating the meaning of the demands or invitations that one faces, so that they better fit one's motives. For the purpose of this chapter, intentionality will serve as an analytical awareness that will allow me to track minor changes and transformations over time; and as such point to developmental processes in a concrete youth life setting, namely that of Peter and his lifeworld.

Intentionality means to be directed towards something; be that an object of sorts, another person, a task, or an aspiration to become or obtain something specific; it is in other words goal-directed behaviour (Leontjev 2002). According to Bertelsen (1994[2], 2003), it is formed in the process of 'reaching out' into the environment in order to satisfy one's needs[3] (thus very similar to Leontjev's understanding of a conative relation to the world. See also Engelsted (1983, 1989) for a further elaboration of this point). The intentional connectivity that arises between person and environment will:

> a) make **impressions,** meaning that the intentionality is **about** something in the environment, and that also b) release **expressions** in the way in which the person

---

[2] Bertelsen's work (which he refers to as anthropological psychology) seems largely inspired by cultural-historical activity theory; however, he adds a more existential-phenomenological aspect (compared to Leontjev) by introducing the notion of 'life projects'. By 'life project' Bertelsen refers to the idea that man has his life as his assignment, for which he is inspired by Sartre's notion of *la projette* and the existentialist tenet that 'l'existence précède l'essence' (see, e.g. Sartre & Elkaïm-Sartre 1946). This implies that 'the particularly human aspect' of life relates to the projects that we have *with* and *for* each other and ourselves. It is through our efforts (concrete actions and activities) to fulfil or complete these life projects that we transcend our conditions and transform the environment (or societal conditions) (Bertelsen 1994).

[3] Whereas plants are limited to a *functional connection* with the environment (as they are passive receivers of light, air and water), humans (and other animals) are also *intentionally connected* to their lifeworld or environment in the sense that they must reach out and beyond themselves to satisfy their needs. Quite similarly, Leontjev describes how humans, just as other animals as well as plants, have a vegetative physiological level, where physiological needs are satisfied without any effort (of will) (such as breathing air, or blood pumping around the body, etc.). As soon as we move beyond the level of 'automatic' (or metabolic) activity, we see a *conative relating* to the environment in the fulfilment of needs (Leontjev 2002). Leontjev divides the psyche into four levels of becoming (besides the vegetative level), starting with the sensory level, followed by the perceptual, the intellectual and the conscious level, of which only the conscious is specifically human (Leontjev 2002).

seeks out, contacts and handles this 'something' in the environment, implying that intentionality is also characterized by **intention**.

(Bertelsen 2003:98, my translation)

Here there is an inherent doubleness: intentionality can be thought of as directed *towards* something (*intentio:* a movement 'from within'), but at the same time *by* something (*intentum:* a movement 'from without') (Bertelsen 2003:99). Hence, intentionality does not refer to an 'inner' directedness alone; on the contrary, it connects the inner directedness (e.g. feeling hungry and wanting to eat) to the concrete and immediate environment (e.g. whether there is food available). As a whole, this makes 'intentionality' an ecological concept: it implies the concurrent 'directed towards' and 'directed by' something and thus connects the inner subjective 'state' or agenda with the concrete environment and its possibilities and invitational character or affordances.

The way in which standards are often referred to – as something external to concrete persons – indicates that standards are to be perceived as something working *on* persons (almost with a will of their own) or something that persons may (or may not) use or refer to in their everyday lives: working through processes of subjectification through which subjectivities are standardized (see also Busch 2011). Therefore, it is easy to analytically reproduce an axiom of immediacy (see Leontjev 1977) by drawing forth the way in which persons respond to standards in their environment. However, as I have argued thus far, the person is active in (re)producing, negotiating and altering the environment, including standards, in an ongoing exchange with the world. An understanding of standards as something working 'on' persons creates a potential division between the 'standard' and the person, as the standard becomes limited to an object of sorts, working on the individual from the outside. As such, standards easily come to represent 'external' perspectives, while the person represents 'internal' perspectives, suggesting that the person acts on needs, thoughts, and feelings that are centred in, defined, or delimited by the body. Hence, an all-too-familiar person-environment dualism would be just around the corner. In this regard, Bertelsen's conceptualization of intentionality is a productive contribution, as the 'inner' perspective, *intentio*, is always co-defined by an external component, *intentum*. If we insert 'standards' in the intentum-position we see how standards may come to be an integral part of intentionality, which means that we can surpass the dualism, as we maintain a comprehension of the individual as being connected with the environment (as inseparable from it). With this nuancing in mind – proposing intentionality to be ecologically constituted – we are able to study the more subtle, dynamic changes in motive orientation (in an individual perspective) without installing dualisms between individual and environment.

Peter; Subjective Meaningfulness and Clear Priorities

To create a starting point from which to analyse Peter's ways of subjectively relating to standards (and his eco-niche at Northside High), I will begin by presenting the part of Peter's lifeworld that relates to his family and his ontogenetic history. This has the threefold purpose of (1) connecting Peter with concrete environmental conditions that extends beyond high school (an ecological comprehension of Peter), (2) providing insight into Peter's self-understanding, as it appears before he starts high school and (3) demonstrating how Peter is subjectified as sensitive in the family practice (as this will influence his participation in the high school practice). The first part will provide a description of Peter to account for his self-understanding and the activities that he is primarily engaged in, in his daily life. From there I will proceed to explore how Peter is subjectified as sensitive, and what this means to him.

Peter is sixteen years old and lives with his parents (and their cat and Peter's pet snake) in a three-room apartment in a suburban area, north of Copenhagen. Peter's father is a carpenter and works on the other side of Copenhagen; he bikes back and forth to work, most of the year, which is a rather substantial bike ride of approximately 35 kilometres each way. Other than that, he is very passionate about baking buns, and according to both Peter and Peter's mother, these are the best buns in the world and something that he evidently takes great pride in. Peter's mother works as a kindergarten teacher in a local kindergarten. On the side, she has a private practice offering healing, coaching and reflexology, and in the long run her dream is to be able to combine that work with a part-time position in the kindergarten.

In our first email-contact, when Peter is still in elementary school, he provides the following description of himself:

In my own opinion I am always happy, or at least I try to be. I find that life is best that way ☺. *I will describe myself as a caring person as I actually find great joy in helping others. Whether it would be with math homework or just a tip on life in general is not so important. But to be able to help people means a lot to me. This of course doesn't mean that I am never pissed off, or that I always agree to help people with their homework; everything in moderation!*

Peter's room is in one of the apartment's two en-suite living rooms. It has a big closet, a desk in the middle of the room, a one-person bed, a digital piano with a small stool and a small table carrying a terrarium with his snake. Peter is contemplating selling the snake to save up money to buy a real piano. The walls are decorated by four guitars, and music is clearly his great passion:

When I am not at school or burdened by homework, I play a lot of music and I will also have music as my priority in high school.

(email correspondence)

Music is a priority in his spare-time, as he likes to sit and play guitar or piano in his room. He also takes lessons and spends his money on new instruments and gear. As he writes in the email, he has prioritized music in high school and will be attending the music line.

Peter is an only child, however, according to his mother; he is very close to his cousins – as if being an only child is somehow problematic. Peter does not seem to mind being an only child, so it appears to be more a concern of his mother's, than an actual problem for him. He presents as a self-assured person, who is very comfortable with his life situation. He openly says that he does not have many close friends, which is not problematic for him, but rather a consequence of his own choice. Prior to starting high school, he explains this to me:

> *I like my own company a lot if I can put it like that. Not to be smug or anything, but ahem ... I was never one of those who needed to hang out with someone after school every day. I usually just like to go home and watch a bit of TV and play some music or something like that. I also have kind of had a need to do that. Or else I 'go completely flat'* (burn out). *It doesn't take much really. I easily feel worn out.*

Peter is used to spending time alone and even prefers his own company (as opposed to being social). He has been attending a private school in another city, which means that he spends 30 minutes each way with public transport (which, in a Danish setting, is quite a lot). Consequently, he does not have many friends in the neighbourhood. He will be attending the local high school, which is just a ten-minute walk from where he lives, but seeing that he has attended a private school further away, the number of people he knows, who will be attending the same high school as him, is rather limited.

From the initial encounters with Peter and his parents, it is clear that Peter is very comfortable in his own company and prefers to have, as well as *needs* to have, a lot of time to himself. His subjectivity reflects an ontogenetically developed meaningfulness related to the need of spending time alone, closely linked to his family practice and its subjectification processes, as we shall see next.

A Sensitive Child

During my first visit to Peter's home, I am told by his parents that Peter has always been a *sensitive child*. This information is passed on with the greatest of ease and with Peter present and consenting; obviously a fully accepted subjectification of Peter, which seems to be completely integrated in his self-understanding (as subjectified subjectivity). This co-construction of Peter as a sensitive person – and here I mean to acknowledge the interplay of Peter's way of being-in-the-world with, e.g., his priorities and needs for time alone, and his parents' understanding of him (and associated actions) as sensitive – is reflected in several aspects in his life world. Firstly, in his parents' choice of school for him; he moved to a private school in another suburb that they found better suited for him than the nearby local school. This necessitated a daily travelling time of one hour in total and implied that his geographical basis for establishing friendships has been rather far from home, considering his age. As his hobbies and preferred activities outside school have always been directed at activities that were easily pursued individually, such as learning to play musical instruments, the basis for establishing and maintaining friendships in his local community has been limited. At this point in time, one can only speculate as to what extent the lack of local community integration has contributed to a preference for activities that were primarily individual; in any case, Peter seems very well-grounded in his current situation and the way his everyday life is structured. Secondly, the sensitivity subjectification is deeply embedded in the family practice, also on a practical level. As mentioned, Peter's father bakes on a weekly basis to ensure that there are home-baked buns for Peter to take to school.

(An afternoon after school, at home)

Peter and I are in the kitchen, and Peter's father joins us. '*I think I may have promised some of your buns to someone*', Peter says to his father while nodding towards me. Peter tells his father how I got jealous at school because he was always bringing these delicious looking buns. His father laughs and says that then he better go and bake some. He goes to the bedroom and returns with a bowl full of dough that has been rising in a warm spot for a couple of hours already.

We all hang around in the small kitchen while Peter's father starts kneading the dough. He is using expensive biodynamic flour and at some point, he adds a white liquid. Peter asks what it is and his father answers that it is a mix of vitamins and minerals that he adds, so Peter can 'grow big and strong and have strong legs'. Peter says that his gym teacher will probably appreciate this effort and laughs. His father agrees. He then splits the dough in two portions; in one half he mixes raisins and in the other half he mixes sunflower seeds. My facial expression reveals an impending question, and he explains that Peter likes raisins while he himself prefers sunflower seeds, so he is making half of each. Luckily, Peter's mother does not have a preference, he says. I want to know if it is always him doing the baking, which he confirms. It started out with rye bread, but Peter preferred white bread and that began the quest for finding a recipe for a white bread that was still good and sufficiently nutritious.

From this glimpse of the current baking practice, we can see how Peter is subjectified as someone who needs extra minerals and vitamins, despite the fact that he is sixteen and not a small child, and for whom special recipes are developed to meet his specific needs and preferences. It does not suffice to buy ordinary bread, or to bake by ordinary recipes, or to use standard supermarket flour. This practice indicates the parents' way of caring for Peter. However, care and awareness of the needs of the other is not a one-way practice in the family, as the next excerpt will show:

Coming home from school, we let ourselves into the apartment. '*No one's home*', Peter says. From the bedroom Peter's father answers: '*yes, there is*' and he comes out to say hello. '*Oh, I had forgotten that today was your day off*', Peter says. '*Go have a look in your room. I have made something for you*', his father says. Peter goes to his room and looks around but does not seem to notice anything new. '*What is it?*', he asks. '*You already passed it*', his father says. Peter turns around and inspects the area by the door: '*Oh … cool*'. He notices the new light switch with a dimmer that his father has installed by the door. His father turns to me: '*Yes, well, the young gentleman prefers to be able to dim the light nowadays. He says he is blinded by it otherwise* (He rolls his eyes in a teasing yet loving way). *He is after all a sensitive kid*'. Peter does not comment but looks satisfied. After a brief silence he turns to his father: '*So, did you relax today like I told you to?*' '*No, because I went to buy the switch, so I could fix this. But it is quite alright*', the father answers.

Here we see how both Peter and his father are oriented towards, and very much in tune with, the needs of the other person. This indicates a family practice in which sensitivity in general, towards the needs of the family members, is conspicuous. The well-being of one person is closely related to the well-being of the other.

The way in which Peter's parents subjectify Peter as 'sensitive' is thus twofold: on the one hand they are aware that he is a sensitive person and they are cautious to both protect him (changing schools to find a suitable one) and nourish him (adding vitamins and minerals to the buns that are baked weekly), as well as installing light dimmers in his room according to his wishes, as an awareness of his changing needs. These small gestures of care provide Peter with a very safe environment, where he clearly relaxes and can unwind. At the same time, it also serves to reproduce a subjectification of Peter as *sensitive*. This concurrent production and reproduction (in terms of subjectification) of Peter as sensitive between Peter and his parents elegantly demonstrates the nature of subjectified subjectivity; as a dynamic interplay between a person and his (in this case: relational and material) environment. Peter experiences himself as sensitive, and this *subjectified sensitivity* is thus integrated in his self-understanding. With reference to Bang (2009b), we can observe how 'sensitivity' resonates in various activity settings in the home practice, and how there is a certain affordance quality to it that is continuously reproduced as meaningful via material artefacts (the special buns, the light dimmer), social others (the parents) and self (Peter).

Projected Sensitivity

In relation to starting high school it follows from the above description of Peter that young people (as exemplified by Peter) do not start high school 'out of nowhere' or as 'empty vessels' in terms of subjectivity. Rather, subjectivity needs to be comprehended as already shaped and subjectified by, and through, past (and accumulated) experiences, which implies that the ontogenetic history of the person influences the way in which high school, as a new environmental setting, is encountered and made sense of. In Peter's case, this is reflected in the way he projects his 'subjectified sensitivity' onto his expectations for high school life, as the following excerpt will show:

> Me: *How do think it will be when you start high school, in relation to friends?*
> Peter: *How it will be? …. It will be both good and bad, I suppose. I suppose it will be okay to withdraw a bit* (based on needing time alone), *but it might also be rather annoying* (to have that need) *in the first couple of weeks. Here, I am thinking of the first weeks where you're supposed to say hello to around 350 new people, right. 'Hey, I am Peter … So, should we do something after school …* (he cuts himself off) *… ahem … No!'* (indicating that he prefers *not* to do social things after school). He laughs. *'Well, not today at least' … But I don't think it will be that bad. Let's say that I am looking more or less forward to it … The different aspects, that is …. some things more than others.*
> Me: *Right. So, what is it you are not looking so much forward to in particular?*
> Peter: *Having to say hi to 350 people. That thought doesn't appeal to me at all.*
> Me: *So, you'll feel better after a few weeks, you think?*

Peter: *Yeah, I am pretty sure of that (...) I think it requires a lot of energy to find out who it is among 350 people that you feel like hanging out with.*
Me: *Definitely*
Peter: *But I mean that is the way it is. It is an experience after all.*

Peter's self-understanding as being sensitive and needing time to himself is clearly a co-construction based on his own experience of easily feeling tired or 'burned out' (subjectivity), and his parents' way of relating to him and meeting his needs (subjectification). This will provide a challenge for him when he starts high school, as he already knows that there are expectations of social participation outside school hours that he will not be able to meet, or that will directly contradict his need for time alone (expectations he picked up, among other places, at the introduction event at the school). This implies that in addition to the subjectified sensitivity that Peter brings with him to high school, we can also observe an indication of the dynamics of his directedness towards high school. Peter is clearly guided by his experience of his needs (for relaxation, time alone); his 'intentio'. At the same time, he is aware of the potential invitational – and possibly demanding – character of high school standards (as e.g. demands and possibilities for social participation), as an 'intentum'. Yet the social demands of high school are not integrated into his directedness (as something that will guide his actions), nor reflected in his self-understanding at this point (e.g. he does not expect himself to be a participant in social events, but more relates to the exacting task of having to decline to invitations). As I shall further explore in this chapter, Peter's self-understanding and his subjectified sensitivity will largely guide his way of *navigating* through the standards of the high school practice and influence his way of prioritizing and participating in the high school setting.

Entering a New Institutional Setting

With Peter's subjectified sensitivity in mind, I will now explore his meeting with the high school to see how this *changes the dynamics* of his subjectified subjectivity. I will begin by introducing Peter's high school, Northside High, and account for the manner in which the high school presents dominant standards to new students. Just as with the description of Peter's family practice, I find it necessary to introduce Peter's high school briefly to emphasize that it is a particular high school he attends, and not just high school as an abstract institutional setting (to underline the ecological person-environment reciprocity).

Northside High: A Space of Contradictory Invitations and Standards

Peter attends Northside High, which is located in the same suburb north of Copenhagen where he lives. It is an area inhabited mainly by middle- and upper-middle-class families. As Northside High is close to Copenhagen, there are many high schools within a 10–15 km radius, and thus students have to prioritize their high school applications; Northside High has a good reputation and it a sought by many, including some who do not live close by. Peter is happy to attend this particular school, which was his first choice, as it is very close to where he lives (limits transportation time) and as it has a good music line (which enables Peter to combine his hobbies with school).

As we recall from the introduction event at Northside High from Chapter 1, the school presents a myriad of often contradictory invitations to new students, of *how* to be a high school student, or how to do youth life in a high school setting. We can list some of the invitations and expectations conveyed to new students, as they were presented by student representatives and the principal of the school:

By student representatives:

- Youth life is important!
- Participating in parties is essential (to social integration)
- You are expected to get very close with your classmates
- The school takes care of you
- Develop friendships for life!
- Develop your talents!

By the school principal:

- Manage high school life!
- Show up prepared!
- High school will take care of you
- Participate and show commitment!
- Create networks for life!
- Discover what you are good at

Firstly, it is conveyed that it is of utmost importance to *participate in the parties* and social events ('parents should expect not to see their children every weekend'). Secondly, that the school could (and maybe *should*) become the new most important arena in your life ('school before family') and thirdly, that it is important not only to follow the classes and complete high school, but to (1) *discover* and (2) *develop* your talents as well. Here there is an inbuilt assumption that one has (special) talents that need to be uncovered or discovered and nurtured and put to use. This emphasis on 'talent' clearly resonates with a timely societal awareness of the importance of pursuing individual talent, standing out, and actively using individualism to your advantage. Allow me to make a brief comparison with my own time in high school in the late 1990s: back then, the individual pursuit of (academic) talent was more likely to be regarded as over-achieving and unnecessary, also reflecting the fact that we were – back then – children of smaller generations (of the early 1980s), indicating that there would be sufficient jobs and numerous job opportunities for us, almost regardless of how well or poorly we would do in terms of education. At least that was the assumption and the projection of our future opportunities back then (needless to say that this projection did not hold!). This appears to no longer be the case in a post-financial-crisis educational setting, where the message conveyed beneath the invitation to discover and develop your talent also resonates with a fear of being left behind in the (now global) competition for (fewer) well-paid jobs; the average performance may no longer suffice, or in any case, it comes with less certitude in the pursuit of future success and happiness. Although I suspect that few high school students, teachers or parents for that matter, reflect upon the meaning of historical timing in the course of everyday life, its influence is indisputable (cf. Elder 1998, and Wartofsky 1983).

The presentation of expectations (and invitations to think oneself as a high school student in specific ways) by current students conveys a credibility and makes it easier for new students to relate, and to identify with these images of how one ought to be, or of what one can expect of high school and what high school expects of you. These expectations are validated by the principal and further expanded with regards to what, more specifically, the school expects for students to deliver: (1) to show up prepared, (2) to hand in things on time, (3) to show commitment to the classes and (4) to discover what you are good at. In addition, one is expected to *manage* everyday life, on both an academic and personal level and one should expect to be 'pushed and pulled', while 'nurtured' and 'cared for'.

Obviously, no lifeworld is free from conflicting invitations or demands; however, it is interesting how the high school presents an image of the 'successful' student as someone meeting both social standards for partying (and a particular kind of social participation) while at the same time showing up prepared, handing in on time *and* taking extra master classes (to pursue one's talent). This may be an alluring image to mirror one's future self in, however it is – perhaps – unrealistic for a majority of the young people. That this image (or perhaps more adequately, mirage) comes with an expectation that the school (as both institutional setting and concrete persons at school) should gradually replace the family as the primary care unit and the setting in which to handle the difficulties that may arise, is an interesting addition.

A comparison of Peter's subjectified sensitivity (established in the home setting), and the dominant standards of social participation (parties, kissing, friends for life) and academic engagement offers potential discrepancies or tensions. First, as just mentioned, there is a potential discrepancy between the two dominant standards (they afford different and potentially incompatible activities), and secondly there are potential tensions between Peter's subjectified sensitivity and the standards. However, the two dominant standards convey very different affordings for Peter and relate differently to his already established subjectified subjectivity (as e.g. sensitive). If we start by the standard of social participation (as in parties), it is evident from the introduction event at the school that the students are invited to be *not sensitive*, and *not* 'tied' to the home setting ('out partying', not depending on parents, etc.). This fits poorly with the subjectified sensitivity that Peter brings into the high school setting. On the other hand, the standard of academic engagement ('show up prepared', 'hand in on time', etc.) seems to provide a better fit with Peter's self-understanding and his awareness of his own need for time alone. This could indicate that the standard of academic engagement will be more easily integrated in Peter's intentionality in comparison to that of social participation. However, as already emphasized, standards are not fixed entities that are either adopted or rejected; rather, they are the result of ongoing negotiation processes. Therefore, the rest of this chapter will, in different ways, explore how Peter relates to the invitational character of standards in the high school practice, and how he negotiates their meaning, all the while trying to look out for his own interests.

Navigating the High School Setting

The following data excerpts take us through the first school year: the first excerpt is from September, the second from January and the last from May. Here we are therefore, as in the case of Anna, following Peter chronologically to get an idea of subtle changes in his motive orientation, intentionality and way of participating. The excerpts from Peter's everyday life all reflect Peter's way of relating to the invitational character of the dominant standards of social participation and of schoolwork, respectively. The purpose of the extended temporal perspective is to illuminate the (micro-genetic) transformations that occur, in terms of how the aforementioned standards are reflected in Peter's intentionality; and to track how the intentio/intentum dynamic fluctuates over time. I will begin with a data excerpt from September, where Peter and I are walking to class in the morning.

> September:
> Me: *So, did you have a nice weekend?*
> Peter: *Yeah, quite a lot of homework and then nice to catch some sleep. It was needed*
> Me: *Oh, you had a lot of homework ... with lots of hand-ins and such?*
> Peter: *Yeah, we do, and then it's just a good thing to get the hand-in over and done with Sunday already, so it's done. Then we also had a Latin translation and stuff ... .*
> Me: *Oh, you had one of those too?*
> Peter: *Yeah, and then I had to go to the living room to tell my dad to turn down the music, so I could concentrate on the Latin!*
> (a little silence)
> Me: *So, was there a party on this weekend?*
> Peter: *No ...* (he hesitates) *... or yes actually, but I kind of blew it,* he says (without sounding upset about it).
> Me: *Oh?*
> Peter: *Yeah, I thought I would just take a nap, right* (he laughs) *and then I fell asleep and didn't really wake up again that evening, so ... I was really tired. ... But I think the others had a pretty good party ... or most of them anyways.*
> Me: *Oh well, it happens ... So, what, you mean, the ones who didn't throw up or something* (had a good party)?
> Peter: *Nah, I don't think it was that bad this weekend, but it might have been ... ,* he says and shrugs.

Peter's recount of the weekend offers insight into where his intentions are directed and what he is preoccupied with. From the excerpt follows that the academic-engagement-standard is largely integrated into his intentionality (as intentum) ('get homework done in time', 'tell dad to turn down music so he can concentrate'), along with his persistent need to relax (intentio). At the same time, he is directed towards a party (and thus the invitational character of the social-participation-standard); however, his need of sleep takes over, and he misses out on the party ('I made the mistake of falling asleep'). This indicates that Peter's intentio 'weighs heavier' and is more directing for him, than the need to participate in the party (intentum), but also, it is illustrated how these are concurrently present as differently directed aspects of his intentionality. At this point in time, we are therefore left with the impression that Peter, in effect, has not really changed his priorities in terms of concrete activities, albeit the awareness of what 'the others' are doing is largely present, even though he is not taking part himself. As if he senses the importance of more actively relating to the social aspects of high school life that takes place outside the school setting. From his account that 'I kind of blew it', it is difficult to know whether he originally had the intent of attending the party, or if he merely recognizes the importance of framing it as such. However, we sense minor and very subtle dynamic movements in Peter's intentionality, albeit his motive orientation largely appears unaltered. We also recall how Peter, before starting high school, was anticipating a certain pressure to participate in social events that he would want to decline.

Jumping forward a few months, it is January, and a one-week winter break is just around the corner. Peter and I are waiting in the hallway for a class to start:

January:
We start talking about the winter break: Peter plans to spend the week 'doing nothing', relaxing and having some actual time to 'muck out' his room, as he puts it. He finds that he has no energy for this on an average weekday. It is always the same routine, he says: '*school, home, relax a bit, do homework, eat, relax a bit more, sleep*'. He is also contemplating getting ahead on his homework during the break – perhaps. He seems very content with the prospect of a week without plans.

A lot of the other first-year students from Peter's school are going to Prague for a week. You hear people talking about it during the breaks at school, in the hallway, and in class. It appears to be a big thing, and some mention that there will be around 10,000 high school students from Denmark participating in total (it is the same trip that was mentioned at Southside High, among Lisa's friends). It appears that everyone from Peter's class is going except Peter and a girl, Rebecca, who happens to wait around for class right next to us. However, they have very different reasons for not attending the trip: to Peter, the trip is not appealing at all; it does not interest him. He prefers to relax, he says. For Rebecca, on the contrary, the reason relates to her afterschool job at the local bakery where she cannot find a replacement to cover her shifts. She depends on her job for earning money to finance the partying, and to buy clothes etc. But unlike Peter, she is absolutely devastated about not going, as she feels that she will be missing out of one of the most important social events of the year.

Here, around halfway into the school year, Peter's conduct of everyday life and general motive orientation has not changed much: he alternates between home and school, and between doing homework and relaxing. However, there is a change in relation to the social life at school. Whereas earlier we could see social life reflected in Peter's intentionality, now it appears *almost non-existent* in terms of significance. Peter's way of relating (or lack of relating) to the trip to Prague is contrasted by Rebecca, who is devastated about not going, indicating that she clearly has a different directedness towards certain parts of youth life in high school than Peter. This excerpt thus shows how Peter's self-understanding appears to be predominantly informed by the subjectified sensitivity (grounded before starting high school) rather than by the subjectification of social participation that Peter encounters at high school. At the same time, the subjectification related to being an academically engaged student seems to be highly integrated into his self-understanding at this point; homework is clearly integrated into his daily routine ('relax, homework, relax'). This suggests that the standard of academic achievement has worked to not only *solidify*, but also *magnify* its importance and meaningfulness to him.

We see the same tendency reflected towards the end of the school year. In the situation depicted below, we are in music class where Peter and his classmate Oliver are rehearsing a song together for the upcoming exam. We have the small rehearsing room to ourselves:

May:
Peter and Oliver pick up their guitars and start rehearsing the song 'House of the Rising Sun', which was assigned to them for ensemble playing for the exam. They are both rather skilled guitar players, and it is mostly the singing part that is challenging them.

After the first take, Peter says with a content tone of voice: '*Well, that went pretty well, actually!*' The boys take a break from rehearsing and start talking about the upcoming exam, when Oliver suddenly changes the subject: '*Say, Peter, why weren't you at Maria's barbecue thing on Sunday?*' he wants to know. '*Oh, it was just a bit too much you know ... I hadn't finished reading my book yet* (a mandatory reading assignment for Danish class) *and I kind of also had to clean up my room and stuff.*' Peter says. Oliver shrugs and nods his head in recognition of the answer, then picks up on the topic (of the homework) and they continue talking about the books they are reading.

In this situation, Oliver confronts Peter with not attending a barbecue at Maria's place; an event that the whole class was invited for. Peter answers in a straightforward way that '*it was too much*' and that he '*had to finish some homework*'. There are no excuses or circumlocutions to make it sound better; it is formulated from a different – and more securely grounded – *subjective stance* than the one we saw in the beginning of the school year (where not attending a party was 'a mistake'). The standard of academic engagement is fully integrated in Peter's intentionality alongside his need for rest that is unaltered. The competing standard of participation in social life outside school is, on the other hand, disregarded as being irrelevant in terms of intentionality (and self-understanding): it no longer appears to be reflected in Peter's directedness. This implies a synthesis of the subjectified sensitivity that characterized Peter prior to starting high school, and the subjectifications tied to being an academically engaged student that Peter has encountered in the high school setting. This forms the basis of his current subjective stance, where he appears at ease with his way of 'doing-high-school-student', and where the contradictions between the different invitations and expectations to participate in specific ways have been largely resolved.

What Do We Learn about Peter from This?

When we follow Peter's way of navigating the affordings of standards he encounters (in high school) over time, we can see how he manages to relate to them in subjectively meaningful ways. Hence, furnishing his self-understanding and conduct of everyday life with the aspects that are meaningful to him (thus in accordance with his motive hierarchy), while gradually rejecting others. Tracking these subtle transformations in Peter's way of relating to high school standards (and himself as someone attending high school) in a chronological way illustrates how change is not necessarily a matter of appropriation of existing high school standards, but also, and no less, a way of subjectively creating a meaningful space for oneself, where subjectified subjectivity is in accordance with actions and values. In Peter's case, the slight transformations in his intentional dynamics suggest that the encounter with the academic-engagement-standard serves to *reinforce* the subjectified sensitivity that Peter brought with him to high school; as the affordings of this particular standard are highly compatible with Peter's need to be alone and legitimizes this need in a high school setting ('my time is spent on homework', 'I *need time alone* to do homework').

The inclusion of temporality (here the time that passes from September until May) as an analytical awareness serves to underline the dynamic movements that occur between Peter and the classmates/standards/environment. We see a movement from September ('I made the mistake of falling asleep'), through January ('I prefer to have time to clean up my room and get ahead on homework') to May ('it didn't fit my agenda'). Had the analysis been limited to the latter data excerpt (Peter and Oliver) it would be impelling to conclude that Peter was merely not paying an interest in the social life at school; that it was not meaningful to him. Such an analysis would fail to account for the dynamic process that Peter has gone through in order to acquire this particular position in relation to high school life. On the other hand, I could have concluded that this position was a direct prolongation of his self-understanding before starting high school and as such, nothing had changed for Peter. However, this would offer a similarly limited comprehension of the developmental dynamics that have taken place over the course of the first school year.

If we return to the model of subjectified subjectivity, the examples in this section suggest that the main transformations for Peter are taking place on level (b) and (c) in the model. Peter relates to his own experience of high school standards (level b) and in the beginning reflects upon this by being aware of how he might be perceived from the outside by others (level c); e.g., 'falling asleep was a mistake' (it was not a deliberate choice). Over time, the dynamics of especially level (c) changes in the sense that Peter cares less about how others might perceive him in relation to the standard of social participation. This suggests an altered meaning of this standard, and of Peter's way of relating to himself (as someone not directed towards this particular standard). In his way of participating in the high school practice (and *not* participating in the social life after school), Peter thus actively negotiates the meaningfulness of standards (level d) with his classmates; both in relation to the standard of academic engagement (which he values), and that of (a specific kind of) social participation (which he values less and less over time).

The Continuous Collective Negotiation of Meaning

Thus far I have examined how Peter relates to the dominant affordings of standards in the high school setting, and how the way he relates to them changes dynamically over the course of the first year in high school. From this, one might primarily consider the person-standard relation in isolated manners, as disconnected from social dynamics. However, with reference to the model (Figure 7.3), this is hardly the case, as young people concurrently negotiate the meaningfulness of standards in a more general or distributed sense, in the process of relating to various aspects of their concrete lifeworld. In the remains of this chapter, we shall therefore look at how these negotiation processes of shared meaning unfold as woven into the fabrics of everyday life. Not as something extraordinary or limited to special occasions, but as deeply embedded in and inseparable from participation in social and material life.

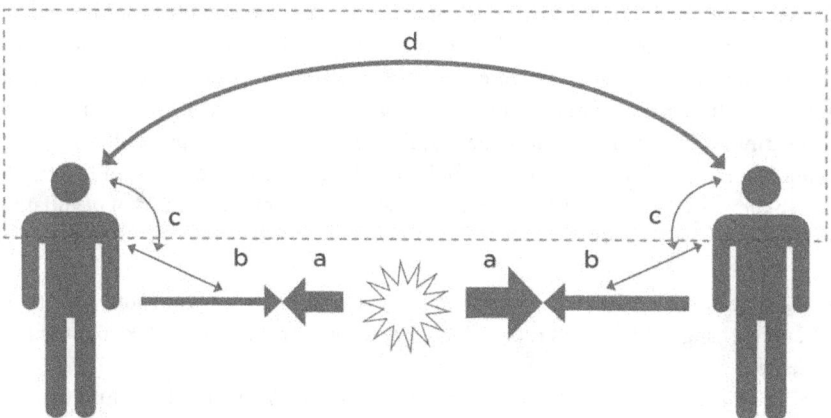

Figure 7.3 The dialectical-ecological model of subjectified subjectivity (Pedersen & Bang 2016a). Analytical emphasis on the negotiation of meaning.

The ongoing negotiations of standards – including appropriations and alterations, as well as challenges to them – relate to the creation of shared meaningfulness and ultimately contribute to the (co)production of how one *ought* to be or do high school student. This is elegantly illustrated by the interplay between Peter and his friend Eric, who co-reflect upon the space of possibilities that high school entails, and how one *ought* to prioritize. Their dialogue reveals the social character of meaning making processes and demonstrates how the two boys use each other, and their long friendship, as a basis from which to reflect upon different available 'positions' in relation to high school – in addition, their dialogue serves to comprehend multiple levels of relating to 'self', cf. the model of subjectified subjectivity. Towards the end of the chapter, I will explore how Peter negotiates socially accepted participation with a group of boys in his class. This will particularly emphasize how processes of transformation (on both an individual and collective level) do not imply that one must *adopt* a specific standard, but rather that processes of transformation occur constantly as they are connected to ongoing and multiple processes of negotiation, of 'who are we' and 'who am I in relation to you'. Peter's use of the kendama (a Japanese wooden toy) will serve as illustrative case. This part of the chapter will thus emphasize the multiplicity of levels in which negotiation processes occur, and how materiality is an integral part of self-understandings, social dynamics and negotiations in the classroom setting.

Friendship: An Intimate Space for Co-reflecting and Negotiating the Meaning of Standards

Although Peter does not know many people from his local community, one of his old childhood friends, Eric, attends Northside High as well. Mostly they attend different classes, but they do attend the same French class. They often hang out after school, and over the course of the school year they increasingly hang out *at* school as well. Their friendship combines activities that were established before they started high school (such as playing online games, cooking noodles and relaxing together), as well as relating to the challenges of managing the new demands and possibilities of high school life. In the following, I will unfold their shared practice to focus on the way in which they *co-reflect* on how to best handle high school demands, as part of negotiating meaning, values and motives.

> After school, Eric, Peter, and I go to Peter's place. Peter's parents are both at work and we hang out in Peter's room, where Eric and Peter are quick to take out their laptops.
>
> '*What would you prefer (as subject) for the exam this year*[4]*?*' I ask Eric (as a follow-up on our talk on our walk home from school). '*Music! … But that's because I think it's fun to play*' he says. '*But you really ought to take your exam in the subject where you get the worst grade*', Peter says. '*That would be biology …* ' Eric says. '*Noooo …. Then you made a really poor choice in skipping the last class* (which is taking part as we speak),' Peter proclaims, while laughing. '*I am sure it will be fine*' Eric says and shrugs indifferently.

---

[4] In the Danish high school system, students do not have exams in all classes, but only about half of them. The exam subjects are assigned randomly.

They are playing the same online game from their respective laptops and their eyes are fixed on their screens: they (verbally) coordinate a few strategic moves. A few minutes later, we pick up the conversation about the French class we attended before coming home: '*Is it divided according to academic skills?*' I want to know, as there are two different beginners' classes in French. '*Yes, that's understood*' Peter says, '*but we could choose ourselves* (between beginners' level one and two).' '*I couldn't care less ... you can't be good at all subjects*' Eric says. '*What about the level?*' I ask. '*I think she* (the teacher) *is exaggerating*' Peter says, referring to a comment the teacher made on what academic level to expect in the second year of high school. He continues: '*But no doubt that second year of high school will be the toughest!*' '*But it was like when they said that starting high school would be difficult, compared to elementary school ...* ', Eric says and adds: '*I think the biggest challenge (for me) was to handle my finances, so I could afford to buy beer!*' Peter laughs: '*Ha ha, was that what you had to prepare for?*' '*Yes*', Eric says smiling and adds: '*but to me it's mostly about the teacher, you know ... if it's a good teacher or not.*' '*Yeah, it means everything*' Peter says. '*It depends on the teacher whether I learn something or not*' Eric says. '*Ok, so let me get this straight, if you guys have a bad teacher that means you are less likely to learn anything in that class?*' I ask. '*Exactly*' Eric says. '*For sure*' Peter adds and continues: '*So I have a bad teacher in one class ... I mean she is nice and stuff, but I am not learning anything. ... I started reading this book ("The game of grades") and it also says that you don't have to show up for class to get a good grade. Instead, it might actually be better to stay at home and focus on doing the homework for a class that you are completing that year* (and where the grade will therefore be final)' '*Well, I show up just to be there, you know and then maybe I will learn a little, right?*' Eric says and continues: '*Well, it's like, I have certain goals about what I want in life, you know, but high school years kind of constitute my youth ... and there I am supposed to have fun*'. '*Have fun, have fun ...* ' Peter says in a mocking tone.

They are still both playing the online game, while we are talking. '*Do you do your homework every day?*' Eric asks Peter. '*You mean if I prepare for all classes?*' Peter replies. '*Yes*'. '*No, I don't. I don't have the time for that*' Peter says. '*Neither do I ... I can call a tower, if you want* (game-talk)' Eric says. They play silently for a few minutes then Eric says: '*Your class is the laziest at school!*' '*Yeah, it's super lazy ... I mean it is not like people are stupid or not intelligent or anything like that, but they just don't do much. ... Well, yeah, they smoke quite a lot and stuff ...* ' Peter says as if he is not part of the class himself. '*Yeah, they're known as the potheads*' Eric says, and Peter adds: '*Many probably choose the music class because they think it's easier ...* '.

As this illustrates, general standards of 'youth life' and 'high school life' coexist and are produced, reproduced, debated and altered in situated manners, that take on concrete forms. Intermingled with a multitude of other strategic and value-laden reflections on how to best spend your time, and what matters the most.

Eric and Peter's interplay illustrates a collective, cooperative meaning-making process, whereby the two boys try to make sense of the practice they currently take part in. As their dialogue reveals, they each had ideas and expectations prior to starting high school, just as they have (different) strategies for how to best succeed with 'being-a-high-school-student' at present and different ideas of what this entails. An additional layer can be added pertaining to the different value sets they impose on high school life: from their motive orientations follows that they clearly value different aspects, which also reflect their different subjectivities. For Eric, high school is primarily about having fun ('high school years constitute youth') and therefore he has a far more relaxed attitude towards the affordings of the academic-engagement-standard than Peter: grades are not important, and his strategy is to just 'show up' and hope that it will not be a waste of his time. Peter, on the contrary, who has fully integrated or aligned with the affordings of the academic-engagement-standard, is preoccupied with *creating the best conditions* for himself to serve his interests; have more time to relax, all the while learning something and achieving good grades. To self-optimize, he has been reading a book ('The game of grades') with the purpose of enhancing his strategies in relation to time management, and thus secures good grades with a minimal effort. Here Peter actively tries to gain control or influence over his concrete conditions by expanding his possibilities for action in ways that will allow him to maintain a space for himself and his needs to stay at home, relax, unwind, all the while meeting academic demands at school – along with his own aspirations for academic proficiency. Eric, on the other hand, evaluates both the affordings of the high school practice, as well as his own activities, engagement and choices, in relation to a parameter of 'fun'; a parameter that does not seem to figure in Peter's motive hierarchy.

These differences in intentionality or motive orientation reflect how the boys have developed different subjectified subjectivities; Eric has readily embraced the standard of 'high school as fun' into his self-understanding, whereas Peter appears to reject this as meaningful. This dynamic appears to be reversed when it comes to a high school standard of academic achievement. The emphasis on 'fun' correlates with the standard-of-social-participation that appears as highly valued among a majority of students at their school. Eric seems well-aware of this even prior to starting high school, as his main concern beforehand related to the question of how to earn enough money for beers (implying a clear expectation of an increase in social gatherings and parties). Despite their differences in orientations (and values), they still directly compare and try to 'tune in' with one another on 'how much one should prepare', or where to draw the line between time spent on homework and time spent on other things. Towards the end of their conversation, we see how Peter clearly distinguishes himself from the rest of his classmates, who are all categorized as 'lazy', 'potheads' or someone who may have chosen the music line for the wrong reasons (to get off easy, rather than to play music). These categorizations present as speculations to the boys, as they both positions themselves as outsiders in relation to this group. What follows from their interplay is how they have furnished themselves with different high school standards, hence integrating different subjectifications into their self-understandings, concurrently impacting on, as well as reflecting, their values, activities and motive orientations. As the boys attend the same high school and are therefore part of the same environment, it is fair to assume that they encounter the same standards and must relate to similar affordings, however, given their different subjective orientations, what stands out as having affordance-quality for them in the environment varies. This underlines how the (ontogenetically distinct) subjectivity becomes a navigation tool in relation to the diverse and possibly contradictory space of possibilities that high school constitutes. The boys' friendship allows them to co-create a space for negotiations and appropriations of meaning with one another. In other words, they use their well-established relation to make sense of a practice that is still new to them, and where, perhaps, their expectations do not always meet reality, which implies a need to reconfigure orientations or probe new understandings. There is sense to be made, and priorities to evaluate or confirm. It is obvious how they allow for each other's differences while also gently making a mockery of one another's priorities; hence using this shared space for simultaneously aligning meaning and emphasizing or confirming demarcation lines ('that which you are, I am not').

By comparing the standards revealed in the boys' conversation and the invitations from the introduction event at their school, we can see how the boys (rather directly) relate to – and re- and co-produce – well-established standards of high school life, albeit different ones, reflecting their intentional differences ('having fun/drinking beer' vs. 'committed to schoolwork'). Standards are thus not just *transferred* to or *adopted* by new students in high school; instead, they are *actively approached* in different ways, depending on the subjectivities brought in by the students. Or, we could say that what becomes meaningful in the sense of acquiring directional significance depends on the interplay between already established motive orientations and new invitations or demands (reflected as the intentio and intentum aspects of intentionality), and thus cannot be reduced to either the individual (needs) or the institutional standards (here as demands) as isolated entities. In terms of subjectified subjectivity, this implies that the subjectification processes that are integrated into subjectivity (over time) are the ones that somehow resonate with the subjectivity already developed (levels b and c). This reinforces the notion that persons are *not passive receivers of subjectifications* offered by the environment, but rather *active producers of (subjectified) subjectivity*.

Thus, subjectification does not necessarily equal adaptation, but rather points towards *differentiated subjectivity*, where part of the original (subjectified) subjectivity is strengthened (more than transformed). In the case of Peter, his subjectified sensitivity (developed prior to starting high school and continuously reproduced in the home setting) is not transformed in the encounter with high school; rather it is reinforced, and additional meaning is added to it qua the meaningfulness available in the affordings of the standard-of-academic-engagement. The self-understanding and the values that guide Peter in his everyday life are recognized in a high school context ('we expect you to hand in on time, show up prepared, etc.'), and thus serve to intensify the meaning that is attributed to these priorities and activities. Therefore, Peter's subjectified subjectivity is not 'the same' after the first year of high school as it was prior to the beginning of the year; additional and new meaning (and new activities) have been added to Peter's self-understanding as sensitive, which can be understood as changes on levels (b) and (c); in Peter's way of experiencing – and relating to – himself as a participant.

Mastering the Kendama: Negotiating Standards of Participation

Negotiations are not limited to the intimate spaces of friendship, nor do they solely unfold as verbal exchanges on meaning-making. As we shall see next, they also occur as deeply connected to materiality and ways of participating in the high school practice.

As was illustrated earlier in this chapter, Peter is not particularly oriented towards social activities taking place outside the formal school setting, such as participation in various parties, music cafés, etc. What changes throughout the first year – as we have seen so far – is therefore not so much his level of social engagement, as one might have expected (based on Anna's developmental trajectory from the previous chapter), but instead his directedness towards, and way of relating to, the school and his classmates. The following empirical excerpts will explore the dynamics between Peter and his classmates further. They are excerpts from a math class, on two different days (one week apart); these will be referred to as 'Math class A' and 'Math class B', respectively. Here we will see how Peter's kendama, a traditional Japanese wooden toy, comes into play, interwoven with expendable drum sets, different and competing priorities, and ongoing positionings among the boys:

Math class A

Math class is starting up; it is C-level math, which only 8 of them (from the class) attend. Peter sits with Benjamin and Martin, and the other students sit scattered in the room. Today's topic is the sine relation, and the teacher starts demonstrating different proofs on the blackboard while the students are taking notes. Peter raises his hands and when called upon, he points out a mistake made by the teacher. The teacher quickly agrees with him and thanks him for being awake. Benjamin turns to Peter: '*Well done, dude!*'

They have a small break. Peter picks up his kendama that is placed on the table next to his computer. He starts playing with it and silently performs different tricks while hanging with the group of boys who are discussing which concerts to attend in the near future. At some point Martin turns to Peter and friskily says: '*How is your damned piece of hipster toy doing?*' He laughs and his tone of voice clearly indicates that his comment was meant as an insult or provocation. As Peter does not respond, Martin turns to one of the other boys and makes a comment about his younger brother having that same kind of toy. Peter does not comment; he just shrugs and continues to play.

After the break Peter and Martin go to work at one of the bigger tables in the hallway. Benjamin and Alexander join them. Peter is focused on the assignments they were given, while the three others are listening to music (on the computer) from a comedy show, singing along and laughing – and not making much progress on the math assignment.

As soon as Peter has finished with the assignment, he starts playing with the kendama that he brought with him to the hallway (it is always within reach). Benjamin has started working on the assignment as well, while still listening to music from his computer. Martin and Alexander (who are still not working on the assignment) are having a conversation on this week's music café at school and who will be performing there. Martin turns to Peter: '*Say, how would you like to borrow one of my drum sets?*' he asks. '*One of them?*' Peter replies in a surprised tone. '*Yeah ...* ' Martin says, as if it was not a big deal to have two drum sets. '*Well, I live in an apartment ... don't think my neighbours would approve much ...*', Peter answers. Martin shrugs, indifferently.

Ten minutes later, Martin picks up the topic again: '*If I were you, I'd be really unhappy about not playing the drums*', he says to Peter. '*Well, if I were you, I'd be really unhappy about not playing the guitar ... or the bass ... or the piano and other instruments requiring being able to weave your hands in different ways*', Peter replies in a calm tone of voice. Benjamin comments: '*Ah, knock it off, guys! What you are doing is big time bullying ... !*' Martin laughs but says nothing. Peter nor laughs or comments.

When math class ends, Martin tries to persuade Peter to come with him to the music room to jam, but Peter declines as there is too little time until the next class starts. Peter and I then head for French class, and Peter is playing with his kendama as we are walking. '*Do you get bored when you are done with the assignments and the others are not?*' I ask. '*A bit*' he answers and continues: '*It's just that I prefer to do as much as possible at the school, so I don't have to spend time doing it when I come home.*' (a little silence) '*Is there a music café at the school tonight?*' I ask. '*Yeah, I do believe so*' Peter answers. '*Are you going?*' '*Nah ....*' he says, while shrugging. '*How is that?*' I ask. '*Because it is Thursday*', he says and explains to me how it would be too much for him, as he gets way too tired – he also has his piano lessons and stuff on Thursday afternoons, he explains. At this point in time (towards the end of the school year), he has not yet participated in any of the music cafes, he tells me.

As the excerpt shows, Peter is actively engaged in the content of the teaching session, for which he is also credited (by both the teacher and Benjamin). At the same time, he is part of a social group that forms in math class, which includes him, Benjamin, Alexander and Martin. Whereas Peter continues his engagement with the academic content of class in an undisturbed manner, the three others alternate between 'having fun' and doing the assignment, reflecting the coexistence of two different standards and the entangled nature of practice (the math class setting allows for several activities to coexist and overlap, to various degrees reflecting school demands and subjective motive orientations).

In the negotiation process that unfolds between the four boys, both positions and activities are negotiated. In this specific activity setting, they clearly have different social situations, albeit facing the same institutional demands. When Peter is not directed towards the math assignments, he is playing with the kendama; a way of participating that clearly provokes Martin. It is obvious that Martin is interested in Peter ('he ridicules the kendama', 'he offers him a drum set'); however only when it comes to the topic of music will Peter engage in an actual conversation with Martin about what they can, or cannot do, together. The manner in which the negotiation process unfolds, in particular between Peter and Martin, indicates two things: (1) that the standards of academic engagement and social participation often coexist and overlap in highly entangled manners in the activity settings that unfold at high school, but that (2) the different orientations afforded by each standard (in terms of participation) may be conflictual and cause tensions between the participants in a concrete (social) situation. For instance, it appears to be problematic for Martin that Peter is not directed towards the same artefacts (the computer playing music; various (present, albeit absent) instruments) or activities (not working on the assignment, but having fun) as himself, which is a constant reminder of what they ought to spend their time doing in class. This way, Peter's motive orientation and adjacent behaviour in the specific situation thus come to embody and presence another impending standard, namely that of academic engagement that the other boys, and perhaps Martin especially, are keen to reject or at least downplay the importance of. The coexistence of different standards – here reflected in the concrete artefacts and activities in which the boys engage – is equally discernible in Peter's way of participating; he too alternates between academic engagement and fun, however in a different order and with different means than the other boys. For Peter, listening to music from the computer, while singing along does not constitute fun. However, playing with the kendama does. Hence, multiple negotiations are concurrently unfolding: (1) on an individual level, for each of the boys in relation to how to spend their time and whether to meet demands for academic engagement or the invitations to create a space for 'free time' within the confined space of the math class setting (allowing for 'fun' in various forms), and (2) on an intersubjective level, the negotiation of how 'to be' in class; a question of participation and what one *ought* to engage in – and how much. These negotiations unfold, in entangled manners, on a material level (of manipulating various artefacts), as well as on a verbal level (as dialogue).

One week later, we are back in math class and here we see minor alterations in the group dynamics:

Math class B

Math class starts up and Peter begins to work on today's calculations. Alexander, who is sitting on top of the table next to Peter (thereby signifying that he is not ready to start class yet), picks up Peter's kendama and begins to play with it. He is demonstrating rather poor skills and he leans over and whispers to Peter: '*But you are crazily good at this! Do you have any tricks for me?*' Peter answers: '*Yes, first thing is to not shoot it forward …* ' Alexander tries again, but still has a hard time mastering the kendama.

In the break, Benjamin starts asking around, who will join him to the canteen: '*Hey, Simon, wanna come to the canteen?*' Simon says yes and moves towards the door and Benjamin continues: '*What about you, Alexander; are you coming?*' '*Of course, I'm coming*' Alexander says and puts down the kendama (that he has been playing with on and off during the first lesson). '*What about you, Peter? Are you joining us, or do you prefer the peace and quiet in the classroom?*' Peter displays no intention of standing up: '*Yes, you are right, no one can contest the peace and quiet in here …* ' he says. The other students leave the room and Peter stays in the classroom to work. Two other classmates have also stayed in the classroom working. None of them speak to each other during the break.

This second excerpt shows a slight change in the meaning of the kendama, and the positions ascribed among the boys. In 'Math class A' the kendama was discredited as being a 'hipster toy' or a 'children's toy' by Martin. At the same time, it was an integral part of Peter's way of participating and having fun. In 'Math class B', we see how Alexander is taking up Peter's interest in the kendama, and desires to master it. The kendama thus becomes a *shared object* (of interest; of fun) between Peter and Alexander, which implies that the meaning ascribed to the kendama is altered, just as 'ways of having fun' is now co-created by Peter and Alexander in relation to the kendama. The invitational character of the kendama is no longer rejected on the basis of instating a not-appropriate-kind-of-fun but embraced and acted upon. Also, Peter is invited to join for the canteen in the break, however with an additional comment acknowledging and obliging Peter's preference for 'peace and quiet', also implying his preference for doing as much schoolwork while at school as possible.

From these micro-genetic excerpts, one cannot readily establish an irreversible change in the social dynamics, and yet a qualitative change is noticeable. Rather than demonstrating development as linear progression, the social dynamics between the boys illustrate how these subtle processes of transformation does not equal adaptation to a particular standard or norm of behaviour, but rather how transformative processes unfold as concrete and continuous negotiations of meaning in practice, relating to central questions of 'who we are and who we can be, in this particular setting, together'. Peter's way of participating displays his subjectivity in an active, albeit mostly non-verbal manner, by demonstrating how he insists on acting on his own preferences (playing with the kendama, spending time on the assignment), while also meeting the challenges thrown at him by Martin by standing up for himself and setting limits. Here we can return to Bang's (2009b) point about how not only concrete materiality carries affordance character, influencing how behaviour unfolds in a particular activity setting, but also how social others act as affordances, and how one learns about 'who I am' and 'who the others are' from taking part in such social interactions. Together, concrete artefacts, institutionally arranged settings and demands form a space of possibilities in which the boys negotiate meaning and ways of doing 'high school student', each with their own motive hierarchies. In entangled manners this becomes a space for not only the negotiation and production of shared meaning, but also of individual agency and self-understanding. According to Wartofsky (1983:204):

> [...] agency does not operate in a vacuum as sheer wilfulness or whim. Agency requires an object to be acted on; it requires means of acting and acquired discipline of effective action. Therefore, the child's possibilities of exercising and developing its modes of activity are subject to the constraints, influences, or opportunities that a particular social-historical context presents.

And furthermore (1983:197):

> What it is to be human is thus objectively given in the artifacts that constitute the inherited objectifications of past action (as history and culture) and in the modes of permitted and prohibited actions, that is, the norms and rules in accordance with which anticipated actions and interactions are regulated.

Wartofsky (1983:197) clearly emphasizes how '*the extended or social self is not simply a creature of consciousness, but of practical activity*'. Artefacts thus play a significant part in the development of self, of self-understanding and of agency. In other words, we are *externally embodied* in and by the activities we engage in, and by the objects we make use of.[5] We come to be and to know ourselves – and others – through our practical engagements with the world, whereby we co-constitute ourselves and the world in dialectical manners. The negotiations of *who* and *how* to be that unfold dynamically between Peter and his classmates are not abstract, disconnected philosophical co-reflections in verbal forms that can be solely and fully accounted for as cognitive processes or exchanges. Rather they are *fully embodied* and *material* negotiations that unfold *as entangled* with practical activities and active relating to various artefacts, that in themselves carry (historically situated) meaning that may be discussed and negotiated. We saw how, in Math Class A, Martin's ascribing of meaning to the kendama was a dichotomous *either* 'a childhood toy' *or* 'a hipster toy', both carrying connotations[6] of something 'not to be'. And how, by not responding to any of these potential insults, Peter negotiates a different meaning of the kendama, and simultaneously, a different space for participation and for self-understanding (as something concurrently individual and dependent on social recognition from others, following Wartofsky (1983)). Not by verbal argumentation primarily, but by practical, object-related doing. With reference to Barker & Wright (1966, 1971), we can see how the boys take part in the same behaviour setting, albeit make use of and orient themselves towards differentiated behaviour objects; therefore, the behaviour setting in itself (as a frame) cannot explain behaviour, but still works as a conditioning force that invites, urges, or, in Wright et al.'s terms (1951:189), *coerces* the boys to relate to 'doing math class' together, which implies relating to one another and concurrently reproducing, and slightly altering, *how* to do math class. And by doing so, they also continuously negotiate, produce and reproduce understandings of self – amidst social dynamics of potentially competing with and positioning oneself and others, and by the use of concrete artefacts that are not neutral objects, but imbued with social (and historical) meaning.

Negotiations as Multi-Layered and Entangled Participation

Regarding the coexistence of standards of participation (as e.g. either oriented towards 'having fun' or 'being academically engaged'), these are not mutually exclusive forms of participation but rather coexisting, and continuously negotiated between participants in a given practice, in relation to meaning and relevance. This indicates the dynamic

---

[5] See also Costall & Richards (2013) and Heft (2001) for similar points.
[6] A quick Wikipedia search determines that the term 'hipster' may convey several references; however, in this case, it refers to what could also be called the '21st century hipster' or contemporary subculture, signifying a subculture, where the emphasis on being unique and authentic is foregrounded, while, ironically few 'members' of this subgroup display much uniqueness, as they all value similar things. For example, the culture is known for fixie-bikes, beanies, long beards, lumber jack shirts, drip coffee and alternative music.

nature of standards. In the intersection of the social dynamics in the two math classes and the conversation that unfolds between Peter and Eric, in Peter's home setting, we get a glimpse of how different groupings exist at Peter's school – as we also saw earlier in Anna's class. The tension we sense between Peter and some of his class mates, in relation to priorities (doing, or not doing, the academic assignments at school), intentionality (towards social participation outside school or relaxation at home), and ways of having fun (singing along to music or playing with the kendama) reflects a multitude of possibilities that coexist in the various activity settings of high school, and in which ongoing negotiations of 'who' and 'how to be' unfold dynamically between the boys. Eric's comments about the majority of Peter's class 'being lazy' and how they are known as 'the potheads', as well as Peter's comment about how the music line at school is often chosen to 'get off easier', reveal that different groupings exist at school. Groupings[7] that may readily be categorized based on their different priorities and orientations. This resonates with the ongoing negotiations between Peter and his classmates on what to prioritize and how to participate.

Despite the fact that Peter's developmental trajectory over the course of the first school year may, on the surface, appear as him mostly 'remaining the same', this is hardly the case, and hence limiting our analysis of him to a strictly individual level would be a simplification. Even though Peter's motive orientation and his self-understanding remain largely the same, the micro-genetic processes in his everyday life demonstrate how he is not only continuously negotiating standards and self with others around him – verbally and through his concrete and object-related actions – but that there are also slight alterations in his directedness. As this chapter has tried to illustrate, Peter's intentionality reflects an ecological relation of self and environment; an inseparable self-world reciprocity. For analytical purposes, this was depicted as intentio/intentum dynamics; of the constant tension and simultaneity of being directed 'by' or 'towards' something. Perhaps, we could state that this reflects the ongoing synthetic movement of subjectivity-subjectification dynamics, where one is always 'the same', in the sense of being a recognizable 'me', all the while in the process of constant *becoming*.

The relational interplay between Peter and the other boys points to the relevance of transcending dichotomies such as 'boring' versus 'fun', 'concentrated' versus 'not-concentrated', 'engaged' versus 'not-engaged' and so forth. Such positions are not necessarily mutually exclusive categorizations, nor definable as constants, but rather they are *fluid* and *dynamic*, just as they are *co-constructed* in everyday life settings, through the participation in concrete activities and through the use of various artefacts (such as the kendama).

---

[7] Such different groupings in high school have long been identified by prominent researchers such as Eckert (1989) and Willis (1977), who, in different ways, point to the influence of socioeconomic status, structural variations and more general group dynamics.

8

Interweaving Analytical Threads

This chapter will sum up on the findings of the previous two chapters and reflect upon how these may contribute to a dialectical-ecological understanding of developmental processes. Furthermore, to reflect upon the perspective of such an understanding, I will briefly revisit a few earlier theoretical understandings of youth development. But first, let me reflect upon what we learn about developmental dynamics from the exploration of Anna's and Peter's subjective processes of transformation over the course of the first school year.

The Meaning of Subjectivity

When a person starts high school, she or he does so with her or his particular ontogenetic history as the basis of self-understanding and intentionality (a particular subjectified subjectivity, or subjective stance, realized in particular motive orientations and hierarchies); this constitutes a particular basis from which to *encounter*, *perceive* and *negotiate standards*. Standards are thus perceived – and dealt with – differently, just as they become more or less meaningful to the person according to the manner in which they correlate with subjectivity and intentionality – and this may change over time (as we saw with Anna and her relation to beer-drinking). As I have tried to demonstrate in the two previous chapters, following Anna's and Peter's developmental trajectories, respectively, is how young people *actively* (although not necessarily deliberately) engage in negotiating the meaning of standards. This implies that the invitational character of standards reflects a dynamic relationship between persons and their environment, referring to the way in which a multitude of ontogenetic histories are interwoven with each other and with institutional practices (in a specific time and place). Furthermore, it points to the meaning of subjectivity and directedness in relation to the development of subjectified subjectivity; as the case of Peter illuminated, not all affordings of standards are integrated into neither self-understanding, intentionality, nor the activities that a person engages in. However, this does not imply that standards are without significance even if they are not integrated, but rather that they are context-dependent and dynamic. For instance, Peter also engages in fun activities both in and after school, even though he is not directed towards an overall standard of social participation.

What I have tried to argue is that only *some* standards are integrated into the self-understanding of the person (as subjectified subjectivity), and this is not something that happens from one day to the next, but as a process (of various duration) that depends on the correlation between the subjectification and the already developed subjectified subjectivity of the person. This implies that 'standards' as an analytical tool may have the disadvantage of primarily bringing attention to the unified expressions of subjectivity (through activities and behaviour), which carries the risk of disregarding the ongoing and active processes of negotiation that are taking place in practice and through which standards are reproduced and transformed. Hence, a balanced analytical grip is pivotal in the sense of not reducing our comprehension of youth development to neither the meeting or deviance from norms (here: standards), nor to mere expressions of individualized agency.

Throughout this book, I have tried to explore and illustrate the meaning of the environment – the 'coercive' nature of the behaviour setting, following Wright et al. (1951) – hence pointing to a somewhat 'determining' aspect integral to the environment, inviting young people to take part in practices that, over time, unify their motives, actions and ultimately their subjectivities. However, discounting agency from the analysis – the 4th principle of Elder (1998) – we would be left assuming that young people would undergo *the same* developmental process, engage in the *same* activities, in *similar* ways and with the *same* outcome, regardless of who they are and where they live their everyday life. Thus, it would become challenging to analytically comprehend the nuances that emerge in the ways in which young people relate to their concrete environment, its invitations and possibilities for action, how they continuously negotiate meaning and self-understanding, struggle to hold on to themselves while allowing themselves to be moved by the demands and spaces of opportunities they encounter. This sets demands for the concepts or models we employ when attempting to grasp development; they need to enable and support a wholeness understanding of developmental processes, in their complexities.

In the following I shall look at how Anna and Peter display two different tracks of development after starting high school; examined as dynamics of intentionality. The purpose of this is to elucidate how processes of standardization do not equate a dichotomous adoption or rejection of existing standards, but rather imply transformation of subjectified subjectivity through ongoing negotiation of meaning.

Anna and Peter; Two Different Tracks of Development

Anna

As we saw in Chapter 6, Anna's directedness, her way of participating and her self-understanding co-developed through the first year of high school, and it was proposed to see this as 'subjectified subjectivity'. When Anna started high school, she was preoccupied with her clear goal of becoming a kindergarten teacher and her time was structured around different activities that resonated with this ambition. Anna thus started high school with a subjectivity that had been largely subjectified in relation to working with children (as a babysitter, an assistant kindergarten teacher, as a children's gymnastics teacher), which was reflected in Anna's self-understanding and her motive orientation. When Anna started high school, she encountered numerous invitations to participate in specific ways and in particular activities (partying, drinking beer, caring about fashion, etc.), as well invitations to perceive herself in specific ways (e.g. through the health profiles). Some of these invitations were presented as social invitations from her peers, whereas others were more formalized institutional demands. Over the course of the first year of high school we see how Anna's motive orientation changes, as the new invitations from the school setting (e.g. beer drinking) are gradually integrated into her self-understanding and intentionality (she develops a subjectified subjectivity in relation to beer-drinking). This does not change her goal of becoming a kindergarten teacher, but it has an impact on the way she conducts her everyday life; how she structures her time, what activities she is directed towards and how she participates in them. These transformations in intentionality (the dynamic between intentio and intentum) concurrently open up and close down 'spaces of action', making different possibilities to act more and less perceivable, accessible and relevant to Anna. That some actions are 'closed down' as possibilities due to changes in intentionality does not involve them being unavailable to Anna on a permanent basis but rather implies an altered connection between intentionality and possibilities for action.[1]

If we should graphically display Anna's development in intentionality (in a simple way), it could look like this (Figure 8.1):

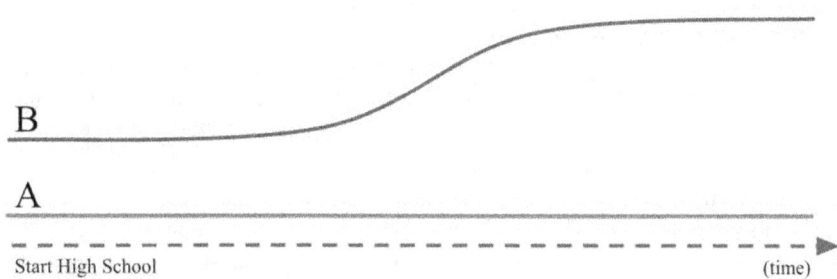

Figure 8.1 Anna's directedness. (A) reflects Anna's directness as she starts high school. (B) reflects how Anna is gradually more directed towards the social life (and beer-drinking practices) in high school.

---

[1] This resembles Hundeide's (2005) take on 'opportunity situations': an opportunity situation contains the concrete possibilities for action that exist for a person, in a specific existential situation, at a specific time. Some of these possibilities for action are available, but not perceived, some are not available. Others are available but not congruent with current life-tracks, and finally some are congruent and perceived. This means that the concrete opportunity situation is always somewhat biased by the individual's own experience of a 'fit' between actual opportunities in the environment and what the individual perceives as relevant (Hundeide 2005). This does not imply that nothing new can occur or that the other possibilities cannot be accessed; however, there will often be a tendency to pursue the life-tracks that fit with what you know or how you know yourself.

The line (A) represents Anna's primary motive orientation and directedness before she starts high school. She has a clear goal of becoming a kindergarten teacher, or a pedagogue, and many of her actions are thus directed towards spending a lot of time with children (gymnastics, babysitting), in addition to spending time at home with her family or seeing her grandmother. Along with her participation in the new practice (high school), Anna's subjectified subjectivity changes and she becomes increasingly directed towards some of the affordances she encounters (here depicted as the line (B)); we see how she is increasingly interested in – as well as participates in – parties and social gatherings with her friends (as well as drinking beers, something that she did not like at the beginning of the year). This does not imply that Anna's goal of becoming a kindergarten teacher has changed, or that she disengages in the activities connected with this goal. What changes is the meaning she ascribes to beer and beer-drinking, and the way in which this new meaning is gradually integrated into her intentionality. The dynamic displayed by Anna – the gradual appropriation of dominant standards or group behaviour – correlates with a mainstream understanding of youth orientation towards social life, and from Anna's developmental trajectory one could infer that development could be understood as simple socialization. Yet this dynamic is not representative of all developmental dynamics in youth life, nor does it fully account for the developmental dynamics that Anna engages in. However, it would be the 'easy' and less nuanced 'outside' gaze of what has been happening for Anna over the course of the year. Rather, I would argue that Anna was subjectified by standards that were affording a certain kind of behaviour and directedness from her. However, this is not meant as a deterministic one-way relation since Anna was actively negotiating ways to participate that resonated with her self-understanding – all the while her self-understanding also transformed. Her active negotiation along the way influenced not only her self-understanding, but also the standards she was relating to.

If we recall the interplay between Anna and Clara, the standard of social participation (parties and beer-drinking) may appear as relatively fixed and obvious, both to high school students and to an outsider. However, when explored concretely, as part of everyday life settings in and outside high school, its demarcations appear permeable and the details up for concrete negotiation. The descriptive power of a standard, as well as its potential to standardize, depends on people's reproduction of it in practice, and it is thus susceptible to alterations. Whereas this particular standard comes to act as a dividing practice in the beginning of the school year, grouping apart those who readily meet and adopt it and those to whom it did not make sense, its meaning has changed – albeit slightly – towards the end of the school year. Now the emphasis seems to have shifted towards uniting Anna, Clara and their classmates as a class who share social experiences, more so than partying for the sake of partying alone. It becomes evident that not only Anna, but also Clara and the new shared practice of partying have undergone small alterations that can only be understood in their reciprocal relation.

What is important to emphasize in relation to comprehending the processual aspect of development is that to herself, Anna 'remained the same' – only through her mother's reflection of her was she able to see that a transformation had occurred. This suggests for the first-person givenness of the person to potentially remain unaltered and requiring the assistance of a third-person perspective in order for the transformations to become noticeable. This indicates that Anna changes without noticing it, but through her mother's reflection (which could just as well have been through the eyes of her friends, or her grandmother), a reflection of herself as a participant (level (c) of the model of subjectified subjectivity) is installed, recognizing differences in directedness, participation, not to mention in her self-understanding. What Anna comes to reflect upon is thus how that which appears obvious in terms of 'what I do' and 'who I am' has changed; gradually, and unnoticeably. Not by itself as an automatism, but as the result of taking part in and making sense of concrete activity settings, and standardization practices, with others.

Peter

With Peter the transformations that occur over the course of the school year appear different than for Anna. He is to a lesser extent than Anna guided by standards of social life at high school. Instead, he is directed by the standard of academic engagement, which does not involve significant changes in behaviour or directedness; it would almost appear as if he 'remained the same' throughout the first year of high school. However, we know already, from studying the micro-genetic alterations in Peter's directedness, that transformations did occur and that Peter, in fact, did not remain the same. Figure 8.2 illustrates how Peter's directedness towards the standard of social participation appeared over the course of the school year:

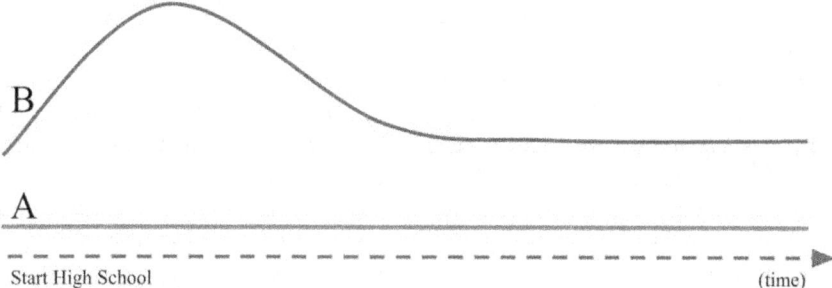

Figure 8.2 Peter's directedness. (A) depicts Peter's self-understanding and his directedness when he starts high school. (B) depicts his increased orientation towards the social life and the standard (of social life) at high school in the beginning of the school year, and how, over time, this orientation is transformed and approximates his self-understanding as it was when he started high school.

If we look at Figure 8.2,[2] we can see the dynamic in Peter's intentionality over time. In the beginning of the school year, he is orientated towards the social life at high school, and the standards of how to participate, even though he most often does not take actively part. Yet, the affordings of this standard still play an important role in his

[2] When we regard the transformations of intentionality (towards social life at high school), as depicted in Figures 8.1 and 8.2, they display different courses of transformation over the school year. These are comprehended in their variability, and as dynamic. It is important to note that these graphs do not demonstrate the development of Anna and Peter in their entirety, but *solely in relation to the standard of social participation*; for other areas of Anna and Peter's lives these graphs would look different.

orientations, his reflections about his actions and priorities and in the way he presents himself – he is well aware of how he is perceived from the outside. Over time, depicted in the line (B), his orientations change, in the sense that he is less and less oriented towards the standard of social participation, but increasingly manages to integrate the affordings of the academic-engagement standard with his already developed subjectified sensitivity (reflected in the line (A)). As we recall from Peter's initial self-presentation before starting high school, he highly values his own company and time to himself. We also saw how Peter was continuously subjectified as sensitive in the family setting, which revealed a synthesis between Peter's self-understanding and his family dynamics. Peter's self-understanding and subjectification as 'sensitive' and needing time to himself correlate well with the also ever-present standard of academic performance in high school, and so, over time, Peter manages to negotiate a way of participating that strengthens the position he had prior to starting high school. Albeit now with the potential contradictions (between the two dominant standards) cleared away. This is evident in how Peter no longer makes excuses towards the end of the school year, and how his classmates also seem to respect his preferences (about not participating in social gatherings outside school).

As the expectations inherent in the standard of academic engagement and Peter's subjectified sensitivity do not conflict, they are integrated in a synthetic manner, which indicates that even though it appears as if Peter's subjectivity is unaltered, it is very much the result of a transformative process, whereby the subjectified sensitivity is reinforced through Peter's way of participating and the choices he makes along the way. This way, he is not only informed and guided intentionally by his intentio (his needs) but also by an intentum (of academic engagement). The lines A and B (in Figure 8.2) do not end up at the same point. Although Peter's self-understanding and his needs (e.g. to be alone) remain rather intact and act as strong motives for him, they are also dynamic and change slightly (as already described).

Peter's development of a subjective stance in relation to the demands and expectations of the new setting of high school reflects not only an active relating to standards, in the sense of opposing (some of) them, but also an *ongoing negotiation* of their meaning and relevance with others, in different settings. We see how Eric and Peter, in the home setting, rather specifically discuss various aspects of high school life, pertaining to values and meaning. And similarly, albeit with different means, how Peter negotiates participation and priorities with his classmates in math class, e.g., by the use of the kendama. Their negotiations transcend the meaning of the kendama (as a kids' toy, a hipster toy or something that is cool to master) and the concrete time-space interface of the math class in the sense that what they are negotiating, on the bigger scale, are ways of 'being' a high school student; of *how one ought to be*.

All in all, Peter's transformative process firstly reflects alterations of intentio/intentum dynamics on a subjective level, and secondly that he is negotiating new ways of participating (on an intersubjective level); thereby creating, if not entirely new standards, then at least (re)producing standards of participation in slightly different manners to better fit his needs and interests (which implies that the standards of participation at school also come to reflect his subjectivity). This implies that intentionality is a dynamic developmental concept that can inform us of some of the transformations taking place on a subjective level, *without* disconnecting the person from the environment.

The developmental dynamics of actively *meeting, making sense of, negotiating* and *holding on to oneself*, I would argue, are the same for Anna and Peter on a dynamic level, albeit they concretize and are enacted differently, demonstrating dissimilar outcomes.

Expanding Our Comprehension of Youth Development – beyond Empty Vessels and Identity Crises

The subtle and yet persistent transformations of subjectivity that have been illustrated in the past two chapters shed light on the micro-genetic dynamics that unfold among young people. This is one way of comprehending development. However, youth development has already been studied and theorized from a range of theoretical stances, and therefore, to understand the contribution of this present study, and its theoretical implications, I shall briefly revisit some of the dominant voices that have co-shaped youth development as a concept and phenomenon.

A historically well-anchored understanding can be traced back to the work of G. Stanley Hall (here referenced in Lesko 2001), who in 1904 proposed that adolescence was most adequately understood as a time of 'Sturm und Drang', with reference to Goethes' infamous work 'Die Leiden des Jungen Werthers'. To Hall, the 'Sturm und Drang' reference depicted the phylogenetic reminiscence of human evolution – from beastlike to civilized behaviour – and thus described a developmental stage largely characterized by the raging hormones of puberty (see also Lerner & Steinberg 2004; Poulsen 2010). In Hall's words, youths were ' ... *ships without mooring, tossed on tempestuous seas of sexuality*' (Lesko 2001:93).

From a present-day perspective, I am sure we can agree that this is a rather reductionistic and simplified account of young people that, despite bringing to the fore the influence of hormones, presents little predictive and analytical value. Considering the historical time however, this view largely resonated with Freud's and later Erikson's theorizing on youth development. Here the hormonal influence is also drawn forth as a major factor in the developmental dynamics, and it is, in itself, the biological influence that initiates the identity crisis, central to Erikson's understanding. And yet there is a doubleness to detect in Erikson's theorizing (1971) that is perhaps not as far from some of the tensions or contradictions presented in this book. Erikson describes how:

> Youth is the last stage of the childhood and here the young person must – in order to complete development – arrange his or her childhood identifications under a new form of identification that is achieved among peers, during intense interaction and work preparation under competition. These new identifications are no longer characterized by childly play or youthful experimentation: with bitter eagerness, these identifications compel young people to make choices and decisions that all too directly may have an impact for life.
>
> (translated from the Danish version, 1971:149)

At the same time, and on the same page even, Erikson writes the following, again in my translation (1971:149):

> *This period can be regarded as a <u>psychosocial moratorium</u>; during this period, the young adult can, through free role-experimentation, look for a shelve in some section of society, a shelve that is clearly defined and yet looks like it was made exactly for him.*

Here, Erikson brings forth a contradiction between the idea of youth as a time of free experimentation – a moratorium – that ultimately leads you to find that 'perfect place' in society, and on the other hand the inbuilt pressure – the competition – to make the right choices and succeed with what, in effect, must be understood as an individual endeavour. This contradiction is a conflict to be solved properly, if one is to successfully transition on to adulthood. Erikson stresses the influence of peers and, in his own words, the influence of what could be read as standards or norms of 'how' and 'who' to be or become:

> *The adolescent mind is essentially a mind of the <u>moratorium</u>, a psychosocial stage between childhood and adulthood, and between the morality learned by the child, and the ethics to be developed by the adult. It is an ideological mind – and, indeed, it is the ideological outlook of a society that speaks most clearly to the adolescent who is eager to be affirmed by his peers, and is ready to be confirmed by rituals, creeds, and programmes which, at the same time define what is evil, uncanny, and inimical.*
> (Erikson 1970:254)

Erikson here touches upon a readiness to be guided and affirmed by the social and societal invitations that one encounters, albeit they, in this theoretical understanding, remain relatively abstract. The notion of the 'moratorium' has persisted and, in my opinion, has contributed to an image of youth (at least in the Western world) as a time to be 'free of responsibility' and free (and at the same time forced) to explore identity options. An image that is still outspoken in terms of cultural images, albeit increasingly challenged in practice.

How youth (as a developmental period) plays out for a person depends, according to Erikson, largely on how she or he has mastered the developmental crises, or stages, prior to adolescence. 'Identity' for the adolescent is built on the grounds of the identity work already completed in childhood, which implies that in case there are conflicts still unresolved, these will have to be handled in adolescence, before a final identity can be developed, or settled on (Erikson 1971). Although we can easily recognize the dynamics described by Erikson on a more general level, the inherent linearity in his developmental theory may be challenged, along with the assumption that development is ever 'complete', and hence 'over'. As we see from the young people in this book, their developmental paths are not linear and not directed towards a certain endpoint necessarily. Rather the paths are tortuous, dynamic and highly entangled with a multiplicity of everyday life aspects that need to be understood concretely. Erikson's point about the influence of previous childhood identifications resonates with the ontogenetic aspect of subjectivity that directs individual participation and co-shapes self-understanding. Here it is, however, important to emphasize the dynamic aspect of subjectivity, implying that subjectivity is not static but a constant *relating* to the concrete lifeworld – carrying the past, envisaging the future, and navigating complex spaces of possibilities (see also Stetsenko 2013).

The understandings of youth based on the works of Hall and Erikson with concepts such as 'Sturm und Drang', 'moratorium' and 'identity crises' share the commonality of being induced by bodily changes of puberty, which emphasizes a physical, biological component in the conceptualization of youth (e.g. raging hormones). They depict a time of uncertainty, which contains both an openness to exploration and a pressure to 'land somewhere' (resolve or master the identity crisis), or 'make it through' (the storm and stress of the hormonal chaos). These descriptive conceptualizations of youth are presented as universal stages of development, characterizing universal similarities for a given age group, offering an understanding of 'youth' in general terms (with a reference to the biological fact of puberty). This certainly has value as overall descriptors of general age-related, biological facts and conditions, but, I find, provide little insight into the developmental dynamics as they take place in concrete everyday life settings, just as I would shift the seemingly chronological age-thinking to a comprehension of age-periods as connected to concrete life situations (and institutional demands), cf. Vygotsky 1998; Hedegaard 2012, 2014; Bozhovich 2009.

To Have, or Not Have, Agency

Another aspect that resonates across theories and time relates to agency, or the adolescent's lack thereof. This is partly hinted in Hall's description of young people being 'tossed on seas of sexuality', implying little control or free will. Such a view is perhaps understandable historically, situated more than a hundred years ago, but interestingly this understanding bears striking resemblance with more recent reports from the influential Carnegie Council on Adolescent Development in 1986 and 1995, respectively, as is pointed out by Lesko (2001) in her extensive work on the cultural construction of youth. In their first report from 1986, 'Turning Points: Preparing American Youth for the 21st Century', the Carnegie Council presented an image of youth as ' ... *youth adrift, tossed on seas of sexuality, drug and alcohol use, and peer pressure: disequilibrated and needing to be guided into responsibility and productivity*' (Lesko 2001:93). The Turning Points report disseminated a concern that a fair number of adolescents were at risk of not becoming responsible adults – able and willing to contribute to a democratic society – due to the '*erosion of traditional moorings (close-knit families, stable neighbourhoods, plentiful low-skilled jobs) ...* ' (Lesko 2001:94). As a solution to this potential problem, school was seen as the most powerful force able to steer adolescents adrift back on track. The report concluded that it was necessary for the organization and curricula of the school to meet requirements in order to provide the foundation for ensuring a stable socialization, with the overall goal of securing the future of a democratic society. This necessitated the acquiring of assistance of medical, psychological and political experts, in order to help reform the school system. In 1995, the Carnegie Council presented their second report: 'Great Transitions', which made a turn away from the overtly behaviouristic and economic approach which had characterized 'Turning Points'. Yet, even though the 2nd report broadened the perspective to include social, environmental and hormonal factors in understanding and shaping development, it maintained a view of adolescents as *'trainable beings ... empty vessels to be filled with the most current and productive skills'* (Lesko 2001:105). On a political level, the 1980s as well as the 1990s contained a significant concern for the maintenance of economic productivity and social unity, and in order to fully comprehend the Carnegie Council reports, this specific historical time and place need to be taken into consideration. Even so, the presented view of young people as 'empty vessels' is nevertheless noteworthy.

These reports illustrate how subjectivity, agency and meaningfulness have been downplayed, or even absent, in relatively recent comprehensions of youth. One may argue that the comprehensions displayed in the reports are not theoretical accounts of youth. Still, as politically motivated documents, they influence how societal institutions (such as school) are shaped and what actions spaces are created on an institutional level. In turn, said action spaces, or spaces of possibilities, largely influence youth development on a concrete level, as we have seen throughout the book, and as Barker and Wright (1971) has well established elsewhere.

Of course, it must be recognized that there is no direct correlation between the Carnegie Council reports and the Danish schooling system, hence the Carnegie Council reports merely serve as a concrete example of the persistence of specific, rather problematic, conceptualizations of youth throughout history, depicting young people as somewhat *moldable entities*. It furthermore serves to emphasize how understandings of youth, as well as high school as a societal institution for educational purposes, are politically influenced and sculpted. According to, e.g., Lesko (2001) and Mørch (1985, 1990, 2010), there is a close connection between societal developments, political interests and youth understanding. The impact on youth understanding is twofold: initially by influencing the policies and regulations, as well as institutional settings and educational agendas surrounding youth, and then by shaping the particular activity settings that form the basis of the development of self(understanding) for young people in their daily lives, which can be seen in, for instance, the works of Eckert (1989) and Willis (1977), to reference some classical works.

Penelope Eckert (1989) conducted her research on youth cultures in an American high school. Her work centred on the way in which group-belonging was created and maintained, and how personal identities were created in relation to specific group belongings. Eckert conducted a thorough study of the students at Belten High School in Michigan, exploring the way in which social categories were produced and reproduced in the high school setting and how the different groups of young people made use of the environment in different ways. She pointed out that the challenge of identity work arises when one does not belong to a particular group, or when one partly belongs to a group but chooses to act in discordance with the group values (or identity). Similarly, Willis (1977) demonstrated a connection between socio-economic class and how you could benefit from the school system. He proposed a connection between 'working-class kids' and 'working-class jobs', and similarly between 'middle-class kids' and 'middle-class jobs', pointing to the school system's contribution to economic and cultural reproduction. The works of Eckert and Willis both point to the necessity to include concrete social, economic and cultural conditions in the understanding of 'socialization', identity and youth development, and it is to this tradition that I hope to make a contribution.

As we saw in some of the earlier chapters, what can be identified as a neoliberal agenda seems to play a part in the governing of young people today: the use of various self-technologies, and the conduct of conduct by means of, e.g., grades, health profiles illustrates this tendency. Neither high schools, nor the standards of youth life, are neutral places or spaces of possibilities and cannot be understood in history-less manners, or 'outside' societal tendencies or pressure. Similarly, agency needs to be understood in situated manners, taking into account the forces that shape the institutional action spaces and co-construct discourses, standards and activity settings; all aspects of the human lifeworld that work on an over-individual level. Hence the need for a theoretical conceptualization that allows for the concurrent presence and interplay of subjectivity and subjectification – or between the person and the environment in a broad sense. Clearly, we can no longer cling to the illusion that young people can be understood as 'empty vessels' or as someone who can, or will, easily and opinionlessly be moved according to, e.g., political interests. However, at the same time, we must recognize that young people are never *not* part of society and are therefore always and already co-shaped by societal structures, politics, institutional demands, etc. We cannot understand neither Anna's nor Peter's development solely by looking at agency or subjectivity in isolated manners and neither by looking merely at group dynamics, socialization or standardization.

Subjectified Subjectivity Revisited

Looking at youth development as a field of enquiry over time, it is clear that some foundational conceptualizations tend to dominate: (1) that young people are 'influenceable' and can be shaped according to the needs of parents, institutional interests or society at large. This reflects a classical socialization thinking emphasizing the meaning of the educational system as a socializing instrument or structure. And (2) that youth, as a specific life period, (automatically) constitutes a 'free space' – a moratorium – where young people are free to experiment and look for the right place for them. The transformative processes of Mia, Anna, Emily, Matilda, Lisa and Peter, respectively, illustrate that obviously we can recognize both tendencies, but we can also discard them for being inadequate. The developmental processes of these six young people throughout the school year in no way supports the idea that they should be 'empty', without motives, directedness, or agency. Their self-understanding is already formed reflecting their participation in a number of different settings and practices, and yet they remain 'formable'. Nor is there anything to suggest that they will reach a 'final' and fixed identity by the end of high school, or whenever we determine the end of youth to be. The developmental dynamics they embody and take part in are of a general kind and require their individual and unique expression, as they (the young people), continuously, meet and actively relate to invitations and demands in various settings, and thus incessantly must be considered ongoing syntheses of subjectivity and subjectification. Anna's, Peter's, as well as Mia's, Emily's, Lisa's and Matilda's, development can thus be explained by the same dialectical-ecological model of subjectified subjectivity, albeit they demonstrate rather different developmental paths.

In the previous chapters, we saw how Anna developed subjectified subjectivity in relation to a dominant high school standard of drinking beer, and how Peter resisted a very similar subjectification (of the social participation standard), thereby suggesting that subjectivity, expressed as self-understanding and intentionality, becomes equally important in relation to how young people perceive, and participate in, the high school setting. They are not merely 'empty vessels' (to paraphrase the Turning Points' report) to be filled with whatever high school offers in an uncritical manner. On the contrary, they carefully *select* and *pursue* those activities and subjectifications available in the high school setting that resonate with their needs, plans and self-understandings, all the while they collectively negotiate and (re)produce social meaning. Or as Stetsenko (2013) would say, they are *always* engaged in actively transforming the world.

At Peter's high school the introduction event presents new students with dominant standards of how to become a 'successful' high school student; however this analysis shows how the meaningfulness of standards – and thus their 'impact' in terms of shaping directedness and intentionality – can only be understood in relation to the self-understandings and subjectivity displayed by concrete individuals, who relate to them in different ways; thereby reproducing and altering them as part of their practice. Peter's participation in high school throughout his first year is largely structured by his self-understanding (subjectified sensitivity), which shows us that 'self' also has affordance quality; not only artefacts and social others (with reference to the work of Bang (2009b)). This suggests that the manner in which a person understands him-/herself guides not only his/her way of relating to (a) artefacts, and (b) social others, but also (c) him-/herself (indicated by level c in the model of subjectified subjectivity): my self-understanding, and my way of relating to myself as a person who relates to, e.g., high school, fosters expectations to myself of how I will most likely participate, and relate.

If we for a minute return to Lisa at Southside High, it is evident how she is also largely guided by her self-understanding, and corresponding need, of being different, that she traces back to being conceived by IVF, indicating a lifelong personal signifier of her self-understanding. As we recall from Chapter 2, the need and expectation to continuously stand out or be different at times contribute to the production of contradictions or ambivalences in her practice (e.g. in relation to the use of Facebook).

If we look at Peter, we see how his self-understanding largely guides his interactions with (a) artefacts, such as the kendama, etc., and (b) social others, such as his parents, Martin, Erik, Alexander and all the others at school, but also c) himself as a participant. Furthermore, the self-understanding largely influences the manner in which these different levels (a, b, c) are entangled and how meaning is ascribed to them. What stands out and becomes standards to Peter – that come to function as something he is directed towards and that structures his time and priorities – are primarily aspects of the environment that coincide with his self-understanding.

To conclude, the developmental dynamics displayed by Anna and Peter respectively demonstrate how artefacts and standards do not afford the same from everyone when they enter high school. Therefore, it does not suffice to talk of 'the affordance quality of something' as static or irrespective of the concrete person that interact with this 'something'. Consequently, we need to abandon any idea of high school students all being similar, with more or less the same opportunities and capabilities for participating in high school life. Participation is not a matter of *the will* to participate – or of a dichotomizing of participation or non-participation – but rather about differences in self-understanding, meaningfulness and the configuration of the subjectified subjectivity that the person brings into the school setting, and the continuous negotiations and synthetic processes between subjectivity and subjectification in concrete high school settings.

Concluding Thoughts and Perspectives

The study and understanding of youth and youth development has a long tradition of treating developmental processes on a continuum ranging from social (or societal) determinism to biological individualism (Hall 1904; Erikson 1971; Willis 1977; Ziehe 1983, 1989; Lesko 2001; Poulsen 2010). However, as I have tried to illuminate in this book, dynamic developmental processes in youth cannot be sufficiently accounted for by explaining the social conditions, let alone an individual biological maturation process.

In my opinion, a dialectical-ecological perspective on youth development is much needed. More specifically, a dialectical-ecological theory of youth development must take the societal realities of youth life into consideration. Being young and starting high school is not merely a matter of biological maturation or adaptation to societal values; rather, it is about navigating through – and negotiating – a myriad of invitations and possible self-understanding- and self-realization options in concrete practices, in concrete socio-material settings. Today – as opposed to few generations ago – young people are expected to take responsibility for many aspects of their lives on their own: their learning process and learning outcome, their social life, their health and their future. And they are expected to do so embedded in ambivalent dominant discourses concerning youth: one the one hand, they are expected to view their lives and their life chances in very positive manners, stressing the seeming individually open possibilities that lie before them; endless possibilities that are equally available and at reach, if the motivation is right. On the other hand, there is a pressure towards performing the self and celebrating talents and superiority within certain educational standards. This ambivalence is wonderfully performed at the introduction events at the schools, where students, teachers and headmasters (re)produce the idea that 'you can become what you want' in an endless space of possibilities, and that you need to take this self-realization (and potential self-optimization) task upon you, as an implicit part of embracing youth life and approximating adulthood. This double discourse (and demand structure) comes to constitute standards in youth life which are perceived, and need to be managed, by the young people. Not as a one-off, but as something that is continuously interwoven into the fabrics of everyday life. Not only does this emphasize that ambivalence and ambiguities are part of the developmental challenges that young people must handle as an integral part of their transitory processes. It also implies that youth development is often made identical with the project of both constructing and optimizing oneself in a performance culture, which indicates a gap between the actual challenges in youth life, on the one hand, and theories of youth development, on the other hand. This calls for the need to further develop our theorizing of youth development.

A Dialectical-Ecological Comprehension of Developmental Processes

Part of the motivation for this book was a desire to challenge the universal and decontextualized preconceptions of 'youth' and 'high school life'; these are not the same regardless of where (and when) they are encountered and studied. The exploration of the everyday life of Anna, Peter, Mia, Matilda, Emily and Lisa during their first year of high school has served to illustrate how developmental dynamics unfold in different manners, depending, inter alia, on the personal motive orientations of the young people and the respective practices in which they participate. This calls for theoretical approaches that can comprehend such developmental dynamics in their simultaneity without foregrounding the subjective aspect at the expense of the environment, and vice versa. Despite my efforts to do so in this book, I believe that this ambition may be hard to fully honour. Most likely the balance will always favour one 'side' of the person-environment reciprocity in our analytical efforts. However, what we can do – and this is important – is to be mindful about where we place the point of intersection, and to continuously strive for a dialectical-ecological comprehension. This requires first and foremost the employment of theoretical concepts or 'grasps' that enable us to work with reciprocal matters, and throughout this book, I have presented some that I propose to have potential in this endeavour. These are my suggestions for units of analysis that may enable a comprehension of developmental dynamics in a non-reductive manner, and thus add productively to the already well-established body of writing within a wholeness approach – or more precisely, a multitude of wholeness approaches, each emphasizing various aspects of the person-environment dialectics.

First, there is a challenge in encompassing an abstract 'societal level' in our analysis. Here, I have suggested a concept of standards to be helpful. The reason for this is based on the premise that all people grow up surrounded by an environment that has been largely shaped by other people; this is reflected in the societal institutions in which we participate, the artefacts we encounter, the activities we engage in with others, our language and eventually also in the way we relate to ourselves. Over the course of time, various aspects of practice are reproduced enough times for us not to question them – and some we never questioned to begin with. They simply become practice, as a *taken-for-grantedness*. For instance, we do not necessarily reflect upon how teaching is conducted at high schools, unless you are, like me, bestowed with the teaching responsibility yourself. Or, for that matter, on how many hours high school students are expected to spend at school every day, how long a high school essay is supposed to be, what it takes to achieve a top grade in physics and French and so forth. Some of these standards were originally decisions on a political level – and at times they are reassessed and altered – which reflects how some of the standards that young people encounter in their daily life are also means of political governing and, as such, they carry political (and historically anchored) motives. Nevertheless, these standards are perceived and experienced as more or less 'natural' in the course of everyday living; they have become an integral part of the high school practice, in the sense that they facilitate and constrain various aspects of agency and activities, and thus, in a larger perspective, the possibilities for life that are created for young people in a high school setting.

In this book, I refer to the notion of standards as a way to conceptualize the ever presence of societal ideals and pressure to perform or consider oneself in specific ways. This is an inevitable part of practice, in youth life and elsewhere, but in themselves standards are neither fish nor fowl. And in that sense, I am not proposing to problematize particular standards. Rather, it is the manner in which standards come to work – by which they standardize subjectivity and participation – and the strength with which a particular standard *invites* for reproduction, that we need to sharpen our analytical gaze. What has become irrevocably clear from entering the life-worlds of Anna, Peter, Mia, Matilda, Lisa and Emily is that standards are often contradictory, and the invitational character of the environment is ambiguous. In addition, standards are not necessarily directly point-out-able, to borrow Gibson's terminology, as formal rules or regulations. Often, they are elusive and very present at the same time, making them hard to pinpoint, but even harder to escape. This puts it upon young people, together and on their own, to make sense of their environment(s) and navigate a variegated landscape of possible self-realization options and normative expectations (on multiple concurrent and overlapping 'levels') on how to participate and consider oneself and the world.

To comprehend the manner in which standards are present – elusive or not – and become meaningful (or not) in the lives of young people, concepts are needed that can account for (1) the invitational character of the environment (including standards), and (2) the unceasing presence of dynamic standards. For this purpose, I shall briefly recapitulate the considerations in relation to the two conceptual propositions that have been presented: the human eco-niche, and the affording of standards.

Human Eco-niches and the Affording of Standards

Throughout the book, I have examined concrete lives of young people, in four different high school settings; based on ecological notions of high school as part of (and constituting) different *eco-niches*, and always connected to the activities and directedness of the individuals who inhabit these niches and participate in the particular activity settings of the school. The notion of eco-niche refers to *how* people actively construct their environment while, at the same time, being oriented towards the concrete possibilities for activities that the (close) environment offers. By developing and employing a notion of the human eco-niche, it is possible to grasp how young people take part in (local) shared life-worlds where collective meaning is historically developed (and developing). This offers a way to comprehend the taken-for-granted-ness of the immediate environment and *what matters in it*, as a historical and social dynamic (between persons and their environment). The notion of the human eco-niche may be a productive addition to cultural-historical activity theory in relation to theorizing the environment. 'The environment', just as the notion of 'societal', tends to become abstract and broad, and therefore difficult to analytically grasp. Here, seminal work has already been established by, e.g., Hedegaard (2009, 2012, 2014) amongst others, who proposes ways in which to operationalize institutional and societal aspects of the human lifeworld, thereby adding productively to the creation of (a multitude of) wholeness approaches to the study and comprehension of human development. As I see it, the environment, however, remains a little less theoretically nuanced and hence could be further operationalized, which is where I see the potential of the integration of cultural-historical activity theory and ecological psychology, in the pursuit of contributing to said wholeness approaches (see also Pedersen & Bang 2016b).

The environment encompasses more than material surroundings, and here I argue that what we, advantageously, could direct our attention to is the *collective ideality* that exists as part of an eco-niche. Or, that in many ways delineates the permeable borders of an eco-niche. Taking the environment seriously in our analytical endeavours implies the acknowledgement that a high school is *not just* a high school. Rather, it is a specific school with its own historicity and concrete material conditions, all of which feed into a particular way of doing high school, presenting a certain space of possibilities to the young people who inhabit it, while they, concurrently and in ongoing manners, negotiate and (re)produce the collective idealities that make up the school atmosphere. The notion of the *human eco-niche* therefore permits a level of analysis that indicates the situated character of high school practices, in a historical and geographical time and place, which allows for a study of variability in youth life – and youth life conditions – in high schools in Denmark, enabling us to transgress the notion of school as an abstract societal entity (see also Pedersen 2019).

My conclusion in relation to variations in youth life is not that the eco-niche (as a concept) can account for the variations alone, but rather that an understanding of human eco-niches may offer valuable insights into the meaning of *where* and *how* youth life is lived. In my opinion, it is therefore not only relevant, but paramount that the human eco-niche is taken into consideration in the study and comprehension of the developmental dynamics and variations in youth life, including in our understanding of the challenges and problems that young people experience and struggle with, in relation to the standards they encounter in their respective high school settings (or environments).

This leads me to the 'affording of societal standards'. I started the book, in Chapter 1, by trying to give the reader an idea of the invitational character of the high school environment. Throughout the book, it became clear that not only materiality or social others had a certain affordance quality, but that also standards of 'how' and 'who' to be in a high school setting played a part in the developmental dynamics that unfolded. This necessitated the need for a further development of the conceptual comprehension of the invitational character of the environment – one that surpassed material conditions alone, and that could account for the substantial historical and societal nature of the human lifeworld in a more elaborate manner than proposed by Gibson. With reference to the shared work of Jytte Bang and myself (see Pedersen & Bang 2016b), I proposed for the notion of *affording of societal standards* to be of theoretical value. This notion reflects an integration of ecological psychology and cultural-historical activity theory, what I believe to be not only a fruitful way for especially affordance theory to move forward, but also, and perhaps most important here, a way to theoretically nuance developmental theory in relation to the environment. When young people enter high school, they encounter a multiplicity of societal standards of how to be a high school student. And, as we have seen, these standards are not necessarily aligned, but often imbued with ambiguousness and ambivalence, if not downright contradiction in their invitations. Despite being encountered on a level of immediacy, these standards also reflect the mediated societal and historical character of the practice in which they are embedded. Therefore, the invitational character of the high school not only entails the immediate possibilities for action (as direct affordances), but it also conveys different levels of expectations and demands to the students, which may be better encompassed by the 'affording of societal standards'. In addition, the change from the noun 'affordance' to the gerund 'affording' reflects how societal standards must be thought of as *negotiated* and processual rather than fixed and prefixing. For instance, we saw how the standard of beer-drinking was continuously negotiated between Anna and Clara, implying slight alterations both on the level of persons and standard. This was further illustrated in Peter's way of encountering ongoing invitations to take part in social life outside school hours: through his way of participating, Peter demonstrated how standards are not blindly or passively accepted and reproduced by all participants in a given high school practice, but rather, that their meaning is meticulously negotiated in relation to personal motive orientations, just as they may be challenged and rejected, as part of the ongoing developmental dynamics that unfold between persons and their environments.

Person-Environment Reciprocity and the Dialectics of the Self

By stressing 'the environment' and 'standards' as influential in relation the development, the risk is, inevitably, to obscure the meaning of subjectivity or human agency. As I just outlined, a high school is a specific setting offering particular, historically and societally developed conditions for development, conveyed through its invitational character, the possibilities for action that it provides, and the objective meaning sets that is embedded in its way of practising high school (as collective ideality). At the same time, young people are not 'blank sheets' or 'empty vessels' entering high school; they enter with their ontogenetically developed subjectivity and self-understanding, reflecting their (historical) participation in numerous institutional, societal settings and interpersonal relations. Nor are they directionless or unmotivated, waiting to be filled with whatever the high school practice dictates. All this influences their meeting with the high school and opens up a comprehension of the person as a historical becoming. To better comprehend the concurrence and entangled nature of these various aspects of the human lifeworld, I – again with a reference to my shared work with Jytte Bang (Pedersen & Bang 2016a) – proposed a dialectical-ecological model of youth development, and the notion of *subjectified subjectivity*. Here, subjectification indicates that subjectivity, as essential as it is to any person, over time furnishes itself on the basis of available standards, which implies that the standards available in the high school setting are potentially integrated into the self-understanding of the person. Subjectivity is understood as multidimensional in that it refers not only to the experience, but also to the engagement, action potentials and initiations of a person. In Chapter 6, I explored how Anna, over time, became a *subjectivity-subjectification synthesis*, in relation to the practice of beer-drinking. Through an analysis of Anna's way of relating to beer and the high school practice of beer drinking, we saw how the different levels of analysis (of relating to self and the world) dynamically influenced each other over the course of time, and how Anna's way of relating to herself transformed; both with regard to her environmental activities (in what she took part), to what appeared meaningful and of value to her (what did she allow herself to do), and to herself (who 'is' Anna). In these transformations, Anna did *not* let go of her ideals (of how to be) or her overall idea of who she was becoming (a pedagogue, with time), but rather was oriented towards finding pragmatic solutions to the (existential) challenges imposed by the alcohol culture at school. Therefore, her subjectivity became *subjectified* through environmental artefacts, practices and standards, but her subjectivity was not *reduced* to subjectification.

This brings forth the following comprehension of developmental change: most often developmental change on an individual level is understood primarily in individual ways, as something occurring *within* an individual. Anna's transformation in terms of self-relation (and relating to beer) cannot be sufficiently comprehended by regarding it as mere adaptation to dominant standards and as something occurring solely *within* Anna. This is demonstrated through the relation between Anna and Carla and their joint way of relating to beer; both Anna and Carla are changing over the course of the first year, and therefore their respective processes of change are necessarily *dynamic* and *interrelated*, just as they cannot be comprehended apart from the concrete material artefacts and historically developed practices and values in relation to which they unfold. The proposed conceptualization of subjectification-subjectivity syntheses is thus an attempt to theoretically account for the way standards come to influence youth development (and how standards, in turn, are continuously negotiated, reproduced and altered). Subsequently, I suggest that we conceive of the developmental 'situation' as numerous people's simultaneous co-construction of social spaces of participation and ways of relating, which can be seen as a result of ongoing processes of negotiation of standards among young people, as they participate in youth life in high school.

Whereas one of the developments that occurred for Anna over the course of the school year, namely that of gradually approximating and engaging in the social life outside school, was rather apparent, this was not the case for Peter's development. Unlike Anna, Peter's subjective transformation did not approximate a high school standard of beer-drinking and social participation, which lead to an obvious change in his conduct of everyday life or his motive hierarchy, but rather demonstrated what appeared as a rejection of the aforementioned standard. What gradually manifested was how Peter remained grounded in his self-understanding (which I analytically conceptualized as subjectified sensitivity), by way of approximating other available invitations or standards in the high school setting, and how he engaged in subtle and ongoing negotiations of the shared meaning of standards with his close friend Eric, as well as his classmates. This does not indicate that no change occurred on a subjective level, but rather that Peter's developmental transformations were mostly visible on a level of intentionality. The transformations in Peter's intentional dynamics over time suggested that the encounter with the affordings of the academic-engagement-standard (as part of his environment) served to reinforce the subjectified sensitivity that Peter brought with him to high school, as the affordings of this particular standard were highly compatible with his need to be alone. It further legitimized this need in a high school setting, thereby consolidating Peter's understanding of self.

Through the various processes of negotiation that young people engage in – here exemplified by Anna and Peter – it follows that the affordings of standards are not just automatically transferred to, or adopted by, new high school students. Instead, I suggest, they are *actively* approached and ascribed with meaning, relating to (and completely inseparable from) the subjectivities and motive orientations of the young people who face and engage with them (in line with Vygotsky's (1994) point about the inseparability of the person and her/his environment). The negotiation of (shared) meaning is intrinsically embedded in concrete settings and practices, and inextricable from ways of relating to each other in the course of daily life. We see numerous examples of the concurrence of multiple negotiation processes, e.g., in relation to the meaning of a specific artefact (beer, kendama, granola bar, health profile, grades, clothes), entangled with overall and way more subtle negotiations of 'who *we* are, in this setting'.

Despite what we might refer to as the 'standardizing force' of standards, in the sense that they do have a tendency to promote certain aspects of practice over others, the individual variations between young people, in their way of relating (to standards), cannot be disregarded. One can be drawn to *some* aspects of practice or respond to *only some* affordances of the environment, and not others. This depends largely on the subjective motive orientation, or, as Wright et al. (1951) phrased it, the 'psychological habitat' of the person. But it also indicates that standards *co-exist* and *overlap* in the high school setting, and that they are not mutually exclusive even though they are often contradictory in their invitations or directions for ways of participating. This co-existence implicates possible tensions that the young people are left to handle – often on their own – through negotiations of meaning and participation with each other. These negotiation processes occur as mediated by subjectivity, which indicates that subjectivity influences the meaning of standards and therefore also contribute to their transformation. In that sense, standards, like artefacts, are not 'outside' the human lifeworld, but dialectically spun into practice.

From the manner in which transformative processes occurred during Anna, Peter, Mia, Emily, Matilda and Lisa's first year in high school, I want to definitively put down the misconception of young people being, in anyway, 'empty vessels' (to paraphrase the Turning Points' report, that I referred to earlier), who uncritically adopt whatever high school, or other educational institutions, throws at them. There is no way (!) in which we can comprehend the developmental dynamics that unfold, neither on an individual nor on a social/societal level, as disconnected from subjectivity. Indeed, young people are actively meeting and engaging with the high school practice. They are open to the world and seem to spend quite a lot of energy in making sense of that which they encounter, collectively and by themselves, probing new self-understandings and ways of participating. If we were to register their time spent on various activities, the negotiation of meaning would certainly light up.

From an outside perspective, it is fairly easy to identify or recognize overall patterns or tendencies that make the majority appear as if they are doing 'the same', while those who fail to do so are seen as somewhat deviant from the norm. But for neither of the six participants can we disregard the meaning of subjectivity and still acquire an adequate comprehension of their developmental trajectories. As was illustrated by, e.g., Matilda and Emily, they both, on the outside, adhere to a general image of successful ways of doing 'youth' at Westside High, but, when we ask into their reasons and motives on a subjective level, we see how they both, in their own way, struggle to keep up this appearance, and let alone their self-understandings. And at Southside High, Lisa demonstrates how, despite appearing – and finding pride in being – a norm-breaker (in multiple senses), she also abides to very normative standards of youth life, pertaining to academic achievement. Therefore, it is impossible to neglect how young people carefully select and pursue the activities and possibilities in the high school setting that resonate with their motive orientations, their plans and aspirations, and their self-understandings. What follows from the ways in which Lisa, Matilda, Emily and the others meet standards (as part of their environments) is that *only some* subjectifications come to matter and are integrated into the self-understanding of the person (as subjectified subjectivity), which is not something that happens from day to day, but as a process (of various duration) that depends on the correlation between the subjectification and the already developed subjectified subjectivity of the person. And a process in which said standards seldomly remain unaltered. For example, Peter's participation in the high school setting throughout his first year is largely structured by his self-understanding (subjectified sensitivity), which implies the rejection of some of the dominant standards that clearly appeal to his classmates and his friend Eric. This suggests that 'self' also has affordance quality, by indicating that the self-relation reflects a person-environment reciprocity, and that the environment is thus not 'external' to the person. The analyses presented in Chapters 6 and 7 indicate that there is no such thing as 'a universal young person'; the manner in which young people relate to the standards they perceive and experience in the high school practice is highly subjective and connected to their subjectified subjectivity (reflecting their ontogenetic development). Furthermore, it suggests how part of comprehending developmental processes consists of theoretically and analytically grasping *the developing relation* between a person and their respective environment, as both person and environment – as well as their interconnectedness – need to be understood as dynamic and interdependent.

The Meaning of Where Youth Life Is Lived

In my introduction to this book, I drew reference to the work of Elder (1974, 1998), and the four principles he outlines in relation to life-course development, namely those of (1) Historical time and place, (2) Timing in lives, (3) Linked lives and (4) Human agency. What I have been attempting to analytically explore is how these principles or aspects interrelate in young people's lives in a time of transition. What do we learn about developmental dynamics when we take the situated character of the human lifeworld seriously?

The backdrop for this enquiry was a theoretical framework that insisted on a wholeness approach and a genuine interest in *the developing relation* between person and environment, implying an analytical interest in multiple interconnected, dynamic factors. Here, I drew reference to, among others, the work of Hedegaard (Hedegaard 2003, 2009, 2012, 2014; Hedegaard et al. 2008) and Lewin (1935, 1946/1954). My ambition in this book has been to add productively to the awarenesses already instated by, e.g., Hedegaard and Elder, in particular in regard to the developmental processes that occur in the transition from one educational setting to another. As the book has sought to illuminate, the meaning of historical time and place (cf. Elder), as well as the societal conditions and institutional values (cf. Hedegaard), becomes a backdrop in relation to which one must comprehend the entangled life-worlds of people in situated manners. What this book may contribute with or elucidate – and I will leave it to the reader to assess whether or not this is achieved – is the necessity of encompassing, and further theoretically nuancing, the environment as concrete conditions that make a difference in the developmental dynamics that unfold. This is not, I will argue, satisfactorily achieved by including (abstract) descriptions of historical time and place alone, but must also, to the extent possible, consider and include how materiality and (human) geography become a factor – and possibly make a difference – in the developmental dynamics in young people's lives, and not least in the challenges and ambiguities that they encounter. These cannot be comprehended apart from the particular institutional practices in which young people participate and the manner in which particular high schools locally handle and embody societal pressure that is (historically) built into their structure and commission. The empirical body of this book suggests that there are significant variations in how Countryside-, Southside-, Westside-, and Northside High, respectively, institutionally arrange and frame youth life, which points to the meaning of *where* youth life is lived, or the meaning of 'place', as also emphasized by Elder.

In my view, the meaning of place indicates that young people are offered different conditions and diverse spaces of possibilities depending on the location of their school. This approximates the insights proposed by Barker and Wright (1966, 1971), who pointed to the almost peremptory quality of the concrete surroundings, suggesting that behaviour settings are coercive. Not in the sense of determining people's actions in a one-to-one relation, but as an indicator of how influential the invitational character of the (concrete) environment can be. Some of these differences were studies extensively as the variations that occurred between, e.g., bigger and smaller schools in relation to the behaviour settings they offered and the differences these variations produced (see, e.g., Wright et al. 1951; Gump 1965; Wicker 1968).

To fully comprehend the meaning of place, we need to transcend a question of geography and include both the concrete availabilities in the environment (*at*, and *in proximity to*, the school), the concrete architectural layout of the school, and the overall historically developed local sets of objective meaning reflected in the school atmosphere. For instance, we saw how the architectural layout at Countryside High co-constructed differentiation in relation to the students with Asperger's syndrome (sound-proof classroom), just as the large communal space that was the very heart of the school contributed to an outspoken atmosphere of communality. Or, how, at Westside High, the distributed character and the rather limited communal spaces perhaps served to reinforce a predominantly individualistic school culture that, evidently, has little to do with the school as a material entity or geographical location alone, but reflects the entanglements of location (in the heart of the capital), material conditions, as well as historical and societal developments at and around the school (over time contributing to an elitist school identity).

The meaning of place further indicates that the high school is *part of* and *co-constitutes* a particular eco-niche, implying differences in what general conditions students are offered in terms of possibilities for orientation, participation and self-understanding. Hence, I return to my proposition of understanding variations in youth life as connected to different eco-niches. As I see it, this enables an understanding of the underlying *collective creative processes* of the concrete and local ways of practising high school – and of the way in which meaning differs across the different high schools. These differences cannot be explained merely as the high school's way of practising high school, nor as reflecting the actions of individuals (the young people), but rather they (the differences) must be comprehended in their *dialectical* and *historical* connection, where both high schools and young people historically have co-created (and continuously co-create) themselves and each other – thereby reflecting locally anchored and mutual *processes of becoming*.

Different Historical Time, Similar Challenges

On the last page of her seminal publication, *Jocks & Burnouts - social categories and identity in the high school*, from 1989, Penelope Eckert writes:

> *Improving education for the adolescent population depends on the creation of an atmosphere in which all adolescents are equally receptive and equally privy to the resources of the school. This atmosphere does not depend simply on interaction between individual school personnel and individual students or even groups of students, but depends far more on interaction among students. Although an individual may be strongly influenced or even transformed by one teacher at some point in life, the average adolescent probably learns more from peers than from any other category of people. There is a wide gap in our knowledge of the structure of adolescent society, and this gap prevents us from understanding the broader issues in problems that face adolescents. Ignorance about adolescents leads us to trivialize their experience, and our efforts to take them seriously are frequently misguided by our stylized notion of their social relations. It is particularly ironic that, in considering 'the youth of today', we seem to translate and apply our own adolescent experience in all the wrong ways. We focus on the surface (although admittedly serious) issues of substance use and abuse, increased pregnancy and childbearing, and alienation, and fail to concentrate on the underlying social processes that are common to at least the current generations.*
>
> (Eckert 1989:184)

Undeniably, historical time is a factor that cannot be ignored which becomes especially apparent when regarded retrospectively. Much has changed since 1989, when Eckert's book was published, but the tendency that she problematizes remains. In my opinion, there is still a vast tendency to focus on the surface phenomena when it comes to youth life and youth life problems, in terms of both comprehension and intervention. In a current Danish context, it is not, as in Eckert's case, teenage pregnancies, drug abuse or alienation that present as the concern-raising surface problems, but rather the dramatic rise in mental health issues among young people and, perhaps on a more political level, drop-out rates and failure to proceed straight through the educational system. However, as in 1989, the diagnosing of the problem is (still) not on point. We tend to focus on what presents as problematic on the surface – what manifests on an individual level in terms of deviances from the (politically desired) norm – instead of enquiring into or critically exploring the concrete conditions in relation to which young people are conducting their everyday lives, and in relation to which they develop. These conditions seldomly form part of our analysis, which implies that the interventions we set in motion to alleviate the (individual) pain are often oblique. We live in a time where the answer to most problems can be found in individual therapy, in meditation or mindfulness exercises, in medication, or in the exacerbation of structural demands for progression, limiting individual freedom all the while upholding the discourse that anything is possible and that current youth generations have *all the possibilities* in the world. And no doubt that these different interventions have their relevance and their audience, and even their beneficial effects. However, none of them address the reciprocity of person and environment and the specific, situated developmental dynamics that unfold for young people in their concrete educational settings. And just as we cannot place the blame for whatever happens here, e.g., in the high school setting, nor can we disregard the relevance of said dynamics and the concrete developmental space that the environment co-constitutes. As Eckert, I will therefore point to the need of further exploring, not only social processes, but the *concrete person-environment reciprocities* as they are embodied, enacted and realized in the life-worlds of young people. In my opinion, this requires a renewed interest in, and an obligation to include, the situated character of the human lifeworld, which must consider the meaning of where youth life is lived – the meaning of place – an integral part of the analysis.

In the analyses presented in this book, I have tried to follow and prioritize that which arose as significant or meaningful over time, in relation to comprehending different aspects of the developmental dynamics. Methodologically, this was an attempt to comprehend developmental change as it was happening, in the micro-genesis of everyday life. And many aspects proved meaningful, which meant that what is presented in this book does not focus in depth on one aspect of the lifeworld alone, but rather the simultaneity and interconnectivity of various aspects – as they appear in entangled manners in everyday life. Thus, one may critically argue that I could have further unfolded and enriched, e.g., the material aspects of the life-worlds of the participants, and I would not oppose to such a criticism. However, the ambition of this book was to explore and enlighten developmental dynamics embarking from the respective lifeworlds of the participants, inspired by – and at the same time hoping to contribute to – a wholeness approach. In my view, the exploration of developmental dynamics entails the integration of multiple aspects of practice that each, in their own right, could readily have been further analytically nuanced, but that never appear separate or isolated in practice. Hence, an attempt to further disentangle singular units for the sake of analysis would, I fear, be at the expense of comprehending and acknowledging how various aspects of the individual lifeworld, such as a kendama, a self-understanding as being 'sensitive', clear expectations to take part in social gatherings, societal demands for academic achievement, dad's baking practice, collective meaning making of what to prioritize, online gaming and a pet snake cannot be understood apart, as they are, in fact, part of one individual's lifeworld, constituting that person's reality, and hence the wholeness of this person's life, intersecting in various ways – messy, as Law (2007) would say – and never static.

Implications for the Comprehension of Developmental Dynamics and Transitory Processes

Part of what surprised me during my time spent at the four different high schools was the variations that emerged, in relation to the ambiguities of practice. A few dominant standards pertaining to youth life became identifiable across the different schools, and although we can name them in decontextualized manners, they are continuously met and (re)produced in local settings, which tend to bring about variations in the meaning that accompanies these standards and the spaces of possibilities that they entail. In Chapters 2–5, I explored these as ambiguities and ambivalences that exist in practice. Here, a remarkable difference presented in relation to the way in which performance pressure was – or was not – part of the school atmosphere or culture. I could not help but notice how this was outspoken at Westside High and Southside High, but not something I would notice at neither Northside High nor Countryside High. This suggests a difference in inner-city versus not-inner-city location. If I, for a second, play the devil's advocate with myself, I could infer that the difference between Northside high and the two inner-city schools could also be explained by the fact that at Northside High, I was part of a boy's group, following Peter in his everyday life, and that, had I followed a girl here, I might had observed different tendencies. Perhaps. Perhaps not. This is an argument that one could present in relation to all the schools, as of course, it would have made a difference to follow *someone else*, but this argument surpasses a question of gender. And perhaps, if I had followed Clara, instead of Anna at Countryside High, I might have ended up with a different impression. Surely, to some extent, as all individuals are different and therefore the person-environment dynamics will play out in slightly different manners. However, this does not exclude the possibility, or diminish the relevance, of pointing towards developmental dynamics that transcend the analysis of the individual. My point in drawing out variations in youth life and coupling them with the variations in high school's ways of 'doing high school' is not to install categorizations or suggest an environmental determinism. On the contrary, I do believe that all schools may foster and enable *a plurality* of self-understandings, meanings and developmental trajectories.

The point I wish to make is that we *cannot* understand the developmental dynamics that occur *detached from the environment in which they occur*. This does not imply that the environment, or a high school setting to be more precise, invites for one thing alone and produces 'one kind' of high school student, to reintroduce the machine metaphor. But it means that what happens on a subjective level, as well as on a collective level, does in fact happen in coherence with the material, relational and social realities of the school setting, and to fully comprehend this, we need to take seriously the historicity as well as the manner in which a high school, e.g., translates and communicates societal pressure to young people. As Ingold (2004:215) writes:

> (..) there is no way of describing what human beings **are** independently of the manifold historical and environmental circumstances in which they **become** – in which they grow up and live out their lives.

This has implications. One of them being the need to extend the analytical unit when it comes to the challenges or problems that young people increasingly seem to present. It would be senseless to claim that the potential ambiguities or contradictions that young people may experience in their high school settings are *causing* their personal problems – such ambivalences, ambiguities and contradictions are part of that which enable and (co)constitute spaces of development, and hence give way to new motive orientations, etc. In that sense, these are not (necessarily) problematic on their own. There is no causal relation between the introduction of a mandatory health profile as part of gym class and an increased awareness of healthy food among a group of girls, or between the health profile and an eating disorder. People are not that simple. Development is not that simple. Nor can we solely ascribe the individual pressure felt by Matilda and Emily of keeping up appearances, all the while feeling anxious, to the outspoken performance culture at their school, although this seems a more straightforward and obvious analysis. However, the problem arises, when in trying to comprehend young people's occasional problems or difficulties, such environmental aspects seem to vanish from the equation. We cannot and, I would argue, *should not* ignore the inherent person-environment reciprocity at play. These aspects of the school practice *do* form part of the building blocks – or the wholeness – from which young people are trying to construct themselves and their foundation for adult life, and although they have the freedom to choose, they do not make choices in a limitless, historyless space of possibilities (regardless of persistent discursive illusions suggesting otherwise).

In the introduction of the book, I briefly touched upon the concerning rise in mental health issues among young people in Denmark, and although this book has not addressed this specifically, I do believe that this book *also* concerns this, albeit in an indirect manner. Paying an interest to the developmental dynamics that unfold in young people's transitory processes, between different educational settings, between various activity settings, or in their existential movement towards adulthood serves as a foundational backdrop for the comprehension of youth life, including the problems that young people experience and present. In this book, I argue that we need to understand developmental dynamics dialectically, anchored in a constitutive person-environment reciprocity.

Exploring the person-environment reciprocity concretely enables an understanding of the *subtle, complex, contradictory* and *layered* reciprocities of young people and their specific societal environments. In the intersection between the 'affordings of standards' in a particular setting and the concrete subjectified subjectivity of the person, *particular possibilities for action* and *becoming* are created and facilitated, along with *possible new relations* to 'self' and the world. However, if and when the particularity is taken out of the equation, it becomes difficult to understand '*why am I not like the others*', or '*why can't I just be like the images I see on social media*', or '*why do I experience a lot of pressure, but still act as if I am on top of everything?*' etc. And it may become difficult for the individual to decipher – or see the connections to – the ambiguities she or he experiences in her/his daily life, as these are experienced from a first-person givenness, that is *always* embedded in a given practice. As we saw in the case of Anna, she only experienced her own transformations retrospectively, and when the temporal perspective was offered by her mother. In the same manner, depending on concrete conditions, interpersonal resources and ontogenetic experiences, it may be a challenge for young people to create an analytical distance to the complexities of their everyday lives and the meaning of, e.g., the affordings of various standards, and therefore it may also prove difficult to reflect upon themselves as subjected to the inherent and hidden power that standards contain in terms of dictating how youth life *ought to be*.

As I see it, there are multiple implications here: firstly, this places a responsibility on high schools in terms of (critically) reflecting upon the way in which they conduct and practise high school (e.g. in relation to how societal pressure is translated and built into practice) – and in which way they, for their part, create an ecological setting, containing specific conditions for activities and self-realization options for young people. Secondly, it addresses the need of comprehending various phenomena, such as large alcohol consumption, mental health issues or increasing drop-out rates, as intimately interwoven with the developmental dynamics of everyday life, not separate from it. So, when we do enquire into such matters, we need to consider them part of a wholeness that is far more complex than peer pressure, or individual mental shortcomings. Young people are always engaged in making sense of the world and the specific invitations to 'become' that they encounter, just as they are continuously trying to look out for themselves (and sometimes each other) and pursue the realization of their current motives, whatever they may be – they are never *not* conducting their lives, and never not trying to make sense of questions pertaining to 'who' and 'how' they ought to be, or not be to. And they are never 'placed' outside the influence of the environment. This means that – thirdly – there is a need of promoting and employing developmental wholeness approaches that can, in fact, account for developmental *dynamics* without reducing their complexities and without losing sight of either personal motives and subjectivity, nor the environment, enabling us to move *beyond* individualized problem conceptualizations. In this book, I have proposed a theoretical framework that I believe to have potential in this endeavour.

The premise of this book was to better understand youth development in a time of transition, between different institutional settings and in the overall sense of transitioning from childhood to adulthood. And if we return to Lisa's vest and the statement of being 'under construction', a fair question may be 'so what have I learned about this construction process'? Well, when we look across the chapters of this book, it becomes evident how youth development as well as the challenges that this entails on a personal level must be comprehended as intimately interwoven with a myriad of everyday life conditions. In this book, I have selectively focused on high school as a prominent everyday life setting, and how this setting comes to matter in terms of development, but that is in no way meant as an exclusion of the meaning of other practices or settings.

What I found to be striking in terms of youth development is how young people, regardless of where in the country they are located, experience and consider their high school conditions as ordinary and natural – 'this is the way things are'. At the same time, we can see, from the outside, how high school conditions are in no way 'ordinary', but instead – and on the contrary – highly *local, socio-material, cultural, historical* and to some extent *geographical*. And we see how this has an impact on how developmental dynamics unfold on the level of the individual. This offers a critical perspective and an alternative to general tendencies to regard young people, as well as developmental processes in youth, in decontextualized manners. When compared to dominant and traditional youth understandings, and the current research trends in the field (that tend to highlight problematic youth life phenomena rather than foundational comprehensions of developmental dynamics), it thus becomes evident that a wholeness approach to the study of young people's everyday lives is not only important, but also fruitful and necessary for the understanding of personal variation, and of developmental dynamics among young people.

Here, I will argue that ecological psychology and cultural-historical theory in combination open new doors for the study and comprehension of youth development; and, specifically, I propose for a dialectical-ecological conception along with a revised concept of affordance to have significant potential for the comprehension of the invitational character of the environment and, ultimately, for an ecologically grounded theory of development. While young people may still experience their everyday lives on the level of immediacy, it remains a theoretical challenge to take into account the person-environment reciprocity in the comprehension of developmental dynamics. Only then can we fully understand the complex and situated life-worlds of persons-in-their-environments.

As I began this book with a quote from Lisa, so I shall end it by sharing her reflections on the existential question of 'who I am', pointing to the concurrence of 'being me' and 'being in process':

> Lisa: *All of my childhood, I was like: 'Okay, I'm here, and I'm a human being. And I am me', right. And I didn't really feel the need to have more answers than that, you know. But then when you become more aware – and I think you do in your teenage-years – then something happens where you start to question: 'Who am I? Who is the "me"? what exactly is this me-thing really?' [...] In a way, I think people really want to be put in boxes all the time, right. It is a human need. One hundred percent. And for me, I really needed to know how and who I was.*
> Me: *But how do you know, when you've found out?*
> Lisa: *I don't know ... and I actually don't think one ever finds out.*

References

Aaberg, F. (2005). Skolespredning – en vej til bedre integration. In Etniske minoriteter – et nyt proletariat? *Social Forskning*, (pp. 73–8). Temanummer. Socialforskningsinstituttet.

Aboulafia, A., Hansen, T., & Bang, J. (2003). Betydning og mening fra Leontjev til ny dansk virksomhedsteori. In Aboulafia, A., Hansen, H.H., Hansen, T. & Bang, J. (Eds.), *Virksomhed, Betydning Og Mening* (pp. 7–18). Frederiksberg C: Roskilde Universitetsforlag.

AE (2011a). Arbejderbevægelsens Erhvervsråd p.b.a. Danmarks Statistik, 2 Aug. 2011: http://www.ae.dk/files/AE_nye-tal-viser-stort-frafald-paa-erhvervsuddannelserne.pdf

Andersen, E.S. (2016). Drop klagesangen om, at vi studerende dåner af stress. Newspaper article, *Politiken*, 28 January.

Arnett, J. J. (2004). *Emerging adulthood*. New York: Oxford University Press.

Axel, E. (2011). Conflictual cooperation. *Nordic Psychology, 63*(4), 56–78.

Axel, E., & Højholt, C. (2019). Subjectivity, conflictuality, and generalization in social praxis. In C. Højholt & E. Schraube (Eds.), *Subjectivity and knowledge: Theory and history in the human and social sciences* (pp. 23–40). New York: Springer.

Bang, J. (2008). Conceptualising the environment of the child in a cultural-historical approach. In M. Hedegaard, M. Fleer, J. Bang & P. Hviid (Eds.), *Studying children. A cultural-historical approach*. London: Open University Press.

Bang, J. (2009a). Nothingness and the human Umwelt. A cultural-ecological approach to meaning (pp. 374–92). *Integrative Psychological and Behavioral Science, 43*(4). New York: Springer.

Bang, J. (2009b). An environmental affordance perspective on the study of development. Artefacts, social others, and self. In Fleer, M., Hedegaard, M. & Tudge, J. (Eds.), *Childhood studies and the impact of globalization: Policies and practices at global and local levels. World yearbook of education* (pp. 161–81). New York and London: Routledge.

Bang, J., & Møhl, B. (2010). Ungdom og de unges liv – indledning til temanummer om ungdom. *Psyke og Logos*, pp. 5–11.

Banks, C. A. (2005). Black girls/white spaces: Managing identity through memories of schooling. In Bettis Pamela, J. & Adams Natalie, G. (Eds.), *Geographies of girlhood: Identities in-between* (pp. 177–194). Hillsdale, NJ: Lawrence Erlbaum.

Barker, R. G. (1968). *Ecological psychology*. Stanford: Stanford University Press.

Barker, R., & Wright, H. (1966). *One boy's day – a specimen record of behaviour*. Hamden, Connecticut: Archon Books.

Barker, R., & Wright, H. (1971). *Midwest and its children. The psychological Ecology of an American town*. Hamden, CT: Archon Books. First published 1955.

Bauman, Z. (2005). *Forspildte liv*. København: Hans Reitzels Forlag.

Beck, S. (2006). *En ny myndighed: Gymnasieelevers rusmiddelkultur og skolekulturelle forandringsprocesser*. Doctoral dissertation, Syddansk Universitet.

Beck, S. (2007). I grænselandet mellem fritidskultur og skolekultur. Gymnasieelever og rusmidler i et forandringsperspektiv. *Unge og Rusmidler, STOF* (8).

Beckstead, Z, Cabell, K. R., & Valsiner, J. (2009). Generalizing through conditional analysis: Systemic causality in the world of eternal becoming (pp. 65–80). *Humana Mente* (11).
Bertelsen P. (1994). *Tilværelsesprojektet - Det menneskeliges niveauer belyst i den terapeutiske proces.* København: Dansk Psykologisk Forlag.
Bertelsen, P. (2003). *Antropologisk Psykologi.* 2nd ed. 1. issue. København: Frydenlund.
Boier, P. (2019). Forsker: Unge på gymnasiet føler pres, ensomhed og er dårlige til at snakke om det. *Danmarks Radio,* 9/9-2019.
Borup, D. B., & Pedersen, S. (2010). Er udvikling overhovedet meningen? *Nordiske Udkast,* årgang 38, nr 1 & 2, Syddansk universitetsforlag.
Bowker, G. C., & Star, S. L. (2000). *Sorting things out – classifications and its consequences.* Massachusetts: The MIT press.
Bourdieu, P. (1986/2011). The forms of capital. In Szeman, I. & Kaposy. T. (Eds.), *Cultural theory – An anthology.* Chichester, West Sussex, UK: Wiley-Blackwell.
Bozhovich, L. I. (2009). The social situation of child development. *Journal of Russian and East European Psychology,* 47(4), 59–86.
Brinkmann, S. (2010). *Det diagnosticerede liv – sygdom uden grænser.* Aarhus: Forlaget Klim.
Bronfenbrenner, U. (1977). Toward an experimental ecology of human development. *American Psychologist,* 32(7), 513–31.
Bronfenbrenner, U. (1979). *The ecology of human development: Experiments by nature and design.* Cambridge, MA: Harvard University Press.
Busch, L. (2011). *Standards. Recipes for reality.* Cambridge and London: The MIT Press.
Bærentsen, K.B., & Trettvik, J. (2002). An activity theory approach to affordance. *Proceedings of NordiCHI,* 51–60.
Cahan, E.D. (1992). John Dewey and human development. *Developmental Psychology,* 28(2), 205–14.
Chimirri, N. A. (2015). Designing psychological co-research of emancipatory-technical relevance across age thresholds. *Outlines,* 16(2), 26–51.
Chimirri, N. A. (2019). Generalizing together with children: The significance of children's concepts for mutual knowledge creation. In C. Højholt & E. Schraube (Eds.), *Subjectivity and knowledge: Generalization in the psychological study of everyday life.* Springer (pp. 115–39). https://doi.org/10.1007/978-3-030-29977-4_7
Chimirri, N. A., & Pedersen, S. (2019). Toward a transformative-activist co-exploration of the world? Emancipatory co-research in Psychology from the standpoint of the subject. *Kritische Psychologie,* 16, 605–33.
Collins, D., & Coleman, T. (2008). Social geographies of education: Looking within, and beyond, school boundaries. *Geography Compass* 2(1), 281–99, Blackwell Publishing Ltd.
Costall, A. (1995). Socializing affordances. *Theory and Psychology,* 5(4), 467–81.
Costall, A. (2001). Darwin, ecological psychology, and the principle of animal-environment mutuality, *Psyke & Logos,* 22, 473–84.
Costall, A. (2004). From direct perception to the primacy of action: A closer look at James Gibson's ecological approach to psychology. In G. Bremner & A. Slater (Eds.), *Theories of infant development* (pp. 70–89). Blackwell Publishing Ltd, chapter 3.
Costall, A., and Richards, A. (2013). Canonical Affordances: The psychology of everyday things. In Graves-Brown, Harrison & Piccini (Eds), *The Oxford handbook of the archeology of the contemporary world* (pp. 82–93). Oxford University Press, chapter 6.
Dalgas, J. (2020). Opråb fra eksperter: Gymnasieeleverne er ikke presset af en præstationskultur. For mange elever er dovne og umotiverede. Newspaper article, *Berlingske,* 11/1–2020.

Darwin, C. (1881). *The formation of vegetable mould: Through the action of worms, with observations on their habits.* By Charles Darwin, with illustrations. London: John Murray.

Dean, M. (2010). *Governmentality – magt og styring I det moderne samfund.* Forlaget Sociologi, 3. oplag.

DeWalt, K. M. & DeWalt, B. R. (2010). *Participant observation: A guide for fieldworkers.* Plymouth: Altamira Press.

Dewey, J. (1884). The new psychology. In Boydston, J.A. (Eds.), *The early works of John Dewey, 1882–1897* (Vol. 1, pp. 48–60). Carbondale, IL: Southern Illinois University Press. First published in *Andover Review, 2,* 278–89.

Dreier. O. (1996). Ændring af professionel praksis på sundhedsområdet gennem praksisforskning. In U.J. Jensen et al. (Eds.), *Forskelle og forandring – bidrag til humanistisk sundhedsforskning.* Arhus: Philosophia.

Dreier, O. (2011). Personality and the conduct of everyday life. *Nordic Psychology, 63*(2), 4–23. https://doi.org/10.1027/1901-2276/a000024

Dreier, O. (2016). Conduct of everyday life: Implications for critical psychology. In E. Shraube & C. Højholt (Eds.), *Psychology and the conduct of everyday life* (pp. 15–33). Hove: Routledge.

Dreier, O. (2019). Generalizations in situated practices. In C. Højholt & E. Schraube (Eds.), *Subjectivity and knowledge: Generalization in the psychological study of everyday life* (pp. 177–93). New York: Springer.

Eckert, P. (1989). *Jocks & Burnouts.* New York: Teachers College.

Edwards, A. (2010). *Being an expert professional practitioner: The relational turn in expertise.* Dordrecht: Springer.

Elder Jr., G. H. (1974). *Children of the great depression.* Chicago: The University of Chicago Press.

Elder Jr., G. H. (1998). The life course as developmental theory. *Child Development, 69*(1), 1–12.

Elder Jr., G. H. (2001). Families, social change, and individual lives. *Marriage & Family Review, 31*(1–2), 187–203.

Elder Jr., G.H., Kirkpatrick Johnson, M., & Crosnoe, R. (2004). Th e emergence and development of life course theory. In J. T. Mortimer & M. J. Shanahan (Eds.), *Handbook of the life course* (pp. 23–50). New York: Springer.

Elmeland, K., & Kolind, T. (2012). 'Why don't they just do what we tell them?' Different alcohol prevention discourses in Denmark. *Young, 20*(2), 177–97.

Engelsted, N. (1983). What is the psyche and how did it get into the world? In N. Engelsted, L. Hem & J. Mammen (Eds.), *Essays in general psychology. Seven danish contributions* (pp. 13–48). Arhus: Aarhus University Press.

Engelsted, N. (1989). *Personlighedens almene grundlag: en teoretisk ekskursion i psykologiens historie.* Aarhus: Aarhus universitetsforlag.

Erikson, E. (1970). *Childhood and society.* Middlesex: Penguin Books, (first published 1950).

Erikson, E. (1971). Identitet – ungdom og kriser. København: Hans Reitzel. (English version: Identity: Youth and Crisis (1968). New York: Norton & Company).

Farver, J. A. M. (1999). Activity setting analysis: A model for examining the role of culture in development. In A. Göncü (Ed.), *Children's engagement in the world: Sociocultural perspectives* (pp. 99–127). Cambridge: Cambridge University Press.

Fleer, M., & Hedegaard, M. (2010). Children's development as participation in everyday practices across different institutions. *Mind, Culture, and Activity, 17*(2), 149–68.

Flyvbjerg, B. (2001). *Making social science matter: Why social inquiry fails and how it can succeed again.* Cambridge: Cambridge University Press.

Foucault, M. (1982). The subject and power. *Chicago Journals, 8*(4), 777–95.
Foucault, M. (1995). *Discipline & Punishment – The birth of the prison*. New York: Second Vintage Books Edition.
Frederiksen, N. J. S., Bakke, S. L., & Dalum, P. (2012). 'No alcohol, no party': An explorative study of young Danish moderate drinkers. *Scandinavian Journal of Public Health, 40*, 585–90.
Furlong, A., & Cartmel, F. (1997). *Young people and social change*. Buckingham: Open University Press.
Furlong, A., Cartmel, F., & Biggart, A. (2006). Choice biographies and transitional linearity: Re-conceptualising modern youth transitions. *Papers: Revista de sociologia* (79), 225–39.
Gallagher, W. (1993). *The power of place – how our surroundings shape our thoughts, emotions and actions*. New York: Poseidon Press.
Gibson, J. J. (1986). *The ecological approach to visual perception*. New York and London: Psychology Press.
Gilliam, L., & Gulløv, E. (2012). *Civiliserende institutioner: Om idealer og distinktioner i opdragelse*. Aarhus: Aarhus Universitetsforlag.
Grønborg, L. (2012). Forskeren og felten: et dobbeltsidet spejl – om brugen af subjektivitet i deltagerobservation. In M. Pedersen, J. Klitmøller & K. Nielsen (Eds.), *Deltagerobservation: En metode til undersøgelse af psykologiske fænomener* (pp. 135–48). København: Hans Reitzels Forlag.
Grønborg, L. (2013). One of the boys: Constructions of disengagement and criteria for being a successful student. *International Journal of Qualitative Studies of Education, 26*(9), 1192–209.
Gump, P. V. (1965). *Big schools ... small schools*. Paper published as part of the Chronicle Guidance Professional Service. Chronicle Guidance Publication, Inc., Moravia, New York (a brief paper from the Barker & Wright archives at the Spencer Library at Kansas University, presenting and discussing findings also published in Barker, R. G., & Gump, P. V. (1964): *Big school, small school: High school size and student behavior*).
Hall, G. S. (1904). *Adolescence: Its psychology and Its relations to physiology, anthropology, sociology, sex, crime, religion, and education* (2 vols). New York: D. Appleton.
Harvey, D. (2005). *A brief history of neoliberalism*. Oxford: Oxford University Press.
Harvey, D. (2007). Neoliberalism as creative destruction. *Annals of the American Academy of Political and Social Science, 610*(1), 22–44.
Hasse, C. (2015). *An anthropology of learning: On nested frictions in cultural ecologies*. Dordrecht: Springer.
Hedegaard, M. (2001). *Beskrivelse af småbørn*. Aarhus Universitetsforlag, 2. udgave, 2. oplag.
Hedegaard, M. (2003). Børn og unges udvikling diskuteret ud fra et kulturhistorisk perspektiv. *Nordisk Udkast* (1).
Hedegaard, M. (2008). Principles for interpreting research protocols. In M. Hedegaard, M. Fleer, J. Bang & P. Hviid (Eds.), *Studying children: A cultural-historical approach* (pp. 46–64). London: Open University Press.
Hedegaard, M. (2009). Children's development from a cultural-historical approach: Children activity in everyday local settings as foundation for their development. *Mind, Culture and Activity, 16*(1), 64–82.
Hedegaard, M. (2012). Analyzing children's learning and development in everyday settings from a cultural-historical wholeness approach. *Mind, Culture, and Activity, 19*(2), 127–38.

Hedegaard, M. (2014). The significance of demands and motives across practices in children's learning and development: An analysis of learning in home and school. *Learning, Culture and Social Interaction, 3*(3), 188–94.

Hedegaard, M., Aronsson, K., Højholt, C., & Ulvik, O. S. (Eds.). (2018). *Children, childhood, and everyday life: Children's perspectives*. 2nd ed. Charlotte, NC: Information Age Publishing Inc.,.

Hedegaard, M., Fleer, M., Bang, J., & Hviid, P. (2008). *Studying children. A cultural-historical approach*. London: Open University Press.

Hedegaard, M., & Fleer, M. (2019). Children's transitions in everyday life and institutions: New conceptions and understandings of transitions. In M. Hedegaard & M. Fleer (Eds.), *Children's transitions in everyday life and institutions* (pp. 1–18). London: Bloomsbury Publishing.

Heft, H. (1989). Affordances and the body: An intentional analysis of Gibson's ecological approach to visual perception. *Journal for the Theory of Social Behavior, 19*(1), 1–30.

Heft, H. (2001). *Ecological psychology in context. James Gibson, Roger Barker and the legacy of William James' radical empiricism*. Mahwah, NJ: Lawrence Erlbaum Associates.

Heft, H. (2007). The social constitution of perceiver-environment reciprocity. *Ecological Psychology, 19*(2), 85–105.

Heft, H. (2014). The tension between the psychological and ecological sciences: Making psychology more ecological. In G. Barker et al. (Eds.), *Entangled life. History, philosophy and theory of the life sciences*, Vol. 4. Dordrecht: Springer Science and Business Media.

Hegel, G. W. F. (1807/1979). *The phenomenology of spirit*. Oxford: Clarence Press.

Hermans, H. J. M. (2001). The dialogical self: Toward a theory of personal and cultural positioning. *Culture and Psychology, 7*(3), 243–81.

Hibell, B. et al. (1997). *The 1995 ESPAD report. The European school survey project on alcohol and other drugs. Alcohol and other drug use among students in 26 European countries*. Stockholm: The Swedish Council for Information on Alcohol and Other Drugs (CAN).

Holzkamp, K. (1983). Mennesket som subjekt for videnskabelig metodik. Stencil. Translated from: Braun, K.-H., Hollitscher, W., Holzkamp, K. & Wetzel, K. (Hrsg., 1983): Karl Marx und die Wissenschaft vom Individuum. Bericht von der 1. internationalen Ferienuniversität Kritische Psychologie vom 7–12. März in Graz. Marburg: Verlag Arbeiterbewegung und Gesellschaftswissenschaften, S. 120–66.

Holzkamp, K. (1998). Daglig livsførelse som subjektvidenskabeligt grundkoncept. *Nordiske Udkast, 26*(2), 3–31.

Holzkamp, K. (2013). *Psychology from the standpoint of the subject: Selected writings of Klaus Holzkamp*. Houndmills: Palgrave Macmillan.

Hundeide, K. (2004). A new identity, a new lifestyle. In Perret-Clermont et al. (Eds.), *Joining Society – social interaction and learning in adolescence and youth* (pp. 86–108). Cambridge University Press, chap. 6.

Hundeide, K. (2005). Socio-cultural tracks of development, opportunity situations and access skills. *Culture and Psychology, 11*(2), 241–61.

Hviid, P. (2008). 'Next year we are small, right?' Different times in children's development. *European Journal of Psychology of Education, 23*, 182–98.

Hviid, P. (2012). 'Remaining the same' and children's experience of development. In M. Hedegaard (Ed.), *Children, childhood, and everyday life: Children's perspectives* (pp. 37–52). Charlotte: Information Age Publishing.

Højholt, C. (2005). Præsentation af praksisforskning. In C. Højholt (Ed.), *Forældresamarbejde – forskning i fællesskab* (pp. 23–46). København: Dansk Psykologisk Forlag.

Højholt, C. (2018). Children's Perspectives and Learning Communites. In I. M. Hedegaard, K. Aronsson, C. Højholt, & O. Skær Ulvik (Eds.), *Children, childhood, and everyday life: Children's perspectives* (2 edition., pp. 93–111). Charlotte: Information Age Publishing.

Højholt, C. (2020). Conflictuality and situated inequality in children's school life. *Children's Geographies*, 1–14. https://doi.org/10.1080/14733285.2020.1817335

Højholt, C., & Schraube, E. (2016). Toward a psychology of everyday living. In E. Shraube & C. Højholt (Eds.), *Psychology and the conduct of everyday life* (pp. 1–14). Hove: Routledge.

Højholt, C. & Kousholt, D. (2014). Participant Observations of Children's Communities – Exploring subjective Aspects of Social practice. *Qualitative Research in Psychology*, 11, 316–34.

Højholt, C., & Kousholt, D. (2018). Children participating and developing agency in and across various social practices. In M. Fleer & B. Van Oers (Eds.), *International handbook of early childhood education* (Vol. 2, pp. 1581–98). Cham: Springer International Handbooks of Education Series https://doi.org/10.1007/978-94-024-0927-7_82

Højholt, C., & Kousholt, D. (2020). Contradictions and conflicts: Researching school as conflictual social practice. *Theory & Psychology*, 30(1),36–55.

Ilyenkov, E. (1977). The concept of the ideal. In Robert Daglish (Trans.), *Philosophy in the USSR: Problems of dialectical materialism* (pp. 71–99). Moscow: Progress Publishers.

Ilyenkov, E. (2014). Dialectics of the ideal. In A. Levant & V. Oittinen (Eds.), *Dialectics of the ideal – Evald Ilyenkov and creative soviet marxism* (pp. 25–79). Leiden: Koninklijke Brill.

Ingholt, L. (2008). Samspillet mellem fællesskab og vaner ved deltagelse i gymnasielivet. *Nordiske Udkast*, 36(1).

Ingold, T. (2004). Beyond biology and culture. The meaning of evolution in a relational world. *Social Antropology*, 12(2), 209–21.

Jensen, T.B. (2010). Unge, sprog og begrebsdannelse? – Den "gotiske" knude eller "Unge" i ordets "egentlige" forstand. *Psyke & Logos*, årgang 31, nr. 1, Dansk Psykologisk Forlag.

Jones, K. (2003). What is an affordance? *Ecological Psychology*, 15(2),107–14.

Juhl, P. (2019). Preverbal children as co-researchers: Exploring subjectivity in everyday living. *Theory & Psychology*, 29(1), 46–65.

Karaliotas, L., & Bettini, G. (2013). Everyday environmentalism: Creating an urban political ecology. A book review of book by Alex Lofthus. *Human Geography*, 6(3), 121–4.

Klitmøller, J., & Sommer, D. (2015). Børn i institution og skole: læring, dannelse og udvikling i globaliseringen. In J. Klitmøller & D. Sommer (Eds.), *Læring, dannelse og udvikling*, (pp. 9–38) 1. udgave, 1. oplag, København: Hans Reitzels Forlag.

Kofoed, J. & Søndergaard, D. M. (2009). *Mobning - sociale processer på afveje*. København: Hans Reitzel.

Kono, T. (2009). Social affordances and the possibility of ecological linguistics. *Integrated Psychological and Behavioral Science*, 43, 356–73.

Law, J. (2007). Making a mess with method. In W. Outhwaite & S. P. Turner (Eds.), *The SAGE Handbook of Social Science Methodology* (pp. 595–606). London: Sage.

Leontjev, A. N. (1977). Activity and consciousness. In Robert Daglish (Trans.) *Philosophy in the USSR, problems of Dialectical Materialism* (pp. 180–202). Moscow: Progress Publishers.

Leontjev, A. N. (2002). *Virksomhed, bevidsthed, personlighed*. København: Hans Reitzels Forlag (published in russian in 1975).

Leontjev, A. N. (2005). Study of the environment in the pedological works of L.S. Vygotsky – A Critical Study. *Journal of Russian and East European Psychology*, 43(4), 8–28.
Lerner, R. M., & Steinberg, L. (2004). The scientific study of adolescent development: Past, present, and future. In R. M. Lerner & L. Steinberg (Eds.), *Handbook of adolescent psychology*. 2nd ed. Hoboken, NJ: John Wiley & Sons.
Lesko, N. (2001). *Act your age! – a cultural construction of adolescence*. New York: Routledge Falmer.
Lewin, K. (1935). *A dynamic theory of personality*. New York, NY: McGraw-Hill.
Lewin, K. (1946/1954). Behavior and development as a function of the total situation. In L. Carmichael (Ed.), *Manual of child psychology* (pp. 791–844). New York: Wiley.
Mainz, P. (2014a). Gymnasieelev: »Får du 7, er du tabt for evigt« *Politiken*, 14/1-2014.
Mainz, P. (2014b). Hver fjerde elev i gymnasiet sover dårligt. *Politiken*, 14/1-2014.
Markard, M., Klaus, H., & Ole, D. (2004). Praksisportræt – En guide til analyse af psykologpraksis. *Nordiske Udkast*, 32, 2.
Ministry of Children & Education (2017). https://www.uvm.dk/aktuelt/nyheder/uvm/udd/gym/2017/marts/170320-fortsat-stor-soegning-mod-gymnasiet
Minken, A. (2002). *Alvorlig Moro. Idé og Virksomhet ved Motorsportstiltaket 2&4*. Oslo Kommune, Rusmiddeletaten, 2. udg.
Molenaar, P. C. M. & Valsiner, J. (2008). How generalization works through the single case: A simple idiographic process analysis of an individual psychotherapy. In S. Salvatore et al. (Eds.), *Yearbook of Idiographic Science* (pp. 23–38), vol. 1. Roma: Firera & Liuzzo Publishing.
Mørch, S. (1985). *At forske i ungdom: et socialpsykologisk essay*. København: Forlaget Rubikon.
Mørch, S. (1990). Ungdomsteori og intervention. *Udkast 1*, 18. Årgang. København: Dansk Psykologisk Forlag.
Mørch, S. (1994). Handlingsteorien. *Udkast. Dansk tidsskrift for kritisk samfundsvidenskab*, 1, 3–48.
Mørch, S. (2010). Ungdomsforskningen som perspektiv og mulighed. *Psyke & Logos*, årgang 31, nr. 1, Dansk Psykologisk Forlag.
Nielsen, A. M & Lagermann, L. C. (2017). *Stress i gymnasiet. Hvad der stresser gymnasieelever og hvordan forebyggelse og behandling virker med 'Åben og Rolig for Unge'*. E-book. København: Danmarks institut for Pædagogik og Uddannelse (DPU).
Nielsen, H. B., & Rudberg, M. (2006). *Moderne jenter: tre generationer på vei*. Oslo: Universitetsforlaget.
Nissen, M. (2014). Standarder og standpunkter i psykosocialt arbejde. In M. Nissen & E. Skærbæk (Eds.), *Psykososialt arbeid. Fortellinger, medvirkning og fellesskap* (pp. 81–114). Oslo: Gyldendal Akademisk.
Ottosen et al. (2010). *Rapporten: Børn og unge i Danmark*. Velfærd og trivsel 2010. SFI.
Ottosen et al. (2014). *SFI: Børn og unge i Danmark*. Velfærd og trivsel 2014, Det Nationale Forskningscenter for velfærd.
Pedersen, M. (2012). Triangulær validering. Samspillet mellem deltagerobservationer og kvalitative interview. In Pedersen et al. (Eds.), *Deltagerobservation – en metode til undersøgelse af psykologiske fænomener*. 1. udgave, 1. oplag, København: Hans Reitzels Forlag.
Pedersen, S. (2019). Not just a school: Explorations and theoretical considerations in relation to the human eco-niche. In K. Murakami, J. Cresswell, T. Kono & T. Zittoun (Eds.), *The ethos of theorizing* (pp. 212–21). Canada: Captus Press.

Pedersen, S., & Bang, J. (2016a): Youth development as subjectified subjectivity– a dialectical-ecological model of analysis. *Integrative Psychological and Behavioral Science*, *50*(3), 470–91.

Pedersen, S., & Bang, J. (2016b): Historicizing affordance theory: A rendezvous between ecological psychology and cultural-historical activity theory. *Theory & Psychology*, *26*(6),731–50.

Pedersen, S., & Bang, J. (2016c). Et studie i variabilitet blandt unge i gymnasiet. *Nordiske Udkast*, *44*(1), 85–98.

Poulsen, A. (2010). Ungdommen i udviklingspsykologien. *Psyke & Logos*, årgang 31, nr. 1, Dansk Psykologisk Forlag.

Resnick, L. B., & Perret-Clermont, A. (2004). Prospects for youth in postindustrial societies. In Perret-Clermont et al. (Eds.), *Joining Society – social interaction and learning in adolescence and youth*. Cambridge: Cambridge University Press.

Richter, L. (2017). Gymnasieelever er lige så stressede som de 20pct. mest stressede voksne. Newpaper article. *Information*, 23/11-2017.

Riegel, K. F. (1975). Toward a dialectical theory of development. *Human Development*, *18*(1–2), 50–64.

Rogoff, B. (2003). *Cultural nature of human development*. Oxford: Oxford University Press.

Rose, N. (1996). *Inventing our selves – Psychology, power, and personhood*. Cambridge: Cambridge University Press.

Rose, N. (1999). *Powers of freedom. Reframing political thought*. Cambridge: Cambridge University Press.

Rose, N. (2010). Psykiatri uden grænser? De psykiatriske diagnosers ekspanderende domæne. In S. Brinkmann (Ed.), *Det diagnosticerede liv – sygdom uden grænser*. Aarhus: Forlaget Klim, chap 2.

Rysgaard, K. K. (2009). Unge dropper uddannelse. *Ugebrevet A4*, 19 October 2009.

Sartre, J. P., & Elkaïm-Sartre, A. (1946). *L'existentialisme est un humanisme*. Paris: Nagel.

Schraube, E. (2010). Første-persons perspektivet i psykologisk teori og forskningspraksis. *Nordiske Udkast*, årgang 38, nr. 1 &2, 2010, Syddansk Universitetsforlag.

Schraube, E. (2013). First-person perspective and sociomaterial decentering: Studying technology from the standpoint of the subject. *Subjectivity*, *6*(1), 12–32, Macmillan Publishers ltd.

Schou, M. L. (2012). Jeg skal til at slappe lidt af. *Information*, 20/2-2012.

Schutz, A. (2005). *Hverdagslivets Sociologi*. København: Hans Reitzels Forlag.

Smith, C., Christoffersen, K., Davidson, H., & Herzog, P.S. (2011). *Lost in Transition – the dark side of emerging adulthodd*. New York: Oxford Univeraity Press.

Stetsenko, A. (2012). Personhood: An activist project of historical becoming through collaborative pursuits of social transformation. *New Ideas in Psychology*, *30*, 144–53.

Stetsenko, A. (2013). The challenge of individuality in cultural-historical activity theory: 'Collectividual' dialectics from a transformative activist stance. *Outlines – Critical Practice Studies*, *14*(2), 7–28.

Stetsenko, A., & Arievitch, I. M. (2004). The self in cultural-historical activity theory: Reclaiming the unity of social and individual dimensions of human development. *Theory and Psychology*, *14*, 475–503.

Stetsenko, A., & Arievitch, I. M. (2010). Cultural-historical activity theory: Foundational worldview, major principles, and the relevance of sociocultural context. In J. Martin and S. Kirschner (Eds.), *The sociocultural turn in psychology: The contextual emergence of mind and self* (pp. 231–52). New York: Columbia University Press.

Svendsen, L. Fr. H. (2010). Patologisering og Stigmatisering. In S. Brinkmann (Ed.), *Det diagnosticerede liv – sygdom uden grænser* (pp. 58–74). Aarhus: Forlaget Klim.

Szulevicz, T. (2015). Deltagerobservation. In S. Brinkmann & L. Tanggaard (Eds.), *Kvalitative metoder*, 2. udgave, 1. oplag, København: Hans Reitzels Forlag.

Timmermans, S., & S. Epstein (2010). A world of standards but not a standard world: Toward a sociology of standards and standardization. *Annual Review of Sociology, 36*, 69-89.

Turkle, S. (1984). *The second self: Computers and the human spirit*. New York: Simon & Schuster.

Valsiner, J. (2011). The development of individual purposes: Creating actuality through novelty. In L. A. Jensen (Ed.), *Bridging cultural and developmental approaches in psychology* (pp. 212-34). New York: Oxford University Press.

Valsiner, J. (2014). *An invitation to cultural psychology*. Washington, DC: Sage Publications LTD.

Vinther-Larsen, M. (2011). *Epidemiological studies on adolescents and alcohol – focus on social inequality*. PhD thesis, National Institute of Public Health, Faculty of Health Sciences, University of Southern Denmark.

Von Uexküll, J. (1982). The theory of meaning. *Semiotica, 42*(1), 25-82.

Vygotsky, L.S. (1994). The problem of the environment. In R. Van Der Veer & J. Valsiner (Eds.), *The vygotsky reader* (pp. 338-54). Oxford: Blackwell. First published as the fourth lecture in Vygotsky, L. S. (1935): *Foundations of Paedology* (pp. 58-78). Leningrad: Izdanie Instituta.

Vygotsky, L. S. (1998). *The collected works of L. S. Vygotsky: Vol. 5. Child psychology*. New York: Plenum (Original work published 1932).

Vygotsky, L. S. (1978). *Mind in Society. The Development of Higher Psychological Processes*. Edited by Michael Cole, Vera John-Steiner, Sylvia Schribner, and Ellen Souberman. Cambridge and London: Harvard University Press.

Walkerdine, V. (2006). Uddannelse, psykologi og neoliberalisme. In B. Elle, K. Nielsen & M. Nissen (Eds.), *Pædagogisk psykologi–positioner og perspektiver* (pp. 241-58). Frederiksberg C: Roskilde Universitetsforlag.

Walkerdine, V., & Bansel, P. (2010). Neoliberalism, work and subjectivity: Towards a more complex account. In M. Wetherell & C.T. Mohanty (Eds.), *Handbook of Identities* (pp. 492-507). London: SAGE publications Ltd.

Wartofsky, M. (1979). Perception, representation, and the forms of action: Towards an historical epistemology. In R.S. Cohen & M. Wartofsky (Eds.), *Models – Representation and the scientific understanding* (pp. 188-210). Boston: D. Reidel.

Wartofsky, M. (1983). The child's construction of the world and the world's construction of the child: From historical epistemology to historical psychology. In F. S. Kessel & A.W. Siegel (Eds.), *The child and other cultural inventions* (pp. 188-215). New York: Praeger.

Wertsch, J. V. (1985). *Vygotsky and the social formation of mind*. Cambridge: Harvard University Press.

Wicker, A. W. (1968). Undermanning, performances, and students' subjective experiences in behavior settings of large and small high schools. *Journal of Personality and Social Psychology, 10*(3), 255-61.

Willig, R. & Østergaard, M. (2005). *Sociale Patologier*. København: Hans Reitzels Forlag.

Willis, P. (1977). *Learning to labour, how working class kids get working class jobs*. Aldershot UK: Gower Press.

Winther-Lindqvist, D. A. (2012). Developing social identities and motives in school transitions. In M. Hedegaard et al. (Eds.), *Motives in children's development: Cultural-historical approaches* (pp. 115-33). New York: Cambridge University Press.

Winther-Lindqvist, D. A. (2014). Forhandling af sociale identiteter på tværs af klasserum. In O. M. Spaten (Ed.), *Unges identitet og selvopfattelse: kvalitative og kvantitative studier – aktuel empirisk forskning* (pp. 179-209). Aalborg: Aalborg Universitetsforlag.

Winther-Lindqvist, D. A. (2019). Becoming a schoolchild: A positive developmental crisis. In M. Hedegaard & M. Fleer (Eds.), *Children's transitions in everyday life and institutions* (pp.47-70). London: Bloomsbury Publishing.

Wright, H. F., Barker, R. G., Nall, J., & Schoggen, P. (1951). Toward a psychological ecology of the classroom. *The Journal of Educational Research*, *45*(3), 187-200.

Zahavi, D. (2008). *Subjectivity and selfhood. Investigating the first-person perspective*. Cambridge: MIT Press (first published 2005).

Zeuner, L. (2009). Det interdisciplinære gymnasium: Nye former for marginalisering. In J.E. Larsen & N. Mortensen (Eds.), *Udenfor eller Indenfor – sociale marginaliseringsprocessers mangfoldighed* (pp. 190-209). København: Hans Reitzels Forlag, chap. 10.

Ziehe, T. (1983). *Ungdom og usædvanlige læreprocesser*. København: Politisk Revy

Ziehe, T. (1989). *Ambivalenser og mangfoldighed*. København: Politisk Revy.

Zittoun, T. (2012). Life-course: A socio-cultural perspective. In Valsiner, J. (Ed.), *Handbook of culture and psychology* (Vol. 60, No. 23, pp. 513-35). Oxford: Oxford University Press.

Index

academic-engagement-standard 179, 182, 186, 187, 200, 215
academic lines 9, 63, 64, 66, 68, 70, 115, 131
activity setting 55, 56 n.6, 57
  agent-positions in 170
  concrete 13–15, 17, 100, 110, 119, 120, 199
  demands in 97, 98
  eco-niche variations and 57–8
  gym class 130–1
  home and school 109
  negotiation process 189–90
  notion of 49, 52 n.1, 55–7, 56 n.7
  and possibilities for life 48–9
  teaching situation as 96
  Westside High 92, 94–6, 102
adolescence 201–4
affordances 15, 15 n.8, 50, 141–2, 145, 212–13
  quality 98, 132, 168–9, 175, 187, 206, 207, 212, 216
  self 168–9, 206, 216
  social others 169, 191
affording of societal standards 15, 141–3, 145, 163, 182, 183, 195, 211–13, 215, 222
agency 203–5
  human 16, 168, 213
  intentional 145
alternative normativity 74, 76, 79–84
ambiguity 116–17, 131, 222
  to health profile 128–9, 132
  multitude of 118
  potential 221
  students' motives 130–1
ambivalence 6, 15, 19, 154, 206, 209, 213, 220, 221
anxiety 100–1
artefacts 60, 192, 206, 207, 210, 215
  beer as 139–40, 148, 150, 155, 156, 166
  in classroom 168–9

  concrete 168, 190–2
  health profile as 128, 128 n.2, 132
Asperger syndrome 67–8, 131, 217–18
Aufhebung 142–4, 162

Bang, J. 10, 11, 12, 15, 15 n.8, 19, 23, 39, 40, 53 n.2, 56, 56 n.7, 135, 137, 140, 141, 143, 144, 161, 163, 166–9, 170, 175, 183, 191, 206, 212, 213
Banks, C. A. 58
Barker, R. 12, 15, 48, 49, 52–6, 52 n.1, 53 n.3, 54 n.4, 56 n.6, 58, 71, 84, 88, 114, 119, 192, 204, 217
Beck, S. 147 n.5, 156
beer-drinking 84, 139–40, 147–8, 151–2, 154
  dialectical-ecological analysis 155–7
  existential challenges 148–50
  meaningfulness of standards 165
  partying and 19, 41, 80–1, 149, 154, 157–9
  social participation 147
  societal perspective on alcohol 150–2
  standard of 19, 152–5, 213, 214
  subjectivity 197
behaviour setting 48, 49, 52–7, 53 n.3, 88, 98, 106, 114, 192, 196, 217
Bertelsen, P. 110, 115, 170, 170 n.2, 171
body
  and food 122, 124–8, 130–2
  health and 122, 127–30, 132, 134
  measures 131–4
  monitoring health 122–7
  normality standards 127–31
Bozhovich, L. I. 3, 11–13, 48, 203
Bronfenbrenner, U. 14, 56, 56 n.6
Busch, L. 12, 39, 40, 135, 171

Carnegie Council 203–4
civilization process 133
close-knit community 59–61, 111, 112
co-construction 3, 83, 84, 159, 162, 173, 176, 214

collective creative process 119, 218
collective ideality 50–1, 72, 86, 107, 108, 111, 114, 119, 120, 154, 212, 213
collective meaning 16, 50–2, 58, 83, 85, 88, 133, 155, 159, 162, 211
community
  close-knit 59–61, 111, 112
  dominant sense of 63–4
  feeling 65
  and mutual care 107
  and proximity 60–1
  transparency and 72
  valuing 66
concrete environmental possibilities 57
construction process 1–3, 50, 73, 222–3
contradictions 79, 103, 107, 116–18, 122, 132, 146, 146 n.4, 181, 200, 206, 221
  Erikson's 201–2
  invitations and expectations 41–3, 146, 177, 181
  potential 132, 200
  societal and political interests 122
conversational interviews 21, 22
Costall, A. 14, 15, 141 n.2, 142, 192 n.5
Countryside High 35–8, 43, 58, 62
  Asperger syndrome 67–8, 217–18
  B-class 68–71
  contradictions 117
  eco-niche of 59–61, 107
  familiarity and belongingness 62–3
  health profile 128–9, 132
  proximity (*See* proximity)
  societal demands 118
  Southside High and 84–6
cultural-historical activity theory 14, 24, 56, 141, 143, 211–13, 223
cyto-settings 53 n.3

Danish school system 7, 41, 101 n.3, 185 n.4, 204
democracy 72–4, 80, 82–5, 96, 103, 117
Denmark
  academic lines 9
  alcohol policy 38 n.1
  youth education in 7
  youth life 105
developmental dynamics 2–4, 8–13, 106, 110, 120, 121, 137, 138, 198, 205–7
  comprehension of 210–16, 219–23

developmental process 1–3, 7–12, 19, 120, 139–40, 155, 162, 163, 168, 196, 205, 209–16
developmental theory 136, 202, 213
development of self 146
  Aufhebung and 142–4
  dialectical-ecological analysis 155–7
  diversity of 157–8
dialectical-ecological model 11–14, 156, 209–11, 223
  Aufhebung and development of self 142–4, 155–7
  development of self 155–8
  eco-niches and standards 211–13
  environmental standards 145–6
  historical time and place (Elder) 16–17
  invitational character of the environment 14–15
  person-environment 48, 57, 120, 210, 213–16
  of subjectified subjectivity 140–1, 144–6, 165–8, 183
directedness 20, 56, 110, 111, 115, 148, 149, 169–71, 176, 188, 193, 196–201
double-standard 68–71
down-to-earth-ness 59–61, 68, 85

Eckert, P. 9, 193 n.7, 204–5, 218, 219
ecological 157
  intentionality 170–1, 193
  realities 156, 157
  subjectivity-subjectification dialectics 140–1
ecological psychology 13, 14, 48–9
  cultural-historical activity theory and 212–13, 223
  Gibson's 141
eco-niche 16, 48, 111, 112, 120, 218
  activity setting 56–7
  to behaviour setting 52–5
  collective meanings 51–2
  Countryside High 59–61, 72, 84–6, 109, 131
  Gibson's 48–50
  human (*See* human eco-niche)
  objective meaning 51–2
  Southside High 72–4, 84–6
  variability 57–9, 106–7, 119

Edwards, A. 18
  relational expertise 20
Elder, G. H., Jr. 9, 16 n.9, 47, 106, 139, 143, 168, 178, 196, 216–18
  historical time and place 16–17
  human agency 16, 168
  linked lives 16
  timing in lives 16
emo 81 n.16
Engelsted, N. 168, 170
environment 145, 196, 212
  activity setting 48–9, 56–7
  availabilities 108, 110
  beer and of beer-drinking 156
  child 12–13
  historical time and place 16–17
  human 50, 141, 142, 145
  individual and 13, 50, 136, 141, 171
  invitational character of 14–17, 24, 35, 44, 54, 66–7, 88, 94, 102, 114, 142, 156, 179, 191, 212, 213, 223
  novelty 138
  persons and 4, 8, 11–14, 17, 45, 47, 55, 57, 85, 110, 119, 140–4, 166–71, 213–19
  possibilities for life 48–9
  standards 145–6, 157, 165–6
Erikson, E. 201–3, 209
ESPAD surveys 147 n.5

Farver, J. A. M. 56 n.7
first-person-givenness 140, 198
first-person-perspective 3–4, 20–2, 48, 55, 157
Foucault, M. 5 n.4, 137, 140
friendship 7, 63, 128, 173, 184–8

Gibson, J. J. 12, 16, 53, 57, 58, 119, 134, 141 n.2, 168, 170, 211, 212
  affordances 15, 15 n.8, 141–2, 145, 149, 169
  eco-niche 48–50 (*See also* eco-niche)
Gilliam, L. 133
globalization 94
grades 7, 36, 41, 75–6, 99–101, 101 n.3, 159–63, 186
Great Transitions 203–4
Grønborg, L. 21 n.11
Gulløv, E. 133

Hall, G. S. 201, 203, 209
Hasse, C. 18
health profile 118, 121–4, 126–34, 221
  awareness 122, 124, 127–9, 131–4
  calories and 122, 124, 126–7, 131, 132
  gym class 122–3, 125–33
  measures 131–4
  mental 6, 7, 11, 118, 127, 219, 221, 222
  monitoring 122–7
  motivation 131
  standards of normality 40, 127–32
Hedegaard, M. 2, 3, 5, 8, 10–14, 17, 19–20, 41, 49, 56–8, 56 n.6, 57, 58, 110, 136, 141, 143, 146 n.4, 158, 203, 212, 217
Hegel, G. W. F. 143
high school. *See also individual high school*
  behaviour setting 54–5
  developmental process 7–10
  location, matter of 108–10
  navigation 179–81
  normative and formative project 115
  place, matter of 110–11
  standards and standardization 39–40
  student 21–3
  youth life and 118–20
high school reform 9 n.6, 42, 115
high school students
  academic ambitions 76
  affordings of standards 182
  alternative normativity 80–3
  close family ties 61–6
  development of self 155–7
  different entrances 88–91
  directedness 196–201
  self-understanding 78–9
  Southside High 83–4
  subjectified sensitivity 175, 176, 178, 181, 182, 187, 200, 206, 214–16
  subjective meaningfulness 171–6
  subtle transformation of Anna 147–55
hipster 192, 192 n.6
historical time and place 16–17, 47, 106, 143, 201, 204, 217–20
human agency (Elder) 16, 168
human eco-niche 16–17, 25, 106
  activity setting 56–7
  and the affording of standards 211–13
  behaviour setting 54–5
  collective meanings 51–2

Gibson's eco-niche 50
  humanizing 50–1
  operationalization 52–4
humanistic-linguistic line 9, 42
human lifeworld 168–9, 213
Hundeide, K. 9, 102, 139, 139 n.1, 169 n.1, 197 n.1

ideality 50–1
ideals 6, 11, 40, 214
identity crisis 201–3
Ilyenkov, E. 50, 51
individualized/individualization 47, 91, 102, 107, 113, 115, 118, 132
individualizing gaze 136
Ingold, T. 11, 221
inner-city schools 2, 10, 33, 57–9, 63, 84, 87, 103, 114, 220
institutional demands 1, 4, 5, 8, 10, 13, 56, 96, 98, 189, 197
institutional setting 2–5, 7, 8, 29, 39, 52, 58, 59, 71, 79, 106, 114–16, 121, 133, 176, 204, 222
  affordings of standards 182
  navigation 179–81
  Northside High 176–8
intentio 110, 171, 176, 179, 187, 193, 200
intentionality 27, 49, 110, 111, 169–71, 178–81, 186–7, 193, 195, 197–200, 215
intentum 110, 171, 176, 179, 193, 200
intersubjectivity 20
invitational character 14–17, 24, 35, 44, 54, 66–7, 88, 94, 102, 114, 142, 156, 179, 191, 212, 213, 223
  of the environment 14–15

kendama 3, 184, 188–93, 200, 220
Kono, T. 47, 50

Law, J. 21, 23, 220
Leontjev, A. N. 13, 48, 51, 52, 119, 141, 142 n.3, 170, 170 n.2, 170 n.3, 171
Lesko, N. 8, 138, 143, 201, 203, 204, 209
Lewin, K. 11, 12, 14, 14 n.7, 15 n.8, 24, 40, 55, 138, 141, 217
lifeworld 12, 15, 17, 19, 48, 145, 146, 148, 149, 205, 212, 219, 220
location, matter of 108–10

mental health 6, 7, 11, 118, 127, 219, 221, 222
Ministry of Children & Education, The 7
Molenaar, P. C. M. 24
moratorium 202, 203, 205
Mørch, S. 5, 204
motive orientation 3, 4, 8, 9, 13–14, 20, 156, 163, 179, 180, 186, 187, 190, 193, 197

national debating team 41, 42, 94, 102
natural science line 9, 42
negotiation process 96
negotiations 14, 96, 126, 145, 154, 156, 165, 167–9, 200, 215
  class culture 99
  of meaning 101–2, 158–62, 183–92, 215
  multi-layered and entangled participation 192–3
  of standards 162, 163, 167, 183–4, 188–92, 214
normality 7, 83, 127–31
normativity 74, 76, 79–84, 113, 122
Northside High 30–3, 42, 43
  institutional setting 176–8

objective meaning 105, 108
  and personal sense 51–2
  place 110–11
opportunity situation 197 n.1

participant observation 21, 22
participation 3, 5, 17–18, 20–2
  multi-layered and entangled 192–3
  social 27, 135, 147, 154, 159, 161, 162, 176, 178–82, 198, 214
  standards of 27, 159, 162, 181, 182, 188–92, 198–200
Pedersen, S. 11, 12, 15, 15 n.8, 17, 21, 22, 39, 40, 47, 53 n.2, 115, 135, 137, 140, 141, 143, 144, 163, 166, 167, 169, 183, 212, 213
Perezhivanie 12–13
performance
  pressure 100–3, 113–14, 220
  and self-awareness 111–14
performing normativity 113
personal sense 51–2

person-environment reciprocity 4, 45, 57, 140, 144, 210
  affording of standards 141–2
  concrete 219, 222
  dialectical-ecological model 166–7
  and dialectics of the self 213–16
  subjective and agentive 57
  subjectivity-subjectification dialectics 140–1
person-environment relation 4, 8, 11–14, 17, 45, 47, 55, 57, 85, 110, 119, 140–4, 166–71, 213–19
person-standard relation 183
place 16–17, 105, 108
  and location 108–10
  matter of 110–11
possibilities for life 14, 48–50, 52, 211
practice portrait 58 n.9
Programme for International Student Assessment (PISA) 40 n.2
proximity 26, 63, 90, 105, 217
  community and 60–4, 66, 85, 107, 111–12
  and distance 61–2
  familiarity 62–3
  friendships 63
  and globality 111
  principle 65, 71–2
  provincial 57–9
psychological habitat 53, 98, 119, 215
Psychology from the standpoint of the subject 17
psychosocial moratorium 202

qualitative
  change 191
  differences 68
  leaps 13
  transformation 13

reciprocity. *See* person-environment reciprocity
Richards, A. 141 n.2, 142, 192 n.5
Rogoff, B. 136
Rose, N. 5, 5 n.4, 42, 103, 115, 116, 137

Schou, M. L. 6–7
Schraube, E. 20, 21, 127, 128 n.2, 136
Schutz, A. 56 n.8

second-person perspective 20
self
  affordances 168–9, 206, 216
  development of (*See* development of self)
  dialectics of the 213–16
  performances of 94
self-awareness 91–2
self-monitoring 130–3
self-understanding 78, 84, 85, 119–21, 169, 172, 176, 181, 182, 186, 187, 192, 198–200, 206, 207
sensitivity 178, 181, 182, 200, 215
  projected 175–6
  sensitive child 173–5
social-human life-activity 50–1
socialization 11, 27, 88, 135, 138, 155, 168, 198, 203, 205
social others 169, 191
social participation 27, 77, 85, 135, 147, 158, 159, 162, 176, 178, 198, 199
social situation 20, 24, 56, 57, 98, 102, 110, 156, 161, 189
societal
  demands 72, 79, 114, 116–19, 133
  ecological existence 138–40
  perspective on alcohol 150–2
  and political interests 122
  practice 51, 57, 106, 142, 143
  pressure 8, 82, 217, 221, 222
  standards 15, 27, 84, 117, 134, 135, 147, 212, 213
Southside High 58, 74–8
  alternative normativity 80–3
  community and mutual care 107
  contradictions 117
  and Countryside High 84–6
  eco-niche of 72–4, 107
  performance culture 112–13
  political awareness and engagement 82
  rules and 79–80
  standards and opposition 78–9
standardization 39–40, 84, 136, 196, 199, 205
standards 10, 15, 19, 39–40
  adaptation to 162
  affording of societal 15, 141–3, 145, 163, 182, 183, 195, 211–13, 215, 222
  character of 163

eco-niches and 211–13
environmental 145–6, 157, 165–6
meaningfulness of 165
negotiations of 162, 163, 167, 183–92, 214
normality 127–31
and opposition 78–9
of participation 27, 159, 162, 181, 182, 188–92, 198–200
societal 15, 27, 84, 117, 134, 135, 147, 212, 213
and standardization 39–40
standardizing force 215
Westside High 97–102, 112
standing out 10, 76, 100, 112, 113, 117, 177
Stetsenko, A. 12, 24, 136, 138, 141, 143, 203, 206
stress 6, 78, 90, 97, 119
Sturm und Drang 201, 203
subjectification 12, 39–40, 137, 147 n.5, 171, 187
ambiguous 114–18
self-understanding and 200
subjectified subjectification 136–40, 205–7
dialectics 140–1
dynamics 193
synthesis 137, 138, 146, 214
subjectified subjectivity 110, 155, 158, 162, 163, 178, 195–9, 205–7, 213–14, 216
changes the dynamics 176
dialectical and synthetic process 157
dialectical-ecological model of 140–1, 143–6, 165–8, 182–4
sensitive child 173–5
subjectification processes 187
subjectivity as 137
subjective 12, 19, 20, 27, 136–8. *See also* transformation
level 61, 74, 88, 131, 135, 165, 168, 200, 201, 216, 221
meaningfulness 85, 171–6
meaning of 195–6
sensitivity 175, 176, 178, 181, 182, 187, 200, 206, 214–16
stance 181, 195, 200
sub-setting 53 n.3, 54
superseding 143

supra-individual level 49, 53, 54, 57, 108, 131
Szulevicz, T. 21

taken-for-grantedness 16, 44, 51, 107, 111, 210
talent programmes 32, 33, 36, 41–3, 45, 76, 94, 102, 116
teacher-students dynamics 95–6
temporality 182
third-person perspective 20–1, 48, 55, 157, 161, 198
totality of the situation 12, 17, 20, 40, 55, 86, 167
transformation 135–8, 184
affording of standards 141–2
Aufhebung and the development of self 142–4
beer-drinking 147–55
development of self 155–8
dialectical-ecological model 144–6, 155–7
directedness 199–201, 214, 215
negotiations of meaning 158–62
societal ecological existence 138–40
subjective and collective process 162–3
subjectivity-subjectification dialectics 140–1
transformative process 191, 200, 205, 215
transitory process 3, 5, 12, 24, 209, 220–3
Turning Points 203, 204, 206, 215

uncertainty 118, 138–9, 203

Valsiner, J. 24, 138, 139
variability 57–9, 106–7, 119
Vygotsky, L. S. 2, 3, 5, 8, 11, 23, 47, 48, 56 n.7, 58, 136, 141, 142 n.3, 146 n.4, 148, 203, 215
emotional experience 12–13
person and environment 119, 167

Wartofsky, M. 14, 16, 57, 111, 128, 128 n.2, 138, 141–3, 178, 191, 192
Westside High 33–6, 42, 43, 87–94, 107
ambitions 94–5
competitiveness 99
demands on students 113
democratic rights and awareness 95–6
different entrances 89–91

downside of the pressure 113–14
  eco-niche of 97, 107
  performance culture 112–13
  standards 97–102, 112
wholeness approach 11–13, 17, 143, 146,
   163, 210, 212, 217, 219, 222, 223
Willis, P. 9, 193 n.7, 204–5, 209
Wright, H. 12, 15, 48, 49, 52–6, 52 n.1, 53
   n.3, 54 n.4, 56 n.6, 58, 71, 84, 88, 98,
   106, 114, 119, 192, 196, 204, 215, 217

youth development 4–10, 23–4, 201–5,
   209, 210, 213, 214, 222–3
  comprehension of 201–5
  dialectical-ecological comprehension
   of 11–17

  dynamics of 120
  influence of standards on 136–7
  subjectified subjectivity 205–7
youth life 41, 114, 118–20
  Countryside High 35–8
  environment 166
  meaning of 216–20
  normal 5
  Northside High 30–3
  standardizing practices 82
  variability 212
  variations 10–11, 16
  Westside High 33–5

Ziehe, T. 147 n.5, 209
Zittoun, T. 16 n.9, 47

www.ingramcontent.com/pod-product-compliance
Lightning Source LLC
Chambersburg PA
CBHW062135300426
44115CB00012BA/1930